A Gathering of Voices

The Native Peoples
of the
Central California Coast

Edited by
Linda Yamane

Santa Cruz County History Journal
Issue Number Five
2002

SANTA CRUZ COUNTY HISTORY JOURNAL
Issue Number Five

Issue Editor
Linda Yamane

Associate Editors		**Administrative Consultants**
David Heron	Rachel McKay	Charles Hilger, Museum Executive Director
Winnie Heron	Joyce Miller	Allan Molho, Chair, Publications Committee
Rick Hyman	Frank Perry	Rachel McKay, *History Journal* Coordinator
Joan Martin		Nikki Silva, History Curatorial Consultant

Production and Distribution

Cover Design and Camera-Ready Production:	Karen Barnett
Printing and Binding:	Sheridan Books, Inc.
Distribution:	Otter B Books

Acknowledgements — With Thanks for Assistance

Lee Davis	Edna Kimbro	Daisy Njoku
Lisa Deitz	Sally Legakis	Susan Snyder
Victor Golla	Chris Lydon	Stanley D. Stevens
Cheryl Gomez	Elaine Maruhn	Mark Q. Sutton
Charles Higuera	Randy Morgan	Sandy Taugher
Brother John	Joanne C. Nelson	

Financial Support for Issue Number Five provided by:
The History Forum in memory of Jim Dolkas
Fred D. McPherson, Jr. Publications Fund
George Ow, Jr./Capitola Book Company
The Porter Sesnon Foundation, with special thanks to Jim Dolkas.

Published by:
The Museum of Art & History
705 Front Street
Santa Cruz California 95062-4508
www.santacruzmah.org

The publisher assumes no responsibility for the statements or opinions of the authors.

Printed in the U.S.A.

Address all correspondence to the Journal Editorial Committee, care of the publisher.

ISSN 1081-681X   ISBN 0-940283-11-5

Contents

Profiles:

Cover design by Karen Barnett; front cover art: detail of a mural by Ann Thiermann on display in the Santa Cruz Museum of Natural History; back cover image: photo by Gary Breschini and Trudy Haversat.

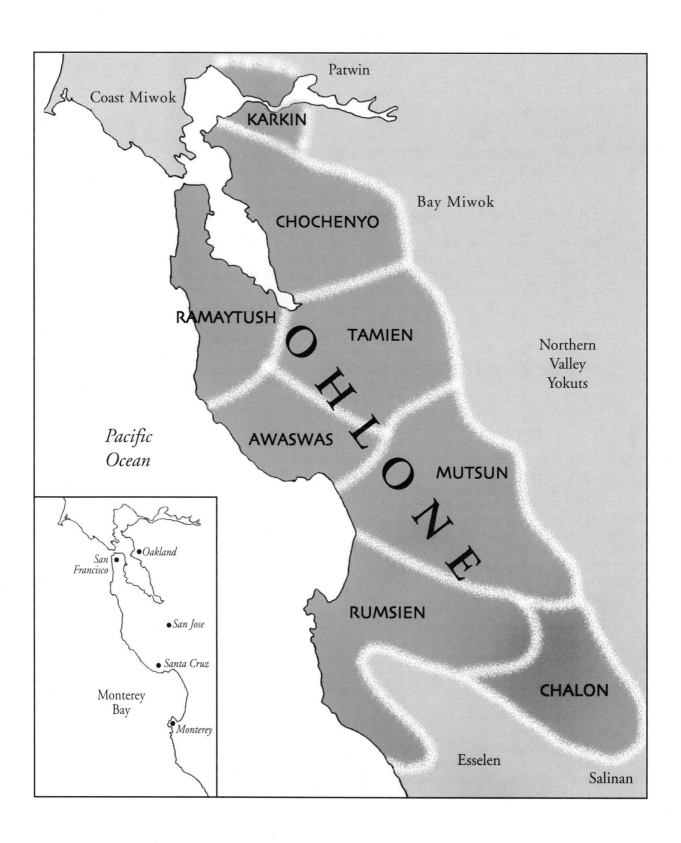

Patwin

Coast Miwok

KARKIN

CHOCHENYO

Bay Miwok

RAMAYTUSH

TAMIEN

Northern
Valley
Yokuts

Pacific
Ocean

OHLONE

AWASWAS

MUTSUN

San
Francisco

Oakland

San Jose

RUMSIEN

Santa Cruz

Monterey
Bay

Monterey

CHALON

Esselen

Salinan

Introduction

The Museum of Art and History is pleased and honored to present this Gathering of Voices. For the first time, native people, historians, educators, archaeologists, and others have come together in one publication to share their knowledge about the Native Peoples of the Central California Coast.

Until now, little has been published about the native peoples of this area, although they lived here for at least 10,000 years before the arrival of Spanish settlers in the late 1700s. The establishment of the Spanish missions brought an abrupt end to their traditional ways of life. Today, the descendants of these indigenous people are doing research to uncover, revive, and preserve their rich heritage.

Initially, the Spanish referred to all the native people living along the Pacific coast as "costeños," meaning literally "people of the coast." Later, the term was anglicized to "Costanoan" and used by linguists to identify the people living in the San Francisco and Monterey Bay regions who spoke common languages. Today, most descendants prefer to identify themselves as "Ohlone." The term "Ohlone" may have been derived from the village of "Oljon" on the San Mateo coast. However, variations of this term have been found in the mission records and early ethnographic literature, making its origin uncertain. When Frederick Beechey visited the area in 1826-27, he referred to the people inhabiting the seacoast between San Francisco and Monterey as "Olchones." As used today, the terms "Costanoan" and "Ohlone" are interchangeable.

The Ohlone languages are part of a larger language family known as Penutian. The other California Penutian languages are: Wintu, Nomlaki, Konkow, Maidu, Nisenan, Patwin, Lake Miwok, Coast Miwok, Plains Miwok, Sierra Miwok, Northern Valley Yokuts, Foothill Yokuts, and Southern Valley Yokuts. The Esselen, Salinan, and Chumash belong to the Hokan family of languages. The sound and structure of these Hokan languages are very different from Ohlone languages.

The Ohlone occupied a vast territory from San Francisco Bay to south of Monterey Bay. In the north, the Ohlone lived on both sides of the Carquinez Strait, including present-day Vallejo, Mare Island, and Benecia. Their territory extended southward along the coast to south of Carmel Bay, and there is linguistic evidence that they lived not only on the western slopes of the Diablo mountain range, but also on the eastward slopes into the Central Valley.

Today it is very difficult, if not impossible, to reconstruct the many Ohlone tribal groups, so people have come to identify with the eight surviving Ohlone languages: Karkin (Carquinez Strait), Chochenyo (East Bay), Ramaytush (San Francisco Peninsula), Tamien (Santa Clara Valley), Awáswas (Santa Cruz area), Mutsun (southern Santa Clara County and San Benito County), Rumsien (lower Carmel Valley and the Monterey area), and Chalon (northern Monterey County east of Mission Soledad).

We hope that the voices in this Journal will not only enrich and enlighten readers but will also provide the seeds for continued exploration into our past.

—The Editors

Santa Cruz
County
History Journal
Issue 5, 2002

2

Listen to the Water

by Alex Ramirez as told to Beverly R. Ortiz

Over the years Alex Ramirez has shared stories of his childhood with a huge variety of groups in countless locales. On August 6 and 22 of the year 2000, he joined me at Coyote Hills Regional Park in Fremont to share some of these stories anew with, respectively, the general public and a group of educators. During these two presentations, Alex told a story about listening that not only relays some of his mother's and grandfather's teachings, but also the keen wit, wisdom, and humor that Alex brings to his storytelling. The following is taken directly from cassette recordings I made of these tellings.

—Beverly R. Ortiz

When I was about four, five or six years old, my mother used to take me down by the river. She would say, "Listen to the water." Then I would listen to the water. When we were going home, we'd be walking under the trees, usually the pear trees in the orchard. You could hear the rustle of the leaves in the trees, and my mother would say, "Listen to the wind." Then I would listen to the wind. When we got home, I would sit around this big old wood stove, with a fire glowing inside, and she would say, "Listen to the fire."

I was a very respectable little kid, or else I would say, "Mom, why do you want me to listen to the water? Listen to the wind? Listen to the fire? Where are we going with all this, mom?" [laughs] But, you know, I didn't. Whatever my mother said to do, I did. She said, "Listen to the water." OK, well I'd listen to the water. But what do we say then? What happens here? Why do I have to listen to the water? And then, four years ago, more than half a century later, I heard a cassette recording from the Smithsonian Institution where my grandfather [Manuel Onésimo] is talking to John Peabody Harrington, an anthropologist who came to this [the Monterey] area in the early 1930s interviewing a lot of Indian people. It's a cassette with my grandfather telling the story of creation to John Peabody Harrington. The cassette was taken from a wax cylinder. I hear my grandfather trying to talk to John Harrington, and he says something to him about a song about the water. And John

Harrington says, "What does a song about the water say?" But my grandfather says, "No, it's not about the water. It's the water singing the song."

Maria Onésimo Ramirez with infant son, Alejandro (Alex), Carmel Valley, 1929. Photo courtesy of Linda Yamane.

Manuel Onésimo of Carmel Valley, grandfather of Alex Ramirez, 1937. Photo courtesy of Linda Yamane.

me, I'll cut through it. I am very strong. I know of no other strength.'" Oh! This is what the water says! That's why I was supposed to listen to it.

Wow! I thought, "Man. How about the wind? Isn't the wind powerful?" Think of those tornadoes going two hundred miles an hour. There's nothing that tornado cannot pick up. How about the fire? A fire can go on and on and on and on. It's very powerful.

When I talk to the kids [during cultural presentations], I ask, "What is the biggest fire you know of?" You know what? It's the sun. If it wasn't for the sun, we wouldn't have these beautiful flowers and trees. And we wouldn't even be here if it wasn't for the sun, that great fire up there. If it wasn't for that, we wouldn't have these things.

How about the wind? Every time you take a breath, that's the wind. That's the air. How about the water? Could we live without the water? Oxygen is our life! Water is our life. Air is our life. Fire is our life.

And I thought, "Wow!" And then he [Harrington] says, "Well, what does the water say?" You know how a dog perks his ears up? Well that's the way my ears came up, really. Because I'm going to hear something that I've been wondering about for so long. So many, many years, I've thought about it. Why do I have to listen to the water? And then he [Harrington] said, "What does the water say?" Am I going to hear what the water says!? Then my grandfather said, "The water says, 'I am very strong. If you put a stone in my path, I will roll it out of the way. If you put a tree across my way, I will wash it out of the way. If you put a mountain in front of

The Indian people felt that way. That's why my mother told me, "Listen to the water. Listen to the wind. Listen to the fire." In other words, she said, "Don't take these things for granted." Consider them all the time. Always take care of it. So that's my experience as a child. That's my experience as an Indian child. I don't have to live like that. I'm not ever going to wear a feather on my head. I'm never going to do that. But I'm still Indian. And the things that I learned are still within me. These are the things that I heard.

Alex Ramirez at the mouth of the Carmel River, November 2000. Photo by Linda Yamane.

3

Santa Cruz
County
History Journal
Issue 5, 2002

4

Walking on the Clouds of Heaven

John Peabody Harrington's Fieldwork on California's Central Coast

by Linda Agren

John Peabody Harrington was born on April 29, 1884 in Waltham, Massachusetts. When he was two years old his family moved from Waltham to Santa Barbara, California. He attended grammar school there and after graduating from Santa Barbara High School in 1902, enrolled in Stanford University in a program of philology, classic and modern languages. He was elected to the Phi Beta Kappa Society and was offered a Rhodes Scholarship in 1905, which he declined in order to study in Germany. In Germany, he was greatly influenced by Franz Nikolaus Finck, a professor of general linguistics. Finck was known to shun university life in favor of working in the field. This philosophy and work habit appealed to Harrington; he adopted it and patterned his life on it.[1]

After returning from Germany, Harrington spent several years working for the School of American Research. During this period, he began his studies among the Chumash Indians and other California Indian groups. In 1915 Harrington took a federal civil service examination and was hired as an ethnologist by the Bureau of American Ethnology at the Smithsonian Institution. A year later he married Carobeth Tucker, and the following year their daughter Awona was born.[2] Carobeth's book, *Encounter With an Angry God*, indicates that even then John Harrington's life was so wrapped up in his work that a successful marriage was impossible.[3]

By 1921 Harrington had become completely focused on the study of native languages. He wrote to his superior, Dr. J. Walter Fewkes, at the Smithsonian:

You recall the discussions that we had last winter with regard to the value of language study to ethnology. One of the lessons which the great out of doors and varied contact with the old Indians has been teaching me is that this value can hardly be overestimated. It is an easy matter to wildly misunderstand an Indian unless you have the language to guide you. Myths in the native idiom often differ widely from the way they are told by the same informant in Spanish or English. We are forced to work through the medium of language for the understanding of the Indian and his life.[4]

During the 1920s and the 1930s Harrington continued his linguistic and ethnographic studies among many California Indian groups. In the early 1940s his interests wandered from California and he conducted fieldwork among Alaska, Canadian, and Northwest Coast tribes. In the late 1940s his interests turned to Latin America and he concentrated on the Quechua of South America and later the Maya of the Yucatan.[5]

Harrington retired from the Bureau of American Ethnology in 1954 at the age of seventy. He left Washington D.C. and returned to California where he continued his life long occupation recording the speech of the last survivors of various California tribes. In 1960 he was living in the Riviera Hotel in Santa Barbara. Stricken with Parkinson's disease, he became too ill to work and was taken to a hospital in the summer of 1961. His daughter, Awona, found him there, being cared for by the family of one of his Chumash consultants. She took him to her home in San Diego and cared from him until he died in October at the age of seventy-seven.[6]

Santa Cruz
County
History Journal
Issue 5, 2002

After over fifty years of work, thirty-nine at the Bureau of American Ethnology, Harrington left perhaps two million sheets of paper scattered across the country. The Smithsonian Institution recently completed microfilming all of Harrington's fieldnotes, correspondence and photographs. He spent much of his life in the field, living with the Indians he studied and staying with them in their homes.[7]

Harrington's Fieldwork in Central California

Harrington's fieldwork with the native peoples of California's central coast began in 1912 when Harrington was 28 years old and just returning from successful linguistic studies in the American Southwest. In addition to his extensive Chumash studies, he began compiling notes on the historical accounts of the Esselen, one of the least-known tribal groups in California.[8] He also began the first of three phases of fieldwork on Salinan dialects.[9] The Esselen and Salinan studies and other fieldwork involving the Costanoan (Mutsun and Rumsen dialects) were to involve him off and on for over 25 years.

John P. Harrington and Isabel Meadows.
Photo courtesy of Linda Yamane.

Esselen

Harrington began a study of Esselen relatively early in his career and maintained a continuing interest in relating it to a recognized language family. Because the language had become extinct in the early twentieth century, he was not actually able to conduct any fieldwork with a native speaker. He did undertake research among the existing primary and secondary sources and attempted to learn what he could from various consultants who he thought might have some knowledge of the language.[10]

The Esselen had inhabited a thickly wooded, mountainous environment on the south-central California coast, south of the present city of Monterey. Their territory included the upper drainage of the Carmel River extending south to the vicinity of Junipero Serra Peak. A 25-mile stretch of this territory appears to have bordered the Pacific coast, from Point Sur to Point Lopez. The Salinan peoples bordered Esselen territory on the south, and there were Costanoan groups on the northern and eastern boundaries.[11]

The Esselen population first moved to Mission San Carlos Borromeo de Monterey after it was constructed in June 1770. The mission was later moved (December 1770) to a new site in the Carmel Valley and became known as San Carlos Borromeo del Carmel. Much of the Esselen population became affiliated with this mission.[12]

Harrington continued revising his notes on secondary sources and in the mid-1930s reviewed his files with his Rumsen consultant, Isabel Meadows, in hopes she might recognize or help him reconstruct various Esselen words. At the end of their work he concluded that she knew only eleven words of the language.[13]

Mutsun/Costanoan

In July 1929 Harrington was excited to learn that Ascensión Solórsano was still living. Unfortunately he also learned that she had a tumor and had been given a year or less to live by her doctors. The doctors could not operate because she was pronounced too old to take a general anesthetic.

Harrington had met her briefly in 1922 when she was believed to be 87 years old. This was to be his first opportunity to record a basic vocabulary of the Mutsun dialect of Costanoan.[14] Harrington himself did not use the terms "Mutsun" or "Costanoan" when referring to native peoples in the area surrounding Mission San Juan Baustista, instead he used the terms "San Juan" or "Juanéo."

Ascención Solórsano was born near Mission San Juan Bautista and lived near it for most of her life. The information that she related to Harrington had been learned from her father and mother. Both her father and mother had also been born near Mission San Juan Bautista; they had married early and spent their entire lives together.[15] Harrington was amazed at Solórsano's knowledge of Mutsun material culture, myths, native plants, ceremonies, customs, and life at the mission.[16] He wrote to the Smithsonian:

> Unless something unforeseen happens, the information of Mrs. Ascención Solórsano, last speaker of the San Juan Bautista language, will be completely recorded and go down to future ages. I feel like humbly thanking God or the universe or something that she is still alive and, feeble and far-gone as she is, able and willing to work.[17]

Much of Harrington's work with Solórsano was devoted to reviewing all historical and contemporary records of Mutsun. To this end they examined such published works as Arroyo de la Cuesta's *Vocabulario Mutsun* and *Gramatica Mutsun*, the manuscript "El Oro Molido," vocabularies recorded by C. Hart Merriam and Henry W. Henshaw, and selected mission records. Some of the information resulting from this work was compiled into a rudimentary dictionary. Apparently Harrington also planned to write "an exhaustive primer and grammar" of the San Juan Bautista language, although there is no evidence of these works amidst the field notes.[18]

During this time period, Harrington boarded at the home of her daughter, Dionisia Mondragon, in New Monterey, where Solorsano was also

Ascención Solórsano Cervantes, daughter of Barbara Sierras and Miguel Solórsano, provided extensive Mutsun language and cultural information to John P. Harrington. Photo courtesy of Linda Yamane.

living. He seemed pleased to be included in their household.

> Well, it is just heart touching how they insisted that I park the machine in the yard, and gave me a room in the house, and insisted that I board with them. . . . She is living at the house of her daughter Dionisia here. Dionisia is married to José Mondragon, formerly *Teniente-Coronel* in the Mexican army. He is Sonoran and is well educated in Spanish. He is a cement worker and has worked here for six years. He is quite a prominent man among the Mexicans of the town.[19]

A number of Solórsano's friends and relatives became involved in the work to varying extents. Her granddaughter, Marta Herrera, aided Harrington by interpreting, translating, and collecting botanical specimens in the field. She also assisted in copying old manuscripts and mission records for use as questionnaires, compiling data for the monographs, and copying Harrington's own field notes. Harrington worked intermittently with Solórsano's daughters, Dionisia

Mondragon and Claudia Corona, and with her grandson, Henry Cervantes, who acted both as a chauffeur and as a major collaborator in preparing the Mutsun data for publication.[20]

Harrington documented their success in a letter to Matthew Stirling on December 29, 1929:

I have completely restored and translated and annotated the Oro Molido of Felipe Arroyo de la Cuesta, a hitherto unpublished and unknown manuscript of 91 pages in the San Juan language, consisting of prayers with Spanish or Latin translations, songs with San Juan words and other unique information written in 1815. This is without any question the most important Indian document from the Franciscan period of California history, and through the work with Ascención every word of it shines forth with brilliancy.

It beats all how this language of her younger years has come back to Ascensión. It is a surprise to her herself. Sick as she is, her mind and memory is as clear as a bell. She is most alert and seems to gain in what you might call spiritual power. Even in the realm of material culture that had mostly vanished before she was born we have several dozen names of artifacts, including almost all the articles used as dancing regalia, two different kinds of bow, two different kinds of arrow, terms for having bow strung and unstrung, a rich assemblage of words and texts on San Juan tobacco, the word for sweathouse, for several different dances, and a lot of fine old words and descriptions dealing with witch doctor practices. The dictionary will be practically exhaustive, the grammar entirely so. Who would have thought that getting this material was possible in 1929! More than this, with my dictionary, I will be able to translate anything into San Juaneno.[21]

Ascención Solórsano died on January 29, 1930. She was buried at Mission San Juan Baustista in a grave just outside the church wall, between the church and the old Indian cemetery of unmarked

graves. Harrington described her grave as being right on the path where tourists visiting the mission walk just after they pass by the front of the church. He stated that a marker was planned with an inscription telling of her work with the Smithsonian Institution.[22]

Marta Herrera, daughter of Maria Dionisia Mondragon and granddaughter of Ascención Solársano Cervantes, with brother Victor Mondragon. Photo courtesy of Linda Yamane.

Rumsen/Costanoan

Isabel Meadows was the daughter of Loreta Onésimo, a full-blooded Carmel Indian, and James Meadows, an English sailor. When Isabel was about ten years old, her parents engaged an elderly Wacharon woman, Maria Omesia, to help at their ranch. The two adult women conversed in Rumsen. Since she spent a great deal of time with Omesia, Isabel learned Rumsen words, gradually building up a comprehensive understanding of the language.[23]

When John P. Harrington began working with Isabel Meadows in March 1932, he was 48 years old. Every morning he would leave New Monterey, stop at a grocery store to pick up the day's provisions and proceed to Carmel where Meadows lived. At 9 a.m. they would commence their work on the Rumsen dialect stopping only when Meadows would step into the kitchen to prepare them their meals. Harrington ate so well during these sessions with her that he complained of his weight ballooning to 190, saying that was the most he had ever weighed. They would work together until 9 p.m. every day that Harrington was in residence at New Monterey.[24]

Harrington had met Isabel Meadows while he was working with Ascensión Solórsano. He cultivated a relationship with her during the later half of 1929 and beyond; he wrote to H. W. Dorsey at the Smithsonian in 1931 "After finishing this work (Salinan), I have old Isabel Meadows, 84 years old, who talks the Carmel language, waiting for me at Monterey."[25]

Assisting Harrington while he worked with Meadows was Claudia Corona, Ascensión Solórsano 's oldest daughter, coming some days to help in the cooking and in gathering and identifying plants with Indian and Spanish names. Also, Andres Gomes, Meadow's nephew, chopped wood and helped by "going all around Monterey town for me trying to locate photographs of old timers and Indians in the old families." During this time Harrington was again rooming at the home of Dionisia Mondragon in New Monterey.[26]

Harrington was concerned over Meadows' health, he wrote to Matthew Stirling, his superior at the Smithsonian that she had nearly died about a month prior to his arrival and had been slowly recovering. Her home in Carmel had photographs of her father and his English relations hung on the walls, as well as pictures of her Indian relatives. Isabel Meadows never married but stayed at home on the ranch and took care of her parents until they died.[27] Of Meadows' knowledge Harrington wrote:

> She knows practically everything her mother knew, and I shall soon have a vocabulary so big that we can translate almost anything into the language. . . . *I have never had such a splendid field season, nothing but one piece of luck after another, without a single disappointment. . . .*it is like walking on the clouds of heaven for me to be getting this Carmel vocabulary from poor old Miss Isabel

Meadows, it is what I have dreamed of doing for years and thought that no one knew the information.[28]

Like Ascensión Solórsano, Isabel Meadows' memories of the past were stimulated by her conversations with Harrington. He said "Many times I ask her a word and she does not know it, and later it comes to her. For instance, she knew how to say bitter and salty, but said she never learned how to say sour; and this morning the old word for sour came to her."[29] Harrington, not content to limit his work with Isabel to California, brought her to Washington, D.C. with him, first in 1934[30] and again in 1936.[31]

Isabel Meadows died in June 1939. Of her funeral Harrington wrote: "Well, you ought to have seen how nice Dona Isabel looked when laid out at the Freeman chapel. They had a rosary in the evening and a big funeral in the old Carmel Mission the next morning with Mass, and burial beside her mother just where she wanted to be buried. Roy Meadows thanked me from the bottom of his heart for prolonging her life and making her last days happy."[32]

Salinan

The terms " Migueleño" and " Antoniano" are linguistic designations for those native peoples who were either born at or lived near Mission San Miguel and Mission San Antonio. Mission San Antonio de Padua was established in the heart of Salinan territory in 1771. Mission San Miguel followed in 1797. Early descriptions of the Salinan language suggest two and possibly three dialects: a Playano dialect spoken on the coast, another in the vicinity of Mission San Antonio (Antoniano) and a third in the area of Mission San Miguel (Migueleño). Detailed linguistic analyses have confirmed only the latter two.[33]

Harrington undertook fieldwork on the Salinan Migueleño and Antoniano dialects during three phases of his career. Beginning in 1912 he worked briefly with two Migueleño speakers. Ten years later he began his most intense work in January 1922 with Dave and María Jesusa Encinales Mora.

Members of the Mission San Antonio Salinan community, including several of Harrington's consultants:
David Mora, Maria de los Angeles, and Maria Mora, 1930s.
Photo courtesy National Anthropological Archives, Smithsonian Institution/ (#91-32718).

Dave Mora provided most of the Antoniano terms, and María, the Migueleño versions.[34] María Jesusa Encinales Mora, was the daughter of Eusebio and Perfecta Encinales; she was raised around San Miguel. Both her father and mother had spoken Migueleño. She was thirty years old when her mother died so she had had an excellent opportunity to learn the language.[35]

María de los Angeles Baylon de Encinales was Harrington's last major consultant on Migueleño. Of her Harrington wrote "I just feel like thanking God that old Maria de los Angeles, aged, nearly ninety years, and David Mora are still alive, for without them the work would be impossible."[36] The primary focus of his study at that time was the rehearing of his earlier field notes and the checking of data from several manuscripts and published sources.[37]

In 1931 Harrington returned to work with Dave Mora as well as with María de los Angeles and her husband, Tito Encinales:

I found the Indians we planned to work with all alive and in fine health, and it is sheer luck, for old Maria (de los Angeles) nearly died last winter and great would have been

the loss. We brought her at once from where she lives at the foot of the great Santa Lucia Peak to David's (Mora) ranch and have about a ton of material from her and Tito (Encinales), her aged husband, already. I have gotten all the names of animals and plants, and very complete and carefully heard, with all kinds of accompanying notes, and supported by a large collection of plant specimens which I will send for identification later. . . . I have brought Marta Herrera here from San Juan to help in the typewriting.[38]

During field visits in 1922 and 1930-32, Harrington recorded approximately 4,500 pages of field notes which provide a wealth of information.[39] The consultants mentioned above provided most of what is known of Salinan cultural survival and much of the recorded language. [40]

Harrington's dedication and enthusiasm for his work shine through his words. As evidenced by his work with Ascensión Solórsano and Isabel Meadows, his coming into their lives, at the end of their lives must have been gratifying to them. Here was a willing ear for all their memories, often bringing back thoughts and words long forgotten and every word recorded for posterity. Harrington

not only worked with his consultants on a scholarly level but he also became lifelong friends with their families. Many of them like, Marta Herrera, Ascensión Solórsano's granddaughter continued to work with Harrington for many years. Academics during this time dismissed Harrington as being too obsessed with recording languages to ever publish or make contributions to linguistic theory. Now, however, there are dozens of scholars working on his linguistic fieldnotes, writing dissertations and papers about the languages portrayed in them.

Maria Encinales de Mora entertaining a young visitor at her ranch, 1923. Photo courtesy National Anthropological Archives, Smithsonian Institution/(#91-32735).

Notes:

1 Jane Maclaren Walsh, "John Peabody Harrington: The Man and his California Fieldnotes." *Anthropological Papers No.* 6, (Ballena Press, Ramona, CA, 1976), p. 10.

2 Ibid., p. 11.

3 Carobeth Laird, *Encounter With An Angry God, Recollections of My Life with John Peabody Harrington* (Malki Museum, Morongo Reservation, Banning, CA 1975) p. 67.

4 Katherine Klar and Elaine L. Mills, "John P. Harrington: A Selection of his Correspondence with the Bureau of American Ethnology supplemented by other documents relating to his field work." Unpublished manuscript. The Papers of John P. Harrington, Smithsonian Institution, Washington D.C. Letter from John P. Harrington to J. Walter Fewkes, December 24, 1921.

5 Walsh, p. 12.

6 Walsh, p. 13.

7 Walsh, p. 13.

8 Ibid., p. 121.

9 Elaine L. Mills, *A Guide to the Field Notes: Native American History, Language, and Culture of Northern and Central California. The Papers of John Peabody Harrington in the Smitsonian Institution 1907-1957*, vol. 2, (Kraus International Publications, White Plains, NY, 1985), p. 130.

10 Mills, p. 121.

11 Thomas Roy Hester, "Esselen." In *California*, edited by R. F. Heizer, Handbook of North American Indians, vol. 8, William C. Sturtevant, general editor. Smithsonian Institution, Washington D.C., p. 496.

12 Ibid, p. 498.

13 Mills, p. 122.

14 Ibid p. 82.

15 Robert F. Heizer, "Ethnographic Notes on California Indian Tribes III. Ethnological Notes on Central California Indian Tribes." *University of California Archaeological Survey.* No. 68, Part III., p. 385.

16 Mills, p. 82.

17 John P. Harrington Papers, Pt. 9, *Correspondence,* [National Anthropological Archives, Smithsonian Institution, Washington D.C.] letter to Matthew Stirling, August 7, 1929, Rl. 17, Fr. 598.

18 Mills, p. 82.

19 Harrington, *Correspondence*, letter to Matthew Stirling, August 7, 1929, Rl. 17, Fr. 598.

20 Mills, p. 83.

21 Harrington, *Correspondence,* letter to Matthew Stirling, December 15, 1929, Rl. 17, Fr. 637.

22 Harrington, *Correspondence,* letter to Matthew Stirling, January 29, 1930, Rl. 17, Fr. 643.

23 Mills, p. 85.

24 Harrington, *Correspondence,* letter to H.W. Dorsey, April 28, 1932, Rl. 17, Fr. 705.

25 Harrington, *Correspondence*, letter to H.W. Dorsey, December 10, 1931, Rl. 17, Fr. 686.

26 Harrington, *Correspondence,* letter to H.W. Dorsey, April 28, 1932, Rl. 17, Fr. 705.

27 Harrington, *Correspondence,* letter to Matthew Stirling, April 2, 1932, Rl. 17, Fr. 701.

28 Harrington, *Correspondence*, letter to Matthew Stirling, May 30, 1932, Rl. 17, Fr. 709.

29 Harrington, *Correspondence*, letter to H.W. Dorsey, May 7, 1932, Rl. 17, Fr. 707.

30 Harrington, *Correspondence,* letter to Thomas Meadows, January 2, 1932, Rl. 12, Fr. 441.

31 Klar and Mills, letter from Harrington to Matthew Stirling, December 27, 1935.

32 Harrington, *Correspondence,* letter to Matthew Stirling, June 14, 1939, Rl. 17, Fr. 792.

33 Betty Rivers and Terry L. Jones, "Walking along Deer Trails: A Contribution to Salinan Ethnogeography Based on the Field Notes of John Peabody Harrington," *Journal of California and Great Basin Anthropology*, Vol. 15, No. 2, Malki Museum, p. 146.

34 Mills, p. 130.

35 Mills, p. 131.

36 Harrington, *Correspondence*, letter to H.W. Dorsey, December 10, 1931, Rl. 17, Fr. 686.

37 Mills, p. 130.

38 Harrington, *Correspondence,* letter to Matthew Stirling, March 30, 1931, Rl. 17, Fr. 667.

39 Rivers and Jones, p. 146.

40 Rivers and Jones, p. 152.

Bibliography

Harrington, John P. 1981. John P. Harrington Papers, Pt. 9, Correspondence. National Anthropological Archives, Smithsonian Institution, Washington. (Microfilm edition, Kraus International Publications, Millwood, New York.)

Heizer, Robert F. 1967. "Ethnographic Notes on California Indian Tribes III. Ethnological Notes on Central California Indian Tribes." *University of California Archaeological Survey.* No. 68, Part III.

Hester, Thomas Roy. 1978. "Esselen." In *California*, edited by R. F. Heizer, pp. 496-499. Handbook of North American Indians, vol. 8, William C. Sturtevant, general editor. Smithsonian Institution, Washington D.C.

Klar, Katherine A. and Elaine L. Mills. n.d. "John P. Harrington: A Selection of his Correspondence with the Bureau of American Ethnology supplemented by other documents relating to his field work." Unpublished manuscript. The Papers of John P. Harrington, Smithsonian Institution, Washington, D.C.

Laird, Carobeth. 1975. *Encounter With An Angry God, Recollections of My Life with John Peabody Harrington;* Malki Museum, Morongo Reservation, Banning, California.

Levy, Richard. 1978. "Costanoan." In *California*, edited by R. F. Heizer, pp. 485-495. Handbook of North American Indians, vol. 8, William C. Sturtevant, general editor. Smithsonian Institution, Washington D.C.

Mills, Elaine L., ed. 1985. *A Guide to the Field Notes: Native American History, Language, and Culture of Northern and Central California. The Papers of John Peabody Harrington in the Smithsonian Institution 1907-1957*, vol. 2, Kraus International Publications, White Plains, New York.

Rivers, Betty and Terry L. Jones. 1993. "Walking Along Deer Trails: A Contribution to Salinan Ethnogeography Based on the Field Notes of John Peabody Harrington," *Journal of California and Great Basin Anthropology*, Vol. 15, No. 2, Malki Museum.

Walsh, Jane Maclaren. 1976. "John Peabody Harrington: The Man and his California Indian Fieldnotes," *Anthropological Papers No. 6*, Ballena Press.

Santa Cruz
County
History Journal
Issue 5, 2002

Profile: Isabel Meadows

Isabel Meadows was born on July 7, 1846, the day the American flag was raised over the Custom House in Monterey. Her mother, Loreta Onésimo, was born at Mission San Carlos in Carmel in 1817, and had both Rumsien (Ohlone) and Esselen ancestry. Isabel's father was James Meadows, an Englishman who jumped ship from a whaling vessel in Monterey. Isabel worked with linguist and ethnographer John P. Harrington for several years, providing thousands of pages of linguistic, ethnographic and historical information, until her death in 1939 at age 93. Photo courtesy of Linda Yamane.

"…The Padre gave the Indians that piece of land that is now called "El Potrero" on Sargent's ranch. And when the Americans came, the Indians were chased out. The padre gave them the land with papers written up, but the signatures weren't held valid when the Americans came. Sargent ran them off when he bought there. They had to leave, and they were gathered together camping at the river—and from there the Indian people dispersed.

The government never helped the Carmel people, not with anything were they helped. The land they were given by the signatures of the padre didn't hold, and they had to disperse to wherever they could. Thrown out, they stayed among the other peoples only to find their life as the most poor. And they were exposed to all kinds of vices and drinking. The American government instead of caring for them like they cared for the Indians in other parts, seemed like it didn't know these Carmeleños existed.

Some died of sadness and others went away from there, dispersed and scattered everywhere. Some ended up living away in Sacramento or in Santa Barbara. Throughout all those places there were Carmeleños hiding that they knew the language. And many died with smallpox also, and with measles—they didn't know how to protect themselves. And years were ended with drunkenness. Before, in Monterey, it seems like every other house had a bar and these poor people drank until they died. Some drank from sorrow because they had been cast out.

The history of the Carmelo and of Monterey tells of many accidents and fights and stabbings and clubbings and everything that happened to the Indians when they were drinking. And many deaths resulted from the drinking of whiskey and wine. In this manner, the Indian people were finished off faster—with the drinking and with so much sorrow that they had been cast away from their land.

They were the first ones that brought the first padres to the Carmelo. They were the first people to be put there in the Carmel Valley. And now there are almost no Indian people of pure Carmel race nor speaking the language. So much have they suffered, forced to mix in with the Mexicans and then with the gringos. I hope that one of the wealthy people of the Carmelo will be able to buy them a good piece of land, at least, to live on, to put their rancheria like before, to revive their language, and to be counted again in the world."

—Isabel Meadows, 1934
(translated from Spanish by Linda Yamane)

C. Hart Merriam and His Friends

by David W. Heron

Clinton Hart Merriam's remarkable career as a biologist began in 1872, when he was sixteen and Spencer Fullerton Baird, Assistant Secretary of the Smithsonian Institution and his father's friend, arranged his appointment as naturalist on Ferdinand B. Hayden's second U.S. Geological Survey of the Rocky Mountains. On this expedition to Wyoming, Montana, and Utah, Merriam established his skill as a collector and taxonomist, discovered his fascination with the West, and became aware of the traumatic effect the flood of westward immigrants had on Native Americans.[1]

After graduating from the Sheffield Scientific School at Yale in 1877 he received his M.D. degree from Columbia University in 1879, and practiced medicine in his home town of Locust Grove, New York, for the next four years. During this period he made time to write the first part of his monumental "Mammals of the Adirondack Region" for the *Transactions of the Linnean Society* (Dec., 1882), twice revised and expanded.

He was dissatisfied with life as a country doctor and, again recommended by the admiring Smithsonian Secretary, Spencer Fullerton Baird, he was appointed surgeon aboard the sealing vessel *Proteus*, which visited the seal fisheries of Newfoundland, Labrador, and Greenland. Secretary Baird subsidized his collection of skins, skulls, and skeletons for the Smithsonian's collections and expressed his pleasure with the results.[2]

After a short sojourn in England and Germany, Merriam went to work for the Department of Agriculture's new ornithology division; this eventually became the Division (later Bureau) of Biological Survey, which he headed from its inception in 1896 until 1910. His travels took him West often, and shortly after the turn of the century he began to devote more and more of his time to the study of western Indian tribes, particularly those of California.[3]

C. Hart Merriam (late 1890s).
Courtesy of Alfred L. Gardner
and the Smithsonian Institution Archives.

The UC Davis Anthropology Department houses the C. Hart Merriam Collection of Baskets of North American Indians. In it are two baskets thought to be of Ohlone manufacture, and reflecting what is known of Ohlone basketry technology. Both were purchased by Merriam in San Francisco in 1901. This basket (CHM-337) was said to have been in the family of Governor Alvarado since 1796. The basket is coiled, with a 3-rod foundation (presumed to be willow), woven with sedge and a bracken fern pattern. There are remnants of feathers in three narrow horizontal stripes. Photo by Linda Yamane, 1996, courtesy of the University of California, Davis.

This basket (CHM-338) was purchased from a man who claimed it was from Santa Clara, but there is no way to verify the statement and there are few extant Ohlone baskets for comparison. The basket is coiled on a 3-rod foundation (probably willow), with sedge and a bulrush pattern. Photo by Linda Yamane, 1996, courtesy of the University of California, Davis.

From this early interest came one of his most important ethnological essays: an estimation of the decline of California's Indian population from 1800 to 1900. He based his estimates on extrapolation from baptismal records of California's Franciscan missions. Merriam calculated that "the Mission strip," as he called the coastal area defined by the missions south of San Francisco, occupied one fifth of the area of the state, and that its native population density (and the decline thereof) was proportionate to that of the rest of the state. He estimated that the total Indian population of California in 1800 was 260,000, and that the area, because of its favorable climate, was once the most populous in North America. He calculated that its biggest decline followed the disestablishment of the missions in 1834, that there were only 100,000 by 1849, that the total in 1856 (the end of the Gold Rush) was 50,000, and that by 1900 the total number of survivors was 15,500.[4] Alfred L. Kroeber published Merriam's figures in his Handbook of the Indians of California, although he was of the opinion that Merriam's initial estimate of 260,000 was somewhat high.[5]

Approaching the turn of the century, Merriam joined a group of people, including Francis Leupp, Hamlin Garland, Charles Lummis, Theodore Roosevelt, and Samuel Brosius (head of the Indian Rights Association) who became active advocates for the Indians. Roosevelt's role in this movement became somewhat delicate after he became president. In 1904, when Merriam proposed firing a couple of Indian Agents whom the IRA suspected of abuses, President Roosevelt chastised him quite bluntly. After that, Merriam became somewhat less active in the politics of Indian rights, though no less concerned.[6]

In 1899 Edward H. Harriman invited Merriam to organize the scientific staff of a large summer expedition to Alaska, and Merriam subsequently edited a twelve volume report, published in 1901. Partly as a result of this expedition, Harriman's widow established, in 1910, a personal trust fund for Merriam, administered by the Smithsonian, which would relieve him of administrative responsibilities so that he might devote his full time to research and writing. Although he did not entirely abandon his taxonomic interests, A. L. Kroeber later wrote that, "From 1910 to 1942 the greater part of his time was spent in the study of historic and living Indians of California, and he was thus *de facto* an anthropologist."[7]

Viviana Soto (also known as Beviana Torres and Viviana Espinosa) was interviewed by both Alfred Kroeber in 1902 and C. Hart Merriam in 1906. She provided each with considerable Monterey area language and cultural information, as well as recording several songs on wax cylinders for Alfred Kroeber. Born in 1823 at Mission San Carlos in Carmel, Viviana was of Rumsien Ohlone and Esselen parentage. She died in 1916 at age 93. She has many descendants living in the Monterey and Salinas areas, and elsewhere. Photo courtesy of Linda Yamane.

In 1911 Merriam built a summer home in Lagunitas near the coast of Marin County, where he and his wife Elizabeth stayed from late spring until late fall. During these long summer months, he traveled on horseback, by wagon, then by car, to Indian villages, particularly in north and central California, where he assiduously recorded the responses to his questions about the life, customs, names, and languages of the survivors he visited. Kroeber later recalled that he conducted his interviews with "patience, tact, and sympathy

Barbara Sierras Solórsano (Mutsun Ohlone/Yokuts) and this unidentified child were photographed at Barbara's Gilroy home by C. Hart Merriam in 1902. While working with Merriam, she provided valuable Mutsun language and ethnographic information. Barbara was the mother of Ascención Solórsano Cervantes, who was an informant to John P. Harrington in 1929. Barbara was born in 1828 and died in 1913. Courtesy of the Bancroft Library, University of California, Berkeley.

which elicited cooperation from his informants. To this I can testify from having spoken to many of them...who always remembered him with affection and approval."[8] An example of his transcripts is that of a vocabulary interview with two elderly Rumsen women, Beviana Torres and her niece, Jacinta Gonzales, in Monterey County. He recorded names of his informants in his transcripts, but seldom included them in his publications.[9] One of his most important contributions was with his camera. He was a skillful photographer, and his pictures of people, their costumes, shelter, artifacts, and places, add immensely to the record.[10]

In transcribing tribal and personal names, Merriam used the simple orthography of Webster's dictionary, rather than that in use by the Bureau of American Ethnology. Kroeber defended this by saying, "Was the name for house, or for, say, jackrabbit, the same here and in the native village ten miles away, or was it similar, or drastically different? For this purpose, Merriam's non-technical means definitely sufficed."[11]

In 1950 Merriam's daughters gave his extensive notes, journals, and photographs to the University of California Anthropology Department. Professor Robert F. Heizer was assigned custody of them, which he transferred to the Bancroft Library in 1977, and from which he published several substantial volumes, supported by the E. H. Harriman Fund and the Mary W. Harriman Foundation. In the introduction to the last of these, *Indian Names for Plants and Animals*, Heizer was less charitable in a frank statement of how professionally trained anthropologists felt about Merriam's orthography:

"There is a point of scholarship involved in presenting the work of a man who has been dead for over thirty years, and particularly the work of a person, however objective, well-intentioned and industrious he was, which is deficient in so many ways. Merriam was a real 'loner,' and as such one might almost say that he invented his own kind of ethnography. He was quite untrained in linguistics and obviously had a 'bad ear.'"[12]

After Merriam's death in the spring of 1942, Charles L. Camp wrote an obituary for the *California Historical Society Quarterly* in which he painted a more favorable picture: "Seldom have so many talents been combined in one person. He was without pretense, with boundless enthusiasm and vigor, and great personal charm. His critical faculties were highly developed, and his views and comments were always acute and wonderfully interesting."[13]

Perhaps most important among Merriam's California friends were his native American informants, many of whom wrote to him after his visits to add to information which they had already given him.[14]

Jacinta Gonzalez, who identified herself as being Kakoon (from south of Carmel near Big Sur), was interviewed by Alfred Kroeber in 1902, at which time he made wax cylinder recordings of her singing a Monterey gambling song with Viviana Soto and reciting part of a coyote myth. C. Hart Merriam interviewed Jacinta and Viviana in 1906, compiling a substantial vocabulary of the Rumsien (Monterey) language. Jacinta is mentioned in No More a Stranger, *a book about Robert Louis Stevenson written by Anne B. Fisher in 1946. Stevenson was forever grateful to Jacinta for treating him with plant medicines during a serious illness during his stay in Monterey in 1879. Jacinta was the great-great grandmother of Lydia Bojorquez. Photo courtesy of Linda Yamane.*

Notes:

[1] Kier B. Sterling, *Last of the Naturalists; the Career of C. Hart Merriam* (New York: Arno Press, 1974) 1-73.

[2] *Ibid..*, 68-75.

[3] Willliam T. Hagan, *Theodore Roosevelt and Six Friends of the Indian.* (University of Oklahoma Press, 1997); 120-122.

[4] C. Hart Merriam, "The Indian Population of California," *American Anthropologist*, vol. 7 (NS), 1905; 594-606.

[5] Alfred Louis Kroeber, *Handbook of the Indians of California.* (Washington: Bureau of American Ethnology, 1925) 880-891.

[6] William T. Hagan, *op. cit.*, 152-155.

[7] Alfred L. Kroeber, "C. Hart Merriam as Anthropologist" in C. Hart Merriam, *Studies of California Indians*, (Berkeley: University of California Press, 1962) vii.

[8] *Ibid.*, x.

[9] Merriam Papers, Bancroft Library (film) Reel 39.

[10] *Studies of California Indians*, various pages. An excellent example is Plate 35a, of a pole and brush Esselen shelter.

[11] Kroeber, *op.cit.*, xi-xii; and C. Hart Merriam, *The Dawn of the World; Myths and Tales of the Miwok Indians of California* , reprint of the 1910 edition. (University of Nebraska Press, 1993) 29.

[12] *Indian Names for Plants and Animals among Californian and other Western North American Tribes, by C. Hart Merriam, Assembled and Annotated by Robert F. Heizer*, (Socorro, New Mexico: Ballena Press, 1979)1-5. Heizer also mentions that neither Merriam nor his friend J. P. Harrington liked Kroeber, which he attributes to professional jealousy .

[13] Charles L. Camp, "Clinton Hart Merriam, 1855-1942," *California Historical Society Quarterly*, vol. 21 (1942); 284-286.

[14] C. Hart Merriam, *Ethnographic and Ethnosynonymic Data for Northern California Tribes...Assembled and Edited by Robert F. Heizer* (Berkeley: University of California Department of Anthropology, 1976) i-ii.

Selected Bibliography

Camp, Charles L. "Clinton Hart Merriam, 1855-1942," *California Historical Society Quarterly*. v. 21. pp. 264-6, September 1942.

Hagan, William T. *Theodore Roosevelt and Six Friends of the Indian*. Norman, Oklahoma: University of Oklahoma Press,1997.

Kroeber, Alfred Louis. *Handbook of the Indians of California* Washington: Bureau of American Ethnology, 1925.

_____ "C. Hart Merriam as Anthropologist," introduction to *Studies of California Indians, by C. Hart Merriam* (q.v.).

Merriam, C. Hart. *The Dawn of the World; Myths and Tales of the Miwok Indians of California* (reprinted from the 1910 Arthur H. Clark edition). Lincoln, Nebraska: University of Nebraska Press, 1993.

_____*Ethnographic and Ethnosynonymic Data for Northern California Tribes—Assembled and Edited by Robert F. Heizer*. Berkeley: University of California Department of Anthropology, 1976.

_____*Indian Names for Plants and Animals among California and Other Western North American Tribes...Assembled and annotated by Robert F. Heizer*. Socorro, New Mexico: Ballena Press, 1979.

_____ "The Indian Population of California," *American Anthropologist* NS, v. 7, pp. 594-606, 1905.

_____*Studies of California Indians, by C. Hart Merriam*. Edited by the Staff of the Department of Anthropology of the University of California. Berkeley: University of California Press, 1962.

Osgood, Wilfred H. "Biographical Memoir of Clinton Hart Merriam, 1855-1842." *Biographical Memoirs of the National Academy of Sciences*, v. 24, Washington, N.A.S., 1947.

Sterling, Kier B. *Last of the Naturalists: the Career of C. Hart Merriam*. New York: Arno Press, 1974.

Profiles: Claudia Corona

Claudia Corona (left) with Isabel Meadows. Claudia was the daughter of Ascención Solórsano Cervantes and granddaughter of Barbara Sierras. Photo by John P. Harrington, courtesy of the National Anthropological Archives, Smithsonian Institution/(#91-30378).

Tony and Melba Corona

Tony and Melba Corona of Hollister are pictured in this 1991 photograph when Tony was 88 years old. Tony's mother was Claudia Corona, his grandmother Ascención Solórsano Cervantes. He knew John P. Harrington, having accompanied Harrington at times as a young man. Tony has maintained a keen interest in his Indian heritage throughout his life, establishing a sizable museum of artifacts and photographs in his garage, much to the delight of his many visitors. Photo by Linda Yamane.

"For my 75th birthday, the kids gave Melba and me airplane tickets to Washington, D.C. We had talked about wanting to go for many years and we thoroughly enjoyed our visit to the Smithsonian in 1978. We spent a whole day looking at Harrington's notes and photographs from the time he spent with my mother and grandmother and other relatives in the area."

—Tony Corona
(Mutsun Ohlone) 2001

Three Poems

by Stephen Meadows

Bert's Wake

Bertoldo Onésimo, son of Manuel Onésimo.
Photo courtesy of Linda Yamane.

I recall your face shining
You were fierce that day
behind the old John Deere
on the tongue
of that man killing scraper
Too young to help
I trailed you through the dust
heard you grunt each time
you threw your body on the iron
Heard the cut sound
the earth made
the hard chuck of stones
and the wheeze of lung muscle
held against the live ground
Forty years of plowing
near that hog fence
laid a hill you moved
in a day
your work shirt stuck
to your black rubber neck
sweating wine

Alejandro

Alejandro Onésimo, son of Manuel Onésimo.
Photo courtesy of Linda Yamane.

The close dark grain
of this antique chair
built about the time
you were born
holds for a moment
your face and its lines
entwining like the years
in my grandfather's field
a transient memory of you
your walk distinctive and measured
along the road
for wine and supper
looking as they all said
like a bear's in the shade
of live oak
you worked with the best of them
and had times been different
you might not have labored for wages
you might have had children
your signature practiced as a youth
more beautiful than my own
your untutored thoughts all those years
like the breathing of the oaks
the plummet and rustle
of an acorn
in a green quiet place

Blues for Juanito

No amenities but cheap wine
and those fits of weeping
the distempered wet look
of some dog and the black
cast stove picked up red hot
with a couple of burlap sacks
thrown smoking on the truck
when they moved you
to the corn crib shack

Son of old Manuel
far down on the ladder
of the children
it was always you and your brother
and the drunks from town
in beaten old cars that limped
through the summer dust
and shimmered in the heat
near the river

When you died on county sheets
of TB and too much wine
no more the soiled blanket
the broken cot crying
to yellow heaven in the heat
the few windows cracked
the lantern too
cracked
and remaining the tin shack
the bad sawhorse leaning
and the white alder
dead in the blackberry vines
like bone

Juan Onésimo, son of Manuel Onésimo.
Photo courtesy of Linda Yamane.

Santa Cruz
County
History Journal
Issue 5, 2002

Profile: Carmen Espinosa Fernandez

24

Carmen Espinosa Fernandez, great granddaughter of Viviana Soto Espinosa, Santa Rita (North Salinas), 1940. Photo courtesy of Carmen Fernandez.

"I've been enjoying learning about my great grandmother Viviana (Soto) Espinosa. It was a big surprise to find out that she had recorded the Indian songs so long ago. I was excited to hear her voice, to hear her sing the songs— it's something I never expected to hear. I'm happy to share this with my children and grandchildren. When I was a child, someone knocked at the front door, asking if there were any California Indians living there. My mother said, "No!" and closed the door. People were afraid to admit being Indian back then. Growing up, I didn't know what I was because nobody wanted to talk about it. But now we can be proud to be Indian."

—Carmen Espinosa Fernandez
(Ohlone/Esselen), 2001

The Spanish Contact & Mission Period Indians of the Santa Cruz-Monterey Bay Region

by Randall Milliken

The Indian people of the California coast from Point Año Nuevo to Point Sur lived a gathering and hunting way of life in 1769, the year that Spanish missionaries and soldiers arrived to settle around Monterey Bay. Forty years later, in 1809, no villages of tribal gatherers remained along the coast or in the adjacent Coast Range valleys. The people had either died of introduced diseases or moved to one of the agricultural communes associated with Franciscan missions San Carlos Borromeo, San Juan Bautista, Santa Cruz, and Santa Clara.

This article describes the lifeways, political geography, and history of the Spanish-contact and Mission Period Santa Cruz-Monterey Bay area Indian People. The article is divided into three parts. The first part briefly describes tribal lifeways, language, and political organization. The second part describes the history of tribal migration to the missions. The third part of the article discusses the fourteen contact-period political groups of the area under discussion, in alphabetic order.

Ethnographic Overview

No Indians or Spaniards of the era wrote detailed accounts of the way of life that came to an end between 1769 and 1809. A general picture of the lost material lifeways can, however, be reconstructed from brief reports in Spanish explorers' diaries and more detailed village population counts provided in mission baptismal registers.

The picture that emerges is one of a light population, varying locally between two and four people per square mile. Villages and campsites swelled, shrank, or were abandoned at various seasons of the year, as families moved about to harvest locally abundant wild plants and animals. Men hunted rabbits, deer, and elk in the fields, ducks and fish in the lagoons. Women gathered greens, seeds, and acorns in their seasons. People wore very little in the benign climate; women wore tule skirts; men and children wore nothing at all. Special feather costumes and shell ornaments were brought forth at festival times, when multiple village groups would meet to share food, trade, and perform traditional ceremonies. In short, the Monterey Bay people lived a gathering and hunting way of life typical throughout California prior to the European invasion.[1]

Spanish reports tell us that all of the people of the coast from Point Sur north to San Francisco Bay spoke closely related languages, with the exception of some villages in the mountains and valleys south of Monterey. Twentieth century ethnographers called the predominant language family Costanoan or Ohlone and the strikingly different southern language Esselen.[2]

Although most of the Monterey Bay groups spoke dialects of the Ohlone (alias Costanoan) language family, none of them thought of themselves as Ohlones or Costanoans. Instead, individuals belonged to local independent political groups led by the elders of extended families. In many areas a number of such extended families joined together in miniature tribes under the leadership of a single multi-family headman. Such miniature tribes were called *tribelets* by anthropologist A.L. Kroeber, who wrote, "I deliberately coined the name tribelet to designate a sovereign though miniature political unit, which was land-owning and maintained its frontiers against unauthorized trespass."[3] Territorial tribelets did not form in rugged and mountainous areas; instead, small family band groups of flexible size roamed the land. In the Monterey Bay area, tribelet organization was the norm. However, in rugged areas, such as the densely forested Santa Cruz Mountains, the more fluid band organization may have prevailed.

Each local group had one, two, or three semi-permanent villages of 50 to 150 persons, as well as numerous temporary campsites. The amount of outmarriage to neighbors varied with group size; in small groups (less than 150 people) as many as half of the married adults came from neighboring groups, while in large tribelets (400 -500 people) as few as 10 percent of the married adults came from other groups.[4]

The Spanish "Spiritual Conquest"

Missions San Carlos Borromeo and Santa Clara
Spanish soldiers founded the Monterey Presidio, a military base, in 1770. Franciscan Junípero Serra established Mission San Carlos Borromeo in the nearby Carmel Valley later in the same year. Serra and the other Franciscans were committed to changing the economy, personal habits, and thought structures of the native people of California by teaching them Spanish Catholicism and small-scale agriculture. By 1777 they had baptized the great majority of the Rumsen tribelet of the lower Carmel Valley, and were turning their attention to more distant peoples (Maps 1, 2). During those years they identified the Carmel Valley Rumsen people in baptismal entries by their specific home villages, not their tribelet group name.[5] From the mid-1770s on, however, people from groups beyond the Carmel Valley were identified by tribelet in the San Carlos Mission registers. Among them were Sargentaruc on the Big Sur coast, Excelen of the upper Carmel River, and Ensen of the Salinas Valley.

In early 1777, the Franciscans founded Mission Santa Clara twenty-five miles north of Monterey Bay in the Santa Clara Valley. The priests at Mission Santa Clara identified the small villages of their initial converts by the saints' names San Francisco

and Santa Clara, without any reference to native village names. The Santa Clara missionaries went on to label the other villages of the Santa Clara Valley with saints' names, including San Jose Cupertino, San Juan Bautista (not to be confused with the mission founded further south in later years), and Santa Ysabel. The Mission Santa Clara priests simplified the geographic picture still further after the mid-1780s, labeling all new Christians from beyond the northern Santa Clara Valley according to one of four saints' names that reflected compass directions, San Antonio to the east, Santa Agueda to the north, San Bernardino to the west, and San Carlos to the south. This practice precluded the use of those registers for directly reconstructing tribelet geography around Mission Santa Clara.

Mission Santa Clara absorbed a total of 133 married couples from its southern San Carlos district from 1785 through 1809. Many of those couples went to Santa Clara from the southern Santa Clara Valley, from San Martin south to Gilroy. Others went to Mission Santa Clara from the high valleys of the Santa Cruz mountains. Even a few coastal people from the Santa Cruz vicinity were baptized at Mission Santa Clara under the broad place name, San Carlos.

Missions Santa Cruz and San Juan Bautista
Mission Santa Cruz was founded in 1791 in an area that had already received minimal proselytization from Mission Santa Clara further north. The Franciscans at Mission Santa Cruz gave saints names to local groups, but also identified the villages by native name. The zone nearest Mission Santa Cruz includes six distinct groups almost completely absorbed between 1791 and 1795. All six groups can be placed near Santa Cruz on the basis of their marriage ties with each other and with more distant groups. They were Uypi, referred to by some missionaries as San Daniel; Cotoni, alias Santiago; Achistaca, also referred to as San Dionisio; Sayanta, alias San Juan Capistrano; Chaloctaca, sometimes listed as Jesus; and Aptos, alias San Lucas. These small groups from rugged areas partially covered by dense and biologically unproductive redwood forests may have been extended family bands, rather than multi-village tribelets.[6]

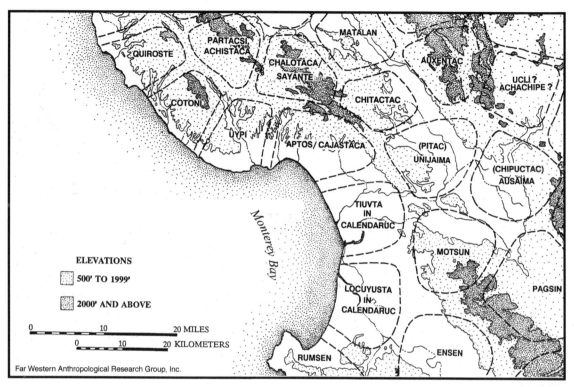

Map 1. General locations of tribelet territories in the Monterey Bay Area

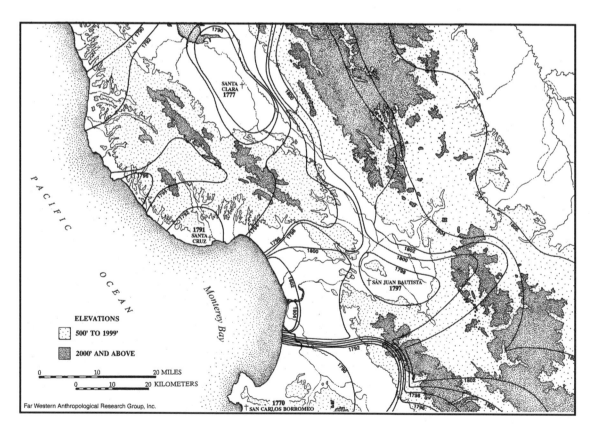

*Map 2. The progressive collapse (in 2-year increments) of
autonomous tribal areas as groups moved to the missions.*

Mission San Juan Bautista was founded in 1797 in the land of the Motsuns, a multi-village group that had already sent people to be baptized at San Carlos Mission. Christian Motsuns moved back home at the founding of Mission San Juan Bautista, where their names appear in marriage and death records. Mission San Juan Bautista baptismal records are excellent for ethnogeographic reconstruction; in them people were identified by tribelet, and sometimes additionally by village within the tribelet. When Mission San Juan Bautista opened, all of the people along the northern shore of Monterey Bay had already been missionized although significant fractions of the Calendaruc and Ensen people of the central Monterey Bay area were as yet unbaptized.

Between 1798 and 1806 Mission San Juan Bautista took in Ausaimas, Tamarrons, Orestacs, and Ochentacs from eastern San Benito and western Merced counties as well as the remaining Calendaruc people along central Monterey Bay. During the same 1798-1806 period, tribal people from the coast range valleys to the east of the Santa Clara Valley continued to migrate to missions Santa Clara, Santa Cruz and San Juan Bautista. The main groups to go to Santa Cruz in those years were Chiputac, Sumu, Tomoi and Uculi from the mountains of eastern Santa Clara County and western Stanislaus and Merced counties (Maps 1, 2). Many people from those same groups went to Mission Santa Clara under the names San Carlos and Tayssenes.

After 1800 immigration to Mission San Carlos Borromeo was limited to a few dozen people from the Santa Lucia mountains and the Big Sur coast. (By 1808 that mission had become the organizational center for other missions and essentially discontinued as a commune for newly arrived tribal people.) By the end of 1803, all of the Coast Range tribelets and bands had moved to the missions. Only a few individuals from the easternmost Coast Range groups moved east to join friends and relatives in Yokuts tribelets along the San Joaquin River.

The Era of Yokuts Missionization

The year 1808 was a watershed for the Monterey Bay Area mission communities. From that year forward San Carlos would discontinue accepting tribal groups, and all newly arriving groups to San Juan Bautista and Santa Cruz would be Yokuts-speakers from the San Joaquin Valley. In 1808 and 1809 Locobos from the mouth of San Luis Creek moved to Mission Santa Cruz. They were followed in 1810 by Yeuratas alias Chanech, and Tejeys alias Mallin from the Los Banos-Gustine area of the San Joaquin Valley. By 1812 trouble had erupted between San Joaquin Valley groups and Spaniards, none of whom had yet moved to San Juan Bautista. Between 1812 and 1817 no large groups arrived at either Mission Santa Cruz or San Juan Bautista. A few unmarried individuals did go to Mission San Juan Bautista between 1812 and 1815 from the "tulares," people identified in subsequent records with the Chanech, Quihueth and Cutocho tribelets of the west side of the San Joaquin River.

Migration of Yokuts-speakers picked up in 1817-1819, following some Spanish military forays into the San Joaquin to arrest runaway Christian Indians.[7] Small groups of San Joaquin River Achils, Chaneches, and Mallins went to Santa Cruz, while small groups of Nopchenches, Eyulahuas, and Copchas went to San Juan Bautista. The major migration occurred in 1820-1823, as almost every group along the San Joaquin River and lower Merced River east of Monterey Bay moved to either Mission Santa Cruz or Mission San Juan Bautista.

Explaining the Process of Missionization

No simple answer exists for the commonly asked question: "Why did Indian people leave their homelands and move to the mission communities?" Catholic baptism was never supposed to be forced upon individuals under the direct threat of gun or sword, and in California it seldom was. The first recruits came to the missions under the attraction of the new and exciting Spanish material technology. As the years went by the negative aspects of mission life became clear; these included high disease rates, an interference in personal lives, an oppressive organization of work, corporal punishment, and the forced return of runaways.

Within the missions, the people were made to feel ashamed of their traditional way of life and envious of Spanish culture. The success of the Spanish assault on native culture is well illustrated by Father Palóu's comment regarding changes in the native attitude toward the naked human body: "It is worthy of notice, that while before baptism, they had no sense at all of shame, these feelings are immediately dominant in them as soon as baptism is received, so that if it is necessary to change the clothing because they have outgrown them, they hide themselves nor will they show themselves naked before any one, and much less before the Fathers."[8]

Many people internalized the belief that they deserved to be powerless, to be ordered about, and to be punished. Missionary president Lasuén wrote in 1793: "They hear Mass every day, and those who accept the Ten Commandments are now convinced that it is right to punish them for their defects."[9]

Yet new tribal recruits continued to join mission communities after the negative aspects became clear. They made that decision within the context of constricting choices caused by a steady deterioration in tribal physical, social, and psychological environments that they were powerless to halt. Most important were the new epidemic and endemic diseases, most notably syphilis, brought by Spanish ships from around the world. The new diseases caused an accelerated infant death rate in native villages. Emigration to the missions by the most easily attracted families also induced a decline in village populations.

Two related problems arose for tribal villages as their populations declined: first, communities that relied heavily on teamwork fell below the minimal size necessary to coordinate food harvest and processing; second, group social organization weakened as trained specialists and community leaders died or moved to the missions. The people who resisted mission attractions, who remained in tribal villages of reduced size, became vulnerable to attacks from traditional enemies in stronger groups situated further away from the missions. At some point, the option to remain in the homeland ceased to exist.

At the missions people sought the familiar within the alien. They placed themselves in the hands of the Franciscan missionaries, and relied upon them—just as they had traditionally relied upon knowledgeable elders in their own lands—to guide them in proper ritual conduct and in respect for the supernatural. Many people became deeply committed to special mission roles, such as those involving church ceremonies, the leadership of work crews, or the acquisition of a mechanical knowledge of the loom or lariat.

Fugitism was relatively common, indicating that the strain of maintaining a new identity sometimes became too much to bear. Overt resistance, although less common, did occur at one time or another at every central California mission. For instance, the first elected native mayor of Mission San Carlos failed to take orders from missionary Father Serra, then ran off to lead a two-year resistance along the Big Sur coast. On December 14, 1793, Quirostes at the Point Año Nuevo area attacked the Spanish soldiers at recently founded Mission Santa Cruz without loss of life.[10] Later, in 1812, a group of Mission Santa Cruz men killed a particularly hated mission priest.[11] Nevertheless, they were not able to forge enduring regional military alliances to oppose the Spanish invasion because they did not consider themselves to be a single people and because they lacked weaponry commensurate with that of the Spaniards. As the years went by, the most common expression of protest against the new authorities was a listless attitude and a lack of cooperation toward work activities.

Missions as Mixed-Language Communities

Intermarriages took place at the missions among groups that had lived too far apart to ever have married in pre-mission times. In pre-mission times intermarriage between language groups had not been uncommon, but they usually occurred among bands and tribelets that faced one another along a language boundary. At the missions, high death rates reduced the numbers of preferred marriage choices and familiarity broke down proscriptions against marriage with strangers from great distances, regardless of language. Intermarriage between Ohlone-speakers and Esselen-speakers became commonplace at Mission San Carlos Borromeo after 1800. Likewise, intermarriage between Ohlone-speakers and Yokuts-speakers became common at Mission Santa Cruz and Mission San Juan Bautista with the arrival of Yokuts groups after 1808.

By the end of 1825 both Missions Santa Cruz and San Juan Bautista had become predominately Yokuts-speaking communes. At Mission Santa Cruz approximately 31% of 429 Indian people were tribally-born Ohlone speakers, another 50% percent were tribally-born Yokuts speakers, and 18% were mission-born children of both groups. At San Juan Bautista 27% of the 1166 Indian people were tribally-born Ohlone speakers, 54% were tribally-born Yokuts speakers, and 19% were mission-born to both groups.[12] As a result of the mixing of people from near and far, many of the Indian people in later mission times and the subsequent Rancho Period were the children of inter-ethnic Yokuts-Ohlone or, at Mission San Carlos Borromeo, Esselen-Ohlone marriages.

We see the multi-lingual background of modern Monterey Bay area Indians illustrated in the genealogies of María Ascención Solórsano, the Ohlone consultant to linguist J.P. Harrington at Mission San Juan Bautista, and Lorenzo Asisara, who remembered his father's stories of the brutality of life at Mission Santa Cruz. María Ascención Solórsano was Ohlone-Yokuts, the granddaughter of Junípero Sierras (SJB-B 1823) of the Ohlone-speaking Orestacs and Sopatra (SJB-B 2766) of the Yokuts-speaking Quithrathres. Lorenzo Asisara (SCR-B 1832) was the son of local Santa Cruz Ohlone Venancio Llenco (SCR-B 215) of Cotoni and Manuela (SCR-B 1803) of the Chalahua, a San Joaquin Valley Yokuts group.[13]

Rancho and Early American Periods

The missions were closed by decree of the Mexican government in 1834-1836. The Indian inhabitants were turned out, landless, to fend for themselves. Many of the Yokuts newcomers returned to their old home lands in the San Joaquin Valley. The old locals, and many of the newcomers, stayed to work on the lands and in the homes of the new landowners, the descendants of the soldiers who had led the Hispanic invasion over sixty years earlier.

A new chapter opened in the history of California Indian people with the declaration of war between Mexico and the United States in 1846. As a result of that war, the rancho lands of central California became part of the United States. For six years, from 1846 to 1852, the Catholic Church in California was in a state of disarray. Many Indian people stopped going to church. Many priests failed to keep adequate records of the births, marriages, and funerals that they did perform. Then, as the civil record-keeping of the Americans began to develop, the marginalized Indian people were often left out of early censuses.

By the time record-keeping restabilized after the Civil War, the paper trail for the life histories of many Indian families seems to have been broken. Because of this legacy of spotty record-keeping, or perhaps because of our society's insistence on proofs from the written record, contemporary political groups of mission descendants have had challenging problems in establishing their historical tribal affiliations. Nevertheless, those affiliations are being established, through a combination of clues from family oral histories, modern civil records, and the early mission records.

Tribal Political Groups of the Monterey Bay Area

Problems of Reconstructing Ethnogeography

Each Indian person who joined a Franciscan mission was given a new Spanish name and listed individually in that mission's register of baptism. The person's guessed age was recorded as well, and typically the person's native name was also recorded. Most important for tribal geography, the priests always recorded the name of the person's home group, sometimes a village, sometimes a region.

Unfortunately, it is impossible to precisely reconstruct the political geography of any vicinity from mission register sources because the missionaries seldom included any clues regarding the direction and distance to the homeland locations they wrote down. Approximate homeland locations can be reconstructed, however, through indirect approaches. Three key rules apply in ethnogeographic reconstruction. First, it is initially assumed that the first groups to appear at a mission lived closer to that mission than groups that appeared in later years. Second, it is assumed that groups that were heavily intermarried lived adjacent to one another, while groups with no inter-marriages lived at great distances from one another. And third, it is assumed that groups that sent members to two different missions lived somewhere equidistant from those missions. The group location reconstruction shown on Map 1 is based upon these three rules.

Brief discussions of fourteen different tribelet (or band district) groups who once lived around Monterey Bay in modern Santa Cruz, San Benito, and Monterey counties are found below in the final section of this article. The inferred group locations are illustrated on Map 1.

Achistaca. Achistaca was one of the local groups of the Mission Santa Cruz vicinity. They were a small group; eighty-five of them went to Mission Santa Cruz from 1791 through 1795 under the name Achistaca as well as San Dionisio. They are inferred to have been in the upper San Lorenzo River drainage in the vicinity of the modern towns of Boulder Creek and Riverside Grove. Achistaca people had four pre-mission marriages with Cotoni of the coast, two with Sayanta, and one with Chaloctac. Some of the San Carlos district converts at Mission Santa Clara may have been from Achistaca.

The Achistacas may be the same group as the Acsaggis baptized at Mission San Francisco between 1787 and 1791. Fifteen year old Ssolcóm, married

at the time to a thirty-nine year old Oljon man, went to San Francisco "from the Acssagis familia in the vicinity of Soróntac at the sourçe of San Francisquito Creek" (SFR-B 676).[14] Although Acsaggis are explicitly referenced in only three other Mission San Francisco baptismal entries, a large unidentified group with links to the four Acsaggis, baptized at San Francisco in early May 1793 (SFR-B 1290-1329), may themselves have been Acsaggis.

Aptos. The Aptos were the largest of the early groups converted at Mission Santa Cruz, with 117 baptisms between 1791 and 1797. They appeared in the Santa Cruz Mission Baptismal Register under the name San Lucas in the margin and Aptos in the text (for instance, SCR-B 4). We presume that Aptos Creek, very near to Soquel Creek in the Uypi homeland, was at the western edge of Aptos lands. The group probably held the shores of Monterey Bay from Aptos eastward about half way to the mouth of the Pajaro River.

Of interest, the people initially identified as Aptos had only four outmarriages to other groups, two to Uypi, one to Cajastaca, and one to Socon (probably Calendaruc). However, numerous Cajastaca people appeared in later death register and padron entries as Aptos, suggesting that the Aptos and Cajastaca may have been a single tribelet. Thus, I treat the Aptos and Cajastaca together on Map 1.

Calendaruc. The Calendaruc area included the central coast of Monterey Bay, near the mouth of the Pajaro and Salinas Rivers, and Elkhorn Slough. A total of 388 Calendaruc people were baptized, 158 at Mission San Carlos between 1783 and 1806, and 230 at San Juan Bautista between 1797 and 1806. Spanish priests at Mission San Carlos distinguished between two Calendaruc groups, Tiuvta on the Pajaro River and Locuyusta somewhere closer to Monterey. At San Juan Bautista the term *Calendaruc* seems to have been applied only to the Tiuvta group of the Pajaro River, while the term *Guacharron* (River People) was applied to the more southerly Salinas River group. Mission records indicate subsidiary village names for both groups. Tiuvta and Locoyusta were alternatively separate tribelets or two main villages of a single tribelet.

Calendaruc people had out-marriages to Motsun (4), Rumsen (2), Ensen (2), Aptos (2), Pagsin (1), and to Ochentac of the distant eastern Coast Range (1). A marginal group at Mission Santa Cruz, "Socon, alias La Candelaria" seems to have been the same people as the Tiuvta group. Only four Socon people were baptized at Mission Santa Cruz, three in 1795 and one in 1797 (SCR-B 378, 407, 409, 763); one of them was married to an Aptos woman, while another moved to Mission San Juan Bautista to marry into a Tiuvta family.[15]

Cajastaca. The Cajastaca (alias San Antonio) group, baptized at Mission Santa Cruz during the late 1790s, are currently thought to be from the lands just north and northeast of the present town of Watsonville in the Corralitos area and perhaps east as far as the Aromas area (cf. Levy 1978:485). The Cajastaca group was baptized at Mission Santa Cruz during the late 1790s, the same years as the Pitacs and the Chitactacs, people of upper Uvas Creek and Gilroy areas. The only people with whom the Cajastacas were married prior to conversion were the Aptos (SCR-M 253). Thus it is assumed that these two groups were contiguous. Of 38 people in the last village group identified as Aptos in the Mission Santa Cruz Book of Baptisms, 11 were identified from Cajastaca in later death records or census lists.[16] This raises the possibility that Cajastaca may even have been a village of the Aptos group.

Chaloctac. The band or tribelet of Chaloctac are thought to have held the rough country around Loma Prieta Creek along the crest of the Santa Cruz Mountains. Only 38 people, they went to Mission Santa Cruz between 1792 and 1795. Their small group size suggests that they were a remnant segment of a group already converted at Mission Santa Clara. In fact, some individuals baptized at Mission Santa Clara in the 1780s under the designation "San Carlos de la Sierra" and "Rancho de la Sierra" have family links to Mission Santa Cruz Chaloctacs. The small Chaloctac group had five pre-mission marriages with the Sayanta people, three with Achistaca, one with Cotoni, and one with

Partacsi of the Santa Clara Valley. I show Chaloctac and Sayanta together on Map 1 because of their exceptionally high number of intermarriages, which may indicate that the two bands lived and worked together seasonally.

Chitactac/Pitac. The Chitactac and Pitac people were baptized together at Mission Santa Cruz between 1795 and 1808 under the Spanish designation San Juan. Although I place the Chitactacs on the upper reaches of Uvas Creek in the Santa Cruz Mountains on Map 1, they may just as easily have held lower lands further to the east in the Santa Clara Valley corridor. The Pitacs, most of whom were baptized later than most Chitactacs, were probably from the San Martin area in the Santa Clara Valley corridor.

San Juan seems to have been merely a directional designation, not an alias for a single tribelet area. Of the first 51 San Juan people baptized at Mission Santa Cruz, on March 20, 1795, most seem to have been Chitactacs. At least the lead individuals in three baptismal groups of the day were specifically identified as Chitactacs. The only clue for the other 48 entries of the day is the word *San Juan* in the register margin. Cross-reference to later death and marriage records indicates that most of these people were Chitactacs, but some were Pitacs. However, to complicate matters further, three people from that first San Juan group (SCB-B 532, 534, 542) were listed as Chipuctacs (an Ausaima alias) in a later Mission Santa Cruz *padrón*.

The Pitacs were first explicitly identified in the 1796 entries at Mission Santa Cruz. In January of that year, 32 children were baptized from the village of Chitactac. Many of these children had Chitactac parents who had been baptized the year before. But the parents of others in the group were baptized in February and identified as Pitac. It is common to find contradictions of this type in the mission registers for Chitactacs and Pitacs baptized at Santa Cruz between 1796 through 1800. This suggests either that the missionaries were confused about political and territorial relationships or that Chitactac and Pitac were two villages of a single tribelet.

A possibility exists that the Pitacs at Mission Santa Cruz were from the same villages as the Uñijaimas at Mission San Juan Bautista. One explicit clue in the Mission San Juan Bautista baptismal register points to it; on October 29, 1819, years after complete tribal absorption in the area, Father Arroyo de la Cuesta baptized a Mission Indian child "born on the 26th at Pitac or La Brea" (SJB-B 2329). La Brea, or Tar Creek, was definitely Uñijaima territory, a clear clue in favor of Pitac/ Uñijaima identity. Yet, other family links between the Mission Santa Cruz Pitacs and the Mission San Juan Bautista Uñijaimas are lacking. The question of the relationship of the Chitactacs, Pitacs, and Uñijaimas remains open.

Cotoni. Cotoni, alias Santiago, is another of the small Mission Santa Cruz groups for which no direct locational information is found in historical sources. They were the last of the first five groups converted at Mission Santa Cruz; 95 of them were baptized between 1792 and 1800. Intermarriage and time of baptism suggest that the group held the Pacific Coast in the vicinity of the present town of Davenport, and probably the inland ridge in the Bonny Doon area as well. Their pre-mission outmarriages were with Achistaca (3), Sayanta (1), and Chaloctac (1).

One of the Cotoni converts was Venancio, whose son Lorenzo Asisara provided many details about mission life which were published in the late nineteenth century. Venancio was listed as a 20 year old from Cotoni in his 1793 baptismal entry (SCR-B 215). Over 80 years later, Lorenzo Asisara did not use the term Cotoni for his father's people. "My father's tribe was Jlli, and he belonged to the tribe that lived up the coast. They lived upon shellfish, which they took from the seacoast, and carried them to the hills, where were their rancherías."[17]

Ensen. The Ensen tribelet, the people of Los Zanjones (The Ditches), had villages in the lower Salinas River Valley from Salinas upstream to Chualar. All but two of 237 missionized Ensen people went to Mission San Carlos between 1782 and 1808. Two others were baptized at Mission San Juan Bautista. The Ensen baptismal pattern was atypical; most of them (188) were baptized between 1782 and 1793, then 47 others straggled into Mission San Carlos over the long period 1797-1808. One baptismal entry refers to a village of Ensen between the places of Buenavista (The Lovely View) and Los Zanjones (The Ditches). Buenavista became a Spanish rancho during the mid-1790s. Perhaps some Ensens found work on the ranch as an alternative to moving to the missions. This interpretation is supported by the fact that two Ensen men baptized between 1806 and 1808 had picked up Spanish nicknames, El Coyote (SCA-B 2671) and El Cabezon (SCA-B 2581).

Motsun. The Motsuns held the site of Mission San Juan Bautista, its environs, and the areas of Aromas and Natividad to the west and south. Some 218 Motsun people were baptized, 22 at Mission San Carlos between 1783 and 1797, 196 at Mission San Juan Bautista from 1797 to 1806. A large village noted by numerous early explorers along San Juan Creek, within a mile south of the mission site, was probably the main Motsun village of Xisca, listed numerous times in the initial baptismal records of Mission San Juan Bautista.[18] It is not clear if the village of Juristac (SCR-B 528; SJB-B 91), later Rancho Juristac, between Gilroy and San Juan Bautista, was in Motsun territory or that of their northern neighbors, the Uñijaima. The Motsuns had marriages with Pagsin (6), Calendaruc (4), Uñijaima (2), and Ausaima (2) at the time of missionization.

Quiroste. The Quiroste were a tribe on the Pacific Coast from Bean Hollow Creek south to Año Nuevo Creek, and inland to Butano Ridge. Occasional Quirostes appeared among the earliest San Francisco Peninsula coastal groups baptized at Mission San Francisco. Sujute, wife of an Oljon, was "from Churmutcé, farther south than the Oljons" (SFR-B 679, October 27, 1787). Uégsém, wife of a Cotegen, was from "the family of the Quirogtes of the village of Mitine to the west of Chipletac" (SFR-B 711, October 19, 1788). A few of them went to Mission Santa Cruz under the designation "San Rafael, alias Mutenne." Most went to Mission Santa Clara from the "San Bernardino" district during the 1790's.

Rumsen. The Rumsen of the lower Carmel Valley and the Monterey Peninsula were the first Monterey Bay area tribelet to be completely absorbed into a Spanish Mission. A total of 436 of them were baptized at Mission San Carlos between 1770 and 1784. At baptism, they were identified according to home village name, Achasta at the mouth of the Carmel River, Tucutnut about three miles inland on the Carmel, Socorronda in the Carmel Valley area, Echilat on a high flat south of the Carmel River Valley, and Ichxenta, location unknown. Only in the 1790s, after Mission San Carlos became the home of people from many neighboring tribelets, were the Rumsen people referred to in mission records by their collective name. The contact-period Rumsen were inter-married with Ohlone-speaking Sargentaruc of the Big Sur coast and Ensen of the Salinas area, as well as the Esselen-speaking Excelen of the Jamesburg area of the upper Carmel River watershed.[19]

Sayanta. This small group went to Mission Santa Cruz between 1791 and 1795, where they were also identified as the San Juan Capistrano group. A total of 69 people were baptized, a small number for an independent tribelet group. To locate them, we start with the inference that they held the Zayante Creek drainage, the present Scotts Valley area and the Glenwood and Laurel areas to the north and east. This is the area of the Mexican land grant Arrollo de Sayante.[20] The Sayanta Creek location is supported by their order of baptism, subsequent to Uypi, and their pre-mission intermarriages with Chaloctaca (5) and Achistaca (2). Other Sayanta people probably went to Mission Santa Clara prior to 1791 under the San Carlos district designation.

Uñijaima. The Uñijaimas held the southern Santa Clara Valley from the present Gilroy vicinity south to the Pajaro River. A total of 141 Unijaimas were baptized, two at Mission San Carlos in the mid-1790s, 135 at Mission San Juan Bautista between 1797 and 1808, and another four at Mission Santa Cruz between 1798 and 1802. Tipisastac, a specific village name, was the term by which the first Uñijaimas at Mission San Juan Bautista were identified from July 1797 until April 1798. Other Uñijaima villages mentioned at Mission San Juan Bautista include Carneadero (The Butchering Place), Saisin, Tebletac (also Teboaltac), and Thirthiri (also Chercheru).

Documented pre-mission Uñijaima outmarriages were to the east to Ausaima (5), to the south to Motsun (2) and Pagsin (1) and to the southwest to Calendaruc (1). The lack of documented marriages to the west and north reflects the fact that people from those areas went to missions Santa Cruz and Santa Clara. To the north, the Uñijaimas would certainly have been intermarried with the Pitacs of Mission Santa Cruz. In fact, it is possible that Pitac was a Mission Santa Cruz alias for the Uñijaima tribelet.

Uypi. Uypi, alias San Daniel, are presumed to have held the mouth of the San Lorenzo River because they were the first group to go in large numbers to Mission Santa Cruz for baptism and the first group completely absorbed into that mission. All in all, 103 Uypi people were baptized at Mission Santa Cruz between 1791 and 1795. Two children of Uypi's captain, Suquer, were baptized at Mission Santa Clara in 1791 under the homeland designation "San Carlos" (SCL-B 1894, 1907). Suquer and his wife were the second and third people baptized at Mission Santa Cruz (SCR-B 2, 3). The town of Soquel almost certainly derives its name from a later Spanish corruption of Captain Suquer's name. Uypi pre-mission outmarriages are documented to Aptos (4), Sayante (3), Cajastaca (1), Chaloctac (1), Cotoni (1) and San Juan (Pitac/Chitactac).

Notes:

[1] Important ethnographic descriptions regarding Monterey Bay area tribal people are found in the 1769 journals of Gaspár de Portolá, Miguel Costansó, and Juan Crespí, translated and published by Frank Stanger and Alan K. Brown in *Who Discovered the Golden Gate?* (San Mateo County Historical Association, 1969). Ethnographic information regarding the southern Santa Clara Valley is found in the 1776 journal of Pedro Font, translated and published by Herbert E. Bolton in Anza's California Expeditions, Volume 4, *Font's Complete Diary of the Second Anza Expedition,* (University of California Press, 1930).

[2] Francisco Palóu first noted the similarities between Monterey Bay and San Francisco Bay dialects in page 270 of his 1774 *Historic Memoirs of New California*, 4 Volumes, Vol. 3 (Berkeley and Los Angeles: University of California Press; 1926). Arroyo de la Cuesta in 1814 described a cline of dialects from group to group from Mission San Carlos north to Mission San Francisco de Asis in pages 20-21 of *As the Padres Saw Them* edited by Maynard Geiger and Clement W. Meighan (Santa Barbara: Mission Archive Library, 1976). By 1910 the language family was most commonly called Costanoan. See pages 237-271 of A. L. Kroeber's "The Chumash and Costanoan Languages" *(University of California Publications in American Archaeology and Ethnology,* Vol. 9(2); 1910). C. Hart Merriam coined an alternative name, Ohlonean, for the language group in his "Ethnological Notes on Central California Indian Tribes" (*Reports of the University of California Archaeological Survey*, No. 68, Part III, Berkeley; 1967). While some Indians still refer to their ancestors as Costanoans, others prefer the term Ohlone. See "People of the West: The Ohlone Story" by Michael Galvan (*The Indian Historian*, vol. 1; 1968) and *The Ohlone Way* by Malcolm Margolin (Berkeley: Heyday Books; 1978).

[3] Quoted from A.L. Kroeber's most developed treatment of the tribelet concept, page 307 of "Nature of the Landholding Group," *Ethnohistory*, Volume 2(4) (University of Indiana; 1955). In that article he suggested that tribelet organization was commonplace across tribal North America, noting as examples Delaware and Cherokee political organization. Kroeber had introduced the tribelet concept in "The Patwin and their Neighbors," *University of California Publications in American Archaeology and Ethnology*, Volume 29(4), pages 253-423 (Berkeley; 1932).

[4] Statistical evidence for tribelet outmarriage in the Southern Monterey Bay area can be found in a limited distribution publication by Randall Milliken entitled "Ethnohistory of the Rumsen," *Papers in Northern California Anthropology,* Number 2 (Salinas: Coyote Press; 1987). For an excellent discussion of general intermarriage rates in small scale societies, see J.W. Adams and Alice B. Kasakoff, "Factors Underlying Exogamous Group Size," *Regional Analysis*, Volume 2, pages 149-173, Carol Smith, editor (New York: Academic Press; 1976).

[5] As found in print today, the term *Rumsen* may apply to the specific tribelet of the Carmel Valley and Monterey Peninsula or to the language spoken by that tribelet and other nearby tribelets with similar dialects which were gathered together at Mission San Carlos Borromeo. See Richard Levy's chapter on Costanoan in *The Handbook of North American Indians,* Volume 8 (California) (Washington, DC: Smithsonian Institution; 1978) for an example of the use of the term Rumsen to designate a multi-tribal language group.

[6] See "Central Ohlone Ethnohistory" by Chester King for detailed genealogies of the local Santa Cruz area groups, pp. 203-228 in *The Ohlone: Past and Present*, Lowell J. Bean editor (Menlo Park, CA: Ballena Press; 1994).

[7] Sherburne Cook translated accounts of some military forays in pages 267-273 of "Colonial Expeditions to the Interior of California: Central Valley, 1800-1820," *University of California Anthropological Records*, Volume 16(6) (Berkeley; 1960).

[8] Quoted from page 211 of Palóu's *The Life and Apostolic Labors of the Venerable Father Junipero Serra*, translated and edited by George Wharton James (Pasadena, CA: Private press of George Wharton James; 1913).

[9] Quoted from Fermin F. de Lasuén, "Ynforme del Estado Espirituál de los Misiones de la Nueva California en el fin del año 1792." *Archivo Generál del nacíon [Mexico].Archivo Histórico de Hacienda Documentos para la Historía de México, Segunda Serie, tomo 2, Misiones de Alta California*, Documento 146. R. Milliken, translator. (Mission San Francisco; March 6 1793).

[10] See pages 88-89 in *Indians and Pioneers of Old Monterey* by James Culleton (Fresno: Academy of California Church History, publication # 2; 1950) for a partial description of the 1780-1782 resistance to Mission San Carlos Borromeo by Baltazar. The Quiroste resistance to Mission Santa Cruz is described in detail in pages 115-120 of *A Time of Little Choice* by Randall Milliken (Menlo Park, CA: Ballena Press; 1995).

[11] See Lorenzo's First Narrative in "The Narratives of Lorenzo Asisara" in this Journal for a complete description by a mission Indian whose father participated in this event.

[12] I derived the year-end language group percentages for 1825 from my own databases for missions Santa Cruz and San Juan Bautista. In those data bases I have transcribed and cross-referenced the baptisms and deaths of individuals at the missions. My Mission Santa Cruz data base lists 461 individuals baptized up to the end of 1825 that have not been reported dead or re-aggregated to another

mission; for Mission San Juan Bautista, I list 1215 fitting the same criteria. Yet the 1825 yearly mission reports, published by Jacob Bowman in "The Resident Neophytes of the California Missions, 1769-1834" in the *Quarterly of the Historical Society of Southern California*, Volume 40(2), pages 138-148 (1958), list only 429 Indian inhabitants at Mission Santa Cruz and 1166 Indian inhabitants at Mission San Juan Bautista at the end of 1825. Obviously, deaths at the missions were underreported, by 6% in the Santa Cruz case and 4% in the San Juan Bautista case. These discrepancies are small enough that we can accept the language group percentages derived from my databases as generally accurate.

[13] The mother of Lorenzo Asisara may actually have been a Southern Miwok speaker who moved to Mission Santa Cruz from the western Sierra Nevada foothills. She was baptized Manuela at Mission Santa Cruz on April 2, 1820 (SCR-B 1803) at the age of 19; her native name was Liutsatme and she was from a group called Chalahua, a tribelet name that appears in no other mission record. However, over a score of Telehua people, probably bilingual Yokuts/Southern Sierra Miwok, were baptized during the 1820's at Mission San Juan Bautista. It is beyond the scope of this paper to document all the evidence for the Telehua as Sierra Miwok. One key piece of evidence, however, is the statement of linguist/missionary Felipe Arroyo de la Cuesta that one of his converts in the year 1827 was of the Telehua Nation which is of the third idiom of his mission (JB-B 3668).

[14] References for individual Franciscan mission baptismal, marriage, and death register entries are:

SCA-B,M,D—San Carlos Borromeo Carmel) Libro de Bautismos, (1 vol.), Libro de Casamientos, (1 vol.), and Libro de Difuntos, (1 vol.). Original registers are under control of the Catholic Diocese of Monterey, 580 Fremont Blvd., Monterey, California. Microfilms are available at family history libraries of the Church of Jesus Christ of Latter Day Saints.

SCL-B,M,D—Santa Clara Mission Libro de Bautismos, 1778-1863 (3 vols.), Libro de Casamientos, 1778-1863 (1 vol.) and Libro de Entierros, 1777-1866 (2 vols.). Original registers are at the Orradre Library, University of Santa Clara, California.

SCR-B,M,D—Santa Cruz Mission Libro de Bautismos, 1791-1857 (2 vols.), Libro de Casamientos, 1791-1802 (1 vol.) and Libro de Difuntos (1 vol.). Original registers are under control of the Catholic Diocese of Monterey, 580 Fremont Blvd., Monterey, California. Microfilms are available at family history libraries of the Church of Jesus Christ of Latter Day Saints.

SFR-B,M,D—Mission San Francisco de Asís Libro de Bautismos, 1776-1870 (2 vols.), Libro de Casamientos, 1777-1859 (2 vols.), and Libro de Difuntos, 1776-1856 (2 vols.). Originals at the Archives of the Catholic Archdiocese of San Francisco, Mountain View, California. Microfilms are available at the Bancroft Library.

SJB-B,M,D—San Juan Bautista Libro de Bautismos, 1797-1874 (2 vols.), Libro de Casamientos, 1797-1860 (1 vol.), and Libro de Difuntos (1 vol.) Original registers are under control of the Catholic Diocese of Monterey, 580 Fremont Blvd., Monterey, California. Microfilms are available at family history libraries of the Church of Jesus Christ of Latter Day Saints.

Numbers that follow register citations in the current article are the unique register entry number that was provided by the missionary scribe of record.

[15] The Socon-Aptos marriage is documented in SCR-M 172 (see also SCR-B 378, 702). The Socon-Tiuvta marriage is documented in SJB-M 148 (see also SCR-B 407, SJB-B 780).

[16] The Aptos people with baptismal numbers SCR-B 676, 682, 687, 689, 691, 692, 695, 696, 702, 718, 719 were noted as being from Cajastaca in their death register entries.

[17] This quote is taken from a nineteenth century published interview with Lorenzo Asisara reprinted by Henry Torchiana in *The Story of the Mission Santa Cruz*, page 284 (Paul Elder and Company, San Francisco; 1933).

[18] The village of Xisca is listed in SJB-B 10, 11, 21, 22, 25-34, 38-40, 45-52, and other records without specific linkage to Motsun. Nevertheless, all of the Xisca converts were members of nuclear families that were otherwise identified as Motsun.

[19] The word Rumsen appears in SCA-B 1528, 1542, SCA-M 399, SCA-D 938, 1078, and 1097, all being entries relating to adults that had been baptized from one or another of the five Rumsen villages. Details regarding the Rumsen tribelet can be found in Randall Milliken's "Ethnohistory of the Rumsen," *Papers in Northern California Anthropology*, Number 2 (Salinas, CA: Coyote Press; 1987).

[20] See page 373 of *California Place Names* by Erwin Gustav Gudde (Berkeley: University of California Press; 1969).

The Esselen Refuge Response to Spanish Intrusion

by Gary S. Breschini and Trudy Haversat

The Esselen were one of the least numerous Indian groups in California, and are often cited in the anthropological literature as the first group to become culturally extinct. Indeed, some researchers placed cultural extinction as early as the 1840s.[1] Reasons given generally include the small size of the group and the close proximity of Esselen territory to two of the three earliest California Missions.

It is now recognized that the group did not become extinct in the 1840s, culturally or otherwise. Rather, it appears that there were fewer surviving descendants of the Esselen than other local groups, and that they were more successful in avoiding the attention of the early anthropologists. Today, there are many individuals who can trace their ancestry back to the Esselen.

The basics of Esselen culture, linguistics, and prehistory are well covered elsewhere,[2] so we have elected to focus on recently acquired information concerning the Esselen's response to the Spanish intrusion into their lands.

The northwestern subgroup of the Esselen, called the Excelen, were the first encountered by the Spanish. There is evidence that one or more skirmishes between soldiers and the Excelen resulted in a number of fatalities, and possibly removal of many of their children to the mission. The Excelen's response was twofold: about half of the group surrendered almost immediately to the missionaries, while other members appear to have sought refuge in the distant mountains.

The southernmost Rumsen (a subgroup of the Ohlone), situated in the Sarhentaruc area between Carmel Highlands and the Little Sur River, appear to have had a similar response. Many went to the missions within a short period, while others appear to have moved south into Esselen lands, where they sought refuge around the Big Sur River and in the rugged coastal mountains.

There were five Esselen districts: Excelen, Eslenahan, Imunahan, Ekheahan, and Aspasniahan (Figure 1). Each district occupied a specific territory with generally-recognized boundaries, and most likely had a reasonably stable resident population. Within each district were a number of villages which were sequentially occupied on a seasonal basis depending on the availability of resources. Food, water, and shelter were the most critical resources, but anyone who has camped in the wilderness can attest that the availability of firewood also would have been a significant factor in village selection. Of these five districts, the boundaries of the Excelen district are probably the best known. The least known boundaries are in the mountainous areas between Excelen, Imunahan, and Ekheahan.

With little land available on the coast, the Esselen Indians made good use of the ridges and the interior. On the coast they established villages or campsites in areas smaller and steeper than used by virtually any other coastal group. Photo by Trudy Haversat and Gary S. Breschini.

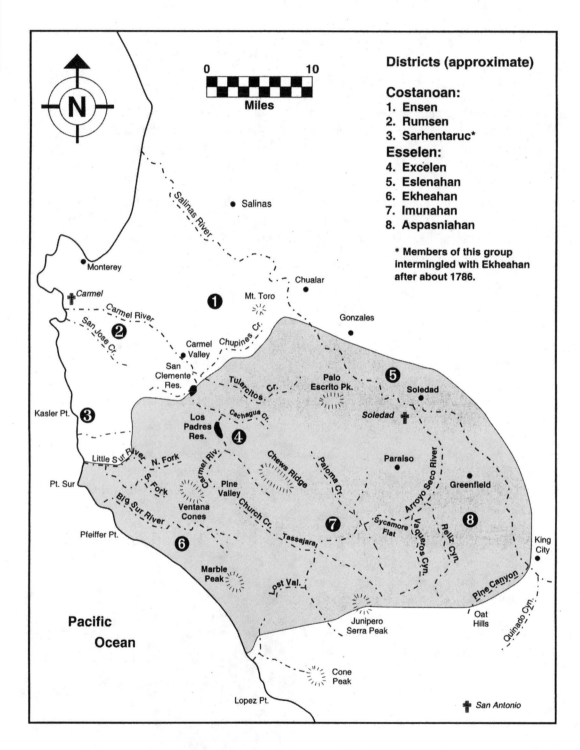

Figure 1. Esselen Territory and Boundaries

Excelen

The first documented meeting between the Spanish and the Esselen comes from Carmel baptismal entry number 350, dated May 9, 1775. On that day, Junípero Serra baptized a 40-year-old man, named Pach-hepas, who was described as the chief of the territory of the Excelen and its rancherias. The baptism took place in the village of Xasáuan, located some 10 leagues (ca. 20-26 miles) southeast of the mission. (The modern name of "Cachagua," a small community in the upper Carmel River drainage, is derived from this Esselen village name.)

> …in the rancheria called Xasáuan in the mountains about 10 leagues distant from this mission of San Carlos of Monte Rey, toward the southeast, I baptized privately a man about 40 years old, in danger of death, married, the headman of the territory of Excelen and its rancherias, named Pach-hepas. I gave him the name Miguel Gregorio.[3]

In the next three years, between 1776 and 1778, an additional 39 Excelen were baptized, including 14 children, but then there was a lull in the baptism rate. Only seven individuals were baptized during the following three year period.

To explain this lull, one has to read between the lines; the early records are poor, and leave out a great deal. However, in the instructions he left to his successor in 1782, Governor Filipe de Neve wrote:

> The repeated patrols that have been sent out to importune them [i.e., runaway Indians] to come back *have resulted in deaths among the non-Christian natives,* due to the poor supervision of the officers in charge. I have refrained to the greatest extent possible from sending out these patrols, preferring other methods for returning runaways to their missions. In those situations in which it has been unavoidable to send them, it has been done with the most detailed instructions to avoid lamentable consequences. It was as much a danger to the little parties which the Presidios were able to send *into the mountains where the natives took refuge.* There was little that our troops could do in that rugged, rocky country, which obliged the soldiers to dismount and enter villages on foot. The non-Christian natives are coming to understand our small number and weakness faster and more frequently.[4]

From this passage, it can be inferred that deaths occurred among the Esselen prior to 1782 because of Spanish attempts to return runaway Indians to the missions. It is also likely that these deaths were at least partially responsible for the lull in baptisms between 1779 and 1782. Within a dozen years after the Spanish arrived, it had become dangerous to send the small parties of soldiers "into the mountains where the natives took refuge" because the soldiers could not make full use of their horses "in that rugged, rocky country."

Another clue to the possible cause for the drop in the number of baptisms comes from a previously unpublished portion of the Galiano manuscript, which notes that at Carmel Mission, Indians speaking the Rumsen and Esselen languages were brought together, and that the two groups were so hostile to one another that reconciling them cost endless labor.[5]

After the lull between 1779 and 1782, baptisms picked up again, with the greatest number occurring in 1783. Culleton notes that there had been a fracas early in 1783 between some men of the mountains (obviously Excelen) and the soldiers, and that a few of the Indians were killed.[6]

While Governor de Neve's account specifically mentions runaways, there is another possible source of friction between the Spanish and Excelen. Many of the Esselen baptized during 1776, and a few of those baptized during the following years, were children. After baptism, children were permitted to live with their parents in their native villages until they reached the age of reason, approximately nine years old. It is possible that the "fracas" mentioned by Culleton resulted when the missionaries tried to force those baptized children to the mission. Not knowing which child was which, the soldiers may have just rounded up all of the children of the appropriate age from the villages they visited. If this was indeed the case, then the large number of Esselen joining the mission during the following months would be understandable—seeing that they could not stand up to the weapons of the Spanish, and they simply wanted to be reunited with their children. Indeed, fourteen of the nineteen Excelen baptisms early in 1783 were of children.

Following this "fracas," a full 40% of the Excelen accepted baptism during the period 1783-1785. But Xasáuan and Excelen were not abandoned immediately after the baptisms of 1783–1785. Carmel baptism 1940, on April 25, 1794, was for José María, interpreter of the Esselen language, who was baptized in the village of Uphahuan (Xasáuan), in danger of death. Three individuals were baptized at Soledad Mission in the early 1790s from Jachaguan (i.e., Xasáuan), and Carmel baptism 1952 shows that the district still had enough people to have a headman in 1794. By 1798 the majority of baptisms had occurred, and it is likely that only a few dozen individuals were left in the mountains of Excelen.

There is evidence that Excelen and the other Esselen districts were not abandoned even after 1798. Only one Excelen baptism occurred during the period between 1799 and 1804, but there was a sudden rise in baptisms between 1805 and 1808 due to the energy of a new priest, Father Amorós, who arrived in September, 1804. In all, 25 individuals from Excelen were baptized during these final four years. In other words, nearly 10% of the total Excelen population which eventually accepted baptism held out for 33 years after proselytizing began in their district. Proselytizing was halted in 1808, and no new converts were baptized after that year.

The last five Esselen to be baptized, in 1808, were mostly elderly individuals. They were: a man whose age was listed as 45 years, two men of 60 years, and two women of 60 and 80 years. It is likely that their children had joined the mission

earlier, and they had no families to support them in their old age, but it is also possible that some of their children were moving into the most rugged interior mountains and these elderly individuals were unable or unwilling to accompany them.

Based on the above information, it appears unlikely that all residents of this mountainous territory went to live at the missions and accepted baptism. But how many individuals managed to avoid the missions? And what eventually became of them?

We know from archaeological evidence that one individual, a girl of about six years of age, was buried in Isabella Meadows Cave (archaeological site CA-MNT-250) in the Church Creek area (see Fig. 1). Based on shell and glass beads, the date attributed to this burial was approximately A.D. 1825. Someone raised the girl and then buried her. In a small cave nearby, another individual was found who had not been buried at all. We do not yet know all the details of this find, but the cranium was reportedly examined by a forensic anthropologist who determined that the individual died approximately 150 years ago.[7] Another clue is provided by Professor Clem Meighan, who noted that "wild" Indians are reported to have occupied the Esselen territory until 1850 or later.[8] Meighan does not provide the source of his statement, but anthropologist Arnold Pilling heard the same story when he worked in the Monterey-Carmel area in the late 1940s.[9] Growing up in the area, the senior author also heard a persistent rumor of a group of Indians still hiding in the hills; it usually took the form, "I never saw them myself, but my cousin saw them once and swore never to tell where they live." This rumor, echoing down the years, may reflect back to the time a hundred years earlier in the 1840s when there actually were Indians hiding in these mountains.

Recent archaeological investigations conducted for the Los Padres Dam project on the upper Carmel River provided additional evidence for occupation of the upper Carmel River during the late Mission Period and perhaps afterward. A change in bedrock mortar usage patterns suggests a short-lived increase in the population in the upper Carmel River drainage. Additionally, four radiocarbon dates from the upper component of site CA-MNT-1601 in this region average approximately A.D. 1815.[10]

With clear evidence for Indian occupation of the mountainous portions of Esselen territory at least into the mid-1820s, it becomes likely that a few individuals survived long enough to bypass the mission system entirely.

As the missions were disbanded in 1834, and in fact had been nearly powerless for years before that date, it would have been possible for Indians to have moved directly from the remote mountains to the newly settled ranchos, where they could have found employment as vaqueros (cowboys) or servants and lived with relatives who were by then free from the missions. It is also possible that individuals released by the missions returned to their original homelands. However, because of the growing settlement of the upper Carmel Valley, it is doubtful that any population of unbaptised Indians survived even in the remotest mountains after the 1850s, although perhaps a few individuals could have held out a little longer.

The Ventana Mountains provided refuge for the Esselen Indians. The Spanish were unable or unwilling to travel very far into the rugged interior. Photo by Trudy Haversat and Gary S. Breschini.

Sarhentaruc

The Big Sur area has been attributed to the Esselen in virtually all the early ethnographic research. More recently Culleton and Cook suggested that the Big Sur area was bilingual and bicultural (presumably some sort of amalgamation of Esselen and Rumsen). Only in the last few years has Milliken's detailed mission record research suggested that the boundary should be placed further south, at, or even south of, the Big Sur River. Milliken also makes a case for bilingualism.[11]

Milliken has made a compelling argument that the Sarhentaruc area was Ohlone (i.e., Rumsen):

> "The village called Sargentaruc situated on the near edge of the great river Jojopan, about eleven leagues from the mission to the south southeast..." [Carmel baptism 1393] was probably near the present town of Big Sur. Some register entries refer to the village itself as Jojopan.[12]

The results of more intensive mission record analyses (using Milliken's database) as well as archaeological research in this area (particularly site CA-MNT-88 on the Post Ranch and sites CA-MNT-63 and CA-MNT-73 at the mouth of the Big Sur River), provide additional details on the nature and location of the Esselen/Rumsen boundary in the area of the Big Sur River.

Locational data for Sarhentaruc are provided in several Carmel mission baptismal and death records (see Table 1).

The records are unanimous that Sarhentaruc lies to the southeast along the coast. A few records refer to the "Sierra de Santa Lucia," but as the coast is extremely steep and mountainous these references are not inconsistent.

There is, however, inconsistency in the use of village and district names. There were apparently two primary villages on the coast south of Carmel mission, Pis (also called Pichi, Pichis, Picho, Piis, and Pys) and Jojopan (also called Jojoban, Joboban, Jojopam, Ojoba, etc.). There is also one reference to the village of "Schascharranta en Sargenta Rucca" (Carmel death 0670). All of these villages are grouped within the district of Sarhentaruc, and in fact, the district name is used in most baptisms.

The name Sarhentaruc is clearly Rumsen. The suffix "ruc" means house, and with a locational prefix refers to a cluster of houses, i.e., a village. Milliken cites Kroeber, whose two Carmel informants equated Sarhentaruc with Sirkhintaruk or Sirkhinta, also called Kakonta, and placed it at Point Sur. The word "kakon" means chicken hawk, and "sirh" means eagle.

However, Henshaw's Rumsen vocabulary gives south as "sir-hin-ti," while his Soledad vocabulary lists "ka-kun." Likewise, Pinart's Rumsen vocabulary gives 'ka koniterx' and "kak kom terx" as the words for south. Another clue as to the location comes from J. P. Harrington's field notes. In April of 1935, Isabella Meadows placed "Sirhin-ta-ruk" in the Palo Corona area, which is just south of the Carmel River. She gave the meaning of "sirxinta" as black oak place. (Linda Yamane, personal communication, 2000.)

The distance for the initial baptisms at Sarhentaruc is most often given as six or seven leagues, or 15.6 to 18.2 miles if the league used measures a full 2.6 miles. However, in rugged terrain, the league is often shorter than 2.6 miles, reflecting the reality of travel.

Measured along Highway 1 from Carmel Mission, 15.6 miles reaches the Little Sur River, while 18.2 reaches the area north of the Big Sur River. If a shorter league is used because of the rugged terrain, this places the location closer to Palo Colorado Canyon. Indeed Carmel baptisms 760 and 1038 and Carmel death 394 each mention a canyon of redwoods or a little canyon of redwoods. These records do not mention a river, which is more consistent with Palo Colorado Canyon's small creek than the much larger Big Sur River. This distance is also more consistent with Palo Colorado than Palo Corona, which is only about two miles south of the mission.

From this, we can infer that the earliest Sarhentaruc baptisms came from the area around Palo Colorado Canyon and Rocky Creek, all north of Hurricane Point and the Little Sur River. In fact, it is likely that the majority of the Sarhentaruc individuals baptized between 1782 and 1785 came from this area. Both the distance and the descriptions match that location better than the Big Sur area. There is also a large archaeological site at Palo Colorado which appears similar to Rumsen sites in the Carmel and Carmel Highlands areas; there are no such sites known from the Big Sur River area. Considerable evidence thus suggests that, as Milliken determined, the initial group of people baptized from Sarhentaruc were Rumsens. A 1789 baptism (Carmel baptism 1393) places Sarhentaruc on the side of the great river Jojopam, and at a distance of 11 leagues (28.6 miles) from the mission. Again using a shortened league, this location should clearly be at the Big Sur River, some 20 to 25 miles south of Carmel Mission. The individual baptized at this location was Maria Felicidad, a 60-year-old woman originally from the rancheria of Ecgeajan of the nation of Esselen, who had lived there for many years because she had a daughter married there.

After the bulk of the Sarhentaruc population was baptized, there were still people in the Palo Colorado area, as well as in the area of the Big Sur River to the south. Ten Esselen and 13 Rumsens were baptized at Carmel between 1786 and 1791. This figure probably includes Rumsens who were missed in the main wave of baptisms, but may also include some who had moved south of the Palo Colorado area previously to avoid the Spanish. This figure also includes Esselen (variously identified as being from Ecgeajan, Excelemac, Excelaux, Ecgeas, Egeac, Egeach, etc.). As noted above, at least one of these, Maria Felicidad (Carmel baptism 1393), was living in the immediate vicinity of the Big Sur River.

From the pattern of baptisms it is clear that Pis/Pichi is on the coast not too far south of Carmel, and that Jojopan is further south, probably at the Big Sur River. The term Sarhentaruc was used as a synonym for both areas.

Table 1. Mission Record References for Sarhentaruc's Location.

Carmel Mission baptisms are abbreviated CA-B, followed by the number, and Carmel Mission deaths are abbreviated CA-D, followed by the number. Please note, discrepancies in spelling reflect those in the original records.

Record	Translation
CA-B 0412	The rancheria named Sargenta-Ruc distant about seven leagues [18.2 miles] toward the southeast from this mission and she is the first Christian from this populous rancheria.
CA-B 0416	Rancheria Pitchi in the place named Sargenta Ruc.
CA-B 0498	The rancheria of Piis in the Santa Lucia mountains.
CA-B 0688	Sargentaruc in the mountains.
CA-B 0760	In the rancheria of Sargenta-ruc in an arroyo of redwoods and laurels about seven leagues [18.2 miles] from this mission by the beach to the southeast.
CA-B 1038	In the rancheria Sargenta-Ruc about six leagues [15.6 miles] following the coast to the southeast in a little canyon of redwoods.
CA-B 1264	On the coast named Sargentaruc to the south of this mission… in that site called Ojoba near a large arroyo.
CA-B 1393	In the rancheria named Sargentaruc, located on the near side of the great river Jojopam, and distant from this mission about eleven leagues [28.6 miles] toward the south-southeast.
CA-B 1428	Originally of the rancheria or Achasta or San Carlos and…living in the rancheria named Jojopan or Sargenta Rucca.
CA-B 1486	In the place named Pis in Sargenta Rucca toward the south.
CA-D 0310	In the fields and mountains of Sargenta-Ruc.
CA-D 0394	About six or seven leagues from here in a canyon of redwoods.
CA-D 0590	Rancheria of Picho (in the margin: Sargentaruc).
CA-D 0649	In the rancheria named Jojopan in Sargenta Ruca towards the south.
CA-D 0670	In the place named Schascharranta in Sargenta Rucca toward the south… native of Jojopan in Sargentaruc.
CA-D 0671	In the rancheria of Sarg.ruc in the place named Jojopam.
CA-D 0742	In the place named Pis in Sargenta Rucca.

Point Sur is a rocky butte extending to a height of 361 feet, and which can be seen for miles in both directions. It is possible that the district of "Ekheahan," or "the rock," was named for this landmark.
Photo by Trudy Haversat and Gary S. Breschini.

Death records show that at least nine individuals (eight adults and one child) were baptized at Carmel Mission but subsequently died and were buried in Sarhentaruc. One individual was not even from that area originally! Culleton notes that the chief of Sarhentaruc and Jojopan, Chilichón (Carmel baptism 1072) left the mission soon after baptism in 1785, and induced his former wife, who was by then married to another, to join him. Culleton also notes that baptisms then ceased for Jojopan for 20 years.[13] Most likely these runaways and a number of other individuals were taking refuge in the southern regions of Sarhentaruc to avoid the Spanish soldiers. The majority of these deaths (7 of 9) were in the years 1786-1790, when, as noted above, there was a very small population in Sarhentaruc, though it was still supplying occasional converts. This is direct evidence of the use of Sarhentaruc as a refuge from the Spanish. But the location was most likely in the area of the Big Sur River than around Palo Colorado Canyon, which, because of the terrain, was much easier for the Spanish to reach. Thus it appears that the term Sarhentaruc was used initially for the populous village at Palo Colorado Canyon, and that later, when some of those individuals moved south, the same name was also applied to the Big Sur area.

After 1792 there was a gap of 12 years with no Carmel Mission baptisms from this area at all (although Milliken lists four baptisms from Jaboban and "numerous" baptisms from Ecgeajan at Soledad Mission between 1796 and 1806). Then, between 1805 and 1808, at the very end of the spiritual conquest, the last individuals to come to Carmel Mission were baptized. As with the Excelen, this can be attributed to the energy of a new priest, Father Amorós. This last group of 45 individuals included 16 who were identified as being from Sarhentaruc and 25 from Egeac, Ecgeas, or Egeach, etc. Four individuals were listed as "Sarhentaruc or Egeac."

This suggests that Esselen and Rumsens were living together and intermixing in some fashion in the Big Sur River area by the mid 1780s, and perhaps intermarrying. Another example comes from the last baptisms in the 1805-1808 period, which included three individuals whose native name was either Mucjay or Mucjas. Two of these were identified as from Sarhentaruc and the third was from Egeach. However, the degree or nature of intermixing is not yet understood.

In the mission records, Ekheahan is occasionally referred to as "Ex'xien" or "the rock." Milliken suggests that this may refer to the distinctive 4,031 foot Marble Peak.[14] Marble Peak is more of a landmark from the interior ridges than along the coast. It is more likely that "Ex'xien" refers to Sur Rock. This is a major landmark in the Big Sur area, and is visible from a considerable distance up and down the coast, as well as from the adjacent ridges. If this is the case, it would place the Esselen boundary toward the northern end of the Big Sur plain, probably in the area of the Little Sur River.

Finally, archaeological evidence casts doubt on the theory that the Big Sur area was inhabited by Rumsens prior to Spanish contact. There is a clear dividing line in archaeological site types at about the Little Sur River. To the north of this point there are sites rich in shellfish remains, as well as large, rich middens. These characteristics are associated with Rumsen sites, such as CA-MNT-12 at Monastery Beach. South of the Little Sur, in the vicinity of the Big Sur River, are sites which contain smaller quantities of shellfish remains, and, while not necessarily physically smaller, contain relatively fewer cultural materials. These can be identified with the Esselen.

There is a large site at the mouth of Palo Colorado Canyon (CA-MNT-186/189) which, in terms of size and surface appearance, resembles Rumsen sites to the north (this site has not been sampled archaeologically). This is most likely the original site of Sarhentaruc, although the village may have also been known by a more specific name such as Pis or Pichi, etc.

A recent excavation at the mouth of the Big Sur River (CA-MNT-63) revealed a clearly prehistoric site with a small, recent feature in its upper levels. The prehistoric site dated several hundred to nearly 2,000 years into the past, while the small feature dated to approximately A.D. 1800-1816.[15] This should represent evidence of the Esselen (the older site) with the recent intrusion of the Rumsen from Sarhentaruc, to the north, superimposed.

Another coastal archaeological site about two miles south of the Big Sur River (CA-MNT-798) also contained a mixture of mission era glass beads and very late radiocarbon dates, suggesting use by Rumsen to the north.

Summary

There is now evidence from two separate areas of Esselen territory which clearly shows its use as a refuge from the Spanish. In both the Excelen and Sarhentaruc/Ekheahan districts the pattern is similar: large numbers of baptisms some years after initial contact, followed by a significant reduction in baptisms, then a last group which accepted baptism between 1805 and 1808. In the Excelen district we have archaeological evidence of occupation beyond 1808, when baptisms of new converts ended. We also have limited evidence from the Sarhentaruc/Ekheahan district in an archaeological feature dated to A.D. 1800-1816.

The Ohlone to the north expressed their distaste for the mission environment by running away, often to the east, where they joined Yokuts groups and engaged in horse raiding. The southernmost Ohlone, the Rumsen in the Sarhentaruc area, perhaps unable to move east, moved south into Esselen territory instead. And the Excelen, in the upper Carmel Valley, moved quietly back into the rugged mountains and passed from the historic record. However, rumors of their survival lasted into the twentieth century.

Notes

1 Kroeber 1925:544; Hester 1978:497; Beeler 1978:3.

2 Breschini 1983; Breschini and Haversat 1994; Kroeber 1925; Hester 1978; Milliken 1990.

3 Milliken 1990:33.

4 Neve 1782:82 in Milliken 1990:56; emphasis added.

5 Culleton 1950:104

6 Tom "Little Bear" Nason, personal communication 1992.

7 Meighan 1955:21.

8 Arnold Pilling, personal communication 1992.

9 Breschini and Haversat 1993, 1995.

10 Milliken 1990:27-33, 73.

11 Milliken 1987:64.

[12] Heizer 1952, 1955.

[13] Culleton 1950:115. Baptisms did not actually stop for 20 years, but rather for 12 years. If years with very limited baptisms are counted the span increases to 16 years. Baptisms from this area continued at Soledad during this period.

[14] Milliken 1990:58.

[15] Jones 1994:42.

Bibliography

Beeler, M. S. 1977. The Sources for Esselen: A Critical Review. *Proceedings of the Third Annual Meeting of the Berkeley Linguistics Society.*

_____1978. Esselen. *The Journal of California Anthropology Papers in Linguistics.* Banning: Malki Museum.

Breschini, G. S. 1973. Excavations at the Church Creek Rockshelter, MNT-44. *Monterey County Archaeological Society Quarterly* 2(4).

_____1980. Esselen Prehistory. Paper presented at the Annual Meeting of the Society for California Archaeology, Redding.

_____1981. Models of Central California Prehistory. Paper presented at the Annual Meeting of the Society for California Archaeology, Bakersfield.

_____1983. "Models of Population Movements in Central California Prehistory." Ph.D. dissertation, Department of Anthropology, Washington State University.

Breschini, G. S., and T. Haversat. 1982. Monterey Bay Prehistory. Paper presented at the Annual Meeting of the Society for California Archaeology, Sacramento.

_____1985a. Radiocarbon Dates and Cultural Models in the Monterey Bay Area, California. Paper presented at the Annual Northern California Data Sharing Meeting of the Society for California Archaeology, Aptos.

_____1985b. Linguistic Prehistory of South-Central California. Paper presented to the Symposium on Central California Prehistory, San Jose State University, San Jose.

_____1993. Phase II Cultural Resources Investigations for the New Los Padres Dam and Reservoir Project, Carmel Valley, Monterey County, California. Submitted to Monterey Peninsula Water Management District, Monterey.

_____1994. An Overview of the Esselen Indians of Central Monterey County, California. Manuscript dated April 24, 1994. Coyote Press, Salinas.

_____1995. Additional Archaeological Investigations Prepared as a Supplement to Phase II Cultural Resources Investigations for the New Los Padres Dam and Reservoir Project, Carmel Valley, Monterey County, California. Submitted to Monterey Peninsula Water Management District, Monterey.

_____2000. Post-Contact Esselen Occupation of the Santa Lucia Mountains. Paper presented at the Annual Meetings of the Society for California Archaeology, Riverside, April 21, 2000.

Breschini, G. S., T. Haversat, and Tom "Little Bear" Nason. 1999. Esselen, Rumsen and the Sarhentaruc Problem. Paper presented at the 14th Annual California Indian Conference, Cuesta College, October 15, 1999.

Broadbent, S. M. 1974. Conflict at Monterey; Indian Horse Raiding, 1820-1850. *Journal of California Anthropology* 1(1):86-101.

Cook, S. F. 1974a. The Esselen: Territory, Villages, and Population. *Monterey County Archaeological Society Quarterly* 3(2).

_____1974b. The Esselen: Language and Culture. *Monterey County Archaeological Society Quarterly* 3(3).

Culleton, J. 1950. *Indians and Pioneers of Old Monterey.* Fresno: Academy of California Church History.

Haversat, T., and G. S. Breschini. 1984. New Interpretations in South Coast Ranges Prehistory. Paper presented at the Annual Northern Data Sharing Meeting of the Society for California Archaeology, Aptos.

Heizer, R. F., ed. 1952. California Indian Linguistic Records: The Mission Indian Vocabularies of Alphonse Pinart. University of California Anthropological Records 15(1).

_____1955. *California Indian Linguistic Records: The Mission Indian Vocabularies of H. W. Henshaw.* University of California Anthropological Records 15(2).

Hester, T. R. 1978. "Esselen." In *California*, edited by R. F. Heizer, pp. 496-499. *Handbook of North American Indians*, vol. 8, William G. Sturtevant, general editor. Smithsonian Institution, Washington, D.C.

Jones, T. L. 1993. Big Sur: A Keystone in Central California Culture History. *Pacific Coast Archaeological Society Quarterly* 29(1).

_____1994. Archaeological Testing and Salvage at CA-MNT-63, CA-MNT-73, and CA-MNT-376, on the Big Sur Coast, Monterey County, California. Manuscript on file, California Department of Parks and Recreation, Monterey.

_____1995. "Transitions in Prehistoric Diet, Mobility, Exchange, and Social Organization along California's Big Sur Coast." Ph.D. dissertation, University of California, Davis.

_____1996. Mortars, Pestles, and Division of Labor in Prehistoric California: A View from Big Sur. *American Antiquity* 61(2):243-264.

Kroeber, A. L. 1904. The Languages of the Coast of California South of San Francisco. *University of California Publications in American Archaeology and Ethnology* 2(2).

_____1925. *Handbook of the Indians of California.* Bureau of American Ethnology Bulletin 78.

Lathrap, D.W., and R. C. Troike. 1988. "Californian Historical Linguistics and Archaeology." In *Archaeology and Linguistics*, A. M. Mester and C. McEwan, eds. *Journal of the Steward Anthropological Society* 15(1&2):99-157.

Levy, R. 1979. A Linguistic Prehistory of Central California: Historical Linguistics and Culture Process. Manuscript on file, Archaeological Consulting, Salinas.

Margolin, M., ed. 1989. *Monterey in 1786: The Journals of Jean François de La Pérouse.* Heyday Books, Berkeley.

Meighan, C. W. 1955. *Excavation of Isabella Meadows Cave, Monterey County, California.* Reports of the University of California Archaeological Survey 29.

Milliken, R. 1987. *Ethnohistory of the Rumsen.* Papers in Northern California Anthropology 2. Northern California Anthropological Group, Berkeley.

_____1990. *Ethnogeography and Ethnohistory of the Big Sur District, California State Park System, During the 1770-1810 Time Period.* Submitted to Department of Parks and Recreation, Sacramento.

Shaul, D. L. 1983. Esselen Linguistic Prehistory. Paper presented at the 1983 Hokan-Penutian Conference, University of California, Berkeley.

_____1988. "Esselen Linguistic Prehistory." In *Archaeology and Linguistics*, A.M. Mester and C. McEwan, eds. *Journal of the Steward Anthropological Society* 15(1&2):47-58.

Santa Cruz
County
History Journal
Issue 5, 2002

48

Mortomar, The Urban Squirrel

by Lydia Bojorquez

I hope, as I write this, that readers will understand my connection to this small Douglas Squirrel who was a great example of life's lessons.

It was two weeks before bow and arrow season opened up for deer hunting. This is the time my husband would go and scout the area that he would be hunting in. He would look to see where the deer were bedding down in the warm afternoons and for the trails the deer were taking. As he was walking he noticed a squirrel run past him, dropping what he thought was an acorn from its mouth. As he looked closer, he realized it was a baby squirrel. He immediately backed away so the mother would come back for it. Finally, he decided to continue his scouting and at the end of his day he went back to see if the mother squirrel came back for her baby. To his surprise, the baby was still there in the exact same spot where she dropped him. Afraid a predator would eat him, my husband picked him up and put him in his shirt pocket and brought him home.

Morty on Mike's knee.
Photo courtesy of Lydia Bojorquez

Our young sons and I immediately fell in love with this baby squirrel and within a few days he received his name—Mortomar.

Mortomar was no more than 2 1/2 inches from head to tail and fit in the palm of my husband's hand. At night Mortomar slept contentedly on my husband's chest. We fed Mortomar by dipping a soft piece of cloth into milk and letting him sip on the cloth. As Morty began to grow we decided to put him in a shoe box beside our bed, only to be waked up by a tiny high pitched chirping sound. Morty continued this sound until my husband reached down to pick him up and put him on his chest to sleep. It was a while before we got Mortomar a house of his own: a large cage complete with a running wheel—two-story even!

At times we let Mortomar out of his cage to run freely in the room and soon he was running throughout the house, knowing all the rooms. He loved to play tag and enjoyed when we would try to catch him. After a year, Mortomar even learned how to unlatch his cage door to get out. He learned this early one morning while we were all still in bed. From our sons' room we heard them cry out that *something* had run across their bed. To our amazement it was Mortomar. He had learned all too well to let himself out of his cage, so we had to secure his door with a piece of wire. We would take Morty outside for fresh air and sunshine, but always in his cage.

It wasn't until several years passed that we decided to let Mortomar out of his cage outdoors so he could feel the earth and grass on his tiny feet. He ran to the tree in an attempt to climb it only to slide back down. We watched with amusement as he did this several times, struggling to climb the tree. After several more attempts, he made it up the tree and we watched as he climbed higher into the branches. All of a sudden we heard the branches as if something was falling through them. To our horror, Mortomar was falling from the tree. My husband quickly put his hands out to catch him, but Mortomar fell into my husband's hands and bounced right off of them onto the ground. He was not hurt—only stunned for a few seconds; then he ran into his safe cage.

It didn't take Mortomar long to master what should have been natural to him and soon he was climbing not only our tree but the neighbors' trees as well. It was at this time I called him Mortomar the Urban Squirrel because he was taken from his natural environment and taught to live in a world both strange and different from that of other squirrels like him.

Native American people from all corners tell their stories, using animals for examples. At that time little did I know the Creator sent Mortomar to us so I could share my own story through him.

Like Mortomar, I was raised in an urban environment and must now learn what Indian girls were taught by their mothers and grandmothers to know, beginning at a young age. I am learning the ways of my grandmothers, singing their songs, dancing their dances and weaving baskets the way they did—traditionally and spiritually. And one day I too will master all that I was intended to know.

My husband Mike would sit back in a chair and listen to music with Mortomar in his cage beside him.
So every time we turned on music, Mortomar would lie on his back in his cage to relax just like Mike.
Photo courtesy of Lydia Bojorquez

The Narratives of Lorenzo Asisara: Three Accounts of Life and Death in Mission Santa Cruz

Editors' Note

Lorenzo Asisara was an Indian who was born and raised in Mission Santa Cruz, lived there as a neophyte until secularization, and continued to live in Santa Cruz for most of his remaining life. He was known to be still alive, living in Santa Cruz, in 1891. During his lifetime he was interviewd three times, twice in 1877 by Hubert Howe Bancroft's historian, Thomas Savage and once in 1890 by E. L. Williams.

For the first time, all three narratives in which Lorenzo Asisara describes life at Mission Santa Cruz are printed in one place. The first two narratives are presented with an introduction and annotation by Edward D. Castillo, who also translated these interviews. The third narrative is presented with no introduction. It was transcribed directly from E. S. Harrison's History of Santa Cruz County, published in 1892.

We hope that presenting these interviews together will provide an insight into neophyte life at Mission Santa Cruz and will also be an incentive for further research into this subject.

Lorenzo Asisara's First Narrative: The Assassination of Padre Andrés Quintana by the Indians of Mission Santa Cruz in 1812[1]

Introduction[2]

Historical literature on the California Indians in the Franciscan mission system has been decidedly unbalanced. For nearly a century the Franciscan historians and many like-minded writers dominated the literature and developed a theory of history that sought to rationalize the mission's destruction of thousands of natives, in order to convert or assimilate them. These works generally approve of European colonization and the triumph of Christianity over "pagans" and their natural world. Some, like Zephyrin Engelhardt, O.F.M., have reflected the outright bigotry that for years typified the stereotypical views of whites about American natives. At one point Engelhardt characterized native Californians as "among the most stupid, brutish, filthy, lazy, and improvident of the aborigines of Americas."[3] To these authors, native society was little more than anarchy; the absence of materialism was indolence; Indian religion was devil worship; Indian cultures and languages were little more than obstacles to native absorption into the Spanish empire as loyal hardworking subjects.

A more modern approach to mission historiography of the Hispanic colonization of California provides a more culturally neutral position that includes a native point of view. Beginning with the pioneering demographic work of Sherburne F. Cook, these authors have not relied entirely upon self-serving missionary sources of data to explain the destruction of native societies and the catastrophic population decline during the mission period in California history.[4] Such non-missionary sources include foreign visitors to missions, as well as early non-Hispanic immigrants to the West Coast. Perhaps the most significant development has been the use of ethnographic data in the reconstruction of California's colonial history. The few scholars who have been able to use both traditional historical sources and ethnographic data concerning this era have provided a new dimension to our understanding.[5]

Sketch of Mission Santa Cruz from an early 1900s postcard. This and similar illustrations were made after the mission chapel had been destroyed and reflect artistic license. Courtesy of the Museum of Art and History.

Few native eyewitness accounts of life under Franciscan authority are known. Pablo Tac's account of Franciscan activities at Mission San Luis Rey is the earliest.[6] Tac's account viewed Franciscan colonization favorably. His narrative was written under the careful tutelage of church authorities who were educating him at the College of Propaganda in Rome. Another Luseño neophyte had his life history recorded by Hubert Howe Bancroft's field historian, Thomas Savage, in 1879.[7] Most recently an account of mission life among the Chumash by Francisco Librado (Kitsepawit) has emerged. This was accomplished by teasing the information from a series of interviews Librado did with the Smithsonian Institution's anthropologist, John P. Harrington, between 1912 and 1915.[8] These native accounts present striking differences to those most frequently consulted as authorities on mission life in California.

The following account of the events surrounding the assassination of Padre Andrés Quintana is taken from the memoirs of the ex-Santa Cruz neophyte called Lorenzo Asisara. Lorenzo's story, transcribed by Bancroft's historian Thomas Savage, is perhaps the most detailed account we have of the motivations, plot, and acts surrounding a neophyte political assassination in Spanish California.

The interview took place on the San Andres Ranch, near Santa Cruz, on July 10, 1877. It was part of a widespread oral history project undertaken by Bancroft's history company. Most likely it was done while Savage was interviewing Mexican colonist José María Amador in nearby Whiskey Hill. In fact, Lorenzo's story is found in two different places within Amador's narrative, where both informants struck common stories.[9]

Lorenzo is unique in that he was again interviewed concerning mission Indian life by E.L. Williams in 1890[10]. This later interview, occurring when Lorenzo was 70 years old, adds more details of his life, as well as corroborates his earlier testimony.

From various sources we can piece together the following biographical data concerning our informant.[11] Lorenzo was born August 10, 1820, at the Mission Santa Cruz, the twelfth such institution established in Alta California. Founded in the fall of 1791 on a hill overlooking the San Lorenzo River,[12] the mission was built next to the local native village called *Aulintac*.[13] Lorenzo was the son of neophyte Venancio Llenco of Cotony and Manuela Liuhatme of the Chalahua rancheria.[14] Lorenzo had a brother called Jacinto, whose fate is unknown. Lorenzo spoke his father's language,[15] as well as Spanish, the language in which the interview was conducted. As a youth he sang in the choir. He remained at Santa Cruz until the winter of 1833, when he was sent by Padre Antonio Real to Monterey, where he learned to play the clarinet and worked for the new governor,

General José Figueroa. He remained at the Mission Carmelo near Monterey for perhaps as long as a year. Lorenzo then returned to Santa Cruz, where Real taught him to read and write Spanish. He became the sacristan and played in the choir. We know Lorenzo witnessed the secularization of Mission Santa Cruz and remained there working as a drover. He married, but by 1845 he was a widower, still living at Santa Cruz.[16] In 1846 Lorenzo went to Yerba Buena [San Francisco], where he was employed by the alcalde. He was serving as an unarmed soldier with other Indians at the San Francisco Presidio when it surrendered to the Americans during the Mexican-American War. Thereafter, Lorenzo returned to Santa Cruz. Lorenzo said he spent three years in San Jose, but it is not clear whether this was before or after the war. Apparently, Lorenzo received no land after the secularization and was forced to work as a ranch hand the rest of his life. Although not allowed to speak himself, Lorenzo shared the speakers' platform at the Mission Santa Cruz centennial celebration in 1891.[17] We know nothing of his death, but we may presume he died a landless pauper.

Perhaps more than any other known neophyte account of life under Franciscan authority, Lorenzo's narrative is rich in detail and comprehensive in its chronology.

—Edward D. Castillo

Lorenzo's First Narrative

The following story which I shall convey was told to me by my dear father in 1818.[18] He was a neophyte of the Mission of Santa Cruz. He was one of the original founders of that mission. He was an Indian from the rancheria of *Asar*.[19] on the Jarro[20] coast, up beyond Santa Cruz. He was one of the first neophytes baptized at the founding, being about 20 years of age. He was called Venancio Asar, and was the gardener of the Mission of Santa Cruz.

My father was a witness to the happenings which follow. He was one of the conspirators who planned to kill Father Quintana.[21] When the conspirators were planning to kill Father

Quintana, they gathered in the house of Julian the gardener (the one who made the pretense of being ill). The man who worked inside the plaza of the mission, named Donato, was punished by Father Quintana with a whip with wire. With each blow it cut his buttocks.[22] Then the same man, Donato, wanted vengeance. He was the one who organized a gathering of 14 men, among them were the cook and the pages serving the Father. The cook was named Antonio, the eldest page named Lino, the others named Vincente and Miguel Antonio. All of them gathered in the house of Julian to plan how they could avoid the cruel punishments of Father Quintana.[23] One man present, Lino, who was more capable and wiser than the others, said, "The first thing we should do today is to see that the Padre no longer punishes the people in that manner. We aren't animals. He [Quintana] says in his sermons that God does not command these [punishments]—but only examples and doctrines.[24] Tell me now, what shall we do with the Padre? We cannot chase him away, nor accuse him before the judge, because we do not know who commands him to do with us as he does." To this, Andrés, father of Lino the page, answered, "Let's kill the Padre without anyone being aware, not the servants, nor anyone, except us that are here present." (This Lino was pure-blooded Indian, but as white as a Spaniard and a man of natural abilities.) And then Julian the gardener said, "What shall we do in order to kill him?" His wife responded, "You, who are always getting sick— only this way can it be possible—think if it is good this way."[25] Lino approved the plan and asked that all present also approve it. "In that case, we shall do it tomorrow night." That was Saturday. It should be noted that the Padre wished all the people to gather in the plaza on the following Sunday in order to test the whip that he had made with pieces of wire to see if it was to his liking.

All of the conspirators present at the meeting concurred that it should be done as Lino had recommended.

On the evening of Saturday at about six o'clock [October 12] of 1812, they went to tell the Padre that the gardener was dying. The Indians were already posted between two trees on both sides that they could grab Father when he passed. The Padre arrived at the house of Julian, who pretended to be in agony. The Padre helped him thinking that he was really sick and about to die. When the Padre was returning to his house, he passed close to where the Indians were posted. They didn't have the courage to grab him and they allowed him to pass. The moribund gardener was behind him, but the Padre arrived at his house. Within an hour the wife of Julian arrived [again] to tell him [the Father] that her husband was dying. With this news the Padre returned to the orchard, the woman following behind crying and lamenting. He saw that the sick man was dying. The Padre took the man's hand in order to take his pulse. He felt the pulse and could find nothing amiss. The pulse showed there was nothing wrong with Julian. Not knowing what it could be, the Padre returned to pray for him. It was night when the Padre left. Julian arose and washed away the sacraments [oil] that he [the Padre] had administered, and he followed behind to join the others and see what his companions had done. Upon arriving at the place where they were stationed, Lino lifted his head and looked in all directions to see if they were coming out to grab the Father. The Father passed and they didn't take him. The Father arrived at his house.

Later, when the Father was at his table dining, the conspirators had already gathered at the house of the alleged sick man to ascertain why they hadn't seized Father Quintana. Julian complained that the Padre had placed herbs on his ears, and because of them, now he was really going to die. Then the wife of Julian said, "Yes, you all did not carry through with your promised plans; I am going to accuse you all, and I will not go back to the house." They all answered her, "All right, now in this trip go and speak to the Father. The woman again left to fetch Father Quintana, who was at supper. He got up immediately and went where he found the supposedly sick man. This time he took with him three pages, two who walked ahead lighting his way with lanterns and behind him followed his Mayordomo Lino.[26] The other two were Vincente and Miguel Antonio. The Father arrived at the gardener's house and found him

unconscious. He couldn't speak. The Father prayed the last orations without administering the oils, and said to the wife, "Now your husband is prepared to live or die. Don't come to look for me again." Then the Father left with his pages to return to his house. Julian followed him. Arriving at the place where the two trees were (since the Father was not paying attention to his surroundings, but only in the path in front of him), Lino grabbed him from behind saying these words, "Stop here, Father, you must speak for a moment." When the other two pages who carried the lanterns turned around and saw the other men come out to attack the Father, they fled with their lanterns. The Father said to Lino, "Oh, my Son, what are you going to do to me?" Lino answered, "Your assassins will tell you."

"What have I done to you children, for which you would kill me?"

"Because you have made a *cuarta de hierro* [a horse whip tipped with iron]...," Andrés answered him. Then the Father retorted, "Oh, children, leave me, so that I can go from here now, at this moment." Andrés asked him why he had made this *cuarta de hierro*. Quintana said that it was only for transgressors. Then someone shouted, "Well, you are in the hands of those evil ones, make your peace with God." Many of those present (seeing the Father in his affliction) cried and pitied his fate, but could do nothing to help him because they were themselves compromised. He pleaded much, promising to leave the mission immediately if they would only let him.

"Now you won't be going to any part of the earth from here, Father, you are going to heaven." This was the last plea of the Father. Some of them, not having been able to lay hands on Father, reprimanded the others because they talked too much, demanding that they kill him immediately. They then covered the Father's mouth with his own cape to strangle him. They had his arms tightly secured. After the Father had been strangled, they took a testicle [*grano de los companonez*] so that it would not be suspected that he had been beaten, and in a moment Padre expired. Then Lino and the others took him to his house and put him in his bed.[27]

When the two little pages, Vicente and Miguel Antonio, arrived at the house, the former wanted to tell the guard, but the other dissuaded him by saying, "No, they, the soldiers, will also kill your mother, father, all of the others and you yourself and me. Let them, the conspirators, do what they want." The two hid themselves. After the Indians had put the Father in his bed, Lino looked for the two pages, and he found them hidden. They undressed the body of Father Quintana and placed him in the bed as if he were going to sleep. All of the conspirators, including Julian's wife, were present. Andrés asked Lino for the keys to the storeroom. He handed them over saying, "What do you want?" And they said silver and beads. Among the group there were three Indians from the Santa Clara mission. These proposed that they investigate to see how much money there was. Lino opened the box and showed them the accumulated gold and silver.[28] The three Indians from Santa Clara took as much as they could carry to their mission. (I don't know what they have done with that money.) The others took their portions as they saw fit.

Then they asked for the keys to the convent or the nunnery.[29] Lino gave the keys to the *jayunte*,[30] or barracks of the single men, to one of them in order to free them and gather them together below in the orchard with the unmarried women. They gathered in the orchard so that neither the people in the plaza nor in the rancheria[31] nor in the guardhouse would hear them. The single men left and without a sound gathered in the orchard at the same place where the Father was assassinated. There was a man there cautioning them not to make any noise, that they were going to have a good time. After a short time the young unmarried women arrived in order to spend the night there. The young people of both sexes got together and had their pleasure. At midnight Lino, being in the Padre's living room with one of the girls from the single women's dormitory, entered the Father's room in order to see if he was really dead. He found him reviving. He was already on the point of arising. Lino went to look for his accomplices to

the tell them that the Padre was coming to. The Indians returned and they crushed the Father's other testicle. This last act put an end to the life of Father Quintana. Donato, the one who had been whipped, walked around the room with the plural results of his operation in hand saying, "I shall bury these in the outdoor privy."

Donato told Lino that they should close the treasure chest with these words, "Close the trunk with the colored silver (that is the name that the Indians gave to gold) and let's see where we shall bury it." The eight men carried it down to the orchard and buried it secretly without the others knowing.

At about two o'clock in the morning, the young girls returned to their convent and the single men to their *jayunte* without making any noise. The assassins gathered once more after everything had occurred in order to hear the plans of Lino and Donato. Some wanted to flee, and others asked, "What for? No one except us knows." Lino asked them what they wanted to take to their houses, sugar, *panocha* [a sugar loaf], honey, or any other things, and suggested that they lay down to sleep for a while. Finally everything was ready. Donato proposed to return to where the Father was to check on him. They found him not only lifeless, but completely cold and stiff. Lino then showed them the new whip that the Padre was planning to use for the first time the next day, assuring them that he [Father Quintana] would not use it. He sent them to their houses to rest, remaining in the house with the keys. He asked them to be very careful. He arranged the room and the Bible in the manner in which the Father was accustomed to doing before retiring, telling them that he was not going to toll the bells in the morning until the Mayordomo and Corporal of the guard came and he had talked to them. All went through the orchard very silently.

This same morning (Sunday) the bells should have been rung at about eight o'clock. At that hour the people from the villa de Branciforte began to arrive in order to attend the mass.[32] The Mayordomo, Carlos Castro, saw that the bells were not being rung and went to ask Lino, who was the first assistant of the Father, in order to ask why the Padre had not ordered him [to toll the bells]. Lino was in the outer room feigning innocence and answered the Mayordomo that he couldn't tell him anything about the Father because he was still inside sleeping or praying, and that the Mayordomo should wait until he should speak to him first. The Mayordomo returned home. Soon the Corporal of the guard arrived and Lino told him the same as to the Mayordomo. The Mayordomo returned to join in the conversation. They decided to wait a little while longer. Finally Lino told them that in their presence he would knock on the door of the room, observing, "If he is angry with me, you will stand up for me." And so he did, calling to the Father. As he didn't hear noise inside, the Mayordomo and Corporal asked Lino to knock again, but he refused. They then left, encharging him to call the Father again because the hour was growing late. All of the servants were busy at their jobs as always, in order not to cause any suspicion. The Mayordomo returned after ten o'clock and asked Lino to call the Padre to see what was wrong. Lino, with the keys in his pocket, knocked at the door. Finally the Mayordomo insisted that Lino enter the room, but Lino refused. At this moment, the Corporal, who was old Nazario Galindo, arrived.[33] Lino (although he had the key to the door in his pocket) said, "Well, I am going to see if I can get the door open," and he pretended to look for a key to open the door. He returned with a ring of keys but he didn't find one that opened the lock. The Mayordomo and the Corporal left to talk to some men who were there. Later, Lino took the key that opened the door, saying that it was for the kitchen. He opened another door that opened in the plaza (the key opened three doors), and through there he entered. Then he opened the main door from inside in front of which the others waited. Lino came out screaming and crying, and carrying on in an uncontrolled manner and saying that the Padre was dead. They asked him if he was certain and he responded, "As this light that illuminates us. By God, I'm going to toll the bells." The three entered, the Corporal, the Mayordomo, and Lino. He didn't allow anyone else to enter. The Corporal and the Mayordomo and the other

people wrote to the other missions and to Monterey to Father Marcelino Marquinez.[34] (This Marquinez was an expert horseman and a good friend.) The poor elderly neophytes, and many other Indians who never suspected that the Father was killed, thought that he had died suddenly. They cried bitterly.[35] Lino was roaring inside the Father's house like a bear.

The Fathers from Santa Clara and from other missions came and they held the Father's funeral, all believing that he had died a natural death, but not before examining the corpse in the entrance room, and had opened the stomach in order to be certain that the Padre had not been poisoned.[36] Officials, sergeants, and many others participated in these acts but nothing was discovered. Finally, by chance, one of those present noted that the testicles were missing, and they were convinced that this had been the cause of death. Through modesty they did not reveal the fact and buried the body with everyone convinced that the death been a natural one.[37]

A number of years after the death, Emiliana, the wife of Lino, and Maria Tata, the wife of the cook Antonio, became mutually jealous. They were both seamstresses and they were at work. This was around August at the time of the lentil harvest.[38] Carlos Castro[39] was with his men working in the cornfields. Shortly before eleven o'clock he returned to his house for the meal. He was a man who understood well the language of the Indians. Returning from the cornfields, he passed behind one of the plaza walls near where these women were sewing and heard one tell the other that she was secretly eating *panocha*. Castro stopped and heard the second woman reply to the first, "How is it that you have so much money?" The first replied, "You also have it because your husband killed the Father." Then the second accused the husband of the first woman of the same crime. The war of words continued, and Castro was convinced that Father Quintana had been assassinated, and he went to tell Father Ramon Olbés, who was the missionary at Santa Cruz, what he had heard.[40] Father Ramon went to tell Padre Marquinez. The latter sent one of his pages to the orchard to warn

Julian and his accomplices that they were going to be caught.[41] At noon, at about the time of the midday meal, Father Olbés spoke to Lino and asked him to send for his wife to come there and also to cut some pieces of cloth. Emiliana arrived, and Father Olbés placed her in a room where there was clothing and gave her some scissors with which to cut some pieces, telling her, "you will eat here." Then he sent a page to bring Maria Tata to take some dirty clothing out of the church to wash. The Mayordomo was observing the maneuverings of the Father. He made Maria Tata stay to eat there. He placed her in another room in order to cut some suits for the pages. The Mayordomo and the two Fathers went to eat. After the meal, and when the two women had also eaten, Father Olbés said to Emiliana, "Do you know who eats a lot of white sugar?" She answered that it was Maria Tata, "because her husband had killed Father Quintana." The Father made her return to the room and called for Maria Tata. The Father asked her, "Tell me if you know who it was that killed Padre Quintana; tell me the truth so that nothing will happen to you." Lino and Antonio often took their meals in the kitchen. Maria Tata replied, "Lino, Father." Father Olbés then sent them to their houses to rest, offering them a present. Then the Father sent for the Corporal Nazario Galindo to arrest the assassins. They began with the orchard workers and the cook, without telling them why they were under arrest. Antonio was the first prisoner. Put in jail, they asked him who his accomplice was. He said who his accomplice was and the man was arrested, and they asked each one the name of their respective accomplices. In this way they were all arrested, except Lino, who was looked upon as a valiant man of great strength. He was taken through the deceit of his own Compadre Carlos Castro, who handed him a knife to pare some black and white mares in order to make a hakamore for the animal of the Father.[42] Suspiciously, Lino said to Castro, "Compadre, why are you deceiving me? I know that you are going to arrest me." There were already two soldiers hidden behind the corral.

"Here, take your knife, Compadre, that which I thought is already done. I am going to pay for it—

and if I had wanted to, I could have finished off the soldiers, the Mayordomos, and any others that might have been around on the same night that I killed the Father."

The result of all this was that the accused were sent to San Francisco, and among them was my father.[43] There they were judged,[44] and those who killed the Father were sentenced to receive a *novenano* (nine days in succession) of 50 lashes for each one,[45] and to serve in the public works at San Diego.[46] The rest, including my father, were freed because they had served as witnesses, and it was not proven that they had taken part in the assassination.

All returned after many years to their mission.[47]

The Spanish Padres were very cruel toward the Indians. They abused them very much, and they had bad food, bad clothing, and they made them work like slaves. I also was subjected to that cruel life. The Padres did not practice what they preached in the pulpit. The same Father Olbés for all his cruelties, was once stoned by the Indians.[48]

(signed) Lorenzo Asisara

Conclusion

The martyrdom of Quintana became a "cause célèbre" among both his contemporaries and Hispanic colonial historians. Part of the aftermath of the assassination was the controversy which arose surrounding the conspirators' charge of cruelty practiced by the Franciscans in California. Franciscan historians are quick to point out that the military governor, Pablo Vicente de Solá, wrote a forceful defense of coercive mission practices under his jurisdiction.[49] Since there was a well-known animosity between the Franciscans and the military, some students of history may be tempted to view Solá's defense of Franciscan corporal punishment as a more or less persuasive denial of the charges against the latter.

While many historians choose to view Solá's letter at face value, there remains a nagging question regarding his motivations. He most certainly knew the Santa Cruz *escolta* (mission guards) were seriously negligent by not accompanying Quintana when he left the mission compound. Yet, curiously, no charges against the military resulted from their rather obvious neglect of duty. Military authorities must also have been embarrassed by the military surgeon's autopsy, which can most kindly be described as incompetent. On the other hand, Franciscan authorities were again faced with the embarrassing revelation of the coercive nature of Christian conversion throughout the Franciscan empire.[50] These church authorities were anxious to preserve and extend their colonial prerogatives. Earlier Father President Lasuén had justified the treatment of neophytes in California this way: "It is evident that a nation that is barbarous, ferocious, and ignorant requires more frequent punishment than a nation which is cultured, educated, and of gentle and moderate customs."[51]

Certainly, Franciscan authorities were aware of the recent actions by the liberal Spanish Cortes of 1813. Reflecting Enlightenment philosophy, this legislative body rejected the view that Indians were inferior. Consequently, they supported a plan to divest the Franciscan empire of its extensive land and labor holdings throughout New Spain's northwestern frontier and to provide mission Indians with land titles.[52] Because of the current revolution in Mexico, The Cortes' decree remained in effect, but unenforced.

Given this situation, it would not seem unreasonable to assume that Franciscan authorities may have agreed not to hold the military authorities accountable for their failure to protect Quintana, in exchange for a report from the military governor that would contravene the Indian charges of cruelty to the neophytes and help redeem Quintana's and his order's reputation.

—Edward D. Castillo[53]

Notes:

[1] Translated and annotated by Edward D. Castillo with the translation assistance of Robert Jackson and Susan and Frank Lobo. Published by permission of the Bancroft Library. The original manuscript and a translation are in the Bancroft Library under the title: *Recollections concerning the History of California by José María Amador*, (BANC MSS C-D 28) 58-77, testimony of Lorenzo Asisara, July 10, 1877.

[2] Editor's Note: This Introduction is excerpted from Edward D. Castillo's article, "The Assassination of Padre Andrés Quintana by the Indians of Mission Santa Cruz in 1812: The Narrative of Lorenzo Asisara," *California History*, (Fall 1989); 117-125. Permission to reprint an edited version of this article is granted by the California Historical Society.

[3] Zephyrin Engelhardt, O.F.M., *The Missions and Missionaries of California*, Vol. II, Part I (San Francisco: James Barry Co., 1912), 224. Examples of other similar works include: E.B. Webb, *Indian Life at the Old Missions* (Los Angeles: W.F. Lewis Co., 1952); Francis F. Guest, "Cultural Perspectives on California Mission Life," *Southern California Quarterly* 65 (Spring 1983); 1-65; Clement W. Meighan, "Indians and California Missions," *Southern California Quarterly* 69 (Fall 1987); 183-201 and Thaddeus Shubsda and Valerie Steiner (eds.), "The Serra Report," Typescript, Monterey, California, 1986.

[4] Sherburne F. Cook, *The Conflict Between the California Indian and White Civilization* (Berkeley and Los Angeles: University of California Press, 1976); 1-194.

[5] The ethnographic data referred to here include physical, social, linguistic studies, and informant notes that broadly describe native economies, religions, technologies, world views, oral histories, and intergroup relations. For examples of such works, see Edward Castillo's "Impact of Euro-American Exploration and Settlement," *Handbook of North American Indians, Vol. 8—California*, ed. R.F. Heizer (Washington, D.C.: Smithsonian Institute, 1978); 99-127; Jack Forbes, "The Native American Experience in California History," *California Historical Quarterly* L (September 1971); 232-242; James A. Sandos, "Levantamiento! The Chumash Uprising Reconsidered," *Southern California Quarterly* 67 (Summer 1985); 109-133; Florence C. Shipek, "California Indian Reactions to the Franciscans," *The Americas* XLI (April 1985), and "The Impact of Europeans upon the Kumyaay" in the *Impact of European Exploration and Settlement on Local Native Americans* (San Diego: Cabrillo Historical Society, 1986).

[6] Pablo Tac, "Indian Life and Customs at Mission San Luis Rey, A Record of California Mission Life Written by Pablo Tac, an Indian Neophyte," in Mina and Gordon Hewes (eds.) *The Americans* 9, No. 1 (1952); 87-106.

7 Julio César, "Cosas de los Indios de California," unpublished manuscript, Bancroft Library, University of California Berkeley.

8 Fernando Librado, *Breath of the Sun,* (Banning, California: Malki Museum Press, 1979).

9 José María Amador, "Memorias de la Historia de California," unpublished manuscript, Bancroft Library, University of California, Berkeley. Within this manuscript is found the two-part interview with Lorenzo Asisara. The first half deals with the assassination of Padre Andrés Quintana on manuscript pages 58-77. The second half is on pages 90-113 of Amador's manuscript. Obviously, Bancroft's field historian, Thomas Savage interviewed Lorenzo at two key points in Amador's narrative where they related parallel stories. Both parts of the interview are reproduced in this journal. The first half immediately follows this introduction. The second half, with its own introduction, is titled "Lorenzo Asisara's Second Narrative."

10 E. L. Williams, "Narrative of a Mission Indian, etc.," in Edward S. Harrison's History of Santa Cruz County (San Francisco: Pacific Press Publishing Co., 1892); 45-48. Williams was a local historian and former clerk of Monterey County.

11 These sources include the second half of the present interview reproduced here in this journal in "Lorenzo's Second Narrative"and the 1890 interview reproduced here in "Lorenzo's Third Narrative;" and also entries from the Santa Cruz Baptismal Register, Vol. I, Archive of the Diocese of Monterey, California.

12 H.A. van Coenen Torchiana, *Story of the Mission Santa Cruz* (San Francisco: Paul Elder Co., 1933), 460.

13 A.L. Kroeber, *Handbook of the Indians of California* (Berkeley: California Book Co., 1953), 465.

14 Santa Cruz Baptismal Register, Vol. I, Archive of the Diocese of Monterey, California, Entry No. 1803. Lorenzo's mother's baptismal record in the spring of 1820 describes her as the 19-year-old daughter of *Hetjeglavihaig*. No record of her native village again appears in the baptismal, marriage, or death journals kept at Santa Cruz or a nearby missions. Nevertheless, a village called *Chalala* appears in the San Antonio Baptismal Register and is described as "above the Salinas River." It is likely, Lorenzo's mother was a Salinan Indian, and her native village was probably *Cholame* near the confluence of Estrella Creek and the Salinas River. Editor's Note: See also Randall Milliken's article in this journal, "The Spanish Contact and Mission Period Indians of the Santa Cruz-Monterey Bay Region," footnote 13, for a different interpretation of the origin of Lorenzo's mother.

15 Alphonse Pinart, "Santa Cruz Vocabularies," word lists manuscript, Bancroft Library, University of California, Berkeley. A comparison between Pinart's Santa Cruz linguistic informants, Rustico's and Eulogia's word lists, and that supplied by Lorenzo in his 1890 interview, demonstrates that Lorenzo spoke the Santa Cruz dialect called *Awaswas*.

16 Robert Jackson, "An Introduction of the Historical Demography of Santa Cruz Mission and the Villa de Branciforte, 1791-1846," University of California, Santa Cruz, Special Collections Library, unpublished senior thesis, 1980. The author cites an 1845 census of ex-missionized Indians that includes a Lorenzo Olivara (sic), age 26. Native county: Santa Cruz; a widower whose occupation is drover.

17 "Mission Santa Cruz: The Centennial Anniversary of Its Founding Celebrated," *Santa Cruz Surf,* Weekly Edition , October 3, 1891.

18 *Santa Cruz Baptismal Register*, Entry No. 1832 (MDCA). Lorenzo's date here is undoubtedly wrong. Baptismal records for the Mission Santa Cruz place his birthdate at August 10, 1820.

19 *Ibid.*, Entry No. 215; and Chester King, "Map indicating approximate locations of many Costanoan and neighboring groups recorded in Spanish mission registers," May 1975, in author's possession; and C. Hart Merriam, "Village Names in Twelve California Mission Records," University of California *Archaeological Survey* No. 74 (University of California, Berkeley, 1968), 41. The baptismal record states Lorenzo's father's village to be *Cotoni*. Merriam's work notes ten Indian baptisms for 1793 from *Cotoni* out of a total of 47 between 1792 and 1800. The village of *Asar* may have been another name for *Cotoni* or that of a satellite village to *Cotoni*. Merriam's study includes one baptism from a village spelled *Asan* or *Axen* in 1829, but given the date it was probably not Lorenzo's *Asar*. The village *Asar* does not appear anywhere in the historic or ethnographic record. King's map locates *Cotoni* along the extreme northern coast of Santa Cruz County, which coincides with Lorenzo's general description of the location of *Asar*.

20 Donald T. Clark, *Some Santa Cruz County Place Names* (Santa Cruz: University of California, Santa Cruz, 1980), 19. Clark notes that the *Rancho Agua Puerca y Las Trancas*, located on the north county coast, was known prior to 1843 as *Rancho el Jarro*.

21 Maynard Geiger, O.F.M., *Franciscan Missionaries in Hispanic California*, 1769-1848 (San Marino, California: The Huntington Library, 1969); 203-206. Fray Andrés Quintana was born November 27, 1777, at Antonossa in the province of Alva in Spain. He joined the Franciscan order in 1794 at the age of 17. He completed his studies for the priesthood in the province of Cantabria in 1804. That year he sailed for Mexico, where he entered the San Fernando College in Mexico City. The next year he sailed from San

Blas, arriving in Monterey in late August 1805. He was given his first assignment at the Mission Santa Cruz, where he remained until his assassination at the age of 35.

[22] Cook, *Conflict Between the California Indian and White Civilization*, 113-134. Cook's balanced discussion of "Delinquency and Punishment" includes Father President Lasuén's spirited defense of mission punishments, which characterizes them as just and mild. Nevertheless, Quintana's wire-tipped whip appears to be an unusually brutal instrument. In the second part of Lorenzo's interview ("Lorenzo Asisara's Second Narrative", translated later in this journal), he describes a later padre who liked to beat Indians on the stomach with a whip.

[23] Geiger, *Franciscan Missionaries*, 205-206; Engelhardt, *Missions and Missionaries of California*, Vol. III, 14; and Bancroft, *History of California*, Vol. II, 389. Both Geiger and Engelhardt make a spirited defense of Quintana's character based on Governor Sola's letter of 1816 to the viceroy. Bancroft notes that officials in Mexico took seriously the Indian charges that Quintana had nearly beaten two neophytes to death before making a new instrument of torture (the wire-tipped whip) that led to his assassination.

[24] This sentence is somewhat jumbled. Its translation here is literal. What it appears to suggest is that Quintana himself admitted to the neophytes that God does not order the punishments; he (God) only prescribes examples and doctrine as means of instruction. Thus, perhaps, the neophytes felt Quintana was solely responsible for the floggings and punishments administered. One must keep in mind this interview was handwritten under field conditions. This sentence may have been shortened by Savage and its obscurity later overlooked by Bancroft.

[25] This sentence also seems disjointed. What it appears to suggest is that Julian's wife suggested the ploy of having her husband, who apparently was habitually sick, play ill to lure Quintana outside the mission compound. The subsequent narrative bears out this contention.

[26] The term *mayordomo* in colonial Spanish California referred to a person with an overseer's authority, sometimes an active or retired member of the mission guard. In this case a neophyte, whom Lorenzo describes as a "man of natural abilities," was in charge of Quintana's personal servants.

[27] Geiger, *Franciscan Missionaries*, 206. This author points out the "deplorable" condition of security at Mission Santa Cruz that fall of 1812. He states the mission gates were supposed to be locked at night, and that "Quintana disobeyed regulations or at least ignored custom in not having at least one soldier accompany him outside the mission."

[28] Robert Archibald, *The Economic Aspect of the California Missions* (Washington, D.C.: The Academy of Franciscan History, 1978); 115-141; and "Santa Cruz Mission Libro de Cuentas," no author, manuscript. The original is at St. Mary's College, Moraga, California. The sources of this gold and silver were numerous and included the sale of surplus grain and manufactured goods, as well as the renting of native laborers to the residents of the nearby pueblo of Branciforte. After 1810 a widespread and illegal clandestine trade with foreign sailing vessels provided a substantial income for the Santa Cruz missionaries. This trade included grain, livestock, tallow, cattle hides, and otter pelts, all, of course, procured by forced Indian labor.

[29] Otto von Kotzebue, quoted in "Footprints of Early California Discovers," *Overland Monthly* (March 1869); 261 and Cook, *Conflict Between the California Indian and White Civilization*, 56-134. The Russian explorer, Otto von Kotzebue, visiting Santa Clara in 1824, described one such convent as a large quadrangular building resembling a prison, without windows and only one carefully secured door. He goes on, "these dungeons are opened two or three times a day, but only to allow the prisoners to pass to and from church. I have occasionally seen the poor girls rushing out eagerly to breathe the fresh air, and driven immediately into the church like a flock of sheep by an old ragged Spaniard armed with a stick. After mass, they are in the same manner hurried back to their prison." Cook's work analyzes both the psychological and biological consequences of this mass incarceration of unmarried neophytes in these unsanitary compounds.

[30] A *jayunte* was a crude, rectangular house constructed like a wicker basket with walls packed with mud. Obviously, at this time no adobe structure had been built to house the unmarried male neophytes.

[31] A rancheria was the Spanish term for an Indian village. The rancheria referred to here was located below Mission Hill, near present-day Harvey West Municipal Park. Residents of this village were married neophytes and their families.

[32] Florian Guest, O.F.M., "The establishment of the Villa de Branciforte," *C.H.S.Q.*, 41 (March 1962); 45-46.

[33] Cook, "Expeditions to the Interior of California Central Valley, 1820-1840," *Anthropological Records XX* (No. 5); 198. Nazario Galindo is described by José María Amador as taking part in a macabre ritual of baptizing gentile Indian captives followed by an orgy of mass murder. Amador boasted they massacred 100 Indians this way in 1837.

[34] Geiger, *Franciscan Missionaries*, 145-146, 204. Marcelino Marquinez was born in Trevino, Spain, in May of 1779. Becoming a

Franciscan in Cantabria, Spain, in 1798, he sailed to Mexico in 1804. After six years in the College of San Fernando in Mexico City, he arrived in California. First serving at Mission San Luis Obispo for a little more than a year, he was transferred in the fall of 1811 to Santa Cruz, where he remained until 1818. Records indicate he was subject to frequent attacks of colic. He was, in fact, ill and receiving medical treatment at Monterey when Quintana was assassinated.

[35] Maynard Geiger and Clement W. Meighan, *As the Padres Saw Them; California Indian Life and Customs as reported by the Missionaries, 1813-1815* (Santa Barbara: Mission Archive Library, 1976), 99. In this collection of responses to a broad question-naire from colonial officials in Cadiz, Spain, Fray Marquinez and Jayme Escude of Santa Cruz describe wailing practices among local natives. Those here described agree with other accounts of mourning behavior which prescribe wailing as a practice to send a spirit away from earth. It did not necessarily suggest any affection for the departed.

[36] Bancroft, *History of California*, II, 387. Bancroft reports that Padres Narcisco Durán of San José and José Viader of Santa Clara chanced to be in Santa Cruz on October 13, the day after the discovery of Quintana's body. Together they presided over his funeral and buried him that same day. Padre Marquinez arrived from Monterey just after the ceremony and prepared the certificate of burial.

[37] *Ibid.*, 387-388; and Geiger, *Franciscan Missionaries*, 204. Geiger reports that before he was buried, a superficial investigation was undertaken which found no cause to suspect violence. But on October 15 the governor of California became suspicious and ordered Lt. José María Estudillo of the Monterey Presidio to investigate. Estudillo wrote to Padre Marquinez that it was imperative that the surgeon Don Manuel Quijano examine the body. Quintana's remains were exhumed, and incredibly the surgeon's investigation again found no trace of violence and concluded Quintana died of natural causes. Bancroft cites Estudillo's report, dated October 23.

[38] Geiger, *Franciscan Missionaries*, 205. All authorities and documents consulted agree that the discovery of the conspiracy to assassinate Quintana resulted as described by Lorenzo. They also agree it was "about two years later." Certainly by the fall of 1814, the conspirators had been arrested. Geiger cites a letter written by Fray Narciso Durán to Noberto de Santiago October 2, 1814, in which he states, "all those guilty are now prisoners."

[39] Leon Rowland, *Santa Cruz the Early Years* (Santa Cruz: Paper Vision Press, 1980), 234. Born on the overland march from Sonora, Mexico, Castro was married at Santa Barbara in 1805. He eventually became Mayordomo of Santa Cruz in 1812 and later held that post at Santa Clara.

[40] Bancroft, *History of California*, II, 625. It is unlikely that Padre Olbés played the role described by Lorenzo in the arrest of the conspirators. Both Bancroft and Geiger agree that Olbés was not stationed at Santa Cruz until June 1818, long after the conspira-tors had been condemned. There is a possibility that he was visiting Santa Cruz at this time, as missionaries sometimes did, yet there is no evidence to support this supposition. The role ascribed to Olbés may have been played by Fray Jayme Escude, who replaced Quintana at Santa Cruz from spring 1813 to February 1818.

[41] Again we find a seemingly incomprehensible statement. It is absurd to suppose that Padre Marquinez would warn the conspira-tors of their imminent arrest, so that they might flee. The only reasonable explanation for this statement is to view it as a mistake on Lorenzo's part or an error in transcription by Savage.

[42] A hackamore is an article of tack used like a bridle. In mission times they were made of twined horsehair.

[43] Amador, "Memorias de la Historia de California," 78. Amador states, "I, José María Amador, was commissioned, along with Jesus Mesa to conduct the prisoners involved in the death of Quintana from Santa Cruz to the Presidio at San Francisco. We took sixteen of them fastened together by their thumbs and to a bar passing along the back of their necks. They were turned over to me in shackles, but I refused to receive them in this condition and I was then authorized to conduct them in such a manner as I saw fit. I ordered the Shackles removed from their limbs."

[44] Engelhardt, *Missions and Missionaries*, Vol. III, 12. The author seems to suggest Quintana's body was again exhumed to confirm evidence given at the trial, but cites no source. Nevertheless, he says the conspirators were found guilty and the sentence sent to the viceroy for final determination.

[45] Bancroft, *History of California*, II, 389. Bancroft noted that evidently officials in Mexico attached some importance to the Indian testimony at the military tribunal in San Francisco that claimed (like Lorenzo) that Quintana was extremely cruel. (See also Note 26.) The author goes on to note that no records exist of the trial. His source relies on correspondence between Governor Solá and the viceroy.

[46] Engelhardt, *Missions and Missionaries*, 12-13. In the spring of 1816, after the case had been reviewed by officials in Mexico, the accused (Lino, Antonio, Quirico, Julian, Ambrosio, Andrés, Leto Antonio, Secundino, and Felguncio) were sentenced to 200 lashes

each and to work in chains from two to ten years at Santa Barbara. However, while awaiting their fate in the San Francisco Presidio, two of the accused died. Engelhardt's source for this data is the controversial defense of Quintana written by Governor Solá to the viceroy, June 2, 1816, which additionally summarizes the Indian charges against Quintana. Engelhardt translates it in full.

[47] Bancroft, *History of California*, II, 388. This author, citing Nazario Galindo's memoirs, notes that Lino died in Santa Barbara in 1817, and only one of the condemned survived his punishment.

[48] See "Lorenzo Asisara's Second Narrative" later in this Journal.

[49] Engelhardt, *Missions and Missionaries*, Vol. III, Part II, 12; and Geiger, *Franciscan Missionaries*, 205.

[50] Bancroft, *History of California*, I, 587-596. While neophyte revolts, fugitivism, and native guerrilla warfare might be dismissed by colonial authorities, serious charges of cruelty and mismanagement originating within the Franciscan order had developed earlier. Padre Antonio de la Concepción Horra of Mission San Miguel in a 1791 memorial to the viceroy specifically charged the order with cruelty to the Indians of California. Although the Franciscan order declared Horra to be insane, a series of embarrassing military and defensive church investigations took place until 1805. By this time Horra had been deported entirely from the New World and returned to Spain and his charges dismissed.

[51] Cook, *The Conflict Between the California Indian and White Civilization*, 124.

[52] David J. Weber, *The Mexican Frontier, 1821-1846: The American Southwest Under Mexico* (Albuquerque: University of New Mexico Press, 1982), 43-68.

[53] *California History Vol. LXX* (Summer 1991). The original publication of this interview triggered a letter containing an unprecedented attack on Lorenzo Asisara's narrative and this author's translation and documentation. The letter was written by Doyce Nunis, at that time vice-president of the California Historical Society. *California History* has a policy of not publishing letters to the editor, but the publishers seem to have made an exception for Nunes. Nevertheless, his attack was simply based upon his personal conviction that Franciscans never abused Indians and that both past and present Indians who make such allegations are lying. This author refutes each allegation point by point. See Communication, pages 206-215 and endnotes, pages 236-238.

Lorenzo Asisara's Second Narrative: Punishment in the Santa Cruz Mission Under Padre Ramon Olbés and Others[1]

Introduction[2]

One of the alleged beneficiaries of the Spanish spiritual and physical "conquest" of Alta California were called *Costaños* (coastal people) by the minions of that empire. Like most California Indian group names, the term *Costanoan* describes a language family associated with a territory. The Costanoan territory encompassed much of the San Francisco Bay and Pacific coast south to Monterey, and was further divided into eight distinct language areas. In precontact times these people lived in at least 50 politically autonomous tribelets. The Mission Santa Cruz was established among the group called *Awaswas*. The total aborigine population of Santa Cruz County was approximately 1,700 persons. Villages ranged in size from 50 to several hundred persons.

Family was the backbone of these societies. Extended family groups governed the conduct of their respective members. Marriage was important because it united two large family groups, which constituted a considerable economic and political force in a small village-based society. Leaders were primarily responsible for organizing ceremonies and coordinating economic activities. Otherwise, individuals were free from religious or political coercion.

The Costanoan economy was carefully maintained by political, religious, and cultural mechanisms. Controlled burning ensured a sustained yield of plant and animal food sources. The native diet was rich in diversity; acorns, grass seeds, berries, roots, deer, elk, antelope, salmon, abalone, sea lion, and whale were eaten. Santa Cruz Indians traded mussels, abalone shells, salt and other coastal resources to their eastern Miwok and Yokuts neighbors.

Much of the tribelet's social, political, and economic order was undergirded by the native religion. These people believed in a creator and a number of lesser deities. Offerings to these gods and a cycle of nature-centered ceremonies were practiced annually. Shamans were consulted to help the ill and insure good hunting and an abundant wild food harvest. Tribesmen were free to choose the depth in which they would become involved in all religious matters.[3]

Nothing in their aboriginal life prepared these happy and robust people for the cataclysmic nightmare triggered by the arrival of Spanish soldiers and their priests.

The Hispanic colonization of Alta California followed a classic pattern for the Spanish Empire in the New World. Lacking a surplus population, Spain initiated a colonial system that utilized both the military and the mendicant orders of the Catholic church to extend and secure its New World conquests.[4] Their plan of empire called for the pacification of Indian tribes, to be accomplished by a Christianization scheme that aimed at quickly converting pagan Indians (or gentiles, as the Spanish called them) who could then be rapidly absorbed into colonial society as "peons" or peasants. The conversion was to be carried out in California by the Franciscan order. Royal military authorities would insure the safety of the missionaries and provide the force necessary to compel Indians to give up their lands, resources, native religion, freedom, and independence. It is essential to a realistic understanding of this process to recognize that once the Indians were baptized, they became unpaid laborers and were not free to leave. The padres established a strict feudalistic regime that sought to control every aspect of their daily lives: where they could live, who they could marry, and the daily labor tasks for men, women and children. A culture of fear was maintained through an elaborate system of native informants and

Indian bullies, who meted out beatings to those who might oppose this brand of "salvation."[5]

No amount of paternalistic moral or legal arguments can blunt the harsh reality of this degrading slavery-like condition.[6] Eventually, nearly 80,000 California Indians (about one-third of the total pre-contact population) were reduced to this humiliating condition between 1769 and 1836.[7]

Considerable native resistance and resentment naturally occurred as a result of this church/military threat. This resistance can be roughly divided between passive and active. Passive resistance included slow and poorly accomplished work habits, abortions, infanticide (especially when the child was fathered by a Spanish soldier), and the belief and practice of native religious movements within the neophyte communities.[8] Active resistance took the form of fugitism (both individual and mass escapes) stock raids in conjunction with interior tribes, assassination of priests, and large-scale neophyte revolts.[9]

As originally envisioned, the Franciscans would convert and train Indians in the missions of Alta California until they were sufficiently Hispanicized to form independent Indian pueblos or municipalities. Legally, this process should be completed in ten years.[10]

The Franciscans would then turn over their positions to regular parish priests and move on to new "pagan conquests."[11] However, a combination of factors caused the Franciscans in Alta California to delay this process for over half a century! The startling mortality rate in the disease-ridden missions fueled nearly continuous military/church "recruitment" expeditions among the nearby healthy interior tribesmen.[12] Furthermore, the padres habitually complained to the governmental authorities that the California Indians were too stupid and slow in adopting Hispanic culture to emancipate.[13] And finally there is good reason to suspect the Franciscans themselves found their vast feudal Franciscan haciendas, with thousands of Indians kept in a state of near slavery, to be simply too wealthy (and not incidentally of considerable political advantage) to give up on this remote rim of Christendom.[14]

Nevertheless, events surrounding the Mexican Independence Wars (1811-1821) soon wrenched control of the 21 Alta California missions from the grip of Franciscan authority. These successful revolutions in Mexico were anti-clerical, anti-Spanish, and imbued with liberal nineteenth century republican ideals. Many of these enlightenment ideas clashed with the earlier Spanish assumptions of the natural inferiority of Indians that underpinned the Franciscan empire in the New World.[15]

Ultimately, the result was a series of secularization laws (1834-1836) that herald the divestiture of the Franciscan estates in Alta California. These laws were supposed to trigger the distribution of mission wealth to the surviving mission Indians. In practice, a secular administrator was appointed to inventory each mission and begin the process of parceling out land, livestock, tools, and buildings to the newly emancipated neophytes. In reality, few Indians were granted lands. The majority of the wealth was stolen by corrupt civil administrators who plundered the Franciscan empire of nearly all its material wealth.[16]

The following eyewitness account of the decline and collapse of the Franciscan empire among the Costanoan Indians is taken from the 1877 interview with the Costanoan Indian and ex-neophyte of Mission Santa Cruz, Lorenzo Asisara. This second half of Lorenzo's narrative deals with missionary discipline, the secularization of the mission, and the melancholy demise of the local Indian population.[17]

Only a handful of California Indian accounts of life in Franciscan missions exist.[18] Taken together, Lorenzo's first and second narratives are without question the most detailed and chronologically comprehensive of this rare body of documentation. Here we have primary data of significant historical events from a native viewpoint. Today's scholars and students of history will now be able to draw upon this material, along with perspectives offered by ethnographers, archaeologists, economists, and a variety of humanities disciplines, to draw a clearer picture of Indian life in the Franciscan yoke. This

material and advances in related disciplines will enable today's readers to move beyond self-serving Franciscan histories of colonial conquest to a more balanced picture of that experience—an experience that nearly annihilated the very Indians the Franciscans hoped to "save."

—Edward D. Castillo

Lorenzo's Second Narrative

After the death of Padre Quintana in 1812, Padre Olbés was the Minister of the mission.[19] As I have said in another occasion, he was a distrustful man and very bad. One night he took in his own hands the key of the *jayunte* to lock up the single men. The corporal of the guard went with him to protect his person. The corporal was Ignacio Peralta.[20] He had a list of all those who were inside the *jayunte*, in order to know if some were absent and who it was. One was absent whose name was Dámaso, who was one who was addicted to playing cards, and who delayed in obtaining some food in order to go to the barracks.

Padre Olbés and the corporal had already been waiting for him for some minutes. Less than half an hour. Dámaso arrived and the Father asked him in exasperation where he had been. The Indian answered that he was waiting for a mouthful [of food] from his relatives. The *alcaldes*[21] said on their part that he had been absent from work from noon to the afternoon in order to occupy himself with the game. Father asked him if this was true, and Dámaso responded that it was—that he had been absent, that he had gone in search of a little wood for the house where they gave him his food.

"Now I am going to punish you," said Padre Olbés, "not on the buttocks, but on the stomach."

Dámaso answered, "No, Father, this is not reasonable, that you punish me on the stomach. I went to look for a little wood for the people who maintain me. I have not committed another fault." The Father ordered the *alcaldes* to arrest him in order to punish him. The Indian resisted, arguing that he wasn't guilty. The Father insisted that he should be punished.

The others who were in the *jayunte* shouted to

Dámaso, in Indian, "Do not allow yourself to be punished."

The Padre turned to see what the Indians told him. He ordered that they take Dámaso by force: this [one] resisted them and he said to the *alcaldes*, "Leave me, let the Father grab me and that he himself punish me."[22] But the Padre insisted that the *alcaldes* do it, and these, inasmuch as they understood what was shouted at them from the *jayunte*, didn't dare to obey Father.

Then an Indian named Crisanto, uncle of Dámaso, shouted to him, "Don't let them."

Padre Olbés then ordered the *alcaldes*, "Bring me that other one as well, "grabbing the *alcaldes* and pushing them so that they would bring Crisanto. The *alcaldes* were fearful of the mutiny of the Indians against the Padre and them.

The corporal descended, saying, "Let's kill them." All of them, [the Indians] in the *jayunte*, rose to attack the corporal, the Father, and the *alcaldes*. They began to grab tiles, and the Padre fled to one side. The corporal threw down his sword and also began to flee in spite of the shouts of the Reverend, "Corporal, Corporal!" But this [one] was more cowardly than the devil and fled with the utmost speed. The *alcaldes* also looked for their salvation. The Indians threw tiles at the corporal and the *alcaldes*, but not one rock was thrown at the Padre nor at the others other than to scare them, not to injure them. Many rocks were thrown at them. Padre Olbés with the cry, "Corporal," ran hard at every minute and didn't stop until he arrived at his house.

The Indians wanted to frighten him so that he would not give them so many lashes, Olbés was very inclined to cruelly whip. He was never satisfied to prescribe less than 50 lashes; even to the little children of eight to ten years he would order 25 lashes given at the hand of a strong man, either on the buttocks, or on the stomach, when the whim would enter him.[23]

After the flight of Father Olbés and his defenders, the single Indians entered the barracks to sleep saying,

"Let us sleep, for tomorrow punishment is sure to follow." On the following morning Father Olbés returned with the corporal to ask who had instigated the rock throwing. Nobody answered. The Father lectured them. From there they went to mass at the church, all pardoned from punishment.

At about the end of the year (now that I remember, it was the eighth day of the Purisima), Padre Olbés made a present to the Indians of one barrel of honey and 100 cheeses divided in two. He began to give them a portion of all this, to all of them after mass. (Because Padre Olbés was cruel in the punishments, on the other hand, he was careful to keep the people well nourished and dressed.) He concluded with the distribution of rations of the same articles to the women as well.

He saw that two of them [neophyte women] were scratched in their faces because they had been fighting out of jealousy. He separated them to ascertain why they had scratched [each other]. One was sterile and the other had children. When the Father became aware of the cause of the quarrel, he asked the sterile one why she didn't bear children. He sent them for the husband, and he asked him why his wife hadn't borne children. The Indian pointed to the sky (he didn't know how to speak Spanish) to signify that only God knew the cause. They brought an interpreter. This [one] repeated the question of the Father to the Indian and that [one] answered that he should ask God. The Padre asked through the interpreter if he slept with his wife, to which the Indian said yes.

Then the Father had them placed in a room together, so that they would perform coitus in his presence. The Indian refused, but they forced him to show them his penis in order to affirm if he had it in good order. The Father next brought the wife and placed her in the room. The husband he sent to the guard-house with a pair of shackles.

The interpreter, on orders from the Father, asked her how it was that the face was scratched. She replied that another woman had done it out of jealousy. The Father then asked if her husband had been going with the other women, and she said yes. Then, he

P. Frenzeny's etching of California mission Indians making baskets and rope. The illustration appeared in Harper's Weekly in October 1877. Courtesy of the Museum of Art and History.

asked her again why she didn't bear children like the rest of the women. Padre Olbés asked her if her husband slept with her; and she answered that yes. The Padre repeated his question, "Why don't you bear children?"

"Who knows," answered the Indian. He had her enter another room in order to examine her reproductive parts. She resisted him and grabbed the Father's cord. There was a strong and long struggle between the two that were alone in the room. She tried to bury her teeth in his arm, but only grabbed his habit. Padre Olbés cried out, and the interpreter and the *alcalde* entered to help him.

Then Olbés ordered that they take her and give her 50 lashes. After the 50 lashes, he ordered that she be shackled and locked in the nunnery. Finishing this, Padre Olbés ordered that a wooden doll be made, like a recently born child. He took the doll to the whipped woman and ordered her to take that doll for her child, and to carry it in front of all the people for nine days. He obligated her to present herself in front to the temple with that [doll] as if it were her child for nine days.[24]

With all these things, the women who were sterile became very alarmed. The vicious Father made the husband of that woman wear cattle horns affixed with leather. At the same time he had him shackled. In this way they brought him daily to mass from the jail. And the other Indians jeered at him and teased him. Returning to the jail, they would take the horns off him.

At last Padre Olbés asked to be relieved and he was sent to Sonoma. He was succeeded by Padre Luis Gil Taboada.[25] This Father quit his habits at night and disguised himself to go and join the games in the rancherias. Many times he did it without being discovered, not even by those who knew him well. He would join the games in order to confiscate the cards. Above all, he would observe who were the players. After this he would place his hand in the center and indicate the number of cards he wanted. As soon as the other players would see his white hand [they] would blow out the light with one blow. He then called by their names those he knew and ordered them to kindle the light. Later he would demand that they hand over the playing cards. They wanted to hand over old playing cards, but they were never able to deceive him. He would always take all the playing cards they had. In this way he went visiting the games of the diverse nations that there were in his mission. They were from the San Joaquin River, of los Tulares, and from these same environs.

The Tulareños were the ones who played *peon*,[26] hidden games. There were two bones about two inches long, one black and one white. The white one was the one that counted. The Father would sit there disguised, watching the game for one or two hours. He would bet them the beads for money, and they covered him with silver. After winning or losing, he would retire to his house.

Under the care of Padre Taboada, the people were much relieved from much of the punishments. He treated them very well. He was very amorous. He hugged and kissed the Indian women, and he had contact with them until he had syphilis and skin eruptions broke out. (Don José María Amador affirmed this, and since they were good friends, he gave him medicines to cure him.) Finding himself in this situation, he would celebrate mass sitting in his house. He was not able many times to celebrate mass standing up because he was all ulcerated. In spite of this, he would still go out to aid the gravely ill. Finally after much time of care, he regained his health, said Amador, being corporal of the guard.[27]

Taboada came to be very well liked by all the Indians, particularly by the Tulareños, whose language he came to understand somewhat. He was rash and happy, and he would go to enjoy himself with the Indians and play *peon* with them.

Rarely did he punish. It was necessary for the crime to be very grave, and then the punishment would not pass 12 or 15 lashes at most. He taught me how to read, write, and play music. He was the one who began to give instruction in the school to the little Indians. He had the Indians taught the prayers and other things of the church in their own language so that they would understand it well.

He treated the Indians well, giving them enough to eat, having the clothing and not having them work to excess.

Padre Taboada was the minister at the mission of Santa Cruz until he was relieved by Father Antonio Jimeno.[28] This Father lasted hardly two years. He was very good and careful, punishing only those that were truly guilty, and for those without any vigor. Addi-

tionally, when he entered, he was jealous and he hurled accusations at Father Taboada in order to compel him to leave the mission immediately. The Indians had already cured Taboada, who left the mission in the middle of the night. I was already at least 13 or 14 years of age or more at this time.

After Jimeno, Padre Juan Moreno came, an excellent horseman.[29] He would leave with his cowboys to lasso bears. One day he lassoed with his first throw a female bear who had just given birth, and many witnessed it. He was at the mission for about three years, and he treated the Indians with the utmost affection. From time to time he stayed to eat with them in their *rancherias*. He was succeeded by Father José Jimeno, the brother of Antonio.[30] Good minister. He lasted until the Zacatecan Fathers came. Padre Antonio Real was the one who relieved José Jimeno.[31] This Real was a rancher. He was an excellent horseman, and he would work a bull like the best cowboy. His brother, José Maria, was the same. Padre Antonio Real was at the mission for many years, until many [years] after the secularization.[32]

I remember the Father being Minister, and I was the sacristan charged with the care of the church and its possessions. General José Figueroa came from San Francisco on inspection. He was accompanied by Captains Nicolas Guitierrez and Agustin V. Zamarano, Eugenio Montenegro, Lieutenant Navarrete, and various others of the retinue, soldiers and settlers. He received the General with great pomp. The Padre dressed in a cape, with a staff and a high cross, received the General at a distance of about 200 *varas* (a vara equals 33 inches) from the church, and accompanied him to the entrance, where a *Te Deum* was sung. Outside he saluted him with cannon and rifle shots and sky rockets. In a word, he was received with enthusiasm and pleasure and with the honor which were due to his high office.

Padre Antonio Real always dealt with the Indians with the greatest liberalness: he rarely punished, and only to the very bad ones. He was very pacifistic, festive, and inclined toward the good life. He dressed the Indians well, each according to his class. He opened the bales that there were in the mission of silk, wool, shawls, and he gave it all to the Indians.

Santa Cruz
County
History Journal
Issue 5, 2002

He already knew that the missions would be secularized. General Figueroa was at the mission for about ten days, inspecting what it possessed. Later he went to the capital.

One month later, Padre Real sent me and four more boys to Monterey under the charge of Sergeant Estrada in order to learn how to play the clarinet. I already knew how to play the flute, and in six months I learned enough and returned to the mission.

Thus like his brother, José Maria was inclined to the vices, especially the women. Antonio, on the contrary, was moderate and moral in his conduct. If sometime he had stumbled, of which I was unaware, he knew how to hide it well from public view.[33]

Finally, the mission was secularized. Don Ignacio del Valle coming to effect it, who entered the drawing room where he was going to be lodged.[34] It was the dinner hour and the Father invited him to it, but he didn't accept. Then the Padre gave him the key so that he could go to his room. He gave me orders to deliver to Señor Valle all that he would ask, and I complied.

Señor Valle asked me if I was the Mayordomo and key bearer. I answered that I was, and he told me to watch close what the Father did that evening, for he had come to receive the mission. I went to my bedroom and took my blankets and placed them to one side of the door of the drawing room, in the inside part. There I lay down to watch.

About two hours later, the Father left to see if the boys were already asleep so that he could carry out his business and take from the mission all that he could. He found me in bed, and I pretended to be sleeping and snoring. He was startled and said to me, "Hairless, what are you doing here?" He didn't touch me, and I pretended not to understand him.

He had a boy name José Aguilar (español), whom he had brought from [Mission] San Luis Rey. He was asleep. The Father awakened him abruptly, and the boy arose very frightened. The Padre ordered him to call his friends that he had there. Juan Gonzalez, the Mayordomo, and his family came. I continued

snoring. They entered Father's room and picked out portions of the most valuable effects, including gold and silver coins, table service.

I myself saw on the third trip between his house and that of the Father with their knots and cargoes, one entered there named Maria Garcia Rodriguez, who was the assistant of the Father left with a bundle of genesis of silk in her hand and others under her arm.[35] I sat up and asked her what she was carrying. She, in a frightened and low voice, said, "Go inside with the Father," and she went out with her bundles.

In a short while, Juan Gonzales and his wife left, weighted down. I was sitting to see the others. They said nothing to me and left, returning to enter immediately without the bundles. I am sure that they told the Father that I was watching. The Father came to me, and I had wrapped my head and all in the blankets and laying down. He called me and told me to go inside. I obeyed.

Then he said to me, "Here you have 40 pesos in pure gold, and a box of beads for your father . . ." This was done so that I would not accuse them. Moreover, he promised me a garment from the feet to the head. He brought out a bottle and a glass, and he gave me half a glass of brandy. The Father continually drank a lot of liquor and wine, although he did not become drunk. He told me to take the beads to my father on that same night so that no one would know it. Thus I did it.

While I was absent, I suppose that they concluded their business; thus when I returned, the door was closed, and the Father was pacing back and forth in the drawing room, waiting for me. Later when I arrived, he said, "What did Don Ignacio tell you?" I told him about it. Then he said to me, "Come here." We went inside; he gave me the 40 pesos in gold. He took out two glasses (it was almost morning)—one for him and the other for me. He gave me the liquor and he also drank. Then he encharged me, saying, "Like a man you should be quiet about what you have seen."

I answered him, "Father, how can you want this, that my father should receive only one box of beads, when all of the interest of the mission belongs to the community?"

He answered me, "I only ask you now that tomorrow you don't talk with Don Ignacio Valle." Saying these words, Valle came, knocked on the door; which he opened.

The Father sent me off to ring the bells, when it still was not time for this. Valle had his sword at his waist, and he told him, "Father, I want the keys to the mission." I didn't go to ring [the bells] because Valle detained me. The Father replied that there would be time enough to transfer the mission and its interests. Then Valle sent me back to sleep. They remained there, arranging their business and drinking.

In about half an hour, I being in my first dream, the Father came and took me by the hands, saying, "Ah, hairless, you are already sleeping."[36] He and Valle had already agreed. The Father sent for Juanillo Gonzalez, the Mayordomo, so that he would come. So I did. Juanillo came. The Father introduced him to Valle as a friend. He and Don Ignacio shook hands. The Father had me bring cheese, buns, and the flask of liquor from his quarters. The three drank. I did not want to drink, pretending that I did not know how to drink. The Father was already happy and so was Don Ignacio, who was also inclined toward drinking liquor. They sent me to ring the early morning bells. I returned to see if the Padre wanted to celebrate mass, but he was unable, being too drunk.[37]

Valle already had the keys to the mission. We went to the storeroom, the Father with us to make the transfer. From time to time, the Father made signals to me so that I would not talk. I remained very silent. Valle asked if all that the mission possessed in effects was in those storerooms, manifesting doubt that it was so, because in reality the storerooms seemed to have been ransacked. The Father and his friends had not had time to rearrange things. If I had not spoken to Maria Garcia Rodriguez, much more would have been taken out of the storerooms. Don Ignacio, nevertheless, saw that he had been compromised.

We retired. From there, Don Ignacio took me to his room. He threatened me with his sword, commanding me to tell him the plain truth. I told him that I had not seen anything out of the ordinary. Then he answered me, "There, you compose yourself. This is all yours; I came to receive it to give to you." He distributed all of the effects to the Indians of the mission, but all the money the Indians will never see. Without doubt, this was all arranged between the two of them.

Additionally, the Father handed over to Valle 5,000 head of cattle, a great quantity of sheep on seven ranches, 11 herds of horses, three herds of female burros, a comparable quantity of oxen, horses at stud. The mission had an abundance of everything.

Valle finished this commission with almost everything. Señor Alvarado governed. Then Francisco Soto came as administrator, and he finished with the rest,[38] even taking the tiles with his drunken feasts. After, he wanted to order the Indians like in the time of the missions, by blows and kicks. The Indians rose in rebellion one evening when he was partly inebriated and grabbed him. They made him understand that if he continued doing this, he wouldn't last many days.[39]

Then he went to Monterey and brought Joaquin Soto, his brother, and Vicente Cantua, his brother-in-law, to keep him company. Francisco Soto was either a lieutenant or civil ensign.

Then the time arrived in which the Robles [Nicolas, Avelino, Secundino, and another that they called Chato] who for some reason that I don't remember, Soto apprehended them and wanted to put a rope around the neck as he had done with the Indians. They resisted. Avelino was the most valiant, and he proved to be the most disobedient. Soto passed by somewhat drunk. He had little soldiers with him. In his drunkenness, he ordered the soldiers to discharge their rifles at Avelino. This [one] separated himself from his brothers and, resting against a wall, he said there they had him and could kill him, but he would not let them put a rope on his neck. The soldiers pointed [their rifles] at Avelino, fired (a majority to the sides), and one of the shots (which was fired by Pantealeon Higuera) hit Avelino in the region of the groin . . . from which wound he died in two or three days.

Because of this event, the widow of Avelino Robles went about disguised as a man with a dagger, awaiting for the occasion to kill Francisco Soto.

The Presidio of San Francisco. Testifying to the climate of force which dominated Indian-colonial relations in Hispanic California, Indians in this 1816-era illustration by Louis Choris are being herded to work. Courtesy of the Museum of Art and History.

Friends and companions persuaded him to flee Santa Cruz in order to escape the fury of that woman and the father and brothers of the deceased. At night he crossed the swollen river and went to Monterey. He did not come back. Joaquin Soto and Vicente Cantua stayed at the mission establishment for a few days.

Then José Antonio Bolcoff became the administrator of the mission.[40] I then entered as the *alcalde* of Indians. He also was the judge of Branciforte. He distributed the moveable assets that remained to the Indians. This was old mares that were no longer productive, very old rams which were retired from stud service. He took for himself some of the animals for his own work. He unearthed the cessions of land which Figueroa had made to the Indians, whose documents had been hidden by Valle and Juan Gonzalez. He showed them to me. He gave the land to the Indians, but it did not do the Indians any good. The smallpox plague came and finished the Indian population.[41]

Bolcoff, finding nothing else to expropriate, carried off to his ranch the used adobes, bricks, roof tiles, studs, and rafters from the mission. This was the conclusion of the goods of the mission. The lands were divided among the Indians. The Indians, those that lived, sold their parcels for liquor. Those who died left their land, and others confiscated the lands for themselves.[42]

(signed) Lorenzo Asisara

Notes:

[1] Translated and annotated by Edward D. Castillo with the translation assistance of Robert Jackson. Published by permission of the Bancroft Library. The original manuscript and a translation are in the Bancroft Library under the title: *Recollections concerning the History of California by José María Amador,* (BANC MSS C-D 28); 90-113, testimony of Lorenzo Asisara, July 10, 1877.

[2] Editor's Note: This Introduction is excerpted from Edward D. Castillo's article, "An Indian Account of the Decline and Collapse of Mexico's Hegemony over the Missionized Indians of California," first published in the *American Indian Quarterly*, Vol. 13, No. 4 (Fall 1989); 391-408. Permission to reprint an edited version of this article is granted by the University of Nebraska Press.

[3] Richard Levy, "The Costanoans," Chapter in *Handbook of North American Indians,* 485-495.

[4] Herbert E. Bolton, "Mission as a Frontier Institution in the Spanish Colonies," *American Historical Review*, 23 (1917); 42-61 and Robert Ricard, *The Spiritual Conquest of Mexico; an Essay on the Apostolate and Evangelizing Methods of the Mendicant Orders in New Spain*; 1523-1572, (Berkeley and Los Angeles: University of California Press, 1966).

5 Sherburne F. Cook, *The Conflict Between the California Indian and White Civilization*, (Berkeley and Los Angeles: University of California Press, 1976); 1-194.

6 Francis F. Guest, "Cultural Perspectives on California Mission Life," *Southern California Quarterly*, Vol. 65 (Spring 1983); 1-65

7 J.N. Bowman, "California Indians Baptized During the Mission Period," *Historical Society of Southern California Quarterly*, Vol. 42 (1960); 273-277. Also see Sherburne F. Cook, *The Population of the California Indians, 1769-1970*, (Berkeley and Los Angeles: University of California Press, 1976).

8 Cook, *The Conflict Between the California Indian and White Civilization*, 56-91.

9 Sylvia Broadbent, "Conflict at Monterey; Indian Horse Raiding, 1820-1850," *Journal of California Anthropology*, Vol. 1, No. 1 (1974); 86-101; Alan K. Brown, "Pomponio's World," *The Argonaut*, No. 6 (May 1975); Edward D. Castillo, "The Native Response to the Colonization of Alta California;" and Jack Holterman, "The Revolt of Estanislao," *The Indian Historian*, Vol. 3, No. 1 (1970); 43-55, and "The Revolt of Yozcolo," *The Indian Historian*, Vol. 3, No. 2 (1970); 19-25. See also Jack D. Forbes, *Warriors of the Colorado, The Yumas of the Quechan Nation and Their Neighbors*, (Norman: University of Oklahoma Press, 1965); 175-220.

10 Gerald J. Geary, "The Secularization of the California Missions (1810-1846)," *The Catholic University of America Studies in American Church History*, Vol. XVII, (Washington, D.C.: Catholic University of America, 1934) and Manuel Servin, "The Secularization of the California Missions: A Reappraisal," *Southern California Quarterly*, Vol. 47 (1965); 133-149.

11 David J. Weber, *The Mexican Frontier 1821-1846, The American Southwest Under Mexico*, (Albuquerque: University of New Mexico Press, 1982); 43-68.

12 Cook, "Colonial Expeditions to the Interior of California: Central Valley, 1800-1820," University of California Anthropological Records, Vol. 16 (1960); 239-292 and Cook's *The Conflict Between the California Indian and White Civilization*, 56-91.

13 Zephyrin Engelhardt, O.F.M., *The Missions and Missionaries of California*, III (San Francisco: James Barry Co., 1908-1915); 477-479; C. Allen Hutchinson, *Frontier Settlement in Mexican California, The Hijar-Padres Colony and Its Origins, 1769-1835*, (New Haven: Yale University Press, 1969); 43-96. Together these works and others like them clearly illuminate the low opinion the missionaries and Spanish colonists in general had of the California Indians. They were astounded that the natives failed to see and emulate the "obvious" superiority of Spanish culture, language, and religion.

14 Robert Archibald, *The Economic Aspect of the California Missions*, (The Academy of Franciscan History, Washington, D.C., 1978); 115-141.

15 Weber, *The Mexican Frontier 1821-1846, The American Southwest under Mexico*, 43-68.

16 Geary, "The Secularization of the California Missions (1810-1846)," 156-190.

17 Robert H. Jackson, "Disease and Demographic Patterns at Santa Cruz Mission, Alta California," *Journal of California and Great Basin Anthropology*, Vol. 5, Nos. 1 and 2 (1983); 33-57.

18 Julio Cesar; "Cosas de los Indios de California," unpublished manuscript, Bancroft Library, University of California, Berkeley; Fernando Librado, *Breath of the Sun*, (Banning, California: Malki Museum Press, 1979); Pablo Tac, "Indian Life and Customs at Mission San Luis Rey, A Record of California Mission Life Written by Pablo Tac, An Indian Neophyte (Rome, California 1835)," Mina and Gordon Hewes, eds., *The Americas*, Vol. 9, No. 1 (1952); 87-106.

19 Geiger, *Franciscan Missionaries*, 167-168. Ramon Olbés was born in Ateca, Spain, February 8, 1786. Joining the Franciscan order in 1802, he arrived at the College of San Fernando in Mexico City in 1810. Arriving in California in 1812, he served at Santa Ines, Santa Barbara, San Luis Rey, and finally in Santa Cruz. He was stationed at Santa Cruz from June 1818 to November 1821. Bancroft elsewhere characterized him as a "monster of cruelty" whose eccentric behavior amounted at times to insanity.

20 Each mission had an *escolta*, or squad of soldiers, stationed there to protect the priests from the Indians.

21 *Alcaldes* refers to Franciscan-appointed neophyte thugs that received official status and small privileges from the padres.

22 Robert F. Heizer, ed., *The Indians of Los Angeles County, Hugo Reid's Letters of 1852*. (Los Angeles: Southwest Museum, 1968), 85. This contemporary observer made these comments about the role of the Indian alcaldes at Mission San Gabriel: "Indian alcaldes were appointed annually by the padre and chosen from among the very laziest of the community; he being of the opinion that they took more pleasure in making the others work, than would industrious ones! From my own observations this is correct. They carry a wand to denote their authority, and what was more terrible, an immense scourge of rawhide about 10 feet in length, plaited to the thickness of an ordinary man's wrist!—They did a great deal of chastisement both by and without orders."

23 Cook, *The Conflict Between the California Indian and White Civilization*, 113-134. This author's balanced discussion of "Delinquency and Punishment" includes Father President Lasuén's spirited defense of mission punishments which characterizes

them as just and mild. He claimed, "It is never ordered to give anyone more than 25 lashes. . ." Cook gently reminds his readers, "We know he must be in error because there are numerous instances on record of floggings amounting to 50 or even 100 lashes."

[24] Heizer, *The Indians of Los Angeles County*, 87. A remarkably similar bizarre punishment is described by Hugo Reid at Mission San Gabriel.

[25] Geiger, *Franciscan Missionaries*, 104-106. Taboada was born in Guanajuato, Mexico, May 1, 1773 of Spanish parents. He attended the College of San Fernando in Mexico City before arriving in California in 1801. He served at Mission Santa Cruz from 1820 to 1827.

[26] Heizer, *Handbook of North American Indians*, California, 465. William Wallace, author of the chapter on Yokuts, describes this common Indian gambling game still practiced today throughout southern California.

[27] Engelhardt, *Mission San Luis Obispo*, (Santa Barbara, 1933), 199. This latter-day Franciscan naturally dismisses all allegations of Taboada's "immorality" as worthless.

[28] Geiger, *Franciscan Missionaries*, 129-130. Padre Antonio Jimeno served at Mission Santa Cruz from March 21, 1828 to December 10, 1828.

[29] *Ibid.*, 157-158. Padre Juan Moreno was stationed at Mission Santa Cruz from August 8, 1829 to October 30, 1830.

[30] *Ibid.*, 131-134. Padre José Joaquin Jimeno served at Santa Cruz from October 30, 1830 to February 17, 1833.

[31] *Ibid.*, 247-249. Padre Antonio de la Concepción Suárez del Real was the first of the Franciscan padres to be assigned to Santa Cruz from the Apostolic College of Zacatecas, Mexico. He was stationed there from 1833 to 1844. Bancroft, *History of California*, Vol. 5, 689, wrote of him, "Padre Real was a dissolute man addicted to more than one vice, and even accused of theft, but credited with having been kind and indulgent to his neophytes."

[32] *Ibid.*, 248-249. Geiger notes several other disparaging descriptions contemporaries wrote about this priest. He was described as a publicly wenching, slovenly drunkard not above thieving from local merchants.

[33] Bancroft, *History of California*, III, 694.

[34] *Ibid.*

[35] Edna Kimbro, Mary Ellen Ryan, Robert Jackson and Randy Milliken, *Restoration Research, Santa Cruz Mission Adobe*, (Sacrament: California State Department of Parks and Recreation, 1985), 65. Chapter Five of this Parks Department study summarizes nearly all that is known of secularization at Santa Cruz. This study identifies Maria de Alta Garcia Rodriguez Gonzales as Juan Gonzales' sister-in-law.

[36] Geiger and Meighan, *As the Padres Saw Them*, etc., 48. Costanoan dreams are discussed in the reply to the Interrogatorio of 1812 by Padres Narciso Durán and Buenaventura Fortuny.

[37] See notes 30 and 31.

[38] Kimbro, et al., *Restoration Research*, 65. Despite Valle's records that claim to have distributed $10,576 to the rapidly declining ex-neophyte population, little convincing evidence exists that this distribution actually occurred. When Soto became mayordomo (1839), he made no land grants to the 71 remaining Indians, instead giving grants of the so-called mission lands to Mexican colonists or "gente de Razon" (men of reason), as they called themselves.

[39] *Ibid.*, 66.

[40] *Ibid.* By the fall of 1839 Soto was replaced by Don José Bolcoff, the *juez de paz* at Santa Cruz.

[41] Robert H. Jackson, "Disease and Demographic Patterns at Santa Cruz Mission, Alta California," *Journal of Californias and Great Basin Anthropology*, Vol. 5, Nos. 1 and 2 (1983); 36-40. This important study notes the 1838 smallpox outbreak at Mission Santa Cruz took eight Indian victims in the first two weeks of July. By September the outbreak had spent itself, leaving 30 Indian victims in its wake. Between 1834 and 1839 the surviving Santa Cruz neophyte population suffered a staggering 70 percent decline. These unfortunate natives now stood at the brink of extinction. Padre Real attributed the 1838 smallpox outbreak to God's anger over the disrepaired condition of the mission church.

[42] Kimbro, et al., *Restoration Research*, 66-69. This study carefully reconstructs what is known of the distribution of ex-mission property. While secularization land records were destroyed during the Mexican War, these authors were able to show only 25 of the 49 adult males living at Mission Santa Cruz in 1839 were granted "mission" property. Within 25 years these natives were completely dispossessed of their native soil.

Lorenzo Asisara's Third Narrative[1]
Narrative of a Mission Indian
[Translated from an interview in 1890 by E. L. Williams.][2]

There is now living in Santa Cruz an old Indian who was baptized at the Santa Cruz Mission about the year 1819. He was educated by the priests, and sang in the choir. He possesses extraordinary intelligence for an Indian, as indicated by the education which he has obtained. He reads and writes the Spanish language. In many instances have I found corroborative evidence of what he has said, particularly in the chapter of Perouse's history descriptive of mission life in Monterey in 1786, which the publisher has deemed of sufficient interest and importance to incorporate in this volume, and which follows the narrative of the Indian Lorenzo.[3]

Lorenzo Asisara's 1890 Interview

I was born at the Mission of Santa Cruz on Monday, the tenth day of August, 1819,[4] and was given the name of Lorenzo by Padre Ramon Olbéz. Three days afterward I was baptized at the baptismal font. My father's name was Venancio. My mother's name was Maria; my brother's name was Jacinto. I was with the reverend Fathers of the Mission of Santa Cruz until I was grown up, and then I went to Monterey, and was employed by General Figueroa, and was taught to play the clarionet by Sergeant Rafael Estrada. There were other military officers there, named Eugenio Montenegro, captain of infantry, Augustin Zamarano, captain of cavalry, and Lieutenant Colonel Nicolas Guitierrez. The barracks and officers' quarters were where now is the church at Monterey. Afterwards I lived at the Mission of Carmelo for one year, during the time of Padre Rafael Moreno, who was a missionary.[5] I conversed at that time with the Indians of that mission about the death of Padre Junipero Serra. They told me they were at his funeral, and for three nights the corpse was watched, and afterwards he was interred, as some of them thought, at San Antonio Mission. Others insist the corpse was embalmed and sent to New Spain (Mexico). When Figueroa died, the corpse was embalmed and taken to Mexico.[6]

Afterwards I came to the Mission of Santa Cruz, and was instructed how to read and write in Spanish by Padre Antonio Real. I was the sacristan, and sang and played in the choir. There were about twenty of us that composed the choir, of which I am the only one living.

The land cultivated in those days was all of the tract between the hill at the end of Pacific Avenue and the hill where the public school now is. There were eight hundred and thirty-six who received rations as I read from the roll. The list was kept by Padre Jose Jimeno, and one day, he being out, I counted the names. They all slept in houses where now is the Sisters' school. All the space about there was covered with dormitories. Some of them were engaged in weaving blankets, others were carpenters, others blacksmiths, tanners, and many worked in the field, cultivating and harvesting. The women prepared the wool for the weavers, did much of the sewing of clothes, and also at times worked in the field. The tanyard was near to the adobe house owned by Mrs Boston, formerly belonging to Rafael Castro, who

Native Americans of San Francisco. In October of 1816 a Russian expedition to the Pacific Northwest entered San Francisco Bay. Aboard the Russian ship were four scientific observers and an artist named Louis Choris. This image by Louis Choris is from the French publication, Voyage Pittoresque Autour do Monde (Paris, France: 1822), which was noted for its colorful pictures. Courtesy of the Museum of Art and History.

was the grantee under the Mexican Government of the Rancho Aptos, now owned by Mr. C. Spreckles.

The names of the Fathers whom I remember were, first, Francisco Moreno, following him, Luis Altaguada, Juan Moreno, Antonio Jimeno, Jose Jimeno, and, lastly, Antonio Real. These were missionaries belonging to the Santa Cruz Mission. There was a tribe of Indians living up the coast called Jaraum. The Indian children were brought to the mission, and afterwards came the grown ones. They were all Christianized by being baptized. Another tribe called Esuans also lived up the coast, and another tribe living farther up the coast was called Joali; another tribe, living at Soquel, had for their captain Balthazar, a name given by the Fathers. These different tribes fought with each other with bows and arrows. Those of Soquel had for their boundary what is now known as Arana Gulch. Soquel is an Indian proper name, so also is Zayante, and are not translatable. The names of the Indian tribes were given them from the names of the lands they occupied. Santa Cruz was called Aulinta in the Indian tongue. I will give you in their language some words: One, *hinumen*; two, *uthiu*; three, *caphau*; four *catwaz*, five *nissor*; six, *sacen*; seven *tupucy*; eight *nizatis*; nine, *nuku*; ten, *iwes* (beyond this there are no numbers, but in counting, twenty, for instance is called *uthinues*, meaning two tens); *mancharas*, woman; *ketchkema*, boy; *ciui*, girl, *atchsema*, wife; *hounsen*, husband; *maco*, knife; *chipay*, ax; *hatis*, arrows; *temo*; bow; *liti*, come here; *hai*, sick; *ena*, dead; *esu*, hand; *coro*, feet; *uri*, head; *hein*, eyes; *ochi*, ear; *uss*, nose; *hais*, beard; *summup*, eyebrow; *siit*, teeth; *tur*, nails of the hand.[7]

I have always lived in Santa Cruz, except a time in Monterey, and San Jose three years, and at the presidio, San Francisco, four years. I was employed at the latter place by Jesus Noe, who was alcalde. This was in 1846 and 1847. I worked about his house and milked the cows and did the chores. When Fremont came, I was made a soldier, and served in the presidio with other Indians at San Francisco. Afterwards I returned to Santa Cruz. There were too many people in San Francisco for me. At the presidio, Francisco Sanchez was our captain. One day there came a man-of-war vessel,

flying the Mexican flag. We were in doubt about her nationality, because she also had the American flag flying lower down the rigging in the stern. Soon the vessel came to anchor, fired their guns, lowered their boats, hoisted the American flag on top, and we knew then it was an American war vessel. What could we do? There were fourteen Indians of us, without arms, shoes, or much clothing. The crew then commenced to ascend the hill of the presidio. Our officers were Francisco Haro, Francis Guerrero, and Jesus Noe. They were obliged to put down their arms and surrender. We said one to the other, 'Now we shall be killed.' We were made to stand to one side, and then we were laughed at, not having hats, shoes, nor arms. They told us not to be afraid, we should have clothing and plenty to eat, and soon we had a grand feast. We got drunk, and then we were very brave. The next day came three more vessels, and thus was San Francisco taken by the Americans.

The Indians at the mission were very severely treated by the padres, often punished by fifty lashes on the bare back. They were governed somewhat in the military style, having sergeants, corporals, and overseers, who were Indians, and they reported to the padres any disobedience or infraction of the rules, and then came the lash without mercy, the women the same as the men. The lash was made of rawhide. I was never punished except a few slaps for forgetfulness. I was always busy in the padres' house, doing the work of a house servant. Sometimes the padres would leave a *real* [silver coin, one-eighth of a dollar] in some corner, or under the bed, to see if I would take it. I was never tempted in that way, but often others were, and then punished. It was the custom of one of the padres to go about at night disguised, and he would come upon his Indian officers playing cards by the fire. One would say during the game, "I play this card!" another some other card. He would approach nearer and say, "I play this card," showing his hands in the light of the blaze of the fire, when the others would discover by his white hands that he was not one of them.

The Indians at the Mission of Santa Cruz, after prayers in the morning at church, received their orders as to their labors, at the church door; then they went to breakfast, and had their meal altogether of boiled barley, which was served out to them from two large caldrons by means of a copper ladle. This full was the ration to each in a *cora* (a small kind of basket), from which they ate with a shell or the fingers. Some had small gourds into which they received their rations. Boiled barley was all they had in the mornings. The labors were in the field mostly. All of the land where Santa Cruz is was cultivated, also the meadow near Kron's tanyard. At eleven o'clock A. M. the bell was rung to call them together—the same bell that was on the church a few years ago. The dinner consisted of a mixture of cooked horse beans and peas. At the end of an hour the bell was rung again, and all went to work until about sunset, when each received his rations of boiled corn. Such of the Indians as had families were given meat also. A beef was killed every eight days.

The land cultivated was all fenced with posts driven in the ground and tied with hazel bark, and a ditch outside They worked in plowing-time from one hundred to one hundred and thirty oxen. The surplus products were sold to vessels that came to buy. the Russian vessels carried away the wheat and barley, Spanish vessels taking beans, corn, dried peas, and dried horse beans. English vessels carried away hides and tallow.

The Indians were dressed with pantaloons of coarse wool, and a blanket over the shoulders. The women wore a skirt of the same material and also a blanket. We had no shoes or hats. If any of us entered the church with a dirty blanket, he was punished with fifty lashes, men and women alike. We were always trembling with fear of the lash. The padres nominated an alcalde and assistant for each of the different bands, of which there were about thirty. Those tribes nearest to the mission, such as up the coast a way, and as far south as Aptos, could understand each other, but those from a few miles farther off did not. Those of Gilroy were in their own language called Paxen; San Juan, Uiuhi; Pajaro, Nootsum; Aptos, Aptos; Soquel, Soquel; up the coast Tili and Ulsicsi; at Red Bank Dairy, up the coast, Posorou; on the San Vicente Creek, Sorsecsi; near the old limekilns of Williams' Landing, Coyulicsi.

To capture the wild Indian, first were taken the children, and then the parents followed. The padres would erect a hut, and light the candles to say mass, and the Indians, attracted by the light—thinking they were stars—would approach, and soon be taken. These would bring in others, such as their relatives. My father's tribe was Jlli, and he belonged to the tribe that lived up the coast. They lived upon shellfish, which they took from the seacoast, and carried them to the hills, where were their rancherias. The remains of the shells are there now, and can be seen in numerous places. They made their huts of branches of trees, which they cut down by firing and then using sharp stones. They also had acorns to eat, which they ground in stone mortars, called *urwan*. The pestle was called *packshan*. To

Santa Cruz from High Street. Late 1800s. Courtesy of the Museum of Art and History.

cook the acorn after being ground, the mass was put into large baskets, which were made water tight, being woven with grass roots of a kind very long and tough. Into these were put hot stones, which caused the water to boil, and so the meal was cooked. Their meat was deer, killed by the bow and arrow, also rabbits, rats, elk, and antelope.

There were many bears in those days; they used to come and sit on their haunches on the hill where now is the water reservoir and residence of J. H. Logan, watching for a chance to kill one of the calves of the mission. The Indians killed bears with bows and arrows and clubs. The wine the padres had to drink was brought from the Mission of San Gabriel on mules, being a journey of nearly one month. There were no vineyards about Santa Cruz. Afterwards a vineyard was planted in San Jose. My father planted and cultivated the orchard of apple and pear trees at Santa Cruz, known as the Mission orchard. The trees were brought to the mission very small, in barrels. so that the roots were kept damp. My father told me they had been brought from New Spain.[8]

Notes:

[1] This article was first published in Edward S. Harrison's *History of Santa Cruz County, California,* (San Francisco: Pacific Press Publishing Co., 1892); 45-48. The article was transcribed and annotated by Joan G. Martin for this journal.

[2] For information on E. L. Williams, see his biography and photo in the *Santa Cruz History Journal, No. 4* (Santa Cruz, California: Museum of Art & History, 1998) 256-258. See also the two earlier interviews with Lorenzo published in this journal.

[3] E.S. Harrison, *History of Santa Cruz County*; 48-58; and J. F. de L Pérouse,*"Monterey in 1786, The Journals of Jean Francois de La Pérouse"* ed. Malcolm Margolin (Berkeley, California: Heyday Books, 1989).

[4] Santa Cruz Baptismal Register, Entry No. 1832, Monterey Diocese Chancery Archive, Monterey, California. Baptismal records for the Mission Santa Cruz place his birthdate as August 10, 1820.

[5] Maynard Geiger, O.F.M., *Franciscan Missionaries in Hispanic California, 1769-1848* (San Marino California: The Huntington Library, 1969); 159. According to Geiger, Father Moreno was in Monterey only very briefly.

[6] Edna Kimbro, in unpublished biographical data on Lorenzo, says the corpse was actually sent to Santa Barbara.

[7] Editor's note: Lorenzo's vocabulary words are transcribed exactly as they appear in Edward S. Harrison's *History of Santa Cruz County, California*. The original transcription appears to be inaccurate in some cases, probably a result of misplaced punctuation. For reference see the word list in the article on the "Awáswas Language" in this Journal.

[8] Edna Kimbro, unpublished biographical data on Lorenzo "In 1837 Lorenzo and his wife Tomasa were listed as fulfilling their church obligations in the Libro de Padrones. In a terrible smallpox epidemic the following year, Benancio, Lorenzo's father died on September 20."

Some Effects of Statehood on California Indians

by Jacquelin Jensen Kehl & Linda Yamane[1]

"Under the Native American Graves and Repatriation Act (NAGPRA), Native American human remains and associated grave objects held by federally funded institutions are required by law to be returned to culturally affiliated tribes. In Ohlone territory, this has become impossible because we are no longer federally recognized and therefore cannot rebury our ancestral remains through federal channels. I believe that with some active effort, we can resolve this problem through research into the historic records."

—*Jacquelin Jensen Kehl (Mutsun Ohlone), 2001*

Under Spanish and Mexican rule, California Indians were considered citizens, although voting privileges were reserved for land-owning citizens. At the time of California's constitutional convention in 1849 just prior to statehood, it was decided that citizenship was open only to whites and that only white males could vote.

On April 22, 1850 the California State Assembly and Senate passed "An Act for the Government and Protection of Indians."[2] The law mandated humane treatment of minor Indian children, but in spite of its title, this new law was little more than legalized slavery. It reads in part:

" Any person having or hereafter obtaining a minor Indian, male or female, from the parents or relations of such Indian minor, and wishing to keep it, such person shall go before a Justice of the Peace in his Township, with the parents or friends of the child, and if the Justice of the Peace becomes satisfied that no compulsory means have been used to obtain the child from its parents or friends, shall enter on record, in a book kept for that purpose, the sex and probable age of the child, and shall give to such person a certificate, authorizing him or her to have the care, custody, control, and earnings of such minor, until he or she obtain the age of majority. Every male Indian shall be deemed to have attained his majority at eighteen, and the female at fifteen years.

"Complaints may be made before a Justice of the Peace, by white persons or Indians; but in no case shall

a white man be convicted of any offense upon the testimony of an Indian.

"Any Indian able to work and support himself in some honest calling, not having wherewithal to maintain himself, who shall be found loitering and strolling about, or frequenting public places where liquors are sold, begging, or leading an immoral or profligate course of life, shall be liable to be arrested on the complaint of any resident citizen of the county, and brought before any Justice of the Peace who shall examine said accused Indian, and hear the testimony in relation thereto, and if satisfied that he is a vagrant shall make out a warrant to hire out such vagrant within twenty-four hours to the best bidder for the highest price that can be had, for any term not exceeding four months."

In 1860, the Act of April 1850 was amended. The amendments pertinent to this discussion follow.

"County and District Judges in the respective counties of this State shall have full power and authority, at the request of any person having or hereafter obtaining an Indian child or children, male or female, under the age of fifteen years, from the parents or persons having the care of such children, with the consent of such parents or persons to bind and put out such Indians as apprentices for the following terms of years: under fourteen years of age, if males, until they attain the age of twenty-five; if females, until they attain the age of twenty-one; over fourteen and under twenty years of age, if males, until the age of thirty; if females, until

the age of twenty-five. Indians over the age of twenty [may be indentured for a] term of ten years."

There was no limit to the number of Indian people that could be indentured in this fashion, creating a free and abundant source of labor of which many people took advantage. In fact, in many cases the men who profited most from this law were the very men who helped create and implement it.

An 1861 newspaper article in the San Francisco Bulletin proclaimed: "This law works beautifully. A few days ago V.E. Geiger, formerly Indian Agent, had some eighty apprenticed to him. We hear of many others who are having them bound in numbers to suit. What a pity the provisions of the law are not extended to greasers, Kanakas, and Asiatics. It would be so convenient to carry on a farm or mine, when all the hard and dirty work is performed by apprentices!"[3]

The gold rush era brought mass destruction to California Indians, with some of the newcomers clamoring for their extermination. The new state government tried to accommodate them. California's Governor Peter H. Burnett made the following statement in his annual message of January 1851: "That a war of extermination will continue to be waged between the two races until the Indian race becomes extinct, must be expected; while we cannot anticipate this result with but painful regret, the inevitable destiny of the race is beyond the power and wisdom of man to avert."[4]

Theodora Kroeber and Robert F. Heizer describe the California situation in this way:
"...new missions were filled with Indians rounded up from villages beside the sea, from valleys, from foothill country, from any nearby area. This was done without reference to tribe, tongue, or personal willingness,

without concern that Indians from different places spoke mutually unintelligible languages, were total strangers to each other, and could not form a society forcibly thrown together as they were. Whole nations, languages, and cultures were in this manner wiped out. The Anglo-Saxons made no place for the Indians in their dreams of wealth and expansion; they set out to enslave them, herd them onto reservations out of the way, let them die, or better, kill them, exterminate them. By and large, they succeeded. In their ignorance and their intolerant racism, the white men called the Californians 'Diggers,' regarding them as scarcely human. Indian-killers were tolerated, their profession considered an honorable one by many of their fellows."[5]

It is no wonder that Indian people chose to identify as white at the earliest opportunity, as research into area census records reveals. But in spite of the need to assimilate into evolving California communities, they nevertheless retained knowledge of their ancestry and their cultural heritage—we are living proof. It is important, and long past due, to honor the people of the past by acknowledging them. People with names and ages, villages and parents, are more easily perceived by us as the very human individuals they were. They each had families—parents or children—and the spectrum of human feelings and experience that can so easily be overlooked when we only consider them in abstract and impersonal terms. Through our involvement in projects such as educational programs, cultural exhibits, protection of burials, and consulting and monitoring of development on cultural sites, we honor and bring recognition to our ancestors. We are grateful for the opportunity to tell at least a part of their story and to keep their memory alive—for it is time that they be counted again in the world.

Notes:

[1] This article is excerpted from "Ethnohistoric Genealogy Study" by Jacquelin Jensen Kehl and Linda Yamane for *Tasman Corridor Light Rail Project*, Santa Clara County, CA, 1995. Published as a companion to *Iñigo of Rancho Posolmi: The Life and Times of a Mission Indian and His Land* by Laurence H. Shoup and *Indians Listed in Mission Santa Clara Baptismal Register 1777 to 1849* by Randall Milliken.

[2] The complete text of this law and two amendments to the law are published in this Journal under the title: *Text of "Indian Protection" Act and Two 1860 Amendments to the Act.*

[3] *San Francisco Bulletin*, March 2, 1861 (Quoting Humboldt Times, Feb. 23) quoted in Robert F. Heizer, *The Destruction of California Indians*; University of Nebraska Press (1974, 1993) p. 240.

[4] Robert F. Heizer & Alan F. Almquist, *The Other Californians;* University of California Press (1971) page 26.

[5] Theodora Kroeber and Robert F. Heizer, *Almost ancestors; the first Californians*; ed. by F. David Hales; San Francisco Sierra Club (1968).

Maria Soledad (Mutsun Ohlone) was baptized in 1849 at Mission San Juan Bautista. Her mother, Guadalupe, was godchild of Quintin Ortega, grandson of José Francisco Ortega, scout for the Portolá expedition and the first person to sight San Francisco Bay by land. Guadalupe and Soledad were closely associated with the Ortega family throughout their lives, even taking the Ortega surname as their own. Their Mutsun lines trace back to several native villages: Unijaima, Ausaima, Ochentac, and Guachirron de la Sierra. Soledad later married Catarino Gilroy, son of John Gilroy and Maria Clara Ortega. John Gilroy, after pledging allegiance to the Spanish Crown in 1813, was the first non-Hispanic European allowed to remain in California. It is from this family that the city of Gilroy took its name. The descendants of Maria Soledad are many, some of whom are active in the Ohlone community today. Those included in this journal are Jakki Kehl, Juanita Ingalls and Kathy Petty.

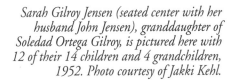

Sarah Gilroy Jensen (seated center with her husband John Jensen), granddaughter of Soledad Ortega Gilroy, is pictured here with 12 of their 14 children and 4 grandchildren, 1952. Photo courtesy of Jakki Kehl.

Jakki Kehl reburying Ohlone remains at a San Jose construction site, 1999. Photo by Lisa Falk.

An Act for the Government and Protection of Indians April 22, 1850 (Chapter 133, Statutes of California, April 22, 1850). The people of the State of California, represented in Senate and Assembly, do enact as follows:

1. Justices of the Peace shall have jurisdiction in all cases of complaints by, for or against Indians, in their respective townships in this State.

2. Persons and proprietors of land on which Indians are residing, shall permit such Indians peaceably to reside on such lands, unmolested in the pursuit of their usual avocations for the maintenance of themselves and their families: Provided; the white person or proprietor in possession of lands may apply to a Justice of the Peace in the Township where the Indians reside, to set off to such Indians a certain amount of land, and, on such application, the Justice shall set off a sufficient amount of land for the necessary wants of such Indians, including the site of their village or residence, if they so prefer it; and in no case shall such selection be made to the prejudice of such Indians, nor shall they be forced to abandon their homes or villages where they have resided for a number of years; and either party feeling themselves aggrieved, can appeal to the County Court from the decision of the Justice: and then divided, a record shall be made of the lands so set off in the Court so dividing them and the Indians shall be permitted to remain thereon until otherwise provided for.

3. Any person having or hereafter obtaining a minor Indian, male or female, from the parents or relations of such Indian Minor, and wishing to keep it, such person shall go before a Justice of the Peace in his Township, with the parents or friends of the child, and if the Justice of the Peace becomes satisfied that no compulsory means have been used

to obtain the child from its parents or friends, shall enter on record, in a book kept for that purpose, the sex and probable age of the child, and shall give to such person a certificate, authorizing him or her to have the care, custody, control, and earnings of such minor, until he or she obtain the age of majority. Every male Indian shall be deemed to have attained his majority at eighteen, and the female at fifteen years.

4. Any person having a minor Indian in his care, as described in the foregoing Section of the Act, who shall neglect to clothe and suitably feed such minor Indian, or shall inhumanely treat him or her, on conviction thereof shall be subject to a fine not less than ten dollars, at the discretion of a Court or Jury; and the Justice of the Peace, in his own discretion, may place the minor Indian in the care of some other person, giving him the same rights and liabilities that the former master of said minor was entitled and subject to.

5. Any person wishing to hire an Indian, shall go before a Justice of the Peace with the Indian, and make such contract as the Justice may approve, and the Justice shall file such contract in writing in his office, and all contracts so made shall be binding between the parties; but no contract between a white man and an Indian, for labor, shall otherwise be obligatory on the part of the Indian.

6. Complaints may be made before a Justice of the Peace, by white persons or Indians: but in no case shall a white man be convicted on any offence upon the testimony of an Indian.

7. If any person forcibly conveys an Indian from his home, or compels him to work, or perform against his will, in this State, except as provided in this Act, he or they shall, on conviction, be fined

Santa Cruz
County
History Journal
Issue 5, 2002

in any sum not less than fifty dollars, at the discretion of the Court or Jury.

8. It shall be the duty of the Justices of the Peace, once in six months in every year, to make a full and correct statement to the Court of Sessions of their County, of all monies received of fines imposed on Indians, and all fees allowed for services rendered under the provisions of the Act; and said Justices shall pay over to the County Treasurers of their respective counties, all money they may have received for fines and not appropriated, or fees for services rendered under this Act; and the Treasurer shall keep a correct statement of all money so received, which shall be termed the "Indian Fund" of the county. The Treasurer shall pay out any money of said funds in his hands, on a certificate of a Justice of the Peace of his county, for fees and expenditures incurred in carrying out the provisions of this law.

9. It shall be the duty of the Justices of the Peace, in their respective townships, as well as all other peace officers in this State, to instruct the Indians in their neighborhood in the laws which relate to them, giving them such advice as they may deem necessary and proper; and if any tribe or village of Indians refuse or neglect to obey the laws, the Justice of the Peace may punish the guilty chiefs or principal men by reprimand or fine, or otherwise reasonably chastise them.

10. If any person or persons shall set the prairie on fire, or refuse to use proper exertions to extinguish the fire when the prairies are burning, persons shall be subject to fine or punishment, as Court may adjudge proper.

11. If any Indian shall commit an unlawful offence against a white person, such person shall not inflict punishment for such offence, but may, without process, take the Indian before a Justice of the Peace, and on conviction, the Indian shall be punished according to the provisions of this Act.

12. In all cases of trial between a white man and an Indian, either party may require a jury.

13. Justices may require the chiefs and influential men of any village to apprehend and bring before them or him any Indian charged or suspected of an offence.

14. When an Indian is convicted of an offence before a Justice of the Peace, punishable by fine, any white man may, by consent of the justice, give bond for said Indian, conditioned for the payment of said fine and costs, and in such case the Indian shall be compelled to work for the person so bailing, until he has discharged or cancelled the fine assessed against him: Provided; the person bailing shall treat the Indian humanely, and feed and clothe him properly; the allowance given for such labor shall be fixed by the Court, when the bond is taken.

15. If any person in this State shall sell, give, or furnish to any Indian, male or female, any intoxicating liquors (except when administered for sickness), for good cause shown, he, she, or they so offending shall, on conviction thereof, be fined not less than twenty dollars for each offence, or be imprisoned not less than five days, or fined and imprisoned as the Court may determine.

16. An Indian convicted of stealing horses, mules, cattle, or any valuable thing, shall be subject to receive any number of lashes not exceeding twenty-five, or shall be subject to a fine not exceeding two hundred dollars, at the discretion of the Court or jury.

17. When an Indian is sentenced to be whipped, the Justice may appoint a white man, or an Indian at his discretion, to execute the sentence in his presence, and shall not permit unnecessary cruelty in the execution of these sentences.

18. All fines, forfeitures, penalties recovered under or by this Act, shall be paid into the treasury of the county, to the credit of the Indian Fund as provided in section 8.

19. All white persons making application to a Justice of the Peace, for confirmation of a contract with or in relation to an Indian, shall pay the fee, which shall not exceed two dollars for each contract determined and filed as provided in this Act, and for all other services, such fees are allowed for similar services under other laws of this State. Provided, the application fee for hiring Indians, or keeping minors, and fees and expenses for setting off lands to Indians, shall be paid by the white person applying.

20. Any Indian able to work and support himself in some honest calling, not having wherewithal to maintain himself, who shall be found loitering and strolling about, or frequenting public places where liquors are sold, begging, or leading an immoral or profligate course of life, shall be liable to be arrested on the complaint of any reasonable citizen of the county, brought before the Justice of the Peace of the proper county, Mayor or Recorder of any incorporated town or city, who shall examine said accused Indian, and hear the testimony in relation thereto, and if said Justice, mayor or Recorder shall be satisfied that he is a vagrant, as above set forth, he shall make out a warrant under his hand and seal, authorizing and requiring the officer having him in charge or custody, to hire out such vagrant within twenty-four hours to the highest bidder, by public notice given as he shall direct, for the highest price that can be had, for any term not exceeding four months; and such vagrant shall be subject to and governed by the provisions of this Act, regulating guardians and minors, during the time which he has been so hired. The money received for his hire, shall, after deducting the costs, and the necessary expense for clothing the said Indian, which may have been purchased by his employer, be, if he be without a family, paid into the County Treasury, to the credit of the Indian Fund. But if he have a family, the same shall be appropriated for their use and benefit: Provided, that any such vagrant, when arrested, and before judgment, may relieve himself by giving to said Justice, mayor or Recorder, a bond, with good security, conditioned that he will, for the next twelve months, conduct himself with good behavior, and betake to some honest employment for support.

Amendments to Act of April 1850

(approved 1860) Chapter CCXXXI-An Act amendatory of an Act entitled "An Act for the Government and Protection of Indians," passed April twenty-second, one thousand eight hundred and fifty. [Approved April 18, 1860.]

The people of the State of California, represented in Senate and Assembly, do enact as follows:

SECTION 1. Section third of said act, is hereby amended so as to read as follows:

Sec. 3. County and District Judges in the respective counties of this state, shall, by virtue of this act, have full power and authority, at the instance and request of any person having or hereafter obtaining an Indian child or children, male or female, under the age of fifteen years, from the parents or person or persons having the care or charge of such child or children, with the consent of such parents or person or persons having the care or charge of any such child or children, or at the instance and request of any person desirous of obtaining any Indian or Indians, whether children or grown persons, that may be held as prisoners of war, or at the instance and request of any person desirous of obtaining any vagrant Indian or Indians, as have no settled habitation or means of livelihood, and have not placed themselves under the protection of any white person, to bind and put out such Indians as apprentices, to trades, husbandry, or other employments, as to them shall appear proper, and for this purpose shall execute duplicate articles of indenture of apprenticeship on behalf of such Indians, which indentures shall also be executed by the person to whom such Indian or Indians are to be indentured; one copy of which shall be filed by the County Judge, in the Recorder's office of the county, and one copy retained by the person to whom such Indian or Indians may be indentured; such indentures shall authorize such person to have the care, custody, control, and earnings, of such Indian or Indians, as shall require such person to clothe and suitably provide the necessaries of life for such Indian or Indians, for and during the term for which such Indian or Indians shall be apprenticed, and shall contain the sex, name, and probable age, of such Indian or Indians; such indentures may be for the following terms of years: Such children as are under fourteen years of age, if males, until they attain the age of twenty-five years; if females, until they attain the age of twenty-one years; such as are over fourteen and under twenty years of age, if males, until they attain the age of thirty years; if females, until they attain the age of twenty-five years; and such Indians as may be over the age of twenty years, then next following the date of such indentures, for and during the term of ten years, at the discretion of such Judge; such

Indians as may be indentured under provision of this section, shall be deemed within such provisions of this act, as are applicable to minor Indians.

SECTION 2. Section seventh of said act is hereby amended so as to read as follows:

Sec. 7. If any person shall forcibly convey any Indian from any place without this State, to any place within this State, or compel him or her to work or perform any service, against his or her will, except as provided in this act, he or they shall, upon conviction thereof, be fined in any sum not less than one hundred dollars, nor more than five hundred dollars, before any court having jurisdiction, at the discretion of the court, and the collection of such fine shall be enforced as provided by law in other criminal cases, one-half to be paid to the prosecutor, and one-half to the county in which such conviction is had.

The Challenges of Interpretation: A Conversation

by Sandy Lydon and Linda Yamane

Historians Sandy Lydon and Linda Yamane have been collaborating for a decade. Frustrated by the traditional "first chapter" practice of writing about the region's Indians, they have been attempting to integrate the story of local Indian people into the whole of the region's history. The following is a recent conversation about the difficulties they are facing in achieving their individual goals.

Lydon: Perhaps we could start by discussing the gaps in the history of California Indian people that start with statehood. And we could also discuss the difficulties in finding and telling the story of this period. With statehood it's as if the Indian story is simply dropped until the civil rights era of the 1960s.

Yamane: For example, a lot of people probably don't know that there were eighteen treaties negotiated by the American government with California Indians in the first years of statehood.[1]

Lydon: Yes, and there's the irony that the indigenous people of the United States were treated as foreigners; you make treaties with foreigners, you make treaties with foreign countries. On the other hand, now it seems that the treaties have become really important, a way to be able to establish a tie with the government.

Yamane: That kind of past recognition by the government is important for groups seeking federal recognition today.

Lydon: By having a treaty, it meant you must have been real. For good or for ill, groups—particularly outside of California—have used treaties to establish their standing before the Bureau of Indian Affairs (BIA) or whatever agency they're dealing with. To be without a treaty makes it much more difficult, and I would think that California Indian groups now are attempting to establish the identity that they would have had if the treaties had been ratified.

Yamane: Contemporary groups still use the existence of those treaties, even though they were not ratified, as a claim of validity through the fact that the government made the agreements. What I find questionable about those treaties is that in many areas there were no intact cultural communities with a central leadership. I wonder who the government agents approached to sign these treaties.[2] In any case, these eighteen treaties involved Indians living the entire length of California.

Lydon: The part that wasn't tied up in Mexican land grants.

Yamane: It's obvious that the purpose of the treaties was to get Indian people out of the way. By signing the treaties, the signatories agreed to give up any claim or title to their tribal lands in exchange for reserve land, the location of which was specified in the treaty. The treaty further specified that they could not move their women and children away from this reserve land. In the years 1851 and 1852, the "tribes" represented by each treaty were supposed to get a hundred head of cattle and a hundred sacks of flour each year. After the treaties were ratified, the people were then supposed to get a long list of material goods such as horses, cows, axes, seeds, blankets, clothing, needles, thread, buttons, and other such things.

Lydon: Of course, at the moment this was happening, in 1851, there's absolute chaos throughout California. Local government wasn't well established, and land titles, even where there were Mexican land grants, weren't clear. The irony is that those Indian people who were able to get a Mexican grant, for a moment, were better off.

Yamane: I believe there were Indian people from the Zayante area who were signatories to one of the treaties, but I've always felt unclear about how the treaties really affected the people of this region.

Lydon: I think that's an excellent point; I don't think it would have made a bit of difference.

Yamane: But here's a strange thing: Isabel Meadows told Harrington in the 1930s that when a chief died, he was buried with an "olla" holding his copy of the eighteen treaties!

Lydon: Around here?

Yamane: Well, that was my impression. Although I suppose she could have been talking more broadly about something she had heard. I can't say for certain that this took place around here, but clearly it was something of great importance to Indian people. And you have to wonder how, in those days, they got a copy of the eighteen treaties? Even if it was symbolic, it blows me away that they would have a copy and that it would be of such importance to put in the burial of a head person.

Lydon: I hadn't really thought it through before, partly because the literature has focused on other parts of the United States and the tragedy of all the broken promises. It's outright duplicity, negotiating the treaties, going back to Washington, and in a secret session throwing them in a drawer and saying, "We're not going to ratify them."

Yamane: Yes, that's the real clincher, that in 1852 the United States Senate refused to ratify the treaties and then ordered them filed under an injunction of secrecy. I understand it was the California legislators who fought hardest to prevent ratification. Do you know if Indian people actually left their lands?

Lydon: I believe that happened in Northern California.

Yamane: They became displaced and then never got anything in return for it?

Lydon: They kept their half of the bargain and did what they were expected to do, and the Yankees that were around behaved as though the treaties were real.

Yamane: The Senate refused to ratify the treaties in 1852, but how long was it before it became publicly known that the treaties were not going to be honored?

Lydon: Over fifty years! It was not until after the turn of the twentieth century that the injunction of secrecy was removed. It wasn't until then that California Indians discovered that the treaties they'd believed to be in force did not exist.

Yamane: What did they have in between?

Lydon: There was an effort to set up a reservation system, but mostly the last part of the nineteenth century was marked by violence. But I think the point you made earlier is very important. I don't think treaties would have made any difference in the Monterey Bay Region. Who would the treaty commissioners have gone to? If they came to the Carmel Valley in 1851, who would they negotiate with? People were scattered and there was already a lot of intermarriage going on. Who would they find to represent the community at large?

That's why the "Act to Protect," this euphemism that was enacted by the California Legislature in 1850, is in some ways of more concern here. *[See text of "Indian Protection" Act of 1850 in this Journal.]* What happens to individuals who find themselves incarcerated is something very real. I've bumped into references to it locally, but never had a chance to go through the specific county records. I've seen references to the fact that David Jacks would go down and indenture Indians who were in jail, then take them out and put them to work. That's what a lot of people did during that period. [3]

Yamane: I would love to find some specific incidents of this Act here in the Monterey Bay Region. It was through the county sheriff that this indentureship took place, so there must be records.

Lydon: The story goes that, like everyone else in the 1850s, Jacks was growing potatoes and a lot of the labor he used was Indian prisoners he had "ransomed" out of the Monterey jail. Under the law you could do that. The practice resembled slavery, but since the indenture was not for life, many Californians thought it was acceptable.

Yamane: In this case, it was for a set number of years or until the person reached a particular age. The act was repealed during the Civil War because it conflicted with the Emancipation Proclamation.[4]

Lydon: Then there was the whole issue of children, where you could actually just acquire children. I'm sad that somebody hasn't had the time to dive into this issue.

For the 1850s through the mid 1860s we have accounts of Indian farm workers coming through, working the wheat and other grains. The sense I have is that these were Indians brought in from elsewhere by labor contractors—that they were migratory farm labor. This means that the Indians were the primary farm laborers for all three periods: Spanish, Mexican and early statehood. The first Chinese came in 1865-66, and up until that time the primary source of farm labor in the Monterey Bay area was Indian. Some were still on the ranches as vaqueros, and some were more Californio culturally.

There's a failing in the way the history of California Indian people has been interpreted. Very rarely are Indians mentioned in the 1850s and 1860s in general history books. Once historians get to California statehood, they drop the Indians' story.

Yamane: It seems to me that one of the reasons the story is not known for this area is that during that period, Indian people as an identifiable group kind of disappeared intentionally. Sure, people recognized those of Indian ancestry locally, but on a broader scale, a governmental scale, I don't think they were ever recognized as a group. That's because they were not an intact group of people living together on a piece of land. They blended in as best they could.

Lydon: They became "Mexicans."

Yamane: You can look at the census records and see someone who's of full Indian blood, yet identifying as white when they married a non-Indian.

Lydon: I think you're right. Some were consciously trying not to be known as Indian and for obvious reasons. I remember Alex Ramirez saying one time, "It was easier to be a Mexican than to be an Indian in Carmel." It seems to me, though, that up until the turn of the century there were still a lot of Indian people around. They were there, it's just that they slid off onto the periphery of everyone's vision. They only appear in newspapers when there's a crime or a fight in the river bottom, and then the papers often conclude with a throw-away line like, "It's no matter because they're only Indians."

They become very quickly marginalized, so quickly it's astonishing. Rarely do you find writers in the popular press saying, "Look what we've done, isn't it terrible." Robert Louis Stevenson said some things in 1879, when he was here, about what a tragedy had happened in the Carmel Valley.[5] But you rarely find voices like that. There's a line in a newspaper article from the *Sentinel* in the 1860s showing concern about the flat land north of Santa Cruz Mission on what was called the Potrero. Apparently the land had been given by the church to the Indians; several Indians had title. Very slowly, but surely, they got squeezed out until, as the editor wrote, "they drop down and perish by the wayside."[6] Their history has also perished—by the historical wayside.

And yet, as you say, they were here; it's not as if they were actually gone. Culturally, a lot of them were trying to "pass," but collectively they were here and everyone knew who they were. The story can be reconstructed, as you're doing it, on the basis of families and individuals. You can follow those threads, they're there.

Yamane: That's what I'm working on, but it's taking a really long time. It's a lot of work to reconstruct the history of the Monterey area Indian community through research into the mission records, the census records, and field notes such as those by John P.

Santa Cruz
County
History Journal
Issue 5, 2001

Harrington. But, oh my, what a rich story is unfolding, and a sad one, too.

Lydon: The tendency has been to focus on what I call the "sexy" stuff, the pre-contact times and early mission period. But after that, it's not "sexy" anymore, because it's so hard. You have to follow all of these threads that are literally buried in the tapestry and pull each one out to see how they're connected. And the people that we find, they're not "sexy" either. They're either regular everyday people or they're not doing well. Their marginalization in society has reflected itself in the way historians deal with it. For example, there's this romantic notion of their pre-contact life that is extremely idyllic and lacks any sense of the true humanity of the Indians—children are always laughing, the sky is always blue and the birds are always singing.

Yamane: Yeah, I know, the sky is so full of birds you can knock them down with a stick.

Lydon: And you can walk across a creek on the backs of fish, and all of those things. But there is this image that people project back to those times, and the reality of what happened later can be so depressing that it's easier to talk about pre-contact. The post-1850 history is not a pretty story.

Yamane: I know. With this work I'm doing now, I'm trying to reconstruct the Indian community of the Monterey area—who they were, from before the missions started, during the mission period, and beyond. For those who lived on, those who physically survived the sicknesses that were rampant, what became of them? Where did they live? What did they do? Mission record data bases can give you statistics, the census records can tell you where they were living, with whom, what they were doing to make a "living." But from Isabel's stories, you get the heart, you get the soul, you get the down and dirty truth. And as you said, this is not going to be a pretty story to tell. It's going to be very sad. It's going to be very real. And it's going to be something that we've never before heard as a whole.

Lydon: And you know what you might find? I look for the heroes in these hard times because there

should be some in both the Indian and white communities. We may find some good people here. There are always people who are kind.

Yamane: Like Schindler.

Lydon: Yes. We've got to find the Schindlers.

You know, we don't pay much attention to the Potrero north of Santa Cruz, that flat, lovely area where San Lorenzo Lumber and the homeless shelter are now. Any morning, you can drive down River Street, and you can see the church which is sitting on the side of the mission up top, and standing along the street are the Indian faces, those guys from Mexico, Guatemala, El Salvador, who are here and are now playing the role of that casual labor pool that we use. They too are off beyond the wayside of our concerns.

Yamane: They're marginalized also.

Lydon: Absolutely. And they're on the same location where Santa Cruz's last Indian community perished. It's a hard issue to deal with, it's complicated, it's human. It's easier to save otters, it's easier to save whales. It's ten times easier to save whales and otters than it is to deal with the complexity of human experience that faces you on the street every morning—those guys standing there looking for work. In a way, that's also happened in the history business. It's easier to deal with these issues at a distance. It's easier because there's no reality to confront.

Yamane: A lot of idealizing and romanticizing.

Lydon: Particularly now, there's that New Age thing that's wandered into our vision with everybody using the era for whatever their purposes are. But to deal with the reality of Indian children being auctioned off by the government in the 1850s and 1860s is very difficult.

You always emphasize this idea of the "first chapter" syndrome: the first chapter's always set aside for Indian people and then that's it, it's over. Sometimes historians will treat the shape of the land—dirt and rocks—first. But then it's the Indian chapter.

Yamane: Yes, and after those two chapters, it's on with the "real" history.

Lydon: At every juncture historically, in some ways we need to use the indigenous people as a litmus test. You get into the 1860's and you ask, "How are we doing? How are those people who are way off on the edge doing?" And if you continue to ask that question, it seems to me it becomes an incredibly useful exercise, because then you begin to realize that they're not gone, they're still here. For the most part, the historians aren't doing very well in this.

Yamane: And we have to remember that most of the history about Indian people is really other peoples' responses to Indian people, not them telling their own story.

Lydon: It reminds me of that Buddhist adage: "Don't mistake the finger pointing at the moon for the moon." Very often when we read accounts, when we hear accounts, we focus on the finger, the describer, and not on the moon. We begin to tell the story of the oppressor rather than the oppressed.

Yamane: I think it's important to acknowledge that, with few exceptions, Indian people in the past have not told their own stories. For one thing, nobody cared what they had to say, because socially they were unimportant. They didn't have status in society. And also for the most part they weren't formally educated, so some didn't know how to write.

At Mission Dolores, we have the testimonies of several Native people who left the mission and escaped to the East Bay. Their testimonies, which were paraphrased at the time of their formal hearing, explain their reasons for fleeing. There are the Lorenzo Asisara interviews from Mission Santa Cruz [included in this Journal]. But there's not much else until Harrington's interviews with Ascención Cervantes and Isabel Meadows in the early twentieth century. Kroeber and Merriam interviewed Ohlone elders early in the same century, but for the most part that material doesn't include personal experiences or feelings. I love where Isabel told Harrington one time, "If I had known how to write, I would have written up the life of those Indians." She did write it, just not in her own hand, but through Harrington.

My point is that rarely do we directly hear a story from the people themselves. That's why, in the research I'm doing, I find it so compelling to run across a story such as the one about Telesforo, whose baby son was buried in the dirt by the other children at Mission San Carlos in Carmel. When the older children went to tell the adults, it was too late, Telesforo's young son was dead and was found with his little hand sticking out of the dirt. Telesforo cried and had the others bring sprigs of wild roses to put over the child. This is real stuff, and we've never really heard the real people stories before. This is a rare opportunity.

Lydon: If you can get down into individual stories, or family stories, then you're not generalizing.

Yamane: That's what's been missing—our specific stories instead of all the generalizations. I don't trust the generalizations. Some of them might be true, but I won't know if they're true unless I hear the individual stories to see if they back up the generalizations.

Lydon: What it will show, when you get it all done, is that there were a multitude of personalities with all the varieties of humanity—from avarice to kindness. You'll find them all represented. First you have to disassemble the record and extract the Indian threads. Then when you weave them together, we'll see the whole story, but with the new added Indian texture. That's the only way it can be done.

Santa Cruz
County
History Journal
Issue 5, 2001

Notes:

1 See Jim Rawls. *Indians of California: The Changing Image* (University of Oklahoma, 1984), 144-148.

2 For an analysis of this issue, see Robert F Heizer and Alan J. Almquist, *The Other Californians: Prejudice and Discrimination under Spain, Mexico, and the United States to 1920*, (Berkeley: University of California Press, 1971), 76-77.

3 A native of Scotland, David Jacks immigrated to Monterey County in 1850 and eventually became the county's largest land owner. For a biography of Jacks see Donald T. Clark, *Monterey County Place Names* (Carmel Valley: Kestrel Press, 1991), 235-236.

4 *Contested Eden, California Before the Gold Rush*, edited by Ramón A. Guttiérrez and Richard J. Orsi (Berkeley: University of California Press, 1998), 220.

5 "San Carlos Day"in the *Monterey Californian*, November 11, 1879.

Profile: Maria Bonillas

Marie Bonillas enjoys the California Indian Storytelling Festival at Indian Canyon outside of Hollister, 1995. Photo by Linda Yamane.

"It's important to me to show others that we're still here, and that our culture's very much alive. We have a lot to learn ourselves, but we have a lot to teach others."

—Marie Bonillas
(Mutsun/Rumsien Ohlone), 2000

Conquest and Destiny:
The Story of "Cache" and "Tahoe"

by Geoffrey Dunn

A series of suspicious fires erupted throughout Santa Cruz and the surrounding vicinity in 1884.[1] In early December of that year, flames engulfed a barn owned by prominent Santa Cruz entrepreneur and politician William H. Bias, reaching into the cold late-autumn night. Santa Cruz's crack fire-hose team, led by Samuel Cowell, the son of local industrialist Henry Cowell, responded to the call, only to arrive too late. The Bias barn lay in ashes.[2]

It was the sixth suspicious fire in recent memory. Deputy Sheriff Henoc "Noch" Alzina, a stalwart of local law enforcement, noticed that two young California Indian men—Joe Lend and Raphael Castro, known throughout the community by the nicknames of "Cache" and "Tahoe"—had been the first observers at several of the fires and, according to the *Santa Cruz Daily Sentinel*, "were not inclined to assist in extinguishing the flames."[3]

At 2 a.m., in the dark morning hours of Friday, December 5, Alzina, by his own account, arrested Lend as he was heading into the train tunnel beneath Mission Hill. Castro was arrested at his home.[4]

Only a few days later, Lend's "confession" was printed in the *Sentinel* under headlines reading: "The Barn Burners: Two Indian Boys Arrested for Arson—One Confesses, the Other Denies."

The accompanying article indicated that the two "boys" had been brought before Judge Edgar Spalsbury in a preliminary hearing and that they "did not want an attorney."

Lend's testimony was published in full detail:

Lend: I am 19 years old. Me and the other fellow [Castro] was on our way home near Kron's tannery, and the other fellow said he wanted to go back to get matches and see the fire boys run…We had no grudge against Mr. Bias.
District Attorney: Who set Towne's barn afire?
Lend: Me and the other fellar. We had nothing against Mr. Towne, we like him.
District Attorney: Why did you do it?
Lend: Just for fun. We was tight and wanted to have a fire…
District Attorney: Did you use coal oil to do it?

The Santa Cruz Alerts Fire-Hose Team: Samuel Cowell is the second firefighter from the right. Courtesy of Geoffrey Dunn.

Joe Lend, alias Cache.
Courtesy of Special Collections, McHenry Library,
University of California at Santa Cruz

Raphael Castro, alias Tahoe.
Courtesy of Special Collections, McHenry Library,
University of California at Santa Cruz

The judge set bail at $2,000 apiece—an enormous sum of money in those days. Lend and Castro awaited their justice in the old jail, near the Mission Plaza. A dog that had befriended the young men waited patiently for their release at the gate.[6]

During the early 1950s, Ernest Otto, the dean of Santa Cruz journalists who had been born at his family home on the corner of Church and Cedar Streets in 1871, recalled the saga of Lend and Castro in his "Old Santa Cruz" history columns that appeared regularly in the *Sentinel.* [7]

Otto had been a 13-year-old boy at the time of Lend and Castro's arrest, and his recollections indicate that he was intimately aware of their circumstances. It is through his eyes and his childhood experiences that we have any sense at all of the lives of the two young men.

Referring to them solely by their nicknames Cache and Tahoe, Otto described them as being "known and liked by everyone" and as "kind and gentle." He recalled that they "knew where fish and game could be found and had friends ready to buy their catches." He described them as "inveterate bird-egg collectors" who could always locate nests, even those "of the rarest birds in this section."

Otto identified both Cache and Tahoe as "two of the best" players on the Santa Cruz Powder Works baseball team that played its games on the present site of Pogonip.

"Cache was a catcher, and Tahoe a shortstop so fast on his feet he could almost keep up with the moving ball," Otto recalled. In another column on the same theme, he described Tahoe as "one of the very best shortstops in the city and moved like lightning when running the bases."

The two young men, according to Otto, were the sons "of the last surviving Indians of the mission," a woman identified by Otto as "Maria" and her sister, whom he did not identify by name. According to Otto's accounts, the two women "always were seen together in their plain skirts and with black shawls over their heads and wrapped around their shoulders. They took in washing and had many customers."

In one column Otto identified them as living on Potrero Street; in another on Evergreen. Both streets were (and are to this day) located on the back slopes of Mission Hill in what was then known as the Potrero—today divided by Highway One, with Harvey West Park to the west and the Sash Mill compound to the east—the common pasture lands deeded to local native peoples following the decline of Mission Santa Cruz.

If Lend and Castro were 19 at the time of their arrest, that would have placed their births in 1865. Baptismal records at Mission Santa Cruz indicate a number of baptized "*indios*" that year. One, in particular, registers the baptism of a boy named José, born illegitimately ("*natural*") *t*o a mother named Maria and a father named Jesus y Maria on June 18.[8] That is likely Joe Lend. County records indicate that the two parents were later married.[9]

The following year, in an article entitled "Lo! The Poor Indian," the *Sentinel* reported that "Jose [sic] Maria and Alajon, two Indians of the Santa Cruz tribe," were arrested for assault and carrying concealed weapons.[10]

"When the Santa Cruz Mission was established," the article continued, "the tribes of Indians at Aptos, Soquel and Santa Cruz numbered nearly 3,000. All are now scattered or have passed away; their tribal character has become extinct—except about forty, who have their houses on the Potrero, within the limits of our incorporation. These few keep up their tribal distinctions."

The article went on to describe in considerable detail how the Indian lands were being usurped by the growing number of both Yankee and European immigrants arriving in Santa Cruz and how that contributed to the Indians' arrests.

Taking a surprisingly sympathetic, albeit stereotypical, stance, the article declared:

Our Indians have not become extinct on account of losses in war, or pestilence, but the grasping avarice of the whites drove them from their lands and happy hunting grounds, and disheartened, they roam unguided through the land, and drop down and perish by the wayside, or become the victim of their white friends who sell them the Indian's curse—whiskey.

Would it not be well for the citizens of Santa Cruz to now determine that the Potrero...shall be forever set apart to those Indians and their children, and that no vandal shall ever despoil them of what the good priest gave them for services rendered.[11]

Speaking directly of the two California Indian men charged with the crimes, the article concluded: "The poor fellows are industrious, earn their own living, are a tax upon no person, and are quiet and inoffensive. Then, for humanity's sake, if not for the sake of law and justice, let us protect them in what is their right, and punish those who do them this great injury."[12]

Two decades later, Joe Lend and Raphael Castro would receive no such sympathy from the local daily.

Immediately after they were arrested, the *Sentinel*—then controlled by Duncan McPherson—fanned the flames of public sentiment against them. Under a headline proclaiming "Bad 'Injuns'," the daily railed, "Now that the two Indians are in a safe place, where they cannot indulge in their propensity to 'have a little fun,' by setting barns and houses on fire for the 'pleasure of seeing the firemen run,' the owners of property can sleep tranquilly."[13]

The paper referred to the two men derisively as "illiterate and drunken," "sons of the forest," "childlike and bland," and "warriors," and to Indian women as "copper-colored squaws."

"The Indian nature," the *Sentinel* opined, "does not understand the duty that is due to civilized society, and it can not fathom the reasons why any respect should be paid to law and order."

Duncan McPherson

The only redeeming description was offered by Mrs. P. B. Fagen, a member of Santa Cruz's crusty elite, and for whom Lend had worked as a gardener and buggy driver. She described "Cache" as "faithful and industrious," as well as "honest." She attributed his errant behavior to "strong drink," and likened his disposition to that of a child.

Her empathy did nothing to stem the tide.

Little more than two weeks after they were arrested—without ever having received legal representation—Lend and Castro were sentenced to six years each at San Quentin Prison by presiding Judge James H. Logan.[14]

 According to the *Sentinel*, "the two dusky 'braves'...received their sentences with a sardonic grin, and with as much nonchalance as if they were going to a place where they would be permitted to set fire to a barn before each meal. Cache and Tahoe calmly smoked cigarettes on the way to jail and seemed to be contented and happy."[15]

On Christmas Eve 1884—19 days following

their arrest—the *Sentinel* reported that "the Indian firebugs were taken to their future home at San Quentin...They regarded their removal to prison more in the light of a 'picnic' than a punishment. Whether they will learn different, time alone will tell."[16]

In the introduction to her important work, *Conquests and Historical Identities in California: 1769-1936*, UCSC associate professor of history Lisbeth Haas recounts the story of Modesta Avila, a young Californio woman from San Juan Capistrano, who, in 1889, nailed a fence post to a railroad track that ran by her home, demanding payment from the Santa Fe Railroad Company for the right of passage.[17]

Avila, born just two years later than Lend and Castro into a similar post-colonial community, stuck a piece of paper to the fence post that read: "This land belongs to me. And if the railroad wants to run here, they will have to pay me ten thousand dollars."[18]

She, too, was sent to San Quentin for her bold transgression against property rights, receiving a sentence of three years.

Were the fires of Joe Lend and Raphael Castro, like the defiant resistance of Modesta Avila, also acts of rebellion against a social order bent on conquest and domination? Or were they simply the frivolous acts of "childlike" and "drunken Indians," as they were attributed in the press and in the courts?

When reconstructing the past it is important not to read into the historical record more than is there; speculation, particularly in history, can be deadly.

At the same time, it's equally important not to accept carte blanche reports or interpretations of historical events, particularly when they are those of those in power who have a stake in the way they are presented. Would anyone today, for instance, argue that the radical political movements of the 1960s in the United States can be accurately recaptured from the pages of *Life* or *The Wall Street Journal*? Hardly. We must look

back at the past with fresh eyes and reconstruct it
for ourselves. To do otherwise is to foster the lies
of the past.

Contrary to wide-spread perception, California's
native population—numbering approximately
300,000 prior to the arrival of Franciscan
missionaries in 1769—was not "wiped out" by
the missions. Many survived well beyond
statehood in 1850. There were concentrated
military and vigilante campaigns directed at
California's native peoples throughout the state
well into the 1870s, culminating with the U.S.
Army campaign against Kintpuash (Captain Jack)
of the Modoc tribe that lead to his capture and
hanging in 1873.[19]

It was more than the introduction of European
diseases that decimated the native peoples of
California; there was a systemic pattern of state-
sanctioned genocide.[20]

Nor were the California Indians passive in the
face of colonial and military aggression. Rebellion
was commonplace throughout the mission era
and early statehood, and Santa Cruz, in particular, had a sustained legacy of resistance. As early as
1793, a tribal leader named Charquin, head of a
Quirosote community near Año Nuevo on the
North Coast that had long resisted the intrusion
of the missions in San Francisco, Santa Clara and,
finally, Santa Cruz, led an assault on the local
mission compound.[21]

Two decades later, members of regional Ohlone
tribes confined at Mission Santa Cruz, strangled
Father Andres Quintana, a mission priest known
for his use of metal-tipped whips and thumb
screws on native peoples. His assailants also
crushed his testicles.[22]

By the time that Lend and Castro lit the fires, the
free-flowing lands of their childhoods in the
Potrero had been significantly diminished. Laws
had been passed severely restricting their hunting
and fishing rights. They had witnessed first-hand
lynchings and other forms of violence directed at
native peoples. And they had been systematically

*Hanging at the Water Street Bridge, May 1877.
Francisco Arias and José Chamales were lynched by an
unidentified Santa Cruz mob. Lend and Castro would
have been 11 or 12 at the time of the lynching.
Courtesy of Geoffrey Dunn.*

excluded from the emerging political and
economic order.

The barns and occasional house that they
burnt—in particular the Bias barn that had been
built on Potrero lands—were symbols of that
encroachment and subordination. Given both
this legacy and these motivating factors, is it really
all that difficult to conceive that the fires lit by
Lend and Castro were, at least in some elemen-
tal aspects, acts of open rebellion?

It is also important to place the story of Lend and
Castro in a larger historical context. It was not
simply an anecdotal local event, as Otto and many
subsequent historians have portrayed it, but part of
a long-term institutionalized assault on local
peoples who were identified as outside the Santa
Cruz mainstream. The second half of the nineteenth century in California, as Haas argues, was a
period of conquest and the subordination of ethnic
identities in local communities. Santa Cruz was

Raphael "Tahoe" Castro's commitment papers to the Stockton Insane Asylum. Courtesy of the California Department of Corrections.

especially virulent in this regard.

Any ethnic group that did not fit into the emerging Protestant and Northern European power structure in Santa Cruz was systematically marginalized and designated as "other." This included not only California Indians, but Mexicans, Californios, African Americans, Chinese, Southern Europeans (most notably Italians) and Irish Catholics.

Almost from the moment that Santa Cruz County was established in 1850, Californios—natives of Spanish, Mexican, Indian or mixed heritage—were targeted. Many Californios lost their land titles through corrupt attorneys and legal proceedings.[23]

Lynchings were also commonplace. As early as 1851, vigilantes pulled Mariano Hernandez from the local jail and hung him; many more were to follow. The last California lynching locally occurred in May of 1877, when Francisco Arias and José Chamales, both suspected of murder, were hung from the Water Street Bridge.[24]

The local legal structure, as well as the *Sentinel,* condoned the lynchings.[25]

The immediate years before Lend and Castro were

sent to prison also saw the uprising of an anti-Chinese movement that would consume the local community for the better part of a decade. Laws were passed that directly impacted local Chinese laundry men and vegetable growers. In 1882, just two years before Lend and Castro were sentenced to prison, Santa Cruz County residents voted 2,540 to 4 to oppose further Chinese immigration to the U.S.[26]

The same Duncan McPherson who would refer to Lend and Castro as "bad injuns" and "dusky braves" had only five years earlier referred to the Chinese as "half-human, half-devil, rat-eating, rag-wearing, law-ignoring, Christian civilization-hating, opium smoking, labor-degrading, entrail-sucking Celestials."[27]

It was the language of conquest and subordination.

The subjugation of ethnic identity was so profound, that by the end of the century, Joséfa Perez Soto, a member of one of Santa Cruz's noblest Spanish families during the Mission era, would be identified as an "old Indian" by people in the community.[28]

Like the Salinas River to the south, whatever remnants there were of local California Indian society and culture were forced to run underground.

And what of Cache and Tahoe? Time, indeed, as the *Sentinel* editorialist portended, did spell out their fates, and in short order.

San Quentin in the late 19th Century—let alone today—was a bastion of brutality and disease. Thousands of prisoners during this era—many of them California Indians—died there, including Modesta Avila.[29]

According to records obtained from the California Department of Corrections, on May 3, 1886, little more than 16 months after he arrived, Joe Lend died from "scrofula," more commonly known as tuberculosis of the lymph nodes. He was 20 years old. [30]

This former baseball catcher and egg hunter known as Cache was buried in a common grave for Indian prisoners.

A year following Lend's death, according to San Quentin records, Raphael Castro went "insane." The speedy shortstop known as Tahoe was sent to the Stockton Insane Asylum in August of 1887. He died there a year later, at the age of 22.

His burial records have been lost.[31]

Notes:

[1] This article is based primarily on accounts taken from the *Santa Cruz Daily Sentinel*, December 9, 10, 16, 23 and 24, 1884. The author would like to thank Father Mike Marini and Phil Reader (both, perhaps not coincidentally, graduates of Holy Cross High School) for their generous assistance in researching this article. Excerpted from *Santa Cruz Is In the Heart: Volume II* (forthcoming). Copyright 2000 by The Capitola Book Company.

[2] For a brief sketch of William H. Bias, see E.S Harrison, *History of Santa Cruz County*, 1892:292. The information about Samuel Cowell is taken from a private photo from the collection of the author.

[3] *Santa Cruz Daily Sentinel*, December 10, 1884. Castro's nickname was spelled both "Taho" and "Tahoe" in various accounts. I have chosen the common spelling of the name used today.

[4] *Santa Cruz Daily Sentinel*, December 9 and 10, 1884; *Santa Cruz Sentinel*, December 15, 1905. There were conflicting accounts of the arrest.

[5] *Santa Cruz Daily Sentinel*, December 9, 1884.

[6] The dog belonged to Dr. and Mrs. P. B. Fagen, for whom Raphael Castro worked as a gardener and carriage driver. Ernest Otto, "Old Santa Cruz," *Santa Cruz Sentinel*, undated history column from the 1940s/1950s.

[7] Ernest Otto, "Old Santa Cruz," *Santa Cruz Sentinel*, undated history columns from the 1940s/1950s. Otto's accounts cited here are taken from three such columns.

[8] Baptismal records located at Holy Cross Church, Santa Cruz, California.

[9] Marriage records for 1867 located at County of Santa Cruz Government Center, Santa Cruz, California. The records indicate that a license was granted on May 18, 1867 and that the marriage took place on May 30 of that year, with Father A.D. Casanova presiding. 1867:0-1:293.

[10] *Santa Cruz Sentinel*, June 23, 1866:2. This is one of the most detailed accounts of life on the Potrero available from the period.

[11] *Ibid.*

[12] *Ibid.*

[13] *Santa Cruz Daily Sentinel*, December 10, 1884.

[14] *Santa Cruz Daily Sentinel*, December 23, 1884.

[15] *Ibid.*

[16] *Santa Cruz Daily Sentinel*, December 24, 1884.

[17] Lisbeth Haas, *Conquests and Historical Identities in California, 1769-1936*, 1995:1-2, 89-91.

[18] *Ibid.*

[19] See Dee Brown, *Bury My Heart at Wounded Knee*, 1971: 213-234; Rupert Costo and Jeannette Henry Costo, *The Missions of California: A Legacy of Genocide*, 1987; and Robert F. Heizer, *The Destruction of California Indians*, 1974.

[20] *Ibid.*

[21] Randall Milliken, *A Time of Little Choice: The Disintegration of Tribal Culture in the San Francisco Bay Area 1769-1810*, 1995:125-136. While I disagree profoundly with some of the analyses in this work, it is one of the most important studies on Northern California Indian life published to date.

[22] See Sandy Lydon, *Santa Cruz Sentinel*, September 8, 1991:D-4. See also "The Narratives of Lorenzo Asisara" in this Journal.

[23] See Neal Harlow, *California Conquered: The Annexation of a Mexican Province 1846-1850*, 1982; Leonard Pitt, *The Decline of the Californios*, 1966.

[24] See Geoffrey Dunn, *Santa Cruz Is in the Heart*, 1989:13-16.

[25] *Ibid.*

[26] See Sandy Lydon, *Chinese Gold*, 1985:115-136; and Dunn, op cit.:17-32.

[27] *Santa Cruz Sentinel*, December 13, 1879.

[28] See Dunn, op cit.:3-12; and Phil Reader, "The Tales of Old Mother Chapar," *Santa Cruz County History Journal*, 1994:91-98.

[29] Fred Harrison, *Hell Holes and Hangings*, 1986:159-167; and Haas, op cit.:2.

[30] Records provided the author by California Secretary of State, Bill Jones, California State Archives, Department of Corrections San Quentin Commitment Papers, No. 11509 and 11510.

[31] Efforts to obtain information on Castro from the Stockton State Hospital Records now housed at Sonoma State Hospital have to date been unsuccessful.

"I'm an Indian, But Who Am I?"

by Patrick Orozco, as told to Lois Robin

In the Central Coastal area of California, the tracing of family lineage is particularly difficult. Here, ninety percent of the indigenous people died by the end of the fifty year Mission period. Following those years, further devastating attacks on Indian life and culture continued. Very few native people have intact family histories.

Patrick Orozco is a descendant who has always known he is Indian, but twenty years ago knew little of his particular background or culture. Through these years with great effort he has recovered pieces of his identity but still continues his search. Oral traditions, memories, intuitions and recorded information are interwoven in the fabric of his identity.

Patrick has been culturally active in the Santa Cruz, San Benito and Monterey County areas. He goes into the schools with remembered songs and stories, dances, and regalia. Helping other Indian people trace their lineages is gratifying to him. He brings an Indian voice into the broader arena, testifying at civic meetings, monitoring with archaeologists and speaking for the needs and dreams of his neighbors and community.

—Lois Robin

"I'm an Indian. But who am I?" This thought comes to me as I sit on the Lee Road[1] burial ground one day in March of 1975. As I sit there with other Indian people, surrounded by policemen, county officers and the Sheriff's swat team, I know that the answer must come. I know if I make it through this showdown alive, I will find the answers to this question.

Our people's graveyard was being excavated by giant machines to lay a foundation for a warehouse. Human bones and skulls surfaced and were being crunched. A judge issued a restraining order to the developer, then rescinded it, succumbing to commercial pressure. Our cemetery would now be bulldozed. We had to take a stand—and we did. With rifles and bows and arrows, we went into the cemetery at night. We would not shoot first, but if someone shot at us, we would return fire. We understood that we might lose our lives defending our religious rights, our culture, our people. When day break came, we faced a sea of law enforcement and weaponry.

Patrick Orozco at the Lee Road site.
Photo by Lois Robin

Santa Cruz
County
History Journal
Issue 5, 2002

*Francisco Rios ("Papa Grande"), great grandfather of
Patrick Orozco. Courtesy of Patrick Orozco.*

At the last minute, the bulldozers were made to
stop further desecration, and the law enforcement
personnel called off by local political leaders. These
county leaders worked out an arrangement with
the property owner who intended to construct his
warehouses over our ancestor's bones. In the
settlement, construction of warehouses was
permitted on the half of the graveyard already
bulldozed, while the remaining half of the burial
ground was given to us Indians along with five
acres of adjacent slough land.

To become an entity and negotiate our situation,
we organized as a local branch of the Northwest
Indian Cemetery Protective Association, as we had
involved this national organization in our resistance.[2] Eventually, this group evolved into the
present Pajaro Valley Ohlone Indian Council. Now
we had a victory, some land, a non-profit status
and even an official designation—Ohlone. But did
we know who we were? At the age of forty I was to
begin a quest that would be more addictive than
anything else I've ever experienced.

My family had always known about this graveyard

and watched over it. Grandma Rios told me how
her father, Francisco Rios, who they called Papa
Grande—Great Father, would come by with his
whole family in the buckboard.[3] He would stop
and go into the graveyard to pray. When he came
back to the buckboard he would tell the family,
"Your people are there. Respect them and protect
them." This is what we were doing at Lee Road,
protecting and preserving our burial ground. My
grandmother Rios told me she was present at the
last burial at the Lee Road site. She was ten years
old. We knew we were Indian people, but this
showdown at Wounded Lee, as it became known,
was the first time I heard us called Ohlone.

The questions burned. What was my tribe? Were
there songs and dances to be learned? What
happened to my people? Who were the conquista-
dores and what happened to us in the missions?
These thoughts and dozens of others consumed
my mind. Somehow, even with the demands of a
growing family, I must find the time, strength and
resourcefulness to address these insistent questions.

Now I began speaking to all the old ones. My first
conversations were with my grandmother, Rose
Rios, my mother's mother. My grandmother
became crippled early in life and was confined to a
wheelchair. Yet with her powerful spirit, she was
able to raise nine children and stay involved and
active in family affairs. Grandma Rose knew that
her husband was Chumash. "But I'm an Indian,
too," she liked to say. Recently I've been able to
prove her statement. Indeed she was from an
Ohlone tribal line. Her father, Francisco Rios
("Papa Grande") was listed in the Monterey Indian
Census of 1880. His father, also Francisco Rios,
was listed in the Carmel Mission records and was
Rumsen Ohlone. On her mother's side of the
family, I have been able to trace and document
family roots that go the Santa Clara Mission
records and indicate Ohlone origins.

I remembered my grandmother using the word
Calentaruc during the time I was growing up.
Calentaruc. Certainly, grandmother, who did not
know how to read and write, had no way of
knowing this word unless it had been handed

down to her by her elders. It rolled on my tongue, *Calentaruc, Calentaruc.* One day I saw the name Calentaruc on a map[4] of Indian villages of this area, and the connection came to me. Grandma must have known about neighbors or people who described themselves as Calentaruc. I realized she knew more about our family than she had ever expressed. I began talking to her, and though she never talked about Indian ways directly, now she began to remember and share valuable information. From this information I began to make family charts. Yet I realized that I would need supporting documents to know if those who intermarried were of Indian origins or not.

Grandma sent me out to gather herbs that could be used for medicines. When I brought them back, she would name them and tell me their uses. There was *yerba buena*, a highly rated herb that could be used for many ailments, such as stomach ache, and was also a soothing drink. There was willow bark for headaches, yarrow for toothaches and *campanoche* or *fireweed* for wounds. And always huckleberries for food and pleasure. Herbs and plant materials through their odors and aliveness connected us to our past. They have been there for a long time, renewing each season.

The most moving moment with grandmother was when she remembered a special song. In my research, I had come on a phrase of a song translated from Spanish to English. In it was the Spanish word *volcano.* That made no sense to me as there are no volcanos here. Grandmother said that in Spanish *vulcano* referred to the river mouth and she began to sing a song about the river mouth of the Carmel River. She knew few Indian songs, but this one, because of its beauty, stayed with her. The song, she said, was about young men and women who meet, coming from the hills toward the mouth of the Carmel River. It is a love song. In it is mention of the abundance of wild rose and the wild grape. The Indian words translate as "From the wet hills, the Indian women come down singing". These are images that come to mind when I sing this song. The words of the song meant so much to me that I learned them in their original language. The time and place of this

Rose Rios, maternal grandmother of Patrick Orozco. Courtesy of Patrick Orozco.

moment, when Grandma began to sing, are etched in my mind. Whenever I sing this song, I am moved to tears by its ancient beauty.

Grandma wanted me to look up relatives from the Rios side of the family. Grandma said, "I want you to go to Los Angeles and look for my Uncle Ramon Rios." On a visit to L.A., I mentioned Uncle Ramon to a friend, Ray Belarde. He said that he knew many members of the Rios family and was related to them. He offered to introduce me to them, but there wasn't time. By now my great uncle must be gone. Grandma herself died in 1987 at the age of 87. Perhaps a Rios reading this article might have known either Ramon or Vicente Rios. They were born in Monterey; their mother was Leandra Soto. I would like to hear from them, as I promised Grandma to follow through on this.

About this time, a relative offered me a very informative book *San Francisco or Mission Dolores* that contained the accounts of Vizcaino, Portola, and de Anza. I learned that these explorers were greeted by a gentle, kind and sharing people. This is what stands out for me, the quality of the native people described by all the explorers. Gifts of food

Santa Cruz
County
History Journal
Issue 5, 2002

Patrick Orozco in regalia, 1991.
Photo by Lois Robin

were given by the natives to these strangers. The strangers were accepted as brothers, though they were odd looking with their white skin and armor. I also read about the experience of my people in the missions. Many of the elders still had a mission fantasy, so I had to find out for myself what the mission experience meant to our people and culture. Little by little over the years information has come to me, so that I have my own under-standing of what happened there.

I also went to the dance lodges held by other Indian people and to the mountains and prayed. An old Indian doing a ceremony at the burial site told me I would be seeing things. She said, "Don't be afraid, you will see your people." I did see the smiling faces of Indians, elders and children. I saw they were old ones because their teeth were missing. First they were smiling. Then sadness came. They were so happy before the contact with the Europeans. But they smiled because they knew

the identity of the Indian people would come back.

As these bits of information about my ancestors came to me, I had many startling experiences. One time, sitting at the cemetery at Lee Road, a shadow fell across the gravestones. It was the shadow of an old lady with a cape. "Am I imagining this or not?" I asked myself. I said to the shadow, "I'm here to protect your place of rest from vandals."

Now we find that not only are our graves vandal-ized, but those of non-Indians are, too. How beautiful it would be to go back to the mountains, to a little cabin, to live there forever and not worry about this world.

My search for genealogical information led me to the churches. I was inexperienced with churches. I began with baptisms and making my own charts. I asked questions: "Where was this person born? What year? To whom?" The family tree grows fast as two sets of parents on both sides are recorded. The old Diocese in Monterey had records from 1769 to the 1900s. Their books are fragile and difficult to read. The other churches have valuable records from the 1900s to the present. The church personnel try to be cooperative, but they are busy with many people coming in. They don't want to take time with you. I always had the feeling that I was a big bother to them. But I persisted anyway. If I couldn't find the information, I had to check with schools to get the names right and with cemeteries to find where they were buried. I also read voting registers and residential directories for each city to clarify addresses. This was a long, slow search with many dead ends.

Randy Milliken, the anthropologist, got the Indian census from Monterey County, 1852-1880. From this I was able to see the Rios family. The first 700 baptisms from Carmel, Santa Cruz and San Juan Bautista Missions came by directly contacting various anthropologists who had access to these records. By reading them, I also found out about the lineage of my great-grandmother on my mother's father's side, Mamita.[5] Unfortunately, Mamita's lineage is still incomplete, and I cannot yet determine her tribal origins. I saw Mamita in a dream. I had this dream four or five years ago. The dream took place in Corralitos Creek. A group of people were sitting under a sand dune along the creek. There was a creek between me and the people. When she saw me, she looked at me. She told me something with her eyes; I didn't hear a voice. She was happy in the work I was doing. The look was of satisfaction.

Although great-grandmother is faded in my memory, I still remember her kind, peaceful face, full of love. Great-grandmother Mamita was a midwife. She was at my mother's birth and assisted the doctor. She was a midwife for her son's and daughter's families and brought many children into the world. She was a healer as well, and gave advice and helped to solve problems. She was held in high esteem, and Indian people and others would bring her gifts as thanks for her healing skills.

I was born 200 feet away from the Pajaro River on Bridge Street in Watsonville, now called Rodriguez Street. Apparently there were birth problems, and Mamita had to call on Dr. Glure for assistance with my delivery. I was only two the last time I saw her, at her death bed. She was sitting up, and my mom said she reached down and patted me on my shoulder and told her "This is the one who will bring all these things back." I was born September 5, 1939, and she died September 20, 1941.

I lived with my mother, Annie Marques, my father, Porfirio Orozco, and grandmother Rose Rios for many years at a great old house in Watsonville. It was a wonderful old house, and I remember every room and corner of it and the garden outside, too. Pleasure and happiness come to me when I think of my years in the old house. Then when I was eight, my mother and father split up. This was largely due to my father becoming involved in gambling. Unfortunately, Keno games were being played almost directly across from the old house. My father became addicted to them and also began to drink.

Then my mother and grandmother moved to a house on East Lake Street. I would go off for hours

Mamita. Mary Dixon, great grandmother of Patrick Orozco. Courtesy of Patrick Orozco.

to play by myself in the land around the house. I had a special hideout. It was in a thicket of willows, where I could move the vines and make a little house for myself. It was my own ruk, as the Indians here called their tule houses. Although at that time, I did not know of ruks, my house evoked the world of my ancestors. Near my hideout, I discovered an old handmade willow bridge. It was crudely made and very frail and provided a path across an old ditch. But the most astonishing experience was finding an old skull lying on the ground there. From its eye emerged a lizard or snake. All these experiences aroused an ancient, dreamlike feeling and had meaning for me. I felt certain I was on the site of an old village.

During this time, also, I hunted little animals with a sling shot or by setting snares, mostly birds. I felt badly about doing this, but I was hungry much of the time. I made a fire in the field and cooked the little birds. I knew at that time my mother had little money to feed us. Grandma used to ask me to bring her mud hens, which I did. She cooked them in a delicious manner. She would skin them and use vinegar to tenderize them. They had a very dark meat. She insisted that I bring no more than we needed, usually about three.

Grandma was always interested in birds. When she heard an owl in the trees she shook her head and said, "Not good. Signe del muerto. Don't ever kill an owl. There is a certain time when an owl approaches you and is singing—it's good luck. Also, when a hawk is singing. When birds are singing, it is always good luck."

I missed my father and rarely saw him. We had hard times; mother could barely support us. Yet, one day, without warning, my father returned and took all of us kids in the car to the Hollister area in the Gavilan Mountains. Our destination was the Almaden Winery, where he was a worker, and where we were to live for the next few years. This was a marvelous place for a young boy. I had a beautiful sense of freedom, and everywhere around us were wild animals; tame deer, quail, coyote, pigeons, mountain lion and bobcat. Many Indian people lived there, and I enjoyed a fine company of boys. I liked the rattlesnakes and king snakes and particularly the tarantulas. I was never afraid of them and could sometimes demonstrate power by handling a tarantula in front of the others. It made them respectful of me.

An elder, Manuel Orango, once pointed to two of the Almaden Mountains and told me that if I listened well, I could hear an Indian shouting to his brother, because the brother had taken his wife. I would listen carefully to see if I could hear him, and I did hear some whispering in the air, but I couldn't swear to it. Apparently these mountains echo, and I was hearing the voices of drunken people and thought it was the brothers shouting.

Trading as my forefathers had done was instinctive with me. Once my younger brother had a tiny puppy that I coveted. I was a good marble player and so had a great stack of marbles. First I offered him a handful of marbles for this dog I called "Tootsie." He declined. When finally I offered him a whole huge sack of marbles, he accepted and Tootsie was mine. She remained with me for many years.

A teacher at the school once took us to a place where there was a cave with hand pictographs on the wall. I was awed but to this day have not been able to find the cave again. But I remember the mark of my people on that cave wall.

Once while attending school, I was chosen to be in a school play about pioneer days. I'll be durn tootin'. I was a real Indian, and they made a cowboy out of me for the play. The incongruity bothered me, but I tipped my hat and slowly rode away.

At this time, my father taught me what I know about hunting, what to wear, how to smell the deer, to make sure it was a buck, important knowledge about hunting. My father was an Indian from Baja California. He knew these arts well, and he was a fine teacher. My father never spanked me, and he kept his word. After he returned us to mother, he and she remained good friends throughout the years.

I came to know my mother's father, my grandfather, Louis Marquez, when we moved around the area picking crops at various ranches. Often we would camp in the middle of a field and build a fire. There grandmother would make very large delicious tortillas. Stories would be told, mostly about animals. One story that impressed me very much at the time and has stayed with me throughout the years was about an Indian boy who was turned into a bear by a bad shaman. My heart would jump as I heard how this bear could only become human again when a person who loved him shed tears for him . . . and how eventually, a woman did.

Grandmother would do her work in the hop fields from her wheel chair. She kept the family together. Her brother, called ChiChi (an Indian name), would bring us watermelons and soda pop. These occasions were very pleasing to me. One place we worked was the McGrath Ranch. McGrath actually funded the funeral for Papa Grande when he died.

At an earlier time, my family worked at the cattle ranches in Monterey County: Rancho San Carlos, Riley Ranch and others. I went there sometimes to trace records.

My grandfather was a strong, vital person and
wonderfully kind. Yet he drank seriously and
heavily. Many years before I was born, he was a
bootlegger. I remember his disinterest in money.
He would throw a handful of coins into the air
and not bother to pick them up. I used to check in
with him, when he was drunk or sober, to see how
he was doing. Even after my grandmother remar-
ried, Louis used to hang out at her place. All three
of them got along well—grandma, her second
husband and Louis.

For a while I stopped working on Mamita's ancestry.
I turned instead to Grandma Rios' ancestry on her
mother's side. Grandma knew that her grandmother
was last married to someone named Flores, and that
she lived in Los Gatos, but she did not know her
maiden name. I went to the *San Jose Mercury News*,
and read in the obituaries that Narcissa Geneve Flores
died in 1915 in Los Gatos. In her obituary I also
learned the name of her brothers and from that
derived her maiden name, Geneve.

Then I went to the cemetery where she was buried,
to verify my information and also pay my respects.
At the location of that cemetery, I found the Los
Gatos Library instead. In the library I was told that
the cemetery had been moved four miles away.
When I found the cemetery, there was an old stone
with the name of Narcissa Geneve Flores, born
1850. It had taken many hours of research to get
to her grave. I prayed and spoke to my ancestor,
talking to her about the things I knew of her from
my grandparents and telling her that I would be
continuing to search for the traces of our family. It
was a high moment.

More remained to be done. I needed to locate the
baptism of Narcissa Geneve in order to learn the
name of her parents. The microfilm at the the
Santa Clara Mission records was not clear, and
although I saw the name of Narcissa Geneve, I
could not read her parents' name. I became
bogged down and did not know how to get
around this problem.

Often when I am stuck, I will give a little prayer
and ask for help. As happened many times during

*Annie Marques Orozco, mother of Patrick Orozco,
1991. Photo by Linda Yamane.*

my search, when this occurred, a way opened up to
me. At a meeting related to archaeological monitoring, a question arose concerning my credentials.
The county planning department asked the
archaeologist on the project to research my
background. A genealogist, Mrs. Edith Smith, was
consulted, and she found the original records I
needed at St. Joseph's church in San Jose. It was St.
Joseph's that recorded baptisms, births and
marriages during this period in Santa Clara
County. These records disclosed that Narcissa's
father was a Frenchman named Alexander Geneve,
married to Juanita Chavoya. They were married in
Santa Clara County. I have a birth certificate for
Juanita Chavoya dated 1835. She was fifteen years
old at the time she gave birth to Narcissa. This was
an important key to tracing the lineage.

Juanita Chavoya's parents, also on the birth or
baptism records, were Jose de la Cruz Chavoya,
from Mission Dolores and Maxima Vasquez. Data
from before this time was to be found in the
mission records. I thought I would have to travel
widely to continue my search, and I doubted that I
could afford to do that. But then I discovered the

necessary records at the Family History Library at the Church of Latter Day Saints. I wondered if I would have to become a Mormon to use the library. Fortunately, it was not necessary. The Library is very helpful. If they don't have it, they'll get it for you. They believe that Indians are the direct descendants of Israel, and so they try to obtain microfilm of birth, death, marriage, baptism and census data. I ordered about twenty reels of different mission records of California.[6]

From the Mormon Library I learned that the father of Maxima Vasquez was Jose Antonia Vasquez from Mission Dolores at San Francisco. The mother's name was not clear. Again, when I hit a snag, help was forthcoming. This time help came from an accomplished woman named Charlotte Farrel. I had met her niece at an Indian gathering. She told me her aunt had been doing California Indian genealogical research, prompted by an interest in her own roots. However, I was not prepared for the extensiveness of Charlotte Farrel's work or the generosity of her help. In her library, she had volumes of hand printed genealogies. She was able to go quickly in her records to Maxima Vasquez, and found that Maxima's mother's name was Maria Leocadia. Next to Maria's name, it said *India*. It was this word that my search was about: *India*. At last, here was proof of Grandma Rios' belief that she was from an Indian family.

Maria's parents were Pedro Pablo and Maria Pelagia and these two were from the village of San Juan Bautista south of San Jose. The people at this village were referred to as the Santa Teresa Hills tribe or "Ritoxci." They must have been baptized in the Mission. Their baptism number of 738 indicates that they were among the earliest converts. It was thrilling to know that the history in my bones was confirmed by the written record.

I sent all these names to Randy Milliken. He wrote me back a letter saying, "Congratulations, Patrick, you have located your family roots." He was able to confirm all the connections. He found that Pablo had the Indian name of "Hugjolis" and that Maria Pelagia was called "Yunen." Their marriage was July 2, 1785. She must have been around

twenty, and he thirty, when they were baptized in the mission. In short, by tracing back seven generations of grandmothers, I came to the point where Europeans made contact with my people, and records confirmed my Ohlone roots. Randy also provided names of the other children of Maria Leocadia. I wonder if her descendants can be located, and if they are aware of their origins.

This is the only lineage I completed. It tells me for sure of a lineage on my mother's mother's side. Other lines are only partially completed, but with each new piece of information, I myself feel more complete. It is an addiction, pursuing these matters, but as the resources become more familiar, and I know where to look, it becomes easier. It is costly, also. I may have spent a thousand dollars in pursuit of this information. This documentation is not only fulfilling to me, but it has been necessary to counter charges that have been made against me. These allegations, that I am not a true Costanoan Indian descendant, are damaging and upsetting. Other people come to believe the false allegations. Much time must be spent in refuting them.

I believe that the least reliable method of documentation is Department of the Interior (BIA— Bureau of Indian Affairs) enrollment lists. You see, those names were gathered because of law suits against the U.S. Government. The government agreed to pay native people a certain amount of money, and it just wanted to take care of the matter. It gave applicants questionnaires and did not require any documentation of their replies. I would not be satisfied with information from roll call records. The ancestry of my mother's father was believed to be Chumash. However, the only documentation I have of it so far is from an enrollment list. While this is a clue, it is not proof. I am still looking at other sources to confirm it.

Anthropologists such as Rob Edwards and Randy Milliken have been helpful to me in my quest for identity and in my efforts to protect grave sites. They have led me to good sources of information, such as J.P. Harrington, Kroeber, Heizer, and other anthropologists. They often know from previous work where burial sites are located. If a burial site is threatened by development, I can ask the County that an evaluation report be filed before any development takes place. Archaeologists and Indians appeared to have opposed interests twenty years ago. The Indians wanted the graves to be untouched, and the archaeologists wanted to expose them for scientific purposes before they were destroyed. Now they have come together to protect resting places from destruction. Archaeologists respect our feelings and value our knowledge; we value the information they bring us.

From my connections with close relatives, from recollection of childhood experiences and talking with the elders, comes the base of my Indian experience. With this base and the genealogical proof of my identity, I am secure enough to continue with other dreams and activities and the continued pursuit of my ancestry. I am an Indian, and I know who I am.

Notes:

[1] Lee Road is in Watsonville near the confluence of the Watsonville and Struve Sloughs. CA-SCR-107 is located there.

[2] The Cemetery Association was formed to preserve and protect Indian burial grounds, villages and ceremonial sites. Victor Cutnose was the director at that time; the organization was based in Arcata, California.

[3] Francisco Rios (Papa Grande) was listed in the 1880 census as Indian. His father, also Francisco Rios, was listed in the Carmel Mission records. The senior Francisco Rios married Leandra Soto at Mission San Miguel. The generation before that is unknown, but a Rios family with apparent ties is mentioned even earlier in the Mission Records of San Luis Obispo and San Miguel.

[4] A map showing the Calentaruc tribelet territory at the coastal plain near the Pajaro River is in Margolin (1978: 2). The map is based on research by C. King and R. Milliken.

[5] Mamita's birth name was Mary Dixon. Her mother, Maria Petra had several partners. The first was Paul or David Dixon. The second was Jesus Romandia, with whom she had Edward Andrew Romandia, the half-brother listed on the Chumash BIA rolls of 1928-1933. The third was Delores Tarango. From this last stepfather, Mamita acquired the nickname "Tarangita." Mary Dixon also had three different partners: Jose Cruz in 1893, Terso Marques in 1898, and Martin Soto in 1918. She had 14 children. She lived in Tortilla Flats in Carmel for most of her life until her house was taken away for nonpayment of taxes. Then she moved to Seaside and died there in 1941 at the age of 64, disheartened from the loss of her house. Mary Dixon spoke Rumsen. Her tribal origins are still uncertain, but she was a well-known and revered Indian elder of her time.

[6] A useful related source is *Spanish Mexican Families of Early California, 1769-1850, Volumes I and II* (Northrup 1976, 1984). It does not have copies of records, but it does give marriage, birth, death, baptism and other data.

Bibliography

Engelhardt, Zephyrin. O.F.M. 1924. *San Francisdo or Mission Dolores,* Chicago: Franciscan Herald Press.

Margolin, Malcolm. 1978. *The Ohlone Way: Indian Life in the San Francisco and Monterey Bay Area*. Berkeley: Heyday Books.

Northrup, Marie E. 1976. *Spanish Mexican Families of Early California, 1769-1850, Vol. I.* Washington: Library of Congress. 1984. *Spanish Mexican Families of Early California, 1769-1850, Vol. II.* Burbank: Southern California Genealogical Society.

Santa Cruz
County
History Journal
Issue 5, 2002

Profile: Ella Rodriguez

Ella Rodriguez. Photo courtesy of Trudy Haversat and Gary S. Breschini.

Ella Rodriguez was raised as a Native American at a time when it was not popular and she was forced to attend the Stewart Nevada Indian Trade School near Carson City in the 1940s. She received her BIA Roll Number in 1951, documenting her ancestry and heritage. Her ancestry is California Mission Indian, with multiple tribal affiliations. Although she was raised as a Costanoan (Ohlone), her ancestry includes a roughly equal amount of Esselen, along with smaller amounts of Chumash, Cherokee, and Yaqui.

Since 1975, with the Lee Road project in Watsonville, she has worked nearly full time protecting Native American cemeteries and cultural sites. She has worked with literally hundreds of separate projects, from small burial encounters to large multi-year developments, both public and private. During her 25 years of experience working with archaeologists (in the early years by herself), she developed relationships with Central California archaeologists that have become standard practice for those managing cultural resources.

Early Peoples of Monterey Bay: The Scotts Valley Site

By Robert Cartier and Victoria Bobo

Introduction

The Scotts Valley archaeological site (CA-SCR-177) is by far the oldest prehistoric deposit discovered to date in the Monterey Bay region, dating beyond 12,000 years ago. It is also one of the oldest and one of the longest continuously occupied sites on the west coast. Excavations and analysis of the site took place over a period of eight years (organized around two periods of excavation, the first in 1983 and a second in 1987 with analysis carrying over until 1991), and brought together one of the largest and most highly trained archaeological crews ever assembled on the West Coast. Over 230 students and faculty from no fewer than a dozen universities and colleges (including University of California at Berkeley, Stanford University, University of California at Davis, University of California at Santa Cruz, Santa Clara University, San Francisco State University, San Jose State University, Hayward State University, Sonoma State University, Cabrillo College, De Anza College, and West Valley College), as well as a number of local professional archaeologists took part in the excavations during each of the two field seasons. During the course of the two seasons, approximately 450 cubic meters of soil were excavated in controlled stratigraphic levels to average depths of over 1.1 meters. The eight years of research produced a wealth of cultural information from one of the earliest documented sites on the west coast of North America.

The excavation at the Scotts Valley site produced over 10,000 stone artifacts, including knives, projectile points, woodworking tools, and milling stones, that revealed a great deal of information about the inhabitants of the area. The site was occupied by several groups over an exceptionally long period of time, and the different types of artifacts found at the site represent not only varied activities, but also gradual changes in stone tool technologies. These changing technologies reflect changes in culture, which are human adaptations to long-term environmental change. In addition to the general array of hunting and gathering artifacts found at the site, a relatively unusual stone artifact was also recovered: an eccentric crescent. The eccentric crescent is a well-known type of artifact that is linked with certain early prehistoric cultures in the western United States (circa 10,000 years before present, or B.P.). The presence of an eccentric crescent at the Scotts Valley site contributes to the evidence for very early settlement patterns throughout California.

As one of the oldest and continuously occupied sites in western North America (from 12,000 to 600 years ago), the chronology of the Scotts Valley site has been one of the most significant aspects of the archaeological research. The chronology of the site was determined by radiocarbon analysis of charcoal materials, artifacts of obsidian (volcanic glass), artifacts such as the eccentric crescent, and soil at the site. All of these analyses have produced a well-rounded picture of the early Native Americans that once inhabited the Scotts Valley region. When the remnants of their early lifeways are compared with archaeological evidence from sites of Monterey Bay, as well as areas such as southern California, we begin to see that the Scotts Valley site represents a uniquely preserved example of early human culture in western North America.

Geographical Setting

The Scotts Valley site is located within the City of Scotts Valley. It is nestled in the Santa Cruz Mountains, one of the mountain ranges of the central California coastline. In its current setting, Scotts Valley is a typical community of the

Santa Cruz
County
History Journal
Issue 5, 2002

Overview of the 1983 excavations at the Scotts Valley site.

Monterey Bay region with developed residential and commercial areas. Scotts Valley also has its share of natural features such as redwood forests, creeks, ponds, and marshes. There are two major waterways in the Scotts Valley area today: Bean Creek, located north of the city, and Carbonera Creek, flowing through the city to the southwest. These creeks are divided by a high rise, or ridge.

Research in the Scotts Valley area has revealed that at various times in Scotts Valley's past, this area contained larger bodies of water than exist today (Vassil 1993; Jones and Wilson 1993). The valley associated with Carbonera Creek is quite large for the volume of water currently flowing through it. Also notable on either side of the creek are well-developed terraces from prehistoric flood events. The size of its valley, and the presence of these flood terraces, indicates that Carbonera Creek once contained much larger amounts of water (Vassil 1993, p. 22). Another contributing factor may have been earthquakes, which affected both Carbonera Creek and Bean Creek. When an earthquake occurs, the ground can liquefy and trigger landslides, and these prehistoric landslides may have been extensive enough to dam the creeks, forming lakes. Rainfall amounts were also higher at the end of the last ice age (circa 12,000

B.P.). Increased rainfall, together with landslide-produced dams, may have created at least one large body of water in prehistoric Scotts Valley.

Soil in the Scotts Valley area also appears to support the theory that a large lake once existed there. The Scotts Valley site had a layer of clean sand at its deepest level of cultural materials, which may be evidence of a lakeside environment. In addition, rich organic material known as "peat" has been recorded in southeastern Scotts Valley (Jones and Wilson 1993, p. 51). Peat is commonly associated with lake and marsh environments, and its presence here strongly indicates that a lake was present.

The people who lived at the Scotts Valley site chose this location not only because of its fresh water and food resources, but also because it was within a transit corridor between the Monterey Bay and San Francisco Bay areas. All prehistoric human traffic between these two regions was likely to pass through the valley, and this would have presented frequent opportunities for economic and social interaction. The movement of people between the two regions is seen in the many artifacts that were made from stone transported from east of the Santa Cruz mountains. At the time of the first occupation of the Scotts Valley site, this area not only had creeks with fresh water, but may have also had a large lake with a continual supply of fresh water resources. This environment was undoubtedly attractive to groups that lived on both sides of the Santa Cruz Mountains. Over time, the climate and environment of the area changed, and the lake receded, but Scotts Valley remained a key transportation corridor between the Santa Clara Valley and Monterey Bay.

Artifacts, Cultural Change, and Related Sites

The Scotts Valley site contains the material remains of one of the earliest known Native American cultures on the west coast. Unfortunately, due to the high acid content of the soil, caused by the presence of coniferous forest in this area, no organic artifacts such as bone or shell were preserved. Although the set of artifacts from the Scotts Valley site lacks organic materials, those items that did remain (over 10,000 stone artifacts) yielded a great deal of information on the lifeways of some of the first Americans.

Analysis of the artifacts from an archaeological site tells part of the life story of the inhabitants of the site. The artifacts from the Scotts Valley site reveal a people who were primarily hunters. These people used projectile points (commonly misnamed "arrowheads," but actually the tips of spears, lances, and darts) and other chipped stone tools, including knives, scrapers, and awls. Different types of stone were used for different purposes. Chert, which flakes easily, was used to make most of the projectile points and large leaf-shaped "bifaces." Scrapers and other tools requiring a stout edge were often fashioned from quartzite. Other stone tools requiring hard, tough surfaces for grinding plant resources (such as manos and metates) were made from sandstone, granite, quartzite, and schist. The obsidian found at the Scotts Valley site indicates that the early Scotts Valley people were traders, exchanging goods for exotic materials. Obsidian came to Scotts Valley from as far away as Napa and the Sierra Nevada region.

One of the artifacts found at the Scotts Valley site is of particular interest; it is a crescent shaped flaked chert tool, known as an eccentric crescent (Fenega 1993a) (see illustration). Although the function of this tool type is unclear, it is likely that it may have been hafted on a wood or bone handle and used to cut or scrape meat and hide. It is also thought that eccentric crescents may have been abstract animal shapes or "zoomorphs" that had some spiritual significance to early Native Americans. Crescents have been found at other early sites in the western United States that date prior to 8,000 years ago. Crescents have been found in early sites of the San Joaquin Valley, the Great Basin of eastern California and Nevada, and throughout southern California (Fenega 1993a).

Recovery of the crescent during excavation changed the entire mood of the excavation. Prior to finding the crescent, debate and controversy over the hypothesized antiquity of the site was continual. There were both ardent advocates and staunch skeptics among the excavation team. Immediately upon the finding of the crescent, all work spontaneously ceased, the entire crew came to share the find, and new feelings about the site were shared by all present. When the crew returned to their work, after the excitement diminished, every excavator and screener looked at the soil with intensified interest. That single artifact changed the course of all work at the site from that time on.

The Scotts Valley crescent is significant on many levels. First, it confirms the early radiocarbon dates and thus the chronology of the Scotts Valley site. Also, the recovery of the crescent in Scotts Valley extends the known geographic range and the understanding of the cultural connection between the prehistoric peoples who used this type of artifact. It also correlates the Scotts Valley site with other early prehistoric sites in coastal southern California where these types of crescents have also been found.

The artifacts that represent a particular culture, cultural phase, or time period (i.e., hunting vs. later hunting/gathering) are said to be diagnostic, as a time frame and cultural group may be "diagnosed" from them. These artifacts possess one or more stylistic or technological qualities that distinguish them from the implements of other time periods within a culture. The Scotts Valley site's eccentric crescent is an excellent example of a diagnostic artifact. A few years after its discovery at Scotts Valley, this type of artifact was designated the official state artifact of California.

Another significant artifact type found at the Scotts Valley site were burins. These artifacts are recognized as characteristic of old sites; the burin tradition comes ultimately from Asia. Burins are small stone tools that are used as part of composite tools and/or in woodworking. For woodworking, burins functioned similarly to chisel blades (Fenega 1993b). These tools are found in very old sites in both the Old and the New Worlds.

It is difficult to compare the artifact collection at the Scotts Valley site with other sites locally, as its chronology extends further back in time and is therefore unique for northern California. Instead, the trends seen in the artifact collection may be compared with patterns at certain sites in southern California and the greater western United States. The earliest artifacts at the Scotts Valley site do not reveal the kind of projectile points as we find in early sites of this time period in other portions of the United States. Based on artifact similarities, the Scotts Valley site appears to have more affinities with the southern California and Great Basin sites, which also often contain eccentric crescents and other types of characteristic stone tools. The nearest sites in California that parallel Scotts Valley in terms of age and artifacts are at Cayucos, Diablo Canyon, Tulare Lake, and Borax Lake. However, the Scotts Valley site's artifacts correlate more closely with the quartzite milling stones, scrapers, projectile points, and especially the crescents of the Western Pluvial Lakes Tradition (Bidwell 1973) of southern California. The Western Pluvial Lakes Tradition is represented by a number of very old sites (7,000 to 10,000 years) east of San Diego collectively called the San Dieguito complex (Moriarty 1987) and coastal sites known as the La Jolla complex (Gallegos and Hector 1987). The Scotts Valley site appears to represent an extreme northern manifestation of an early Native Ameri-can hunting culture that was previously known only in the southern half of the state.

As a reflection of human behavior, the artifacts at the Scotts Valley site represent a pattern of initial hunting activity followed later by an increase in groundstone artifacts which most commonly include bowl mortars, pestles, metates, and other stones used for grinding and crushing. The inhabitants of the Scotts Valley site apparently became increasingly reliant upon ground seeds and other plant resources to supplement their diets; a gradual shift in the proportion of hunting to milling artifacts indicates this change. This may have been a gradual response to a changing environment and/or dwindling animal resources. This trend is commonly found in sites in the Monterey Bay and San Francisco Bay regions as a gradual transition covering several centuries at approximately 3,000 years ago.

Soils and Stratigraphy

As mentioned previously, the Scotts Valley site has several stratigraphic layers which aided in interpreting the age of artifacts and ecology of the site. It is uncommon to find sequential levels of cultural materials at an archaeological site in California and especially in early archaeological sites. However, at the Scotts Valley site there were three general stratigraphic levels and many smaller levels. The three general levels of cultural stratigraphy are extremely useful to archaeologists, as they allow us to observe the sequence of events that occurred at a site, thereby producing a chronology.

The deepest, and therefore the earliest, cultural level at the site contained an unusual pattern of small banded levels in the soil. These banded soils, called fragipan, are thought to be formed when an area experiences long-term fluctuations in the subsurface water table. This situation appears to have been present in Scotts Valley at the beginning of the Holocene period (about 10,000 years ago). Although fragipan soils are not produced as a by-product of human activity, they do help archaeologists learn about the early occupation at the Scotts Valley site. Fragipan soils solidify over time, and

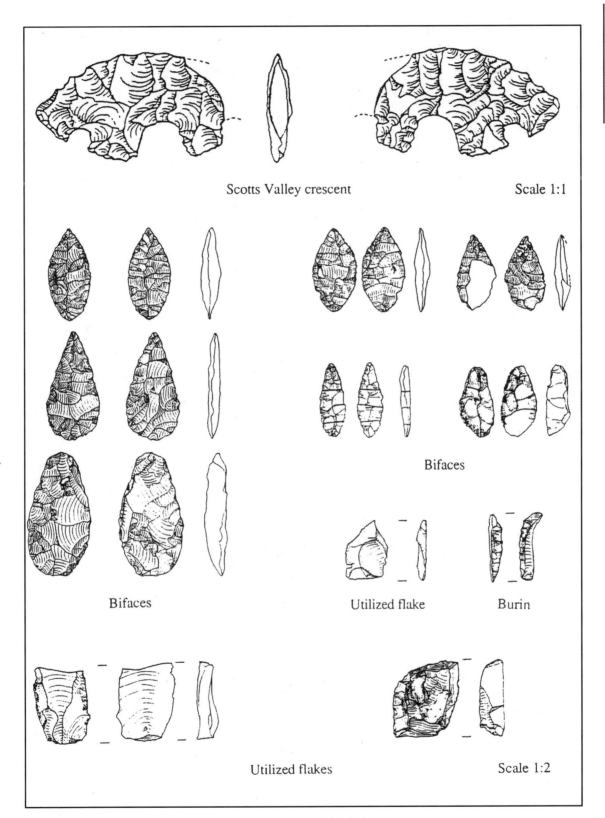

Scotts Valley crescent   Scale 1:1

Bifaces

Bifaces

Bifaces   Utilized flake   Burin

Utilized flakes   Scale 1:2

The Scotts Valley crescent and flaked stone tools.

they effectively seal cultural materials, such as artifacts and the remains of campfires, in discreet layers or strata. Thus, the fragipan soils at the Scotts Valley site sealed in many of the cultural remains left behind by these early people.

In terms of chronology, the fragipan stratigraphy improved the preservation and the sequence of artifact deposition over time, effectively producing an intact record of changing prehistoric lifeways spanning more than twelve thousand years. This allowed analyses and interpretation of artifacts, features, and radiocarbon data from both culturally natural and geologically arbitrary levels, which gave unprecedented precision in developing the site's lengthy and important chronology.

Chronology

Establishing the age and sequence of an archaeological site is done using a variety of methods. The most basic method is relative dating, whereby artifacts from a site are compared with known characteristic artifact types to arrive at an estimated age. Some artifacts, particularly projectile points, have a distinctive stylistic developmental sequence which is often regionally unique. These artifacts are said to have a seriation, meaning that their size and shape changes through time. Artifacts with seriations are particularly useful for relative dating.

Another type of dating is known as absolute dating, as it establishes an age in years for an artifact, soil sample, or deposit. In archaeology the most important and reliable method of absolute dating is radiocarbon dating, which measures the amount of a radioactive isotope (carbon-14) in organic materials such as bone, shell, or charcoal. Radiocarbon dating is possible because the amount of carbon-14 in living tissue is known and it breaks down at a uniform rate after the death of the organism. Radiocarbon dates can be extracted not only from shell or bone, but also from minute amounts of carbonized (burned) wood left in soil from ancient campfires. Obsidian hydration is another method of archaeological dating. It involves the micro-measurement of the absorption of water by obsidian, which also takes place at a

uniform rate. Though not as precise as radiocarbon dating, it is still useful for establishing ages for obsidian artifacts and associated material in deposits.

Since the Scotts Valley site was recognized as exceptionally old and important, all of the above dating methods were used to establish a clear chronology. From the 1983 and 1987 excavations, a total of 37 radiocarbon and 86 obsidian samples were processed, yielding a range of occupation from approximately 580 to well over 12,000 years ago. Radiocarbon dates are the most accurate technique establishing the chronology for the prehistoric past. However, one must be aware that there are several forms of mathematical presentation used for radiocarbon dates. The dates originally generated in the study of the Scotts Valley site were what archaeologists refer to as "raw dates." Since the time that the raw dates were produced for the site, modern archaeology is now able to correlate these raw dates with the common chronology of B.C./A.D. dating. The B.C. corrected date of the earliest raw radiocarbon sample from the Scotts Valley site (12,520 years) is currently adjusted to 13,990 years B.C or 15,940 years ago (Hood, 1999). This calculation uses the internationally adopted baseline of A.D. 1950. This makes Scotts Valley one of the oldest and one of the longest continuously occupied archaeological sites on the west coast. In terms of age and length of occupation, the Scotts Valley site is not only one of the most significant prehistoric sites in the Monterey Bay region, but on the entire west coast of the North American continent.

Summary

The Scotts Valley site has become one of the most thoroughly dated sites, possessing evidence of very early human activity in California and the west coast of North America in general. Its chronology is clearly defined by its sequence of artifacts, its stratigraphy, and the absolute dates produced through radiocarbon dating. The crescent, along with other artifacts, links the site with broader cultural patterns associated with other early archaeological sites in western North America.

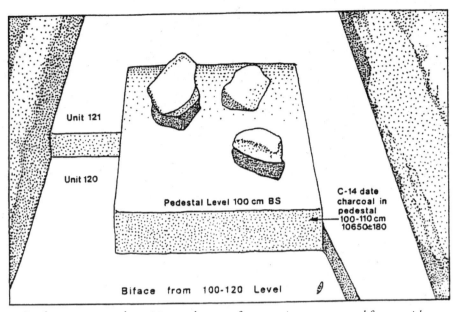

Sandstone metate and granitic trough metate fragments in a concentrated feature with notable charcoal within and underneath artifacts. The C14 date established these artifacts as some of the earliest groundstone in North America and date a biface underneath one of the groundstones as older than 10,650 years before present.

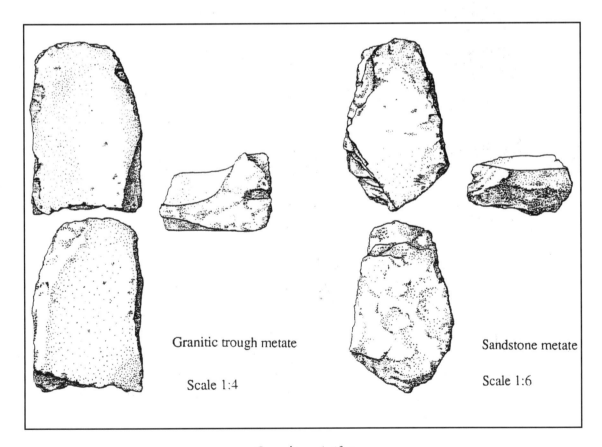

Groundstone Artifacts

Based on the chronological data, the site has been used between 600 and at least 12,000 (perhaps nearly 16,000) years ago, and thus it presents one of the longest chronicles of continued occupation in all of the Americas. The Scotts Valley site is not only intrinsically interesting because of these factors, but also provides substantial amounts of archaeological data that may be well-suited to address future archaeological questions.

The exceptional character of the Scotts Valley site lies in its well documented antiquity and in its duration of occupation during an important and little understood period of the archaeological past.

Comparisons of the Scotts Valley site with other sites in California show it to be similar to those found distributed throughout San Diego County. The site may thus represent the origins of an early cultural tradition that later moved south into San Diego County or that existed simultaneously with the traditions of southern California. We know little of the earliest population of this continent and the lifeways of the peoples who first settled it, and the Scotts Valley site has added substantially to this important topic. A display of the more interesting artifacts found in the excavations along with descriptive explanations is currently located in the entrance to the Scotts Valley City Hall.

Bibliography

Bidwell, Stephen F. 1973. *Fort Rock Basin: Prehistory and Environment*. Eugene, Oregon: University of Oregon Press.

Cartier, Robert, ed. 1993. *The Scotts Valley Site: CA-SCr-177*. Santa Cruz, California: Santa Cruz Archaeological Society.

Fenega, Gerrit L. 1993a. The Eccentric Crescent. In *The Scotts Valley Site: CA-SCr-177*, pp. 94-109. Robert Cartier, editor. Santa Cruz, California: Santa Cruz Archaeological Society.

_____1993b. Paleotechnology at the Scotts Valley Site: 1987. In *The Scotts Valley Site: CA-SCr-177*, pp. 159-242. Robert Cartier, editor. Santa Cruz, California: Santa Cruz Archaeological Society.

Gallegos, Dennis, and Susan M. Hector, eds. 1987. San Dieguito-La Jolla: Chronology and Controversy. *San Diego County Archaeological Society Research Papers, No. 1*. San Diego: San Diego Archaeological Society.

Jones, Terry and Glen Wilson. 1993. Soils and Geology of CA-SCr-177. In *The Scotts Valley Site: CA-SCr-177*, pp. 37-51. Robert Cartier, editor. Santa Cruz, California: Santa Cruz Archaeological Society.

Hood, Darden. 1999. Personal communication. Beta Analytic Radiocarbon Lab. Miami, Florida.

Leventhal, Alan with Beverly Domenech. 1993. 1983 Analysis of the Flaked and Groundstone Tool Assemblage. In *The Scotts Valley Site: CA-SCr-177*, pp. 110-158. Robert Cartier, editor. Santa Cruz, California: Santa Cruz Archaeological Society.

Moriarty, James R. III. 1987. A Separate Origins Theory for Two Early Man Cultures in California. In *San Dieguito-La Jolla: Chronology and Controversy*, pp. 51-62. San Diego County Archaeological Society Research Papers, No. 1. San Diego: San Diego Archaeological Society.

Vassil, B. Vasiliki. 1993. Geologic Factors Potentially Influencing Late Pleistocene/Early Holocene Surface Water Regimes. In *The Scotts Valley Site: CA-SCr-177*, pp. 22-36. Robert Cartier, editor. Santa Cruz, California: Santa Cruz Archaeological Society.

The Rock Art of Chitactac-Adams Heritage Park and Environs

by Donna L. Gillette[1]

Introduction and History of the Park

Chitactac-Adams Heritage County Park is located on Uvas Creek between Gilroy and Morgan Hill in Santa Clara County. This four-acre county park provides an important cultural link to the distant past. The site was the ancestral home of the Mutsun-speaking Ohlone people and was the location of a village apparently known (according to Mission records) as Chitactac.[2] Although the village of Chitactac survived into historic times, archaeological research indicates that people inhabited the immediate surrounding area for at least 3,000 years.[3] Native American habitation sites in the general region can be traced with radiocarbon dates back 12,000 years.[4]

By the beginning of the nineteenth century Spanish missionaries had removed the native inhabitants from the Chitactac area to Mission Santa Cruz.[5] Nevertheless, many of their descendants remained in the surrounding region and have continued to shape the history of California.[6]

Dotted with native oaks and California bay laurels, this rural land was once a portion of the El Rancho Solis. It was granted by Mexico to Joaquin Solis, "convict ranchero," in 1828.[7] In 1829 Solis was returned to San Blas, Mexico, for his part in organizing an ill-fated rebellion against the Mexican government.[8] In 1831 the land was awarded to Mariano Castro by Mexican Governor Figueroa.[9] John Hicks Adams acquired the parcel in 1853 and in 1856 donated the site for the construction of a one-room schoolhouse. Local and migrant-worker children attended the school until 1956, when the last of two Adams Schools to occupy the site burned down. The school building had also functioned as a community center. In 1963 the property was deeded to the County of Santa Clara. The Parks Department began operating the site as a roadside rest in 1966.

For many years the area was referred to as "Indian Rocks," due to the numerous bedrock mortars located in the sandstone outcrops that line the creek bank. In the 1960s Karl Gurcke, then a student at Cabrillo College, reported on an archaeological excavation of the area. Although misidentifying the site as Yokuts9, he noted 500 bedrock mortars in the surrounding area.[10] The exact count of mortars for the Chitactac site is unknown, as many are undoubtedly buried under soil and leaves, but nearly seventy were visible at the time of this writing. This unusually large number of mortars makes the area one of the most significant cultural heritage sites in the San Francisco Bay Region.

In the early 1980s Robert Mark and Evelyn Newman (now Evelyn Billo), while taking an art history class from Dr. John Hestor at San Jose State University, were directed to the then almost pristine prehistoric site. The visit not only confirmed the bedrock mortars, but also revealed the existence of concentric circle petroglyphs and a boulder with cupules.

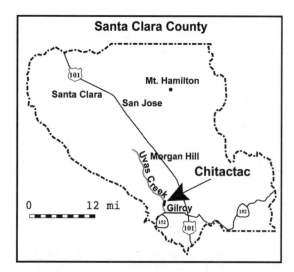

Map showing Chitactac and the surrounding area. Insert with location of Chitactac-Adams Heritage County Park.

In 1984 a team was assembled, including archaeologists and Native Americans, to record the three rock art images (concentric circles) that had then been identified and the cupule boulder. The following year Mark and Newman presented the results of their research and published papers about the site.[12]

By the late 1980s the roadside rest had become an arena for local gang "tagging wars." More spray paint was added to the numerous carvings of initials and other markings that had by this time defaced many of the moss-covered boulders and the interiors of rock shelters. Some of the markings actually damaged the petroglyphs.

Mark and Newman were introduced to local tribal elders by Irene Zwierlein, Chairwoman of the Amah/Mutsun Band of Ohlone, and Alan Levanthal, the tribal ethno-historian. It was Leventhal and others who had determined that the most likely name for the village was Chitactac. Mark and Newman were the impetus for what became a combined effort of Native Americans, park planners, archaeologists, rock art conservation specialists, and community volunteers to transform this neglected eye-sore into a viable family park with extensive interpretive signs and an exhibit shelter. A docent led interpretive program has also begun. Funding for the park was provided by a large federal grant and by county funds. In September of 1998 the Chitactac-Adams Heritage County Park was dedicated, with many Ohlone descendants in attendance.

Petroglyphs are, by definition, carved into the rock (as opposed to pictographs, which are painted). The carving was usually done by pecking, that is, striking the rock with a pointed object. Concentric circle petroglyphs may be defined as concentric rings equally spaced in graduated sizes. They may or may not have a central point—a pecked dot or cupule—and consist of two or more circles. Cupules are defined as "a cup-shaped depression which has been ground or pounded into a rock surface."[11] Cupules may be placed on both vertical and horizontal surfaces, and are usually no larger than 10 cm wide and 4 cm deep. They may or may not form patterns. While the term "rock art" is used to generally identify the prehistoric markings on the stones, the marks were most likely not intended as "art" by the Native Americans who placed them there but were probably ritual related.

*Concentric circle petroglyphs at Chitactac.
Photo by Donna Gillette.*

*Concentric circle petroglyphs at Chitactac.
Photo by Donna Gillette.*

Concentric Circles at Chitactac

The initial study of the petroglyphs identified three sets of concentric circles and a cupule boulder, all located in close proximity to the water's edge. Since that time, Mark, Newman, and others have identified several similar elements elsewhere within the park, with a previously unnoticed series of concentric circles discovered as recently as January of 1999. In the mornings of early winter, when the light of the rising sun is just right, shadows are created which sometimes reveal the faint outlines of the concentric circles. Just as quickly, as if by magic, the circular elements disappear from view. Still more petroglyphs may reveal themselves in the future.

Flooding along Uvas Creek in the spring of 1987 dislodged one of the originally-discovered boulders containing concentric circles. It tumbled to the edge of the creek and was in jeopardy of being lost forever. Mark and Newman solicited the help of members of the Santa Clara County Board of Supervisors, the Park Commission, and members

of the Historical Heritage Commission in relocating the boulder to a safe location. Funds were allocated to move the 1,000-pound boulder from the creek bed by helicopter to a location on the lawn at the Mt. Madonna County Park Headquarters.[13] After a period of time at this location, the petroglyph boulder was vandalized, and it was decided to move the boulder again (this time by truck) to the Morgan Hill House (the former residence of Mr. Morgan Hill and now home to the Morgan Hill Historical Society). In 1999 the Bay Area Rock Art Research Association requested that the County of Santa Clara move the boulder back to its original site at Chitactac-Adams Heritage County Park and place it in the new on-site interpretive shelter, and in December of that year the move was completed.

Concentric Circles in California and their Interpretation

The concentric circle rock art elements that appear at Chitactac are especially significant as they are the most southerly occurrence in the central Coast Range of this style of concentric circle rock art. Additionally, this site is the only one in the Coast Range where concentric circles appear as the only visible elements on the boulders.

Similar motifs are found at four sites in Mendocino County. While the boulders at Chitactac are sandstone, the boulders utilized in the northern Coast Range are schist, which is softer and easier to carve. On these northern sites, all of which are located on private property, the concentric circle motif appears several times along

*Concentric circle petroglyphs in Mendocino County
with other elements present. Photo by Garry Gillette*

A PCN boulder located east of San Francisco Bay Area. Photo by Garry Gillette

with several other styles of rock art elements. These other elements consist of zigzag lines, ladders, spoked circles, linear elements, possible pecked tracks, and many grooves and cupules. Such styles are referred to as rectilinear and curvilinear abstract. It has been observed by one researcher that when other element styles are found on the same boulder, they are super-positioned above the concentric circle motif. This would indicate that the concentric circle was the older of the elements.[14] Also appearing on the Mendocino County sites are Pecked Curvilinear Nucleated elements (or PCNs). The PCN element is characterized by oval or circular pecked grooves which produce a raised (or nucleated) center. Teresa Miller defined the PCN style in a 1977 thesis from San Francisco State University.[15]

One of the northern sites that was recorded in the 1980s did not reveal the concentric circles on the

Painted (pictograph) boulder showing concentric circles. Boulder appears to also be carved. Photo by Robert Mark.

boulder until a group from the Bay Area Rock Art Research Association visited the site in the fall of 1998. Again, certain lighting conditions (late in the day with a western exposure) were needed to see the petroglyphs.

A second important site in Santa Clara County is on a ranch on Mt. Hamilton and also contains concentric circle elements. This site was first mentioned in a 1933 article appearing in the *Oakland Tribune*[16] and has been the subject of research and a paper by Virginia Hotz-Steenhoven.[17] Hotz-Steenhoven has identified two sets of concentric circles located on a schist boulder. The rock was of similar composition to those in Mendocino County. Also present at this site are many circular and oval grooved elements with many cupules, grooves, and PCNs. The circular elements consist of concentric circles and many deep circles with cups (or cupules) in the center. These are referred to in literature as "cup and ring"—a style of petroglyph found world wide. While the concentric circle elements at this site have several rings similar to the Chitactac petroglyphs, they appear to be of a somewhat different style. The grooves appear deeper, with the raised part of the rings wider than the grooves. The difference may simply relate to geology (schist verses sandstone).

Concentric circle petroglyphs are also present on a site in Marin County known as Ring Mountain. The four elements on this site are also very elusive and can only be observed with optimum lighting. This is the same boulder upon which PCNs were first identified. A site in San Benito County, containing numerous circular elements, pie-shaped depressions, cupules, grooves, and PCNs, also exhibits cup and ring petroglyphs.

In Chumash territory in Santa Barbara County there is a boulder which was removed from its original site because of the flooding of the reservoir at Lake Cachuma. Originally located near the Chumash village of Tequepia, this sandstone boulder displays several concentric circles. They differ from the other sites by having a more pronounced and larger cupule in the center of the rings. Many cupules are also in evidence. Mark and Newman had noted that the existence of this petroglyph boulder is a very rare style for the area, as most rock art in the southern Coast Range, with the exception of cupules, is painted. In other words, they are pictographs. However, the difference in medium (carved verses painted) does not necessarily imply that they are the products of a different culture.[18] Georgia Lee believed that the difference might be "the result of contact with another culture, reflect the breakdown of old patterns of behavior, or indicate a search for new ways to cope with unusual events."[19]

Concentric circles are also depicted in pictograph and petroglyph form in other regions of California. In Monterey County there is a site with concentric circles depicted in bands of red, white and bright slate blue paint. The concentric circle appears to also be pecked. There are also several concentric circle sites in Southern California. One particular site near Los Angeles contains a series of concentric circles with both three and five sets of rings. It has been suggested that both the Chumash and Fernandeño conception of the three or five tiered universe may be depicted in these pictographs. The circles may relate to the ability of the shaman (Native American spiritual leader) and the shaman-initiate to travel between the upper and middle worlds. Their travels are for the purpose of obtaining power or knowledge.[20] Others have expanded on this interpretation of the site by suggesting that the concentric circle element can also "function as a metaphor for a tunnel, path, or passageway from one of these worlds to another."[21] Breck Parkman has suggested that concentric circles "might have been used by Native American shamans as ceremonial targets or places of energy focus." They provided a focus when entering a trance state.[22]

The concentric circle motif at this same site in Southern California has also been identified as an archaeoastronomy site. Archaeoastronomy incorporates the belief that prehistoric people used an interplay of land or rock forms (both natural and embellished) to predict a change of seasons by tracking the movement of the sun. Known as solstice sites, these panels of rock art interacted with a shaft of light produced by the sun that hits the "target" or center of a concentric circle element at the extreme periods of the seasonal movement of the sun. Such extreme points would indicate the longest and shortest days of the year. It may have been important for native cultures to determine when to perform certain rituals such as those that brought back the sun. They may have feared that without such rituals the sun would go completely away. Such information was also important in some areas for determining hunting, planting, and gathering times. At this particular site the sun enters the west end of the elongated tunnel shelter and forms a target at the time of winter solstice, which at that time illuminates the second ring of the concentric circle (or universe symbol). This ring is thought to be the sun's ring in the cosmology of the Chumash.[23] Many other rock art solstice sites have been identified around the world.

In the Coso region of Kern County some pictographs containing concentric circles have been identified as being associated with the Ghost Dance Movements of the 1870s to1890s.[24] As European culture and ideals impacted native cultures, movements known as Ghost Dances were organized in an attempt to revive or perpetuate traditional culture in the face of outside pressure to change. Theories about the Coso site were developed based on an early account by Julian Steward which relates how the Ghost Dance was performed for five nights while the dance leader stood near a center pole. As the dead ancestors appeared, they were touched by the leader.[25] Using this theory, the center dot of the concentric circle would represent the pole, and the rings the number of nights that the dance was held. It has also been speculated that the concentric circles may symbolize other round dances held by the Panamint Valley Shoshone Indians for courting or to bring rain, make the seeds grow, provide plentiful deer for hunting, and bring good harvests. All of these themes were also included as a part of the Ghost Dances.

Both Mark and Newman[26] and Benson and Sehgal[27] have discussed the use of concentric circles by the Ajumawi band of the Pit River Indians in northeastern California. Both articles refer to Floyd Buckskin, a tribal member and an archaeological aide to the California Department of Parks and Recreation, who is interested in the relationship between rock art and his people. In the Mark and Newman article Buckskin tried to locate a "power place" with a tribal elder who told of an instance in the early 1900s when a tribal doctor went into seclusion upon entering a trance state to rid his village of a rattlesnake infestation. While in the trance he was directed to carve in the rock a concentric circle and zig-zag lines that would have the power to keep the snakes from the village. In the second article Buckskin had accompanied the authors to a rock art site in Lassen County where he interpreted the concentric circle motifs to mark the place where "spirit beings" or very powerful shamans could pass through the rock from this world into the next.

Concentric Circles In America

Many additional concentric circle sites are located in the Sierra Nevada Range, Oregon, and Baja California. The Southwest is also an area where concentric circles appear in the rock art. An archaeologist in New Mexico has reported concentric circle motifs on the canyon walls lining both sides of a dry stream bed, and has indicated that there are many references to the element involving the location of water.[28] The concentric circle motif is also incorporated into other rock art elements such as the bodies of human figures or their heads. In a study of the line, tree, and circle motif appearing in the rock art at selected sites in the Southwest, two researchers, Granzberg and Steinbring, have suggested that the circle motif may symbolize "points of entry to our world from other worlds, center spots, settlements, places of peace and harmony, the earth itself, fruition, the culmination of a process, and/or the creative source (or womb) of all things."[29]

Elsewhere on the continent, the concentric circle motif is reported from Alaska to Kentucky and Missouri and in the Southern Appalachians of Georgia. Concentric circle petroglyphs are also found in South America.

While the exact meaning of the concentric circle

petroglyphs at Chitactac can never be determined, there may be a connection between the concentric circles and their location near water. Some years ago while at the Chitactac site, I observed a little boy tossing a pebble into Uvas Creek. What appeared as the small stone disappeared from sight was a series of concentric circles with an entrance point in the center. Is there a symbolic connection? In the mind of the Native American could this be representative of an "entrance" point?

Concentric Circles Worldwide

The concentric circle element is most prevalent in the British Isles. Exhibiting a stylistic difference from the Chitactac site, these elements are more appropriately referred to as "cup and ring," differentiated by a distinctive cupule in their center, as is also present in the site in Santa Barbara. Kalle Sogness, a Norwegian researcher, has reported that the motif also appears in Denmark and Norway, with the northernmost example found at the Trondheim Fjord at about 64 degrees North.[30] Similar styles are found in South Africa, Australia, and Galicia (on the Iberian Peninsula). The most important concentric circle site on continental Europe occurs at Carshenna in Switzerland.

Cupules

Cupules are the other style of rock art at the Chitactac site. These are depressions in stones and have been identified on two boulders in the park. The first cupule boulder to be recorded lies near the edge of the creek. Thirty-eight cupules have been identified on the horizontal plane of the

Cupule boulder from Chitactac, with cupules cascading down the sides in lines. Photo by Robert Mark.

boulder.[31] Recording of the cupules was difficult because there were many natural depressions on the water-worn surface, and several of the natural depressions had been enhanced. The second cupule boulder at Chitactac lies near the southern boundary of the park. Exhibiting a different style than the first boulder, the cupules appear to begin on the top of the boulder and cascade down the vertical sides in rows. There is no evidence of cupules occurring on the same boulders that contain concentric circles, or elsewhere in the park. However, it is important to remember that the sandstone composition of the boulders at Chitactac weathers in such a way that all evidence of earlier elements being placed on the rock may have disappeared.

Cupule petroglyphs are found in many parts of the world and are considered by some to be the oldest style of rock art. Those in France date back 40,000 years.[32] They are especially common in the western part of North America, where more that 1000 sites have been identified.[33] Most of these sites are in the Coast Range of California and appear on many different rock types—granite, basalt, sandstone, serpentine, and schist. Some sites, particularly in the northern Coast Range, exhibit more than 100 cupules on a single boulder, while other boulders may only have one element. Frequently the cupules are found in association with grooves, although this is not the case at Chitactac.

While the cupule element is thought to be the earliest (or one of the earliest) forms of rock art in the New World, there is evidence that cupule production continued into the historic period in some northern groups of California Indians.[34] As for the antiquity of the element, cupule petroglyphs have been recorded at sites where there are cultural deposits that date back 10,000 years.[35] The cupules may or may not be in association with the other cultural evidence. Heizer and Baumhoff, who researched and published on rock art in California in the 1960s, believed that the cupule phenomena goes back 5,000 to 7,000 years B.P. (before present).[36]

There are several ethnographic accounts that indicate the possible function of the cupules. An ethnographic account is a description of the customs, beliefs, and social practices of a prehistoric culture group that were recorded from a native consultant at or shortly following initial contact with the Western World. In the Pomo area of Northern California accounts were recorded that linked the production of cupules with human fertility.[37] Several of these cupule bearing boulders have been identified as "baby rocks."[38] Further to the northeast the Indians of the Shasta area used the production of cupules as a ritual to control the weather.[39] The cupules in this area were referred to as "rain rocks," and the ritual of creating the cupules was thought to cause wind and rain. It was believed that covering the cupule boulder would cause the rain to stop. Some of the other ritual uses of cupules involve fishing, territory marker indicators, markers of deaths and burials, vision quest sites, and in some areas represent the footprints of the first people.[40] Parkman writes that "Sacred Thunder" is the voice of a god, who is a spirit inherent in a storm. It was Sacred Thunder, an ally with the local California rain-making shamans, who brought the rain. He wrote that some of the rituals involved shamans repeatedly hitting a boulder with another rock, thus producing cupules; other uses consisted of pounding on the boulder, which was perceived as a "door" through which the shaman entered the supernatural world.[41] Parkman has also suggested that cupules in the Kumeyaay territory of southern California may have been produced in soft powdery soapstone to provide the pigment for body paint used in rituals.[42] Some sites, also located in southern California, may have involved archaeoastronomy, possibly indicating constellations seen in the night sky. With the broad distribution of cupule sites the ritual function of the cupule petroglyph undoubtedly varied from one tribe to another.

Other Rock Art Sites in the Region
Rock art occurs in many central California areas surrounding Chitactac, and these sites reveal several different styles. Some areas, however, are nearly void of identified sites. While this article refers to counties, it is important to remember that

these geographical lines do not represent prehistoric demography. [43]

San Mateo County

San Mateo County is one of the areas that appears to be nearly void of rock art. Although one site has been recorded ("Rap Rock" near La Honda), the integrity of the site is in question, as it lies near the dining room of a youth camp and has acquired numerous graffiti markings through the years. Recorded as a petroglyph, it was listed as containing pits and grooves and scratches, with a deep pit on the top of the boulder. A recent visit to the site failed to identify any markings other than the historical graffiti. Personal communication with Native Americans and archaeologists has indicated that there are, however, some cupule boulders near Woodside.

Santa Cruz County

Similar to its neighbor to the north, the recorded rock art inventory of Santa Cruz County is also very slim. One site in the Santa Cruz Mountains, initially recorded by students in 1969, was reported to contain a faint painting of a thunderbird-type image. But, a return visit to the area in 1972 failed to find the pictograph in the recorded cave.[44] Similar bird images are not known anywhere in the Coast Range of California. An article in 1895 referred to a site that contained rock art which included simple geometric shapes in a small cave four miles from Saratoga in an almost inaccessible part of the Santa Cruz Mountains.[45] This site has not yet been located again and may be in Santa Clara County.

Santa Clara County

In Santa Clara County the inventory of rock art sites, including the Chitactac site, greatly increases, as does the variety. More than thirty-five sites have been recorded, the majority of these containing cupules, with grooves also present in some instances. It is quite possible that many more unrecorded cupule sites are also present. The most frequent style found in the area is the PCN (Pecked Curvilinear Nucleated). There are six identified PCN sites within the county. Most occur in the eastern part of the county along the

Diablo Range, with the smaller sites closer to the valley floor. While most PCNs have been pecked into soft schist, two smaller sites near Santa Teresa consist of one or two elements pecked into sandstone. Some of the PCN sites in the area also contain cupules and grooves. The PCN style petroglyph has been identified at ninety sites from Oregon to the Southern Coastal Ranges, including a recently identified site on Catalina Island. Although the meaning of these elements is not known, one of their functions may have been similar to the "baby rocks" discussed earlier. While this author's extensive research on the PCN phenomena led to a conclusion that they pertained to fertility (whether human or world renewal),[46] others have suggested that the centers may have been quarried for material to make implements such as charmstones, pipes, beads, etc.[47] While quarrying of PCNs may have occurred as a secondary or opportunistic event, this author does not believe that the element itself was produced with quarrying as the intent.

There are three rock art sites of special significance within the county. The first is the previously mentioned site on Mt. Hamilton, which contains PCNs, concentric circles, cup and rings, cupules, and grooves all inscribed on a large schist boulder. A second site, located in Henry Coe State Park, consists of PCNs, cupules, and grooves, also placed on a schist boulder. The third significant site is the village of Chitactac, with several series of concentric circles and two cupule boulders, discussed earlier, that appear on sandstone.

San Benito County

To the south of Santa Clara County and to the east of Monterey lies the County of San Benito. While limited research has been carried out in this rural area populated by numerous ranches, ten petroglyph sites have been recorded. The vast majority of these are small cupule sites. An exception is what this author considers a pivotal site in the study of PCNs and other circular motifs. Usually located underwater in a flooded reservoir, it was recently exposed by a break in the gate of the dam. A 30-meter-long schist boulder reveals a very large concentration of PCN-style

Circular petroglyphs from reservoir in San Benito County. Elements consist of PCNs and pie-tin shaped depressions. Photo by Garry Gillette.

Line of cupules at site in San Benito County. PCNs are visible in the rear of photo. Photo by Garry Gillette.

elements of all sizes and shapes, many circular elements, including some large pie-tin shaped depressions, cup and rings, numerous grooves, and many cupules. A ridge on the boulder contains an alignment of cupules. First identified in 1950, this boulder has been the subject of many studies.[48] While no similar petroglyphs have been recorded in the area, local property owners have mentioned knowledge of a painted limestone cave near the site.

Monterey County

While stylistically different from the rock art to the north, the most colorful sites are found in Monterey County. Although a granite boulder at the Presidio in Monterey contains many cupules, the majority of the more than forty identified sites consist of an abstract polychrome style that was identified as the South Coast Painted Style by Heizer and Clewlow.[49] These pictograph sites are less ornate than the elaborate Chumash (Santa Barbara) style to the south and that of the Yokuts (Southern Sierra) style to the east. They represent the most northern painted sites south of the Bay Area and are numerous.[50] The majority of the sites are located in the Vaqueros sandstone caves of the Santa Lucia Range and consist of red painted elements placed on smoke-blackened walls. Some caves are decorated with polychrome designs in red, black, and white. Elements represented in these caves range from geometric shapes, grids, cross-hatches, and lattice designs, to a few stick figure and animal shapes. Also present are the

Pictographs from Monterey County showing South Coast Painted Style. Photo by Robert Mark.

Pictographs from Monterey County showing South Coast Painted Style. Photo by Robert Mark.

previously mentioned concentric circle elements, depicted in bands of red, white, and slate blue. Many of the recorded sites also include many nearby sheltered areas that also contain pictographs. Several of the sites are located in the ethnographic Esselen territory, south and east of the area prehistorically occupied by the Ohlone people.

Several caves in Monterey County contain numerous hand prints executed in white paint. One of these, known as the Cave of the Hands, contains more than 200 of the hand print elements. The most studied and documented cave in the area is La Cueva Pintada on the Hunter Liggett Army Base. This pictograph site contains hundreds of images and some of the best preserved rock paintings in central California. First recorded by J. Alden Mason about 1910, it has been mentioned in several rock art inventories in the succeeding years. In 1980 an archaeological consulting firm, under the direction of Gary Breschini and Trudy Haversat, and including a large number of volunteers, undertook the task of completely documenting this site, which is listed on the National Register of Historic Places. The result of their monumental research project is contained in a technical report and three large volumes of sketches of the La Cueva Pintada elements.[51]

Summary
The rock art of Chitactac and the surrounding region represents distinct styles that are unique to this immediate area and may provide insight into the early inhabitants of the area. The style of the concentric circle elements, PCNs, and the cupules also link the local cultural groups to the people in other parts of the Coast Range of California. The similarity of the style of concentric circle petroglyphs with the sites to the north in Mendocino County and the existence of several PCN-style sites within the area likely indicate a very early use of the sites. Both of these styles and the cupules are believed to represent some of the oldest rock art of the New World.

The newly dedicated Chitactac-Adams Heritage County Park, with its interpretive signs, shelter, and programs, now provides the public an opportunity to learn more about the people who made them and their way of life. While speculation can be interesting, the true meaning of the rock art elements can only be known through the unreachable minds of those who carved or painted them on the rocks so long ago.

Notes:

1 Breck Parkman, Archaeologist with the California State Department of Parks and Recreation, and former president of the Society for California Archaeology, has reviewed the paper in this journal.

2 Identification of the location of the Village of Chitactac is found on maps appearing in Randall Milliken, "The Costanoan-Yokuts Language Boundary in the Contact Period" in *The Ohlone Past and Present*, ed. Lowell John Bean (Menlo Park: Ballena Press, 1994), p.166; and in Chester King, "Central Ohlone Ethnohistory" in *The Ohlone Past and Present,* p. 205.

3 *Chitactac-Adams Heritage County Park,* brochure prepared by the County of Santa Clara Parks and Recreation Department, 1998 (revised July, 1999).

4 *Phase II Archaeological Testing Report for Santa Clara Parks and Recreation Department*, Submitted by Archaeological Resource Management (Robert Cartier, Principal) 1995, p.7.

5 Patricia Baldwin Escamilla, *A Short History of Gilroy* (Gilroy: Gilroy Historical Society Museum, 1997). See also the chart in King, "Central Ohlone Ethnohistory," p. 207.

6 Information shared in a personal communication with Alan Leventhal of the College of Social Science at San Jose State University, an archaeologist and ethnohistorian for the Amah-Mutsun Ohlone, 1999.

7 Hubert Howe Bancroft, *History of California* (Santa Barbara: Wallace Hebberd) 1825-1840, v. III, p. 68. Joaquin Solis was a convict sentenced to California as a result of "brutal crimes." According to Bancroft, his punishment would have been more severe if he had not previously served his country (Mexico) in the war for independence from Spain. Volume IV of Bancroft (p. 287) provides a further explanation of the practice of sending criminals to settle California. It refers to the formation of a "large force" to be sent to California in 1842. A decree was issued through the minister of justice to select 300 criminals from the prisons of Mexico. Apparently those who had a trade were more likely to be chosen and could be released from the remainder of their prison term if they behaved well on the journey or if they rendered services. Their families would be assisted in joining them in California and they would be given lands and implements to become colonists.

8 *Gilroy Dispatch*, June 6, 1979, 15:1-4.

9 Eugene Sawer, *History of Santa Clara County*, (Los Angeles: Historic Record Company, 1922), p. 1055.

10 Karl Gurcke, *A Yokut Indian Site in the Foothills of the Santa Cruz Mountains*. Manuscript on file at the Northwest Information Center at California State University, Sonoma, Rohnert Park, 1970:S-5316.

11 E. Breck Parkman, "California Dreamin': Cupule Petroglyph Occurrences in the American West," in *Rock Art Studies in the Americas,* ed. Jack Steinbring (Oxford: Oxbow Books, 1995), p. 1.

12 Evelyn Newman and Robert Mark, "Uvas Creek (CA-SCL-111): A Unique Petroglyph Site In The San Francisco Bay Area," in *Rock Art Papers*, ed. Ken Hedges (San Diego: Museum of Man, 1986) v. 3, pp. 191-200; and, Robert Mark and Evelyn Newman, "Computer-Graphics Assisted Recording Uvas Creek" in *American Indian Rock Art*, ed. William D. Hyder (San Miguel: American Rock Art Research Association, 1993) v. 12, pp.137-149.

13 "SCL-111 "Up" Date," *Bay Area Rock Art News* (San Francisco: Bay Area Rock Art Research Association, 1988) v. VI, no. 1, pp. 9-10.

14 The antiquity of concentric circles is based on a personal communication with Mark Gary, 1999, an archaeologist with the California Department of Forestry, Mendocino County, and a rock art researcher.

15 Teresa Miller, "Identification and Recording of Prehistoric Petroglyphs in Marin and Related Bay Area Counties," M.A.Thesis on file in the Department of Anthropology, California State University, San Francisco, 1977.

16 *Oakland Tribune*, August 16, 1933, p. 9D.

17 Virginia Hotz-Steenhoven, "Petroglyphs of the San Francisco Bay Region and Related Areas," *Rock Art Papers* (San Diego: Museum of Man, 1986) v. 3, pp. 175-189.

[18] Robert Mark and Evelyn Newman, "Cup and Ring Petroglyphs in Northern California and Beyond," *Rock Art Studies in the Americas,* ed. Jack Steinbring (Oxford: Oxbow Books, 1995), p. 19.

[19] Georgia Lee, "Two Unusual Petroglyphs From Santa Barbara County," *The Masterkey* 54, n. 1, 1980, pp. 30-34.

[20] Bob Edberg, "Shamans and Chiefs: Visions of the Future," in *Earth and Sky,* ed. Arlene Benson and Tom Hoskinson (Thousand Oaks: Slo'w Press, 1985), p. 91.

[21] Arlene Benson and Linda Sehgal, "The Light at the End of the Tunnel," in *Rock Art Papers,* ed. Ken Hedges (San Diego: Museum of Man, 1987), v. 5, pp. 1-16.

[22] Mark and Newman, "Cup and Ring Petroglyphs in Northern California and Beyond," p. 15.

[23] Benson and Sehgal, p. 10.

[24] Robert Schiffman and Stephen Andrews, "Pictographs of the Ghost Dance," in *Pictographs of the Coso Region,* ed. Robert Schiffman, David Whitley, Alan Garfinkel, and Stephen Andrews (Bakersfield: Bakersfield College Publications, 1982), v. 2, pp. 79-95. The Ghost Dance Indian religious movement, which occurred between 1870 and 1890, was an attempt by the Indians to recover their lost culture which was being displaced by the "white man." While prevalent in many parts of California and the West, there was not much impact within the areas where the Mission system had already influenced native culture.

[25] Julian Steward, "Cultural Element Distributions: XIII Nevada Shoshone," *Anthropological Records,* (Berkeley: University of California Press, 1941), n. 4, p. 267.

[26] Mark and Newman, "Cup and Ring Petroglyphs in Northern California and Beyond," p. 13.

[27] Benson and Sehgal, pp. 6-7.

[28] Personal communication (1999) with Julie McNew, a rock art researcher in southern New Mexico. Julie is the part owner of CRM firm in Las Cruces, and she specializes in rock art of the Jornada Mogollon region.

[29] Gary Granzberg and Jack Steinbring, "The Line, Tree, and Circle in Rock Art and Pictography: Some Selected Examples From the Southwest," in *Rock Art Studies in the Americas,* ed. Jack Steinbring (Oxford: Oxbow Books, 1995), p. 46.

[30] Personal communication with Kalle Sogness, a rock art researcher in Norway and Director of the StjØrdal Museum (located in a small town 30 km east of Trondheim) and a representative to the International Federation of Rock Art Organizations (IFORAO).

[31] Mark and Newman, "Computer-Graphics Assisted Recording Uvas Creek in American Indian Rock Art," pp. 140, fig. 12h.

[32] Campbell Grant, *Rock Art of the American Indian,* (New York: Promontory Press, 1967), p. 152. While Grant refers to cupules as the oldest form in the New World, E. Breck Parkman has indicated that they appeared back at least 40,000 years in France. This reference is found in his article "The Western Rain-Making Process," *Journal of California and Great Basin Anthropology* (1993), v. 15, p. 101.

[33] Parkman,"The Western Rain-Making Process," p. 1.

[34] Ibid, p. 5.

[35] Ibid, p. 7.

[36] Robert Heizer and Martin Baumhoff, *Prehistoric Rock Art Nevada and Eastern California* (Berkeley: University of California Press, 1962), p. 234.

[37] There are several early ethnographic reports that reference fertility rituals in northern California. Two of the most often referred to are: S. Barrett, "Material Aspects of the Pomo Culture," *Bulletin of the Public Museum of the City of Milwaukee* (Milwaukee: Public Museum, 1952), p. 165; and Edwin Loeb, "Pomo Folkways," *University of California Publications in American Archaeology and Ethnology* (1926) pp. 247-248.

38 Ken Hedges, "A Re-examination of the Pomo Baby Rocks," in *American Indian Rock Art*, ed. Frank Bock (El Toro: American Rock Art Research Association, 1983) v. 9, pp. 10-21.

39 Robert Heizer, "Sacred Rain-Rocks of Northern California," *University of California Archaeological Survey Reports* (Berkeley: University of California Press, 1953), n. 20, pp. 33-38.

40 Parkman, "California Dreamin': Cupule Petroglyph Occurrences in the American West," pp. 8-10.

41 Parkman, "The Western Rain-Making Process," pp. 90, 95-96.

42 Parkman, "California Dreamin': Cupule Petroglyph Occurrences in the American West," p. 9.

43 In 1876 Col. Garrick Mallery began recording petroglyphs and published *Picture-Writing of the American Indian* in 1893 (Tenth Annual Report to the Secretary of the Smithsonian Institution). In the 1920s Julian Steward identified 129 petroglyph and pictograph sites in California ("Petroglyphs of California and the Adjoining States," *University of California Publications in American Archaeology and Ethnology*, Berkeley: University of California Press, 1929. v.24, n.2, pp. 47-238). In 1948 Robert Heizer began a more intense recording of rock art sites of California and, with Martin Baumhoff, published the results of their studies in 1962 (Heizer and Baumhoff); and in 1973, with C.W. Clewlow, Jr, Heizer published *Prehistoric Rock Art of California* (Ramona: Ballena Press, 2 vol.). Since that time the inventory of sites has grown dramatically. The publication compiled from notes left by the late Bill Sonin:*California Rock Art, An Annotated Site Inventory and Bibliography* . ed. M. Leigh Marymor (Los Angeles: Rock Art Archive of the Institute of Archaeology, University of California press, 1995) inventories rock art sites by California counties.

44 Bill Sonin, *California Rock Art: An Annotated Site Inventory and Bibliography*,, p. 193.

45 Ibid.

46 Donna Gillette, "PCNs of the Coast Ranges of California: Religious Expression or the Result of Quarrying," M. A. Thesis (Salinas: Coyote Press, 1998).

47 Pete Rhode, "Are Charmstones Hatched from PCNs?" *Bay Area Rock Art News* (San Francisco: Bay Area Rock Art Research Association, 1988) v. IX, no. 2, pp. 8-10.

48 Robert Mark, Evelyn Newman, and Bruce Rogers, "Site SBN12 Revisited," *Rock Art Papers*, ed. Ken Hedges (San Diego: Museum of Man, 1989), v. 7, pp. 49-52. This interesting rock art site was first identified in 1950 by Arnold Pilling as a petroglyph site. In 1960 it was reexamined by Jay von Werlhof and reclassified in University of California, Berkeley records as a bowl quarry. The Mark et al. article listed above was the first to take an in-depth look at the boulder, after it had been flooded by the reservoir. The dam was empty due to a drought. Mark et.al. came to the conclusion that the site was indeed a petroglyph site.

49 Robert Heizer and C.W. Clewlow, Jr., *Prehistoric Rock Art of California* (Ramona: Ballena Press, 1973), 2 v., p. 37-38.

50 Klause Wellman, *A Survey of North American Indian Rock Art* (Graz, Austria: Akademische Druck-u. Vesrlaganstalt, 1979).

51 Gary Breschini and Trudy Haversat, *La Cueva Pintada: A Technical Report on Documenting the Rock Paintings at National Register Site CA-MNT-256* (Salinas: Coyote Press, 1980).

Santa Cruz
County
History Journal
Issue 5, 2001

Santa Cruz Baskets

by Linda Yamane

Few baskets thought to be of Ohlone manufacture have survived into the present. Of these, many are part of European museum collections in Russia, France, Germany, England and elsewhere. In the United States, a small number are housed in east coast museums and there are several within California. In the Monterey Bay area, there are two at Mission San Carlos in Carmel, two at the Pacific Grove Museum of Natural History, one at the Pacific House Museum (Monterey State Historic Parks) in Monterey, one at the Santa Cruz Museum of Natural History, and one in a private collection in Aptos. Another is part of the San Jose Historical Museum collection in San Jose.

Surprisingly, we have four baskets within California that are believed to have originated in Santa Cruz. Here they are, together again for the first time in many years, on the pages of this journal.

This coiled basket is on permanent display at the Santa Cruz Museum of Natural History, where you can visit it without special arrangement. The 3-rod foundation is probably willow and is wrapped with sedge and a small amount of bracken fern at the base. It is ornamented with white and red glass beads and still retains the remnants of three horizontal bands of acorn woodpecker scalp feathers, which once covered the basket surface between the beaded rows. Photo by Linda Yamane, courtesy of Santa Cruz Museum of Natural History.

This small basket, also on permanent display, may be found at the Museum of Natural History in Pacific Grove. It is coiled on a 3-rod willow foundation, wrapped with sedge. The red and green horizontal bands of featherwork are acorn woodpecker and mallard duck. Photo by Linda Yamane, courtesy of Pacific Grove Museum of Natural History.

This tiny basket, which is part of a private collection, is coiled on a 3-rod willow foundation, wrapped with sedge. The outer walls were once covered with white glass beads, many of which no longer remain. The basket was purchased in the late 1960s from a school mate who found the basket in Santa Cruz under a rock shelter, in an area where people dumped their garbage. Photo by Linda Yamane, courtesy of Craig Bates.

Part of the State of California collection housed in a West Sacramento warehouse facility, this basket has an old label attached which reads, "Santa Cruz—La Teresa." It is coiled on a 3-rod foundation, wrapped with sedge. The parallelogram designs, which are now quite faded, are of dyed sedge. The rim and base of the basket are damaged, and the basket is in fragile condition. Photo by Linda Yamane, courtesy of State of California Department of Parks and Recreation, State Museum Resource Center.

Santa Cruz
County
History Journal
Issue 5, 2001

Contemporary Basket Weavers

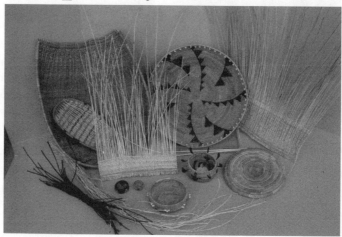

These baskets were made by Linda Yamane using traditional Ohlone materials and techniques. The small one near the center is the first basket she wove. It is made of willow, sedge, and bulrush with quail topknot feathers at the rim. The basket holds a favorite picture of her Grandma, Beatrice Barcelone. Long before starting to weave, she had to harvest and process the native plant materials, a labor-intensive activity. Two of these materials are shown in the foreground; the sedge runners are white, the bulrush roots black. The large basket on the left is called a "walaheen" or "warseen," a basket that was used by the Ohlone for winnowing and for roasting seeds. This basket is significant because it is the first walaheen to be made by an Ohlone person in more than 100 years. Linda says, "When we weave our baskets, we bring honor and respect to our ancestors and keep our ties to them alive." Photo courtesy of Linda Yamane.

"It was really something to learn how to handle the sedge and to see the way it grows—the way Great Spirit has put things and planted it for our people, for all people, to live by."

—Delia Casados
(Costanoan-Rumsen Carmel Tribe), 1999

"Weaving feels so natural—the technique and just the way it feels in my hand, like it belongs there. It brings us together, and it brings us closer to our ancestors and the land.

—Rosalie McCracken
(Costanoan-Rumsen Carmel Tribe), 1999

Delia Casados (left) and Rosalie McCracken of the Costanoan-Rumsen Carmel Tribe learn to gather sedge for basketry, August 1999. Photo by Linda Yamane.

From left to right, Linda Yamane, Lydia Bojorquez and Carol Bachmann share a moment of fun while demonstrating Ohlone basketry at "A Gathering of Ohlone Peoples," Coyote Hills Regional Park in Fremont, October 2000. Photo by Bev Ortiz.

"I enjoy singing and I'm learning the language. This is all very important to me to be able to learn all this and teach it to my family so that they can learn about our people, our ancestors. It's good to be able to bring these songs back to life again. I'm also a basketweaver and I enjoy my basketry and being able to go out and gather the materials."

—**Lydia Bojorquez**
(Rumsen-Kakoon Ohlone), 2000

"Digging the sedge makes me think about and praise our ancestors, what hard work they did. A lot of people say they just relaxed all day long, but I think they were very hard-working people."
—**Kathy Petty**
(Mutsun Ohlone), 1995

'I've been learning how to gather the basketry materials and in the process have learned how hard our ancestors had to work in their lives. I really respect them for that."

—**Juanita Ingalls**
(Mutsun Ohlone), 1995

"My most current effort is to bring back our dances. Based on information pulled from research over the years, a group of us are attempting to reconstruct our dances in the most authentic way possible. With support from a California Arts Council Traditional Folk Arts Program grant, we are learning to make regalia, and are meeting regularly to sort out many complex issues. As always, it is not a simple task, but as we move through one slow step at a time, we find ourselves a little closer to our dream and will soon dance our dream into reality."

—**Linda Yamane**
(Rumsien Ohlone), 2001

"I've been enjoying learning to make baskets and am finishing my third one now. Each one takes a really long time. Besides gathering and cleaning the materials, it's a lot of work to get the sedge ready to weave. I live in Stockton, but gather sedge out at Fort Ord with my friend Linda Yamane. We have a beautiful gathering spot under the oak trees. I also make soap root brushes and have learned to prepare some of our traditional foods. I'm glad to learn these things so we can keep them alive for the future."

—**Carol Bachmann**
(Mutsun Ohlone), 1998

Kathy Petty (left) and her mother Juanita Ingalls learn to dig sedge at Fort Ord BLM lands, 1995. Photo by Linda Yamane.

Santa Cruz
County
History Journal
Issue 5, 2001

134

Quirina Luna Costillas learns the basics of beginning a coiled Ohlone basket, 1998. Photo by Linda Yamane.

Chuck Striplen at California Indian Storytelling Festival, Indian Canyon, Hollister, 1995. Photo by Linda Yamane.

"I've been working on Mutsun language for 4 or 5 years now. As a person, it helps me know who I am. It's filled that gap in my life, and I'm teaching my children as I learn. We speak Mutsun every day in our home. They don't always speak back in the language, but they understand what I'm saying and return with their answer in English. I want my children to have the opportunity to have what I didn't have growing up—to know who they are. A lot of people go through life and never know who they are. I used to wonder, "What am I here for?" Now I know this is what I was meant to do." (Mutsun/Awaswas/Rumsen Ohlone), 2000

—Quirina Luna Costillas
(Mutsun/ Awaswas/ Rumsen Ohlone), 2000

"For me, the basket is a wondrous creation reflective not only of the incredible skill of the weaver, but of the landscape from which its parts were gathered. In that gathering process, a weaver interacts with many aspects of the natural world that reflect not only a need for materials, but an obligation to those resources. The very act of gathering, in almost every case, is beneficial to the plant spiritually AND physiologically. When some of those basket plants are later burned to produce good shoots for next year's baskets, the entire system benefits from those nutrients released by burning. As new weavers, especially as part of a culture in which these traditions are being restored in their entirety, we must relearn not only how to weave a basket, but how to manage and care for that ecological system that gives us our basket materials. That is our obligation, and how we earn the right to weave."

—Chuck Striplen
(Mutsun Ohlone), 2001

Profile: Rico Miranda

Rico Miranda gathering manzanita berries in "walaheen" basket made by Linda Yamane, 1999. Photo by Linda Yamane.

"I'm learning and incorporating traditional values and lifeways into my current life. As a teacher, I bring who I am as an Ohlone person into the classroom as an example of how the kids can be proud of who they are and whatever cultural background they come from. This helps them appreciate the diverse cultures they come in contact with every day. The most important thing I try to teach is to honor who they are, to respect themselves and others."

—**Rico Miranda**
(Rumsien Ohlone), 2001

Traditional Salinan Musical Instruments

by Eduardo José (Joe) Freeman

The ancient civilization and culture of our ancestors developed and flourished on the central coast of California for at least 10,000 years. The modern name that was given to us is Salinan, which is derived from the Spanish word (Salina) for "salt mine." In our language, we referred to ourselves as *T'owt'aa'l* or *T'epot'aha'l* which translate as People.

Katherine Turner, a linguist, studied the Salinan language for her doctorate degree. In 1983, Dr. Turner wrote: "Taken as a whole, the evidence suggests Salinan as the oldest population in this area of California with, possibly, a more eastern and southern extent than historically understood. The Chumash would be the first intrusive peoples between the Salinan speakers and Uto-Aztecan speaking peoples" (Turner, 1983: 231).

In the late 1700s, the millennia-old existence of our ancestors was dramatically altered by the arrival of the Spanish and their mission system. "Naturally, every phase of primitive religion was strictly tabu, and all contra-European customs prohibited" (Mason, 1912: 116). In the missions there was constant pressure to conform to a foreign way of thinking and living in the world. In spite of the pressures and the high death rates in the missions, our people and the culture endured. Our people continued gathering, preparing and feasting on acorns until the 1930s or 1940s. Our language was spoken into the 1950s. Our connections to our native community and our homeland have remained intact. Indeed, more than sixty percent of our tribal members continue to live within the boundaries of our traditional homeland. And, we continue to sing our songs.

Today, our tribal government is working to secure formal recognition of our sovereignty from the United States of America. Our goals are to protect our ancient cultural sites and ancestral remains; revitalize our ancestral culture and language; attain economic and political independence for our community; and, ensure that our elders and children have access to essential services including basic health and educational opportunities.

There is evidence that some Salinans never did enter the missions and that others attempted to keep the traditions alive within the adobe walls of the missions. In 1910, Dr. Alfred L. Kroeber sent J. Alden Mason to Jolon, California to study the Salinan people. A justice of the peace named J. Alonzo Forbes served as a consultant and interpreter for Mason. Forbes apparently understood English, Spanish, and a Salinan dialect. Mason reports that Forbes "was told by elder natives that the Indians who held their ceremonies in this place (Devil's Canyon) belonged to the Bear totem and that they furnished the renegades of the mission, resisted the padres and never became entirely converted" (Mason, 1912: 189).

In 1993, Betty Rivers and Terry Jones wrote, "Throughout Harrington's notes, the descendants refer to Salinan material culture. These individuals were not living in the past; rather the past was more a part of their lives than had been believed. Along with the language and a familiarity with the old ways, the men and women with whom Harrington worked demonstrated a remarkable knowledge of Salinan geography" (Rivers and Jones, 1993:158).

This evidence tells us why the Salinan elders who were alive in the early 1900s spoke the language fluently and still remembered the traditional songs, dances, stories and practices. They were not speaking about something that they had simply heard stories about. They were speaking from live experience. The culture and language were still very much alive and vibrant despite the influence of a foreign culture. What follows is information they shared with researchers about traditional Salinan musical instruments.

On December 12, 1912, the University of California Publications released *The Ethnology of The Salinan Indians* by J. Alden Mason. Much of the material for his publication "was collected in Monterey County, California, during the month of September, 1910." Perfecta Encinales and Jose Cruz, both Salinans, provided the information.

Mason's ethnology quotes a report about Salinans at Mission San Antonio that had been translated by Dr. A. L. Kroeber. The reports states, "They have another musical instrument, which consists of a wooden bow to which a string of sinew is bound, producing a note" (Mason, 1912:157). Mason further states that, "Nothing could be learned concerning the musical bow, except that the mouth supplied the resonance chamber" (Mason, 1912: 157).

Mason summarizes what he learned about Salinan dances and musical instruments from Cruz and Encinales. He states that, "Naturally all dances of a religious significance were strictly forbidden by the Spanish missionaries and have largely been forgotten. Most of the Salinan dances were performed by individuals. The music was supplied by rattles of split sticks, cocoons, or rattlesnake rattles, and by rasps and whistles. Rattlesnake rattles were used by all participants. The flutes and possibly other instruments may have been used at dances" (Mason, 1912:177).

Mason's publication includes a photograph of a Salinan musical rasp that at the time was located at the Dutton Museum in Jolon, California (Mason, 1912: 231). It is possible that the rasp in the photo may still be in existence and tribal members hope to locate it someday. R. F. Heizer and M. A. Whipple state in *The California Indians* that "The

notched scraper or musical rasp has been reported only from the Salinans" (Heizer, Whipple, 1971: 19).

On March 6, 1942, the University of California Press published *Culture Element Distributions: XIX: Central California Coast* by John P. Harrington who had collected data from Gabrielino, Chumash and Salinan descendants thirty years before. The Salinans who provided information to Harrington included Antonio Gomez and Pacifico Gallego.

In his publication, Harrington lists the following Salinan musical instruments (Harrington, 1942: 28-29):

Cocoon rattles attached to stick handles.
Split stick clappers.
Notched musical rasps.
Bull roarers.
Baskets may have been scraped for a percussive effect.
Musical bows played with fingers.
Whistles made from single bird bone.
Whistles made from wood (cane or elder) with asphalt stops.
Wooden flutes that were blown from the end and probably had four holes.
Drums of any kind were noted as absent.

*Split-stick Clappers
Illustration by Linda Yamane*

The summer 1998 issue of *News From Native California* featured a special report on musical instruments of Native California. The report states that the bull roarer is "known in many parts of Native America and the rest of the world. A bull roarer is a flat piece of wood on a string that, when whirled overhead, reverberates at a deep visceral pitch. The length of the wood varies, from under a foot to two feet" (Gendar, 1998: 40).

The report from News also states that the Yurok and Tolowa drums of Northwestern California are "...virtually the only hide-covered drum in California tradition; rattles and clapper-sticks are still the hand-held rhythm instruments of choice in traditional music. The other important drum in California is found in the roundhouses of the central part of the state. Made of planks or a hollowed-out log, and placed over a pit to resonate well when the drummer beats on it with a pole, its deep boom is an essential part of ceremonies" (Gendar, 1998: 30).

None of the Salinan elders who spoke with Mason or Harrington mentioned drums. However, Jose Cruz did tell Mason that Salinans danced the Kuksui. Since the Kuksui dance in central California is generally associated with the type of round-house drum referred to above, it is possible that Salinan ancestors may have used such a drum for our version of the Kuksui. Future research may answer this question one way or another.

Our traditional stories tell us that we are related to all that lives. We remember that when we gather and shape the materials that are used to make our traditional instruments. And, we remember our ancestors when the voices of our singers blend with the sounds of our instruments from the earth.

Bibliography

Gendar, Jeannine. 1998. "California Drumming," *News From Native California: An Inside View of the California Indian World*, Vol. 11, No. 4 (Summer).

Gendar, Jeannine. 1998. "Buzzers, Bows & Bull Roarers," *News From Native California: An Inside View of the California Indian World*, Vol. 11, No. 4 (Summer).

Harrington, John P. 1942. "Cultural Element Distributions: XIX," *Central California Coast*, Berkeley & Los Angeles: University of California Press (March 6).

Heizer, R. F. and Whipple, M.A. 1971. *The California Indians: A Source Book*, Berkeley: University of California Press, 2nd edition.

Mason, J. Alden. 1912. *The Ethnology of The Salinan Indians*, Berkeley: University of California Publications in American Archaeology and Ethnology, Vol 10, No. 4 (December 14).

Rivers, Betty. 1994. "Many Others Dancing, An Ethnography of Obispeno Chumash," *Toward A Prehistory of Morro Bay: Phase II Archaeological Investigations for the Highway 41 Widening Project*, San Luis Obispo County, California.

Rivers, Betty and Jones, Terry. 1993. "Walking Along Deer Trails: A Contribution to Salinan Ethnogeography Based on the Field Notes of John Peabody Harrington," *Journal of California and Great Basin Anthropology*, Vol. 15, No. 2.

Turner, Katherine. 1983. "Areal and Genetic Affiliations of the Salinan," Lawrence, Kansas: Linguistics Graduate Student Association, University of Kansas.

Santa Cruz
County
History Journal
Issue 5, 2002

Profile: Theodore Bonillas

Theodore Bonillas, 2000. Photo by Linda Yamane.

"I learned herbal plant medicines from my mother when I was 7 or 8 years old. She showed me how to pick them and how to use them. It was my job to collect them for her to make medicines for the different people who needed them in our town. Throughout the years, we used these medicines in our own family, but there wasn't much interest elsewhere. Now, people are very interested in traditional Indian ways, and I have a chance to share this knowledge. It's been an honor for me to teach about the uses of herbal medicines and to be able to carry on the traditions my mother taught me."

—**Theodore Bonillas**
(Rumsien/ Mutsun Ohlone), 2001

Ohlone Medicinal Uses of Plants

by Charles R. Smith

"The land abounds in these natural remedies and to classify the plants, give their names and describe their properties, the presence of a botanist would be required. It is certain that many illnesses are cured by these people and they have their remedies for everything, many quite effective. For this reason not a few prefer their herbs and roots to our unguents and salves."

—Reply by Frays Sancho and Cabot,
Franciscan missionaries at Mission San Antonio
as to what knowledge the natives had of medicines.

Geiger and Meighan. 1976: 71

Disclaimer

The purpose of this article is to serve as a reference source on some of the medical practices and medicinal plants used by the Ohlone from the late 18th through the early decades of the 20th centuries. This article is not intended for prescribing medicines nor for curing afflictions. The author is an anthropologist without medical expertise and therefore can render no judgment on the efficacy of the remedies and treatments described. Some of the plants discussed in this article occur only sparingly in the environment today, and should not be disturbed since widespread collection could result in their extermination. Other plants which I discuss are extremely toxic and under no circumstances should they be collected or should one attempt to use any of the plants mentioned in this article in an attempt to replicate Ohlone treatments. I emphasize that the use of any of the information in this article for purposes of self-treatment without consulting a physician can be dangerous.

For clarity I have not used scientific names for plants in the body of the text. All plants mentioned are listed alphabetically at the end of the article with their scientific names.

Introduction

This paper provides a brief overview of semi-traditional medical beliefs and practices, especially those using plants, as they existed in the nineteenth and early decades of the twentieth century among the Ohlone. The overview is based primarily on three data sets: (1) a series of documents known as *Preguntas y Respuestas* (questions and replies), written between 1813 and 1815 by the Franciscan missionaries of the seven missions established in Ohlone territory; (2) information collected during the first three decades of the twentieth century by several scholars including the anthropologist Alfred Kroeber, the ethnographer-linguist John Peabody Harrington, and the self-taught ethnographer C. Hart Merriam; and (3) various archival and published ethnographic and ethnohistoric records, including Kroeber's *Handbook of the Indians of California* (1925), Harrington's *Culture Element Distributions, XIX: Central California Coast* (1942), Merriam's *Ethnographic Notes on California Indian Tribes, III. Ethnological Notes of Central California Tribes* (1967), and Barbara Bocek's *Ethnobotany of Costanoan Indians, California, Based on Collections by John P. Harrington* (1984). Ethnobotanical information acquired from several Ohlone living in the Watsonville, California area during the 1970s and early 1980s by this paper's author has also been included in the present article.

Since most of the data on which this overview is based was collected more than 100 years after the European colonization of Ohlone territory, this paper is not strictly about Ohlone medical beliefs and practices, but rather about "Californio-Rumsen/Mutsun Ohlone" medicine. By the time researchers began working with the native peoples of the Monterey and San Francisco Bay regions, the Ohlone had become well assimilated into California's Mexican-American and Euro-American communities. As a result, non-native medical beliefs and practices had been acquired by the Ohlone. In addition, during the nineteenth century, hundreds of non-native plants were introduced into, and had become an integral part of, the California landscape. The Ohlone added many of these to their already extensive herbal pharmacopoeias. Consequently, Ohlone medical ethnobotanical data combines aboriginal and acquired beliefs about both native and non-native plants. Furthermore, the majority of Harrington's, Merriam's, and Kroeber's Ohlone consultants were members of the Rumsen and Mutsun language groups (whose territories included, respectively, the Carmel and Salinas River valleys, and the upper Pajaro River drainage and the upper Santa Clara Valley and the lower San Benito River drainage), and the bulk of the data those researchers collected reflects the cultural understandings of only two of the traditional Ohlone nations. Except where noted, this data bias is reflected in the present article.

In addition, although both Merriam and Harrington were extremely interested in Ohlone ethnobotanical knowledge, the way in which both researchers collected, identified, and wrote about plant specimens varied from very good to highly questionable. For example, although Harrington collected more than 500 plant specimens from a number of different Rumsen (Monterey and Carmel regions) and Mutsun (San Juan Bautista and Gilroy area) people, none of his specimens were labeled consistently, none of the people who collected the plants were trained in botany, most of

the plants he acquired are poorly preserved, and the majority of the plant names recorded by him were not Ohlone, but what he referred to in his notes as "Cs.," or the local California Spanish. To compound the problem of accurately identifying the plants, while both Harrington and Merriam sometimes had qualified botanists identify specimens collected, the botanical nomenclature, both common and scientific, in many instances has changed frequently since the beginning of the twentieth century. Therefore, in listing herein the plants used by the Ohlone, the common and scientific nomenclature used, no matter how archaic, is in the majority of examples, that of the original fieldworkers. Except in those cases where the author of the present work was able, with complete confidence, to update the original fieldworkers' nomenclature, the plant names which appear in the present paper, whether given in English (such as California walnut) or in California Spanish (such as 'yerba del pasmo'), are those of Merriam or Harrington.

While it is tempting to assume that one can simply translate the California Spanish into English and then look for the correct scientific name, or find the California Spanish name, with its scientific equivalent, in works dealing with other California Indians and apply such a name to the Ohlone data, to do so would be unwise. For example, Harrington (1942) notes that sores were sometimes treated with a healing salve made from a mixture of, among other plants, 'yerba del pasmo.' Unfortunately, Harrington provided no further identifying data. However, 'yerba del pasmo' is mentioned in works dealing with other native Californians. The Salinan, who occupied territory south of the Ohlone, were said to use 'yerba del pasmo', identified as Ribbon Bush, *Adenostoma sparsifolium*, to treat skin abscesses (Weber 1978:17), while the Tipai of extreme southern San Diego County used 'yerba del pasmo', identified as a species of *Haplopappus*, to wash wounds (Hinton 1975 *passim*). Since both *Haplopappus* and *Adenostoma* species grow in Ohlone territory, there is no way of ascertaining with any certainty to which plant Harrington was referring.

In a somewhat similar vein, most early fieldworkers, including Merriam and Harrington, rarely defined what they meant by such terms as 'infusion', 'decoction', etc., when discussing plant preparation. While it is tempting to assume their use of such terms is consistent with modern usages, it is not wise to do so. While to modern herbalists an infusion is synonymous with steeping and is usually done with leaves and flowers, such preparation and use of specific plant parts cannot be assumed to be the same for the Ohlone. Therefore, except in those cases where the ethnographic references were explicitly clear regarding plant preparation, I have chosen to substitute the term 'medicinal liquid' for the terms 'tea', 'infusion', etc.

Medicine Persons

Most of the specifics concerning traditional Ohlone medicine persons are no longer known. But from the data collected by Harrington (1942), Merriam (1967), and Kroeber (1925), it appears that most of the Ohlone nations, like many other California Indian nations, had several types of medicine persons. Some of these medicine persons were well versed in the use of herbs; others could make rain begin or end; and still others could transform themselves into grizzly bears and then back into human form (Harrington 1942:11). Some scholars believe the most prominent medicine persons were the curing shamans (Bean 1992:56). Not only were they the primary healers, intervening with, or influencing or imposing their will on, the personified cosmic forces believed to be responsible for the medical or social problems facing people, but some also possessed the knowledge and power to foretell the future, find lost objects, call in game animals, remove ritual contamination. And some shamans also possessed the ability to bring about disease, misfortune, or even death (Harrington 1942:2, 39).

Precisely how one entered into the shamanic profession, what means of acquiring shamanic power existed, what the shaman's relationship to her/his personified cosmic helpers was, and how cures were effected, "are all matters on which the evidence is lost" (Kroeber 1925:472). It is known that both women and men could become shamans,

and in some instances a novice shaman obtained shamanic power during visions induced by ingesting the hallucinogenic plant Jimsonweed. It is also known that all novices were trained by older shamans (Harrington 1942 39-40).

Theories of Disease Causation

The sorts of beliefs the Ohlone held prior to European colonization concerning the causes of illness and disease is unknown. Data from the mission period and later suggests, however, that they, like most other Native Californians, regarded minor and/or transient illnesses (common cold, common headaches, common childhood ailments, rashes, sores, indigestion from obvious causes), traumas (fractures, sprains, wounds), and muscular and skeletal disorders (such as rheumatism and arthritis), as normal conditions of life. On the other hand, persistent, major, or unusual illnesses were often attributed to "the incantations of their enemies" (Forbes 1839:121-122) or the activities of a malevolent shaman (Harrington 1942:39). In either case, the sickness stemmed from a disease-causing object which the shaman or one's "enemies" had inserted into the victim's body (Harrington 1942:40). While it is no longer known how the Ohlone perceived the disease-causing object, throughout the rest of native California, such objects were often physically manifested as a fingernail, a hair of a dead person, a ball of coyote fur, a small pebble or a grain of sand, pieces of jagged flint, a live lizard, or an insect. A shaman might initiate an intrusion for any number of reasons including: enmity toward the victim, or toward the victim's parents, or because the shaman had been hired to do so, or because the shaman hoped to collect a fee from the victim for removing the illness.

Methods of Treatment

Curing existed along a continuum, with certain variables determining the action of a sick individual, including the number and persistence of symptoms, the perceived seriousness of symptoms, the extent of social and physical disability resulting from the symptoms, and available information and medical knowledge. Some illnesses required the assistance of shamans or herbalists, while others could be self-treated, or tended by members of one's immediate family. If the symptoms were few or mild, or did not require drastic alterations in the individual's everyday routine, then that individual most likely entered into self-treatment. If, for example, a person was suffering from a mild headache, indigestion, or a mild sore throat, the sick individual may not consider disease object intrusion as the probable cause of discomfort, since such causes would be reserved for more serious symptoms. Self-treatment would suffice and the individual would use various home herbal remedies. The headache might be treated by rubbing onto the forehead a paste made from pulverized California Nutmeg nuts mixed with animal fat (Bocek 1984:248), while simple indigestion could be treated by chewing the California Nutmeg nuts, which acted as an antacid (Bocek 1984:248). And the mild sore throat could be treated with any number of gargles including one made from California Hedge Nettle roots (Bocek 1984:253) or, after the introduction of Eurasian oranges and pomegranates, one made by cooking in water a mixture of California Wild Rose hips, small pieces of orange and pomegranate peels, a small piece of alum, and Rattlesnake Weed (Harrington n.d.). However, should the ailment increase in duration or in intensity of discomfort, the individual might then consider consulting individuals whose knowledge of medicines was more detailed and specialized. And if these measures failed, then a shaman might be consulted and asked to diagnose and treat the illness (Harrington 1942:39-40).

As with other aspects of Ohlone shamanism, little is known about the exact procedures an Ohlone shaman followed in diagnosing and curing. According to the priests stationed at Mission San Juan Bautista, in Mutsun Ohlone territory, curing was effected by "chanting and by gestures and shouts" (Geiger and Meighan 1976:78). Kroeber (1925:472) and Harrington (1942:39-40) provide more detail: when a shaman was called upon to treat a patient, the shaman first danced and sang in order to diagnose the cause of the illness. If the diagnosis was disease object intrusion, then the shaman extracted the disease object by applying her/his lips directly to the patient's body and

forcefully sucking the object into her/his mouth. Sometimes the doctor made one or more shallow incisions on the patient's skin over the location of the disease object and then applied suction. Once the object was removed, it was displayed and then the shaman disposed of it (Harrington 1942:40).

Plants and Their Medicinal Uses

The following discussion of Ohlone herbal remedies is intended to acquaint the interested person with some of their methods and plants used and should not be taken as an encyclopedic compilation of the Ohlone's medical knowledge. To do so would require an entire book since more than 100 native plants, plus a host of introduced plants, were used in treating sickness and injury. What is offered, instead, is a glimpse into their herbal pharmacopoeia.

Plant medicines were prepared and administered in many ways. External treatments involved the use of salves, dry powders, pastes, bandages, bathing and/or washing the afflicted area, poultices, both hot and cold packs, soaks, 'infusions' and 'decoctions'. Internal treatments ranged from ingesting various medicinal drinks (prepared as 'teas' and/or 'decoctions'), to chewing various plant parts or inhaling the smoke or vapor from heated plants, to the use of purgatives and enemas. The method used depended on a host of factors including the type of illness and its severity.

Some plants were ailment specific; others were used to treat a number of disorders. For example, Yerba Santa was used to cure headaches, asthma, rheumatism, and colds in their early stages. As a medicinal drink, Yerba Santa was also used for tuberculosis, to purify the blood, wash sore or infected eyes, or when combined with other herbs, to wash infected sores. Three other multipurpose, cure-almost-anything plants were Black Sage, California Wild Rose, and Yarrow. Black Sage leaf preparations were drunk to cure coughs; leaves were placed in a bath to cure limb paralysis; and heated leaves were held against the ear to reduce earache pain or wrapped around the neck to relieve sore throat pain. California Wild Rose was used for treating numerous ailments, including as a paste for sunburns, as a gargle for sore throat or swollen tonsils, as an ointment for scabs, and as medicinal beverages for fevers, indigestion, and kidney ailments. A medicinal liquid made from Yarrow was used to treat a number of ailments: drunk to alleviate stomach aches; as a wash for skin sores, cuts and bruises. Heated leaves were applied to wounds to prevent swelling or held in the mouth to alleviate a toothache (Harrington n.d.). Such multiple uses for a single plant was not unusual; in fact, nearly fifty per cent of all medicine plants used by the Ohlone had more than a single use.

After European colonization, the Ohlone added to their already broad pharmacopoeia numerous non-native plants, some of which were used in treating a variety of ailments. Mention has already been made of a sore throat medicine made from a mixture of the hips of the native Wild Rose and bits of introduced orange and pomegranate peels. Other non-native plants which were used in treating maladies included Lemon Balm, which when brewed into a medicinal liquid was considered efficacious in treating stomach aches and colic in infants. And when boiled with orange blossoms and peels, Lemon Balm was drunk three times a day to ease heart pains.

Skin Disorders. One of the most ubiquitous plants in Ohlone territory was (and still is) poison oak. Contact with any part of the plant, or inhaling the smoke from burning poison oak plants, causes a painful dermatitis for some human beings. The Ohlone treated the rash with washes made from the leaves of either California Coffeeberry or California Bay or the leaves and flowering tops of the Gumweed, which also was used in treating several other types of dermatitis.

Sores were treated in numerous ways. Infected, open sores were washed with the water in which any one of a number of plants had been boiled, including: Honeysuckle (also used for bathing swollen feet), Figwort (twigs), Bird's Foot Fern (leaves; the wash was used primarily for facial sores; or the heated leaves were applied as compresses), Monkey Flower (leaves), California Goldenrod (leaves), Vinegar Weed (leaves decocted

Monkey Flower *Mimulus* sp.
Photo by Frank Perry

with other herbs); the cooked hips of the California Wild Rose (a rose hip wash was also applied to scabbed-over sores to hasten healing), or Yerba Mansa (roots). Sores (and wounds) were dusted with healing powders made from the finely powdered Yerba Mansa roots, or the entire Paint Brush plant, or Monkey Flower leaves or compresses of heated Figwort twigs, or heated Yerba Santa or Angelica leaves. Healing salves were made from the ground seeds of either Wild Cucumber or Pineapple Weed. Toasted and finely ground seeds of Mayweed, mixed with "yerba del pasmo, and oreja de liebre," were fried in melted beeswax and olive oil to make a healing salve, which was smeared on a cloth, then laid on the sore. This treatment was repeated until the sore healed. Left over salve was stored in a bottle or cup for future use (Harrington n.d.). The juice from Violet was applied fresh to sores, and on the following day the plants were boiled and laid on the sores. Several European introduced plants also provided medicines for treating sores. Washes were made from Yarrow (entire plant) and Bittersweet (the leaves, fruit, or both were mixed with the leaves of the native Centaury).

Boils were treated in various ways: sometimes they were lanced, followed by applying warm poultices made from the leaves of either Baccharis (cooked in animal fat), Figwort, or Nightshade; sometimes they were rubbed with a pain relieving salve made of ground Jimsonweed leaves, or bathed with a medicinal wash made from Gumweed.

Hair and scalp care products were made from several different plants. Dandruff was treated using a shampoo made by mixing the pounded stems and bulbs of Soap Root in a little water. Although baldness was uncommon, it was not unknown and at least two herbal treatments were used to treat it. To encourage hair growth, as well as keep the scalp and hair healthy, the roots of either Wild Cucumber and/or Bracken were made into either a hair rinse or a paste to be rubbed into the scalp. Or the scalp was washed with a solution made from the leaves and twigs of Seep Willow. And to rid the scalp of lice a hair wash prepared from California Poppy flowers was applied.

Burns, Wounds, Cuts and Similar Injuries. Burns were treated in a number of ways: washed with water in which California Goldenrod leaves had steeped; or sprinkled with a healing powder made from toasted and ground Sesaña, which permitted burns to heal without scarring. For treating sunburns, an ointment made from California Wild Rose flowers fried in olive oil was used.

A variety of herbs were used in treating wounds. To ease pain and aid the healing processes, leaf compresses made from either California Mugwort or California Sagebrush were applied. Pain-killing medicinal drinks also were made from the root of Yerba Mansa (this same medicinal liquid also was used for disinfecting wounds). Yerba Mansa roots, when dried, were reduced to a fine powder and then sprinkled on wounds to aid in the healing process. Or a wound might be sprinkled with a powder made from the finely pulverized stems and leaves of Baccharis (wounds also were bathed with a healing wash made from the plant) or dried,

powdered Sneezeweed. Other treatments included bathing wounds with medicinal preparations made from any number of plants, including Stonecrop (the leaves and stems were sometimes dried, reduced to powder and sprinkled on wounds), Buttercup, Golondrina (used for washing cuts), and Gumweed; or applying compresses made from a species of native Yarrow or from Bedstraw. To prevent wounds from swelling, heated leaves of either the native or introduced Yarrow were applied as poultices.

Circulatory System. The ethnographic literature contains references to plant-based medicines that were used as "blood" and/or "heart" medicines. Most of these were used to "purify," "tone," "clean," or "freshen the blood," important therapeutic values since many illnesses were believed caused by "bad" blood. In addition, there were some plant-based medicines that were administered for such symptoms as chest or heart pains, while a few were simply said to be "highly regarded as heart medicine."

A number of plants, prepared as medicinal drinks, were used routinely, even daily, for purifying, cleansing, and/or "thinning" the blood. Included among these blood medicines were: Yerba Santa (leaves, fresh or dried); Golondrina (foliage); Rattlesnake Weed (leaves), Leather Root (root), Spurge (various parts), Sea Lavender, California Maidenhair fern (used for purifying the blood), or California Walnut leaves (taken to thin the blood).

Heart pains were treated by drinking three times a day the water in which orange blossoms and peels and Lemon Balm had boiled while other heart disorders were sometimes treated by drinking the water in which the fresh leaves of Black Sage had soaked.

Respiratory System. Respiratory ailments were a common health problem and were treated most often with herbal drinks, some of which were prescribed for their analgesic, or decongestant, or expectorant effects. For example, the leaves of Yerba Santa, a proven expectorant, were either chewed, smoked, or taken in a medicinal liquid form, to cure colds, coughs, and most pulmonary ailments, including asthma and tuberculosis. Respiratory ailments also were treated with herbal poultices and salves, sometimes in conjunction with medicinal drinks, and sometimes as stand alone medicines. Chest pains were treated with compresses of heated Jimsonweed leaves, Virgin's Bower foliage, or Trillium. The roots of Narrow Leaf Mule Ears were pounded to produce a thick lather which was rubbed on the chest as cure for various lung problems. Asthma was treated by drinking medicinal liquids made from California Mugwort (leaves), Yerba Santa (leaves), the roots of a non-native species of Thistle, or California Sagebrush (leaves - the cooked leaves were applied warm to the back and chest). Or asthma sufferers might smoke or chew Yerba Santa leaves or inhale the smoke from burning dried Milkweed plants.

Tuberculosis and pneumonia had a devastating impact on the Ohlone. Various Spanish government documents from the mission period described "with monotonous regularity" the death of the Indians at the missions from consumption and pneumonia (Geiger and Meighan 1976 *passim*). Treatments for both these diseases relied mainly on drinking liquid medicines made from a number of plants including: Yerba Santa (leaves), Nettles (roots), Manzanita (dried bark), or the introduced European native Hedge Mustard (seeds). Hedge Mustard seeds were wrapped in a white cloth, immersed in a hot water, brought to a boil, the sack removed, and the medicinal liquid ingested. Or the cooked plant, in combination with olive oil, was put on a cloth which was then placed on the chest to treat aching lungs: "the mustard is hot and does not let the coldness go to the chest" (Harrington n.d.). Sometimes a drink made from Bird's Foot Fern was prescribed to help cough up "bad blood." Pneumonia was treated variously: drinking medicinal beverages made from Peony roots; making shallow cuts in the patient's back, followed by hot compresses of Coyote Mint "to draw out bad blood." Coyote Mint also was used to make medicinal beverages, poultices and salves for treating other respiratory problems.

Cold and/or coughs were treated in various ways:

Milkweed *Asclepias* sp.
Photo by Frank Perry

drinking medicinal beverages made from any one of a number of plants including Manzanita (flowers), Elderberry (flowers), California Everlasting (leaves and/stems), Vinegar Weed (leaves; leaves also ground and then rubbed on the face and chest to relieve cold symptoms), Rattlesnake Weed (usually taken in the early stages of a cold), or Bluecurls (leaves); salves for applying to the chest and/or back and made from Bluecurls (leaves), or Milkweed (whole plant); or washes made from California Sagebrush (leaves). Persistent coughs were sometimes treated with medicinal beverages made from the leaves of Black Sage, or the leaves of the introduced Horehound (this medicinal liquid was also prescribed for whooping cough), or with cough syrups made from the fruits of Honeysuckle, or the foliage from either Bird's Foot Trefoil or Owl's Clover. Sometimes, cold sufferers rubbed their forehead and nose with a powder made from dried, ground Sneezeweed. The chills that accompany colds were sometimes treated by soaking one's feet in a hot bath made from a mixture of Manzanita (leaves), Elderberry (flowers), and Mallow (plant).

For relieving sore throat pain, poultices of heated leaves of either Black Sage or California Hedge

Santa Cruz
County
History Journal
Issue 5, 2002

148

Nettle were applied to the throat. Or one might gargle with the water in which the California Hedge Nettle roots had been boiled, or the water in which a mixture of California Wild Rose hips, little pieces of orange and pomegranate peel, a small piece of alum, and Rattlesnake Weed had been cooked. Other gargles were made by boiling in water Curly Dock and pomegranate rinds, or the leaves and stems of Stonecrop. Swollen tonsils were treated by drinking a Durango Root medicinal liquid or gargling with the water in which California Wild Rose flowers and Curly Dock had cooked.

The soothing and pain relieving properties of willow bark have been recognized by most peoples around the world, and the Ohlone were no exception. Medicinal beverages made from the bark, young leaves, or flowers of Arroyo Willow were drunk to cure colds, while a drink made from Red Willow bark was used as a fever remedy. Fever reducing medicinal beverages also were made from the diaphoretic Pineapple Weed; Dogwood (inner bark); Elderberry (flowers); California Wild Rose (blossoms and hips); Oregon Ash (twigs placed in cold water until it turned blue, signifying that the medicinal sap had leached out); Phacelia (roots); Common Plantain (roots); Leather Root; Chia (seeds); Rattlesnake Weed; or Bird's Foot Fern (fresh leaves gathered in early winter).

In addition to treating fevers associated with the more common upper and lower respiratory ailments, the Ohlone also attempted to treat "fever" diseases such as scarlet fever and typhoid fever. For dealing with the former, medicinal beverages made from the leaves, or the leaves and berries, of Bittersweet were prescribed or a medicinal drink made from Nightshade leaves, while medicinal beverages made from either Storkbill (leaves) or Verbena were drunk for typhoid fever. The Verbena medicinal drink also was prescribed for an ailment labeled "fever of the stomach."

Ear Disorders. An earache was treated variously: blowing Tobacco smoke into the ear; placing heated Rue leaves inside the ear; applying against the ear heated poultices made from the leaves of either Black Sage, California Hedge Nettle, or California Mugwort; or heated stalks of the introduced Alfalfa.

Eye Disorders. Eye problems were common maladies. Some eye problems, such as sore, irritated and inflamed eyes, may have been due to the Ohlone's almost daily practice of sweatbathing. During sweats, a fire was kept burning in the sweathouse. Since there were no openings through which the smoke could escape, the sweathouse filled with smoke (Harrington 1942:11). Undoubtedly, this contributed to various eye, throat, and lung ailments.

Washes were a common treatment for many eye disorders. Plants used to prepare washes included Yerba Santa (leaves) and Golondrina (leaves). The dew that collected during the night on the inside of the trumpet-shaped Jimsonweed flowers also was used to wash sore and/or infected eyes. For treating poor vision, an eyewash made from the juice of Figwort was used. And Figwort compresses made from the leaves were applied as poultices as a treatment for sore eyes. And for removing foreign particles from the eyes, one or more of the tiny gelatinous Chia seeds might be placed under the eyelid, where they became soft and sticky, causing

Chia *Salvia columbariae*
Photo by Frank Perry

any foreign particles to adhere to them, thus making it easy to remove the irritating matter.

Snake Bites. For the Ohlone, as for most California Indians, rattlesnakes were a fearsome, ever-present threat, just as they are today among modern Californians. Unfortunately, there is little information on how they dealt with snakebites, other than having a person who was bitten by a rattlesnake drink a medicinal liquid made from Rattlesnake Weed. However, it is likely that they also used the common California Indian procedure of making an incision or excision, followed by suction applied to the area of the bite. The Ohlone did, however, protect themselves from possible snake bites by placing fresh leaves of the Oregon Ash tree in their sandals.

Genito-Urinary System. A number of plant species were used in treating various urinary tract disorders. In general, treatments consisted of drinking liquids made from one of any number of plants: California Fuchsia was prescribed for urinary problems, as were medicinal drinks made from a species of California Sagebrush, Sea Lavender (also used in the treatment of venereal disease), and a decoction made from California Buckwheat (Bocek 1984:249). Bladder problems were treated with medicinal liquids made from any one of several plants: Cocklebur (seeds); Horsetail (stalks); or Manzanita. The Ohlone also treated urinary ailments with hot poultices of cooked California Buckwheat stems and leaves, or medicinal liquids made from Curly Dock, although details on the specifics of application are not now known. And for treating kidney ailments, medicinal liquids made from the dried stems of a species of Baccharis, or the berries of Fairy Bells, or California Wild Rose hips were prescribed.

Women's Medicines. A medicinal liquid made from Horsetail was used by women to treat delayed or difficult menstruation, for bladder ailments, and to prevent pregnancy, while menstrual cramps were alleviated by drinking a medicinal liquid made from Yerba Mansa roots. This same medicinal liquid also was used by both women and men as a general pain reliever. The leaves of Toyon were steeped in water to make a medicinal liquid which was drunk by a woman to suppress her menses. This same medicinal drink was considered good for young girls as it cleaned their blood and complexion, as well as promoted regular menses in them. A medicinal drink made from California Maidenhair was used to help expel afterbirth, and as a general post-parturition tonic. Following childbirth, women drank a medicinal liquid made from Groundsel to prevent "lockjaw." Pregnant or lactating women were said to avoid the California Poppy plant, as the smell was believed to be poisonous. And a medicinal liquid prepared from the leaves of False Solomon's Seal was used as a contraceptive.

Disorders Of The Teeth. Several remedies were used to relieve a toothache: warm Yerba Buena leaves were held against the outer jaw, or a strong medicinal liquid was made from the leaves and held in the mouth; Yarrow leaves were placed on hot stones, then transferred to the aching tooth; or Nightshade leaves were rolled into a cigarette and smoked; or Sagebrush leaves were held against the tooth; or a medicinal liquid made from Buckeye bark was held in the mouth. This same Buckeye medicine drink, or one prepared from Tan Oak bark or oak galls, also was used for treating loose teeth.

Population Control and Contraceptives. The Ohlone, like the majority of Native Californians, lived in a rich and varied environment and population densities were very high. However, high population densities can lead to problems. If there is environmental stress, such as a shortage of food, pregnancy may be strongly disapproved of. Having too many children too close together can result in problems, such as lack of food easily digested by nursing newborns. Furthermore, the rigors of supporting a large family in the gathering-hunting economy placed additional stresses if families were too large. In order to keep their population within the carrying capacity of the environment the Ohlone practiced various forms of birth control, including sexual restrictions, infanticide and abortion. They also used at least two plant-based contraceptive medicines: the

Santa Cruz
County
History Journal
Issue 5, 2002

150

leaves of False Solomon's Seal or the stems of Horsetail were decocted in water which was drunk by a woman to prevent conception.

Children's Medicines. Just as parents today treat a sick child with medicines specifically formulated for children, so too did the Ohlone. This is not to say that a medicine used by an adult was never used by a child, or vice versa. However, there were some plant medicines which were used especially for, or only in, treating medical conditions and illnesses in children. Medicinal liquids for treating fevers in children were made from Mallow (roots) or California Fuchsia (stems and leaves). Sometimes when fevers reached dangerous heights in children, convulsions occurred. To treat the convulsions, the child's body was rubbed with a salve made from a mixture of Pineapple Weed, urine and crushed brick. Colicky infants sometimes were given small amounts of a warm medicinal liquid made from the roots of Sagebrush, or, in the post-contact period, a medicinal liquid made from the European Lemon Balm. Or

California Poppy *Eschscholzia californica*
Photo by Frank Perry

they were simply picked up and held until the crying passed. When a child was restless or unable to sleep, one or two California Poppy flowers were placed beneath her/his bed to help relax her/him.

Neurological System Disorders. Headaches were treated by inhaling the smoke from burning Angelica roots, or by placing on the head dampened California Bay leaves or poultices made from heated leaves of Mallow. A Mallow leaf medicinal liquid also was prescribed for migraines. For pain in the limbs, the Ohlone living at Mission San

Carlos at the beginning of the nineteenth century would "bind fast an aching leg, arm, etc., and say that by this means the pain is somewhat alleviated" (Geiger & Meighan 1976:76). To treat numbness or paralysis in the limbs, California Goosefoot compresses were applied, or quantities of Black Sage leaves were placed in the afflicted person's bath water. After European colonization, the introduced Rue was added to the Ohlone's pharmacy as a treatment for paralysis (as well as stomach pains, coughs, and earaches).

Musculoskeletal System Disorders. Arthritis and rheumatism, which result from growing older and reflect the accumulation of wear and tear at the joints, and a suite of physical traumas (fractures, strains, sprains, bruises, and the pain and swelling associated with such traumas) were all fairly common among the Ohlone and were treated using a variety of herbal and non-herbal therapeutics.

Rheumatism was treated in a number of ways. A person could first induce sweating by drinking a hot medicinal liquid prepared from Mallow and Elderberry and when sweating stopped, rub the painful areas with a mixture of toasted California Wild Rose flower petals and the fat from a hog's kidneys. Or various pain relieving medicinal beverages were used: California Wild Rose (hips), Yerba Santa (leaves), Monterey Cypress (needles). Or a rheumatism sufferer could chew Grayleaf Pine pitch or apply compresses of cooked California Mugwort plants or heated Western Ragweed leaves to the aching and painful joints. Rheumatic pains also were treated with washes made from California Sagebrush leaves, compresses of either warmed California Mugwort leaves or Bedstraw, or lightly whipped with either burned twigs of Angelica or bundles of fresh Nettle.

The Ohlone were adept at treating fractures. For example, at the beginning of the twentieth century Ascención Solórzano de Cervantes, one of the last of the full-blooded Mutsun Ohlone and an herbalist, described for Harrington her method of casting, claiming the method was "an ancient Indian one." After setting the fracture she prepared the casting material by boiling the outer bark of

Cottonwood until a thick, syrupy gum formed. This syrup was then spread thickly on a piece of buckskin and wrapped around the fracture, then a splint tied on. The next day, after the gum had solidified, the splint and hide were removed "revealing a cast as hard as a modern plaster-of-paris one" (Martin 1977:17).

Gastrointestinal Disorders. Stomach aches and/or indigestion were usually treated by drinking medicinal liquids made from any one of several plants: a native species of Yarrow (entire plant); Vinegar Weed (leaves); Blue Eyed Grass (roots and narrow, grasslike leaves); California Everlasting; various species of Bluecurls (leaves, sometimes combined with the flowers); Pineapple Weed; and Peony (roots). The Peony liquid medicine was sometimes enhanced with the addition of orange peels, Mayweed, and "well toasted, almost burnt, meat (or else the little skin of the gizzard of a chicken)" (Harrington n.d.; Bocek 1984:251). After cooking for some time, the liquid was strained off, two or three teaspoons of olive oil were added, and the concoction drunk a cupful at a time "while simultaneously keeping warm and rubbing the stomach." This mixture also was drunk to cure constipation, as was a medicinal liquid made from the roots of the introduced Common Plantain.

For treating diarrhea, the Ohlone sometimes prescribed drinking the water used in the acorn leaching process. Usually, however, diarrhea and associated stomach problems were treated with medicinal liquids made from any one of a number of different plants including White Alder (bark), or the rhizomes and roots of various species of the genus Rubus (Blackberry, Raspberry, Thimbleberry). The medicinal drink made from Blackberry was regarded as the most effective treatment for both diarrhea and dysentery. Dysentery also was treated with medicinal liquids made from Sagebrush leaves, or Turkey Mullein roots, or the introduced Shepherd's Purse.

Enemas were used by some Ohlone for treating indigestion and complications arising from overeating. At the beginning of the nineteenth century the priests at Mission San Juan Bautista noted that such ailments were treated by administering lukewarm water via a syringe or hollow cane "applying it to the area they all know ... and thus try to regain their health" (Geiger & Meighan 1976:78). Sometimes the enema solution was made from marine algae, or after the coming of the Europeans, the boiled leaves and roots of Mallow.

Purgatives—A Special Class of Medicines
The Ohlone used a number of plants as purgatives, medicines which stimulated either emesis (expelling from the mouth) or catharsis (expelling from the rectum), or sometimes both. The cathartics were used primarily to treat constipation and included medicinal liquids made from several different plants including Coffeeberry (the dried, ground bark was either cooked or steeped in water), Vetch (roots), introduced Common Plantain (roots), or a mixture of Peony roots, Mayweed, orange peels, several teaspoons of olive oil.

The emetics were more broadly used. Some were used to relieve the uncomfortable feelings of nausea that accompany certain gastrointestinal illnesses. However, many others were used to treat ailments having little to do with the gastrointestinal tract. Why the Ohlone (as well as many other people) held a cultural expectation that one treatment for certain ailments was to induce vomiting is not clear. But that they held such an expectation is clear. For example, they prescribed smoking the dried leaves of Jimsonweed, or drinking a medicinal liquid made from brewed Elderberry leaves when one's health condition required a purgative. Unfortunately, there is no information about what health condition required such a treatment. Similarly, a medicinal liquid made from Clover was drunk as a purgative, while the roots of Wild Pea, or a drink made from cooked Mallow leaves were used to produce emesis, but it is not now known why a purgative was induced. It was quite common for men to use Tobacco as an emetic, either by chewing the fresh leaves or smoking dried leaves. This was done within both social and ritual contexts, but for what

Santa Cruz
County
History Journal
Issue 5, 2002

Vetch *Vicia* sp.
Photo by Frank Perry

numerous herbal medicines used in treating various ailments, the Ohlone also employed a number of non-herbal treatments. Mention has already been made of their ability to set and cast broken limbs. They also treated aching limbs, including sprains and strains, by binding them "and say that by this means the pain is somewhat alleviated" (Geiger and Meighan 1976:73). Missionaries at Missions San Carlos and Santa Cruz noted the use and beneficial effects of sweatbathing: "The men have the daily custom of entering an underground oven known as the temescal. …It is our experience that this is very beneficial for them" (Geiger and Meighan 1976:76). The Ohlone also knew how to induce abortions, both pharmacologically as well as mechanically, as well as control severe bleeding through the use of animal hair compresses. Massages, cauterization of wounds, suturing of wounds, dietary restrictions against fats and salt, massage, enemas, and bedrest, also were common medical procedures and practices.

Conclusions

Ohlone medicine proceeded from their assumptions about the nature of reality and they explained disease by reference to both the natural and supernatural worlds. And even where there seemed to be a "natural" explanation for a disease, there was always the chance that supernatural agents were at work. When a disease was supernatural in origin, the immediate cause was believed to be the presence of a disease-causing object in the sick person's body. This object was placed there by malevolent shamans, or less often by supernatural power beings. It could only be withdrawn by a shaman who employed sucking as her/his primary extractive method. On the other hand, common illnesses and traumas were treated by both shamans and non-shamans with a suite of plant medicines.

exact purposes is not now known. The missionaries at Mission San Carlos said that the Ohlone living there used the juice obtained from the Soaproot root as a purgative, drinking it "freely," along with sea water, to purge themselves (Geiger and Meighan 1976:77). But for what purposes, the missionaries did not say.

Non-Plant Therapies

In addition to shamanic cures involving the application of supernatural power, and the

Bibliography

Bean, Lowell John. 1992. *California Indian Shamanism,* ed. Lowell John Bean, Ballena Press, Menlo Park, California.

Bocek, Barbara R. 1984. "Ethnobotany of Costanoan Indians, California, Based on Collections by John P. Harrington." *Economic Botany,* 38(2):240-255.

Forbes, Alexander, Esq. 1839. *California: A History of Upper and Lower California From Their First Discovery to the Present Time.* Smith, Elder and Co. Cornhill, London.

Geiger, Maynard, and Clement Woodward Meighan. 1976. *As the Padres Saw Them: California Indian Life and Customs as Reported by The Franciscan Missionaries 1813 - 1815.* Santa Barbara Mission Archive Library, Santa Barbara, California.

Harrington, John P. nd. "Unpublished Fieldnotes on the Costanoan." Microfilm, McHenry Library, University of California, Santa Cruz, California.

_____1942. "Cultural Element Distributions: XIX, Central California Coast." *Anthropological Records* 7:1. University of California Press, Berkeley.

Kroeber, Alfred. L. 1925. *Handbook of the Indians of California* (Reprinted 1953 by California Book Company, Berkeley).

Martin, John M. 1977. *Indian Legends from Mission San Juan Bautista.* Mission San Juan Bautista, San Juan Baustista, California.

Merriam, C. Hart. 1942. "Culture Element Distributions: XIX, Central California Coast." *Anthropological Records* 7:1. University of California Press, Berkeley.

_____1967. "Ethnographic Notes on California Indian Tribes, III. Ethnological Notes on Central California Tribes." Compiled and edited by Robert F. Heizer. *Reports of the University of California Archaeological Survey, No. 68, Part III.* University of California Archaeological Research Facility, Berkeley.

Weber, F. J., ed. 1978. *Andrew Garriga's Compilation of Herbs & Remedies Used by the Indians & Spanish Californians, Together With Some Remedies of His Own Experience.* Archidiocese of Los Angeles, Los Angeles, California.

Vogel, Virgil. 1970. *American Indian Medicine.* University of Oklahoma Press.

Santa Cruz
County
History Journal
Issue 5, 2002

Common and Scientific Plant Names

The following list was reviewed and augmented to reflect current nomenclature by Randall Morgan, a botanist and representative of the California Native Plant Society on November 11, 2000. Some of these identifications are tentative because of the difficulty in matching early-day descriptions with modern botanical names.

An asterisk (*) indicates introduced (non-native) plants.

*Alfalfa - *Medicago sativa*
*Angelica - *Angelica archangelica*
Angelica - *Angelica hendersoni, A. tomentosa*
Arroyo Willow - *Salix lasiolepis*
Baccharis - *Baccharis douglasii,*
B. pilularia, B. viminea*
*Bedstraw - *Galium aparine*
Bedstraw - *Galium californicum, G. triflorum,*
     G. porrigens, etc.
Bird's Foot Fern - *Pellaea mucronata*
*Bird's Foot Trefoil - *Lotus corniculatus*
Bird's Foot Trefoil - *Lotus scoparius*
*Bittersweet - *Celastrus dulcamara*
Black Sage - *Salvia mellifera*
Blackberry - *Rubus ursinus*
Blue Elderberry - *Sambucus mexicana*
Blue Eyed Grass - *Sisyrinchium bellum*
Bluecurls - *Trichostema lanatum*
Bracken - *Pteridium aquilinum* var. *pubescens*
Buckeye - *Aesculus californica*
Buttercup - *Ranunculus californicus*
California Bay - *Umbellularia californica*
California Buckwheat - *Eriogonum fasciculatum* & others
California Everlasting - *Gnaphalium californicum* & others
California Fuchsia - *Zauschneria californica*
California Goldenrod - *Solidago californica*
California Goosefoot - *Chenopodium californicum*
California Hedge Nettle - *Stachys bullata*
California Maidenhair - *Adiantum jordani*
California Mugwort - *Artemisia douglasiana*
California Nutmeg - *Torreya californica*
California Poppy - *Eschscholzia californica*
California Sagebrush - *Artemisia californica*
California Walnut - *Juglans hindsii*
California Wild Rose - *Rosa californica*
Centaury - *Centaurium davyi* & others
Chia - *Salvia columbariae*
Clover - *Trifolium* (many species)

*Cocklebur - *Xanthium strumarium*
Coffeeberry - *Rhamnus californica*
*Common Plantain - *Plantago major*
     (also *English Plantain- *Plantago lanceolata*)
Cottonwood - *Populus fremontii* (inland) & *P. trichocarpa* (coastal)
Coyote Mint - *Monardella villosa*
*Curly Dock - *Rumex crispus*
Dogwood - *Cornus sericea*
Durango Root - *Datisca glomerata*
Elderberry - see Blue Elderberry
Fairy Bells - *Disporum hookeri*
False Solomon's Seal - *Smilacina racemosa* (fat), *S. stellata* (slim)
Figwort - *Scrophularia californica*
Golondrina - *Euphorbia maculata*
Gray Pine - *Pinus sabiniana*
Groundsel - *Senecio vulgaris*
Gumweed - *Grindelia camporum* & others
*Hedge Mustard - *Sisymbrium officinale*
Honeysuckle - *Lonicera hispidula, L. interrupta*
*Horehound - *Marrubium vulgare*
Horsetail - *Equisetum arvense, E. laevigatum* & others
Jimsonweed - *Datura meteloides*
Leather Root - *Psoralea macrostachya*
*Lemon Balm - *Melissa officinalis*
*Mallow - *Malva nicaeensis, M. parviflora*
Manzanita - *Arctostaphylos* (many species)
*Mayweed - *Anthemis cotula*
Milkweed - *Asclepias eriocarpa, E. fascicularis* & others
Monkey Flower - *Mimulus guttatus* & others
Monterey Cypress - *Cupressus macrocarpa*
Narrow Leaf Mule Ears - *Wyethia angustifolia*
Nettle - *Urtica dioica*
Nightshade - *Solanum douglasii, S. umbelliferum* & others
*Nightshade - *Solanum nigrum*
*Olive - *Olea europaea*
*Orange - *Citrus sinensis*
Oregon Ash - *Fraxinus latifolia*

Owl's Clover - *Orthocarpus* (various species)
    (now *Castilleja* & *Triphysaria* species)
Paint Brush - *Castilleja affinis* & others
Peony - *Paeonia brownii, P. californica*
Phacelia - *Phacelia* (many species)
Pineapple Weed - *Chamomilla suaveolens*
Poison Oak - *Toxicodendron diversilobum*
*Pomegranate - *Punica granatum*
*Prickly Pear - *Opuntia ficus-indica*
Raspberry - *Rubus leucodermis*
Rattlesnake Weed - *Daucus pusillus*
Red Willow - *Salix laevigata*
*Rue - *Ruta chalepensis*
Sagebrush - see Californa Sagebrush
Sea Lavender - *Limonium californicum*
Seep Willow - *Baccharis viminea* (mule fat)
Sesaña - *Navarretia atractyloides, N. hamata* & others
*Shepherd's Purse - *Capsella bursa-pastoris*
Sneezeweed - *Helenium puberulum*
Soaproot - *Chlorogalum pomeridianum*
Spurge - *Euphorbia* & *Chamaesyce*; many species,
    about half native & half introduced
Stonecrop - *Sedum spathulifolium*
*Storkbill - *Erodium cicutarium, E. botrys*, & others

Tan Oak - *Lithocarpus densiflora*
Thimbleberry - *Rubus parviflorus*
Thistle - *Cirsium brevistylum* (Indian Thistle)
    & probably all others
*Tobacco - *Nicotiana acuminata* & *N. glauca* (tree tobacco)
Tobacco - *Nicotiana bigelovii* (Indian Tobacco), & others
Toyon - *Heteromeles arbutifolia*
Trillium - *Trillium chloropetalum* & *T. ovatum*
Turkey Mullein - *Eremocarpus setigerus* (aka Doveweed)
Verbena - *Verbena lasiostachys*
Vetch - *Vicia gigantea* & others (also many introduced vetches)
Virgin's Bower - *Clematis ligusticifolia* & *C. lasiantha*
Vinegar Weed - *Trichostema lanceolatum* (aka Turpentine Weed)
Violet - *Viola pedunculata* & others
Western Ragweed - *Ambrosia psilostachya*
White Alder - *Alnus rhombifolia*
Wild Cucumber - *Marah fabaceus, M. oregona*
Wild Pea - *Lathyrus vestitus* & others
Yarrow - *Achillea millefolium*
Yerba Buena - *Satureja douglasii*
Yerba Mansa - *Anemopsis californica*
Yerba Santa - *Eriodictyon californicum*

Eating Poison Oak:
Alex Ramirez's Childhood[1]

by Beverly R. Ortiz

When Alex Ramirez was about five years old, he ate his first leaflet of poison oak. "So your nose won't run," his mother told him. "So you won't look like Bobby."

Bobby was the little blond-headed boy from Oklahoma who lived near the Ramirez home in Carmel. He seemed to be plagued with colds. His nose was always running, and he wiped it with his hands and fingers, so Bobby always had sores and scabs on his cheeks. "My mother used to say that was terrible," Alex recalls. "It was nasty to be like that, because his nose was running all the time."

"So you won't look like that, you eat this," Alex remembers his mother saying. "So I ate it." Thinking back to that day, Alex supposes he probably ate his first poison oak while on one of the regular Sunday morning walks he, his mother, his two brothers, and

Xerox of front and back of poison oak leaves: This is the size of the poison oak leaflets Alex Ramirez learned to eat as a child in the late 1930s.

his sister used to take. At that time, there were few houses in Carmel, and dense, Monterey pine forests surrounded the Ramirez home.

She started me eating one leaf. We always ate one leaf. I don't remember how often she had me eat it. It was more than several times in the same year. I don't think it was any particular season, but I found out on my own that the best time was the beginning of spring, when the leaves are tender... When they're tender, they're easier to eat than when they're chewy. You don't want to be chewing on that thing.

I ate it every year for a long time. Then, probably when I went to Mexico in 1959, I stopped. I didn't eat any more until 1975, when I started getting involved in the Indian culture again. I tried to teach my sons, but they thought I was crazy. My youngest was about nine and my oldest about twelve. We went up to Mt. Hamilton, and I told them I was going to show them. They knew a lot about poison oak, because we went camping often, and I said, "This is what my mother had me do, and you can do what you want." I picked it, and I ate it, but they wouldn't.

Driving home down the curvy mountain road, my youngest son stared at me with concern, like he was wondering if I'd be all right. My sons never did try it.

I asked Alex how often he eats poison oak today. "Whenever somebody asks me to, I eat it," he said with a laugh.

Santa Cruz
County
History Journal
Issue 5, 2001

158

Alex Ramirez samples a poison oak leaf.
Photo by Beverly R. Ortiz.

Alex was born on a cold, December day in 1928 to María "Mary" Onésimo (Rumsien) and Pete Ramirez (Rumsien/Mexican).

> We lived with my grandfather on my father's side in Carmel on Santa Rita Street. It was a gathering place for everybody. The Indians who lived in Carmel Valley, when they came down to Monterey, they would come by that house in Carmel, and stop and have coffee. My mother would give them water and food. It was during the depression so my father used to make beer, and all the beer drinkers would gather around the house...

Throughout his childhood, Alex's mother and maternal grandfather Manuel Onésimo exposed him to the cultural traditions upon which he would draw throughout his life. The teaching about poison oak came while Alex was living at the Santa Rita Street home.

Later, Alex's family moved to the property of Loreta and Domingo Peralta, then owned by

Loreta's son, Roy Meadows. The Peralta property had been the only land granted to a Rumsien family after the secularization of Mission San Carlos Borromeo (Carmel) in the 1830s. Although continually threatened with expulsion from their property by civil administrator Antonio Romero, who reportedly "resented the ownership of such an extent of land by a native family," the Peraltas, with the intervention of local resident Juana Boronda, were able to keep the land.

While living at this second home, a ranch, Alex received another important teaching, which came during a rabbit hunting trip with his grandfather:

> We didn't have refrigeration, so we needed fresh rabbits. We wouldn't go very far, but I was such a little kid it seemed like a long ways. I guess he saw me looking back at the house. That's when he told me to talk to the trees. Talk to the plants. Talk to the stones. When you're on the way back, the stones will help you get back. It didn't make sense to me then, but now I realize you get acquainted with the road you're on. If you get lost, you can backtrack.

By the time Alex was school age, he ate poison oak regularly.

> When we used to go on field trips, the teacher would tell us, "Look out children. This is poison oak." Then I would show off and say that I could eat it. I wasn't afraid of it, and I would take bunches of it and eat it. A bunch would be about two or three leaves.

On a beautiful, clear June day in 1994 Alex and I traveled to the important locales of his childhood: his Santa Rita Avenue home; the reconstructed Carmel Mission church, which still holds the font where Alex was baptized; and the Carmel Valley Farm Center building where everybody gathered to celebrate and dance following the cattle roundups. While en route, we visited an intertribal powwow at Mount Madonna where, along the narrow roadway, we found some sticky monkey flower bushes encrusted with orange blossoms. As a child,

*Blossoms of the Sticky Monkey flower.
Photo by Beverly R. Ortiz.*

*Alex Ramirez holds some young poison oak plants.
Photo by Beverly R. Ortiz.*

Alex learned to pluck these flowers and suck the nectar from their base. The blossoms we tried tasted delicious, although Alex assured me they were not as sweet as those picked in his childhood, and they had less juice.

When we reached the Farm Center, Alex located a large bush of poison oak in a nearby field. Upon my request, he had promised to eat some, and so he did. Every poison oak leaf has three leaflets, each of which looks like an individual leaf. It is the latter "leaf" which Alex learned to eat all those many years ago.

On this day, he ate two such leaves, first one, then the other in quick succession. I could imagine how impressed his schoolmates must have been at the sight. I certainly was.

Science has not explained the desensitizing effect of eating poison oak leaves. According to Doctor William Epstein, a U.C. San Francisco researcher, it takes milligrams of the active antigen to produce a tolerance to poison oak, not the

microgram which are found in each leaflet. Studies conducted in the United States have shown that 50% of the population is clinically sensitive to poison oak, another 30% or so are subclinically sensitive (that is, not resistant), while about 15% are tolerant. Although it's difficult for children younger than five years old to become sensitized, after this age those tested react like adults. No attempt has been made to correlate this information with ethnicity, and many questions remain concerning the response of American Indians to poison oak. [2]

As for the Rumsien and Mutsun (San Juan Bautista area), a plant use study conducted by linguist John Peabody Harrington in the early 1930s in collaboration with several cultural consultants, revealed the use of poison oak shoots in local basketry. Yet the Rumsien and Mutsun had some sensitivity to poison oak, since Harrington also listed two local cures for poison oak dermatitis, one a decoction of coffeeberry leaves (*Rhamnus californica*), the other a decoction of California bay leaves used as a wash (*Umbellularia californica*).[3]

Santa Cruz
County
History Journal
Issue 5, 2001

As his mother promised, Alex has been virtually free from colds ever since he ate his first poison oak. He has also been free of the dermatitis, although his mother never stated this as a reason to eat the plant. It was a reason given to Lillian Marshall, a Rumsien elder who recently passed on. Like Alex, his mother, and Margaret Manjares (Alex's sister), Lillian became accustomed to eating poison oak leaves, although she felt it unwise to pass to the tradition on to her grandchildren.[4]

While the consumption of poison oak may leave the modern mind with many questions, it is thanks to the elders' wisdom that this plant, which most contemporary people view as an enemy at worst and a nuisance at best, has been a life-long friend for Alex and so many others.

Notes:

[1] Portions of this article were previously published in *News from Native California* and *The Ohlone Past and Present: Native Americans of the San Francisco Bay Region*.

[2] Special thanks to Dr. William Epstein and Julie Jorgensen of U.C. San Francisco's Department of Dermatology for sharing information about poison oak studies.

[3] Bocek, Barbara. "Ethnobotany of Costanoan Indians, California, Based on Collections of John P. Harrington." *Economic Botany* 38(2):240-255.

[4] Special thanks to Linda Yamane for sharing with me Lillian Marshall's recollection of eating poison oak.

Native Uses of Plants: How to Cook Acorns and Work with Tules

written and illustrated by Douglas J. Petersen

Introduction

Central California, with its mild climate, plentiful winter rainfall and number of different habitats, is home to a great variety of plants and animals. The Native Peoples of this area, who were hunters and gatherers, took advantage of this abundance and lived quite comfortably here for thousands of years.

Plants provided the people with food in the form of nuts, seeds, berries, roots, bulbs and greens. Plants were also a source of medicines and materials for making baskets, hunting equipment and tools. Plant materials were used to make everything from houses and boats to musical instruments and toys. People's lives were deeply connected to the plants that grew around them.

Of the hundreds of plants that were used by the Native Peoples of central California, this article will focus on only two: the oak tree and the tule plant. Each of these plants, in its own way, played an important role in the lives of these early Californians.

Acorns, the seeds of oak trees, provided an abundant and reliable food source that could sustain people throughout the year. Acorns were so plentiful that California had one of the densest Native populations in North America in the late eighteenth century when Europeans first began to colonize the region. Similarly dense populations were found in the four-corners area of the American Southwest and in the North-eastern woodlands, but both of these areas depended on crops of corn, beans and squash to support their large numbers.

Tules, long grass-like plants that grow in freshwater wetlands all over central California, were used to make a great number of things needed for daily life. This abundant and versatile plant was used to make houses, beds and mats, baskets and boats, duck decoys, and much, much more.

By learning something about the foods they ate and the materials they worked with, we can come to understand a little more about the early Native Peoples of this area and appreciate the remarkable culture that developed here over thousands of years. This article will tell you how to collect, process and cook acorns, and how to gather, cure and make a few simple objects from the tule plant.

California, with its ample supply of food, supported a number of different tribes of people. Each of these groups had its own language, mythology, and way of doing things. Each had its own unique traditions as to how acorns were processed and cooked. And each group had its own, unique uses and construction techniques for working with tules. With respect and apologies to the hundreds of Native cultures in California and their centuries-old traditions, here is a simple and generalized way of working with each of these materials.

Santa Cruz
County
History Journal
Issue 5, 2002

Acorns:

Collection, Storage, Preparation and Cooking

There are several steps involved in processing and cooking acorns and many readers will think this is far more work than it's worth. But, since we can't go to the store and buy a container of freshly prepared acorn flour, we have to begin at the beginning. Imagine thrashing and milling the wheat before you bake a loaf of bread. We hope you'll persevere. There are many rewards to be gained from the experience.

The steps for preparing and cooking acorns include the following:

Gathering	acorns ripen and drop from the trees in the fall
Drying	the nuts must be dried in the shell before storage
Storing	they must be kept dry and away from "critters"
Cracking	to remove the hard outer shells
Winnowing	to remove the thin papery husks
Pounding	to produce a coarse flour
Sifting	to separate out the fine flour
Leaching	to wash away the bitter-tasting tannic acid
Boiling	to make acorn mush or soup
Baking	to make acorn bread

The Acorn

There are eight different species of oak trees native to California. The most common oaks in central California include the coast live oak *(Quercus agrifolia)*, interior live oak *(Quercus wislizenii)*, valley oak *(Quercus lobata)*, and the black oak *(Quercus kelloggii)*. The tanbark oak *(Lithocarpus densiflora)*, although it looks like an oak, acts like an oak, and even produces acorns like an oak, is not a true oak. Notice the "fuzzy" cap on a tanbark acorn unlike the smoother caps of all true oaks. California Native Peoples used the tanbark acorn just as they did the others. In fact, tanbark oak acorns were the acorn of choice for many Monterey Bay area Peoples.

Acorns are eaten by a number of different animals,

*Coast Live Oak
Quercus agrifolia*

*Valley Oak
Quercus lobata*

*Black Oak
Quercus kelloggii*

*Tanbark Oak
Lithocarpus densiflora*

including deer, squirrels, jays and acorn woodpeckers. But acorns contain high levels of tannic acid that make them toxic to humans. Fortunately, tannic acid has an extremely bitter taste, so it would be very difficult to eat enough to cause any serious problems.

Hundreds of years ago California Native Peoples figured out a way to leach, or wash the tannic acid from the acorns, resulting in a highly nutritious and abundant staple food supply. Acorns are a good source of protein and are high in fat, vitamins and minerals. They are also a wonderful source of fiber.

Every species of acorn found in California is edible. However, they vary in their tannic acid content and flavor. If possible, try preparing two or three different kinds of acorns separately to compare the flavors.

Gathering

Acorns mature and begin dropping from the trees in the fall. When they were ready, people from small villages all around the area would gather together at their traditional groves to harvest the valuable nuts. This was a time of great excitement as family members and friends were reunited for the First Harvest celebration. It was a time of feasting, singing and dancing, but it was also a time of hard work.

Burden Basket

First the ground beneath the trees was cleared of any acorns that had already fallen. Acorns that drop early are often improperly formed or have become infected by insects. Then several people would climb the trees and shake the branches or use long poles to carefully knock the acorns from the trees. Below, everyone helped gather the nuts. They were collected in large burden baskets that were carried by a tumpline, a wide strap that passed around the basket and up over the forehead or across the upper chest of the bearer. When they were full the burden baskets were carried back to the village where the acorns were dried and stored away for use throughout the year.

The easiest way to gather acorns is from an oak tree that overhangs a driveway, parking lot or playground. Use a broom or rake to sweep them into bags or boxes. Be sure to get permission from the owner if you want to collect on private property, and of course, you may not collect acorns in any city, county, state or national park without special permission.

It's also a good idea to only collect acorns that have already fallen from the tree. Not only is climbing the tree dangerous to the gatherer, but can cause serious damage to the tree by accidentally breaking branches.

Oak trees produce acorns on an irregular basis. Some years the crop is abundant. Some years there are very few acorns. This cycle varies from species to species and from location to location, so watch the trees carefully to see when the acorns are ready to harvest.

Drying
Acorns must be dried carefully before they can be stored away for the season. Reducing the moisture content makes them less likely to mildew in storage. The acorns were again sorted to remove any with signs of insect damage, and then they were spread out on the ground to dry. In the past, children might have been kept busy keeping marauding animals like deer, squirrels and birds from stealing too many.

Inspect the acorns one more time for damage. Discard any that are cracked or show signs of mold or mildew. Small holes in the side of the shell indicate an insect infestation and these should be discarded as well. Spread the acorns out in a single layer on a tarp. This makes them easier to move around and turn each day, helping them dry more evenly.

The drying can take just a few days if it's warm, dry and a little breezy. It can take a couple of weeks if it's not. The acorn is dry when you can feel it rattle inside the shell. Don't be surprised if suddenly more jays, squirrels, and other critters start hanging around the yard. Enjoy their company and let them have their share of the acorns. If they're taking too many, however, the acorns can be spread inside a garage or other covered area to dry.

Fresh acorns contain far too much moisture to be used right off the tree. Instead of grinding to a dry flour, they turn into a wet paste that can be very difficult to leach. It's also not a good idea to try speeding up the process by drying the acorns in a warm oven. The nutmeats can become very hard and difficult to grind into flour.

Storing
Acorns were traditionally stored in granaries. These were specially made structures that kept the acorns off the ground, away from "critters," free of insects and dry until they were needed during the coming year.

Acorn Granary

Granaries could be constructed on top of a flat rock or inside a hollow tree. Others were built around wooden poles stuck in the ground. The body of the granary was loosely woven of sticks to allow air to pass through the acorns and help keep them dry. The roof would be covered with bark slabs or tule or brush thatching to keep the rain off. Pungent leaves, like those of the bay tree, were layered among the acorns to help keep insects away.

Onion sacks from a produce market make excellent storage containers for acorns. The open weave allows air to pass through, and they can be hung from rafters in a garage to keep them away from critters. Don't store acorns in plastic bags or in a plastic garbage can. Excess moisture remaining in the acorns, even after they have dried, will collect inside and cause them all to rot.

Check stored acorns regularly. If little white grubs are crawling around the acorns, or if you notice small moths flying around, it means insects have infested the supply. It will be necessary to put the acorns in a freezer overnight, or heat them in a low oven for about half an hour to get rid of the insects before they destroy the harvest.

Cracking

When needed, a supply of acorns adequate for the family was taken from the granary. The caps were popped off, if they were still attached, and the acorns cracked open between two stones. The shells were discarded and the papery husk was rubbed or picked loose from each nut. Well-made acorn mush was clean and white, with no traces of husk material remaining.

Two small stones still work the best for cracking open acorns. Place a flat-sided stone on the ground. Hold the acorn on this rock, standing on its point, and strike it sharply on the top with the other rock. A small dimple chipped into the lower rock will help steady the acorn. Hit the acorn just hard enough to crack the shell open. Don't crush the nutmeat inside.

Crack enough acorns to make about two cups of nuts. The number of acorns needed for this depends on how large the acorns are. Pick loose as much of the papery husk material as possible. It won't affect the flavor of the acorns, but it does affect the texture of the meal and it really doesn't look very good.

Winnowing

The acorn meats were tossed or rubbed in a winnowing basket to separate the nuts from the husks. As they were tossed in the air, the breeze would blow

Winnowing Basket

away the lighter husks while the heavier nutmeats were caught again in the basket.

Winnow the acorns by putting them in any wide, shallow basket or bowl. Take them outside and toss the acorns into the air, catching them again in the basket or bowl. While they're in the air, the breeze will blow the lightweight chaff away. Continue this process until the nutmeats are clean. It takes a little practice, but is a very effective technique.

Pounding

Acorns were pounded, not ground, into coarse flour using a stone mortar and pestle. These could be large "portable" mortars, chipped and shaped from round boulders, or bedrock mortars chipped

Mortar and Pestle

directly into an outcropping of bedrock. Shallow bedrock mortars were often surrounded with a bottomless "hopper basket" to help keep the flour contained in the hole. The pestles were long, narrow stones that were carefully shaped and highly prized by their owners.

There are several other ways you can reduce the acorns to flour. Put a handful at a time into a blender with some water and run the machine until the acorns are smooth. Don't put in too many at a time; the blender motor could burn out. They can also be ground in a food processor. If the acorns are very dry they will make a lot of noise in the machine and can eventually cause tiny cracks to form in the container. I now use a separate container for this process, wrapped in duct tape to help keep it intact.

Sifting

The coarse flour was then sifted to remove any of the larger particles. It was placed on a special basket tray and spread around with the hands. The basket was then shaken or tapped to loosen any of the

Sifting Tray

larger pieces and they were returned to the mortar for further pounding. The remaining fine flour was swept from the cracks in the basket with a soaproot brush and saved until all the flour was sifted.

If processed well enough in a blender or food processor, the acorns won't need much sifting. However, it's a good idea to run the flour through a sieve to remove any very hard pieces of acorn that simply won't grind, ending up with about a cup or so of fine flour.

Leaching

The finely processed flour was then taken down to the edge of the river where a large, shallow basin was formed in the sand. This basin was lined with leaves and the acorn flour was spread on top. Then, using a small bundle of twigs or cedar branches to break up the flow, water was carefully poured over the flour.

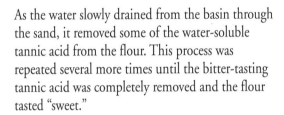

Leaching Basin

As the water slowly drained from the basin through the sand, it removed some of the water-soluble tannic acid from the flour. This process was repeated several more times until the bitter-tasting tannic acid was completely removed and the flour tasted "sweet."

This process can be done at home by lining a colander with 3-4 layers of cheesecloth or an old dishtowel (the tannins will stain the cloth). Spread the flour evenly inside and set the colander in the sink. Then, using a wide spoon or spatula to break the flow of water, turn the tap on slowly over it, just enough to match the water leaking out the bottom. Leave the water running for a few hours and then begin tasting the acorn. It's ready when there is no trace of bitterness left.

Some acorns will take longer to leach than others because they have a higher concentration of tannic acid. The speed at which the water flows through the cheesecloth or towel will also effect the time required, and hot water will leach the acorns faster than cold water.

Boiling

Acorns were most commonly boiled in a watertight

basket to form a thick mush. Because the basket couldn't be put directly over the fire, hot stones were stirred around inside the basket. One by one, heated stones were picked out of the fire with a pair of wooden tongs, dipped briefly in a basket of water to clean off any ashes, and placed into the cooking basket.

Boiling Basket

The rock was stirred with a carved wooden paddle or a looped stick to distribute the heat evenly through the basket. When the rock cooled a bit, it was removed and another hot cooking stone was placed inside. In just a few minutes the acorn mush came to a full rolling boil in the basket. Acorn thickens as it cooks and was served either as a thick mush, or thinned with water as a soup.

Acorn was eaten every day and it was generally eaten plain, without any seasoning or additions. But, as with most staple foods, many other things were eaten with it: deer, antelope, elk, rabbit, squirrel, duck, geese, quail, pigeon, salmon, trout, clams, mussels, snails, nuts, seeds, berries, roots, bulbs and greens.

Acorns can also be boiled in a pot on the stove. Begin with one cup of water to one cup of leached flour, adjusting the mix as needed during cooking. It's important to stir frequently to keep the acorn from burning on the bottom of the pot. The mush will thicken as it cooks, much as cornmeal or oatmeal does. Don't cook acorn mush in an aluminum pot. The residual tannic acid in the acorn will react with the aluminum, causing the pan to turn dark and your acorn mush to take on a slightly metallic taste. Stainless steel or glass pots work best.

Acorn mush, by itself, has a rather bland, cooked cereal taste. At least it does if all the bitter tannic acid has been leached out. Adding a bit of salt, though untraditional, may make the mush a bit more palatable to our "sugar-and-salt-jaded" palates. Try adding a bit of leached flour to soups or stews for an interesting change.

To eat acorn in a more traditional manner, serve it plain, perhaps with baked salmon, a salad of springtime miner's lettuce, and manzanita cider or hot yerba buena tea. Finish the meal with a bowl of blackberries.

Baking

Acorns were also baked into a bread. The leached flour was formed into a thick patty that could be placed on a preheated flat stone and propped at an angle near the fire to cook, or simply be buried in the hot ashes at the edge of the fire and left until it was done. Acorn bread was also sometimes wrapped in broad leaves and placed in a pit oven to bake slowly along with other foods, like meats and vegetables.

Pit ovens were holes dug into the ground that were lined with stones. A fire was lit inside and when it died down, the ashes were removed and a variety of foods were put into the oven to cook. Meats, vegetables and acorn bread were each wrapped in leaves and layered in the oven. The oven was then covered over with plant material and soil and left to sit for several hours while the food cooked. Pit ovens were especially used during times of celebration when larger quantities of food were needed to feed guests.

Bake traditional acorn bread by putting a half-inch patty of leached flour on an ungreased cookie sheet and baking it in a moderate (300-350 degrees) oven for 15 to 30 minutes, or until it "feels" done, slightly moist inside. Acorn bread has little in common with the breads we eat today. Unlike wheat breads that contain gluten and rise with the addition of yeast, acorns bake into a dense, dark bread with a somewhat tough texture.

Acorn flour can be added to any baking recipe, much as one might add a little whole wheat flour or bran. It adds an interesting and unusual touch to a variety of breads, cakes and cookies.

Tules:

Collection, Curing, Preparation and Projects

*Tule Plants
Scirpus spp.*

After the oak tree, with its abundant supply of life-sustaining acorns, the tule was probably the second most useful plant in the lives of the early Native Peoples of central California. This widely available and remarkably versatile plant was used in many different ways, from making string and simple toys to constructing boats and houses.

After the description of the plant and how Native Peoples used it, there follow directions for gathering, curing and preparing tules, and for making a few simple crafts. Familiarization with the material and its potential uses can help us appreciate the remarkable skill and inventiveness of the first Californians.

The Tule Plant

Tules are tall, grass-like plants that regularly grow in wet, marshy areas all over the world. They are common in California anywhere there is a freshwater marsh. Tules can grow from 6 to 9 feet tall, rising as single stems from thick rootstocks and rhizomes under the water, and can form very large and dense thickets.

Tules are in the sedge family, belonging to the genus Scirpus. *They are not rushes, which belong to the genus* Juncus. *Sedges grow tall and produce their flowers at the tip of the stem. Rushes are usually much shorter plants and produce their flowers on the side of the stem, a few inches down from the tip.*

Inside the tule plant are thousands of individual air pockets. Each of these pockets is dry and sealed to keep the air trapped inside. It's this unique structure that gives the tule its lightweight strength, allowing it to stand tall in the sunshine, yet be flexible enough to bend and not break in a strong wind.

The outer skin of the tule is tough, fibrous and water repellent. This tough outer surface helps the plant stand tall while moisture and nutrients travel up just beneath its surface. It also helps keep the air pockets inside the plant dry.

Native Uses of Tules

Because tules grow abundantly in fresh-water, and because the Native Peoples of California always built their villages near fresh water, it's no surprise that over the centuries they developed many different ways to use this versatile plant.

Because of their abundance and water repellency, tules were used in many places to make dome-shaped houses. A thick layer of tules tied to a framework of willow poles made a snug and dry house for sleeping and storing things away from the elements. Long mats or bundles of tules were sometimes tied to upright poles to make wind-breaks in front of the houses, or they were used as a covering for a ramada or sunshade. Tules were also used to cover granaries, keeping the year's supply of acorns dry and safe from the weather.

Because tules are so long and have a tough outer surface, they can easily be twisted into twine or rope for securing a variety of things. A short piece of twine might hold a berry-gathering basket around a person's neck, freeing both hands for gathering fruit. Thicker lengths of rope were used for things like making boats.

Because of the spongy air pockets inside, tules made wonderfully soft mats for sitting on while fashioning a basket or working on an arrow shaft. The air trapped inside these pockets also worked as an excellent insulator against the chill of the ground, so thick pads of tules were sometimes used to make warm, soft beds as well.

Because of their water-repellent covering and the air trapped inside, tules will float. So boats were made by tying several large bundles of tules together. They were used on the rivers, lakes and quieter bay waters of California. Floating decoys were also fashioned from tules to attract ducks and geese on the marshes.

Simple baskets were made for collecting duck eggs or blackberries. Small folding mats were used to store feathers, keeping them straight and undamaged. Women's skirts were sometimes made of shredded tule fibers. In southern California tules were used to make sandals and in northern California some people even made sun visors from them. Tules were used to make a variety of toys for children, and shredded tule could even be used as diaper material.

With all these uses, and probably dozens more, it's easy to see why the tule was such an important plant to these early Californians. It touched almost every aspect of their lives in some way or another.

Gathering Tules

Deer Bone Tule Saw

Tules were harvested in the late spring or early summer when the plants were as tall as they were going to grow, but hadn't started turning brown yet. The tules had to be cut when they were green and then cured or dried slowly before they could be used. Since lots of tules were sometimes needed, all the members of a village would help with the harvest.

For cutting tules many Native People used a special saw made from the shoulder blade, or scapula of a deer. One side of this broad, flat bone was notched to form a serrated edge that worked very well for cutting tules. A loop of twine or leather was tied to the thicker end and around the person's wrist so they wouldn't accidentally drop the saw and lose it in the wet marsh.

Be careful where you gather tules. They are often found in city, county, state or national parks where they are protected and cannot be collected without special permission. If you find some on private property be sure to get the owner's permission before cutting any. Cut them in the late spring or early summer when they are very tall and haven't started turning brown yet. Once the tules have turned brown standing in the water they are too brittle for use.

A small serrated steak knife works very well for harvesting tules. The serrations make a big difference. It's a good idea to tie a cord through the handle and around your wrist to avoid dropping the knife and losing it in the marsh. Also, be mindful of the knife in your hand when you're making your way through the thicket. The footing can be unsure making it easy to trip.

Cut the tules just above the waterline. If you cut them too low the plant could rot and die. If you cut too high you're wasting valuable tule material and being disrespectful. Also, cut winding tunnels through the tules instead of clear-cutting them. These tunnels allow more sunlight into the thicket and the tules will grow more thickly the following year.

After cutting several stalks, carefully carry them out of the patch and lay them all the same direction on a tarp. The tules can then be rolled up in the tarp for easier transportation when the gathering is completed. It is also important not to bend the tules while you're collecting. Every bend results in a weak spot that may break when you're working with the plant later. It helps to carry or drag them thick end first.

Remember that many animals live in the tule marsh and are deserving of our respect and care. Ducks, coots and redwing blackbirds, for example, use the tules for nesting, feeding and protection. Move slowly and watch for birds and their nests. If you encounter one, be careful not to disturb it and move off in another direction.

Curing Tules

Tules were usually dried slowly, or cured, before they were used. They were put in a shady place and turned every day for a week or two until they turned a pale green or light tan color. Then they could be stored in a dry place for future use, or they could be crafted into any of a number of things.

Place the cut tules in the shade of a tree and spread them out to dry for a week or two. If you leave them on the tarp you used for collecting, they can be covered at night to help keep them dry. Turn them daily to assure that they dry evenly and don't mildew. The black, powdery mildew isn't harmful

and the tules can still be used, but unless you wash it off, the powder will rub off on your hands and clothes and doesn't look particularly nice.

Once cured, tules can be tied together in bundles and stored in a dry place until needed. They'll keep this way for a year or two, if not longer.

Using Tules

Although tules are stored dry, they must be dampened well before use. If not, they'll tear and break when bent, twisted or shaped. Soaking for about half an hour in a pond, river or bathtub will usually dampen them enough to use. They can also be put on the ground under a sprinkler for a while, or they can be wrapped wet in a tarp and left overnight.

When securing ends, tules are always wrapped or tucked into themselves. They are never tied. A knot, with its sharp angles and twists, puts too much strain on the tule fibers and they will break.

You'll find that tules are a very forgiving material. Once bundled, wrapped, woven or twisted, tules can be flexed and adjusted to get the desired form. Once they dry, tules tend to keep their shape.

And finally, because tules have been soaked in water, they're a bit swollen when worked with. They'll shrink back again when they dry, so don't be surprised when the nice tight piece of string is a little less so the next day.

Making Tule Twine

Twine was important in the material world of the Native Peoples of central California. It was used to make carrying bags and nets for catching fish.

Making Tule Twine

Twine was used for making small game snares and huge rabbit nets hundreds of feet long. Elaborate ceremonial regalia was made using twine, and it was used to play games of cats cradle.

Materials for making string included milkweed, stinging nettle and dogbane, among others. For heavier cords and ropes, the leaves of cattails or tules might be used.

All string, twine and rope is made the same way, no matter what material is used. Once this skill is mastered with a piece of tule, string and twine can be made out of any strong, long-fibered material at hand.

To begin the piece of twine, select a long, unbent, wet piece of tule. Take the tule and "squiggy" it between thumb and fingers to flatten it and get all the air out. Do this the entire length of the tule stalk to loosen the fibers and make it easier to twist.

Hold the tule in the middle with two hands, about four inches apart. Begin to twist the tule. As it tightens, a small loop will flip over near the center of the twisting. This is the beginning of the piece of twine.

Now take the small loop in one hand and, with the other hand, (this is easier with two people working together) continue twisting the two ends, separately and in the same directions, until they are very tightly wound for a length of 2 to 3 inches. Holding the two twisted ends so they won't unwind, let the loop end in the other hand go and the twine will twist back on itself, locking the newly twisted lengths into place. Work the twine to even out the twists and continue this process until nearing the end of the tule piece.

To splice another piece of tule into the twine and extend its length, simply lay a new piece over the last 4 to 5 inches of the shortest end and twist the two pieces together as one. Keep the splices separated from each other by several inches to avoid weak spots in the cord.

Stagger the thick and thin ends of any added pieces to keep the twine an even thickness. A thick piece of tule can be split the long way if thinner material is needed. Or, 3 or 4 stalks of tule can be twisted together to make rope.

When you've finished your piece of twine, cord or rope, trim off any extra material and go back over it, twisting and shaping it to get a nice even look. A small piece of string wrapped around the end will keep the twine from unraveling.

Making A Tule Mat

Making a Tule Mat

Tule mats were used by the Native Peoples of central California in many different ways. Mats were sometimes laid over the willow pole frames of houses to form the walls and roof, or tied around upright poles to make windbreaks. Thick mats of tules were bundled together for beds, and thinner mats were woven to sit on while working under the ramadas or sunshades.

In some areas tule mats were used as cradleboards for newborn infants until their formal cradleboards could be made, and were sometimes used as backing material for those. Small mats were also made into "folders" for keeping feathers straight and undamaged until they were needed.

To begin a 1-foot square mat, cut several pieces of tule each about 1 1/2 feet long. Cut enough of them to make a single layer mat about 1 foot long. The extra length of each piece allows room to trim the edges when the mat is finished. Lay them out and alternate thick and thin ends so the mat will be even when done.

Now get two pieces of twine, each about 3 feet long. Thin, handmade tule twine can be used, or a heavy jute cord or bailing twine. Fold one piece in half and loop it over the first piece of tule, about 3 inches from the end. Give the two ends of twine a half-twist and set another piece of tule between them. Repeat the half-twist and adding pieces until the end. Weave the two loose ends of twine back through the tules to secure them, or, if commercial twine is used, simply tie a loose knot.

Now repeat the process with the other piece of twine, about three inches from the other end of the mat, keeping the two lines of twining as parallel as possible. At the end, secure the twine as before.

To finish the mat, trim the edges off evenly an inch or so from the line of twining. When the mat dries it may become a little loose. It can be tightened by untying the ends of the twine, pulling the string tighter between each piece of tule, and re-securing the twine.

To make thicker mats or mattresses, use more tules between each twist of the twine. For mats wider than a foot or so put a line of twining about every 8 to 12 inches to give it strength.

Making a Toy Tule Boat

With all the things made from tules by the Native Peoples of central California you can imagine that there were plenty of scraps and odd pieces laying around the village. And the Native

Making a Tule Boat

children, like children everywhere, were good at improvising toys from what they found.

This construction method was devised by Linda Yamane, a Rumsien Ohlone descendant, for its simplicity, enabling even very young children to build a boat with success and with minimum adult help. Because the bundles are not sewn together their entire length, however, this construction technique will not work well for larger models.

To make the boat cut several pieces of wet tule into 8-10 inch lengths. Assemble 5-10 pieces into one small bundle and tie one end tightly with raffia or string. Then wrap the bundle firmly, as illustrated, and tie the other end as well, leaving any remaining cordage attached. The number of tule pieces needed depends on the size of the tules used and how large the boat will be.

Repeat this step, making another bundle the same length and diameter as the first. These will be the gunwales, or sides of the boat so it's important that they be the same size.

Assemble a third bundle, about twice the diameter as the first two. Wrap and tie it the same way. This will become the bottom of the boat.

Hold the two smaller bundles in place, atop and to either side of the larger bundle, and wrap the remaining cordage firmly around all three, tying a knot. If you don't have enough cordage, add another piece so the bundles are secured well.

Trim off any excess cordage and adjust the shaping of the boat until the tules have dried. Use scissors to trim the ends of the tules at an upward angle to finish the boat model. Now test it in the water!

The "Tule Doll" That Never Was

In our quest to learn about the Native Peoples of California, and then share what we've learned with others, we sometimes fail to question the accuracy, or completeness of what we've learned and can inadvertently begin passing on misleading or incorrect information. The

Current Tule "Doll" (misinterpretation)

"tule doll" that interpreters and teachers have been showing children how to make for many years here is a good example of this.

First, some background information. Between 1906 and 1908 R. Stewart Culin, the curator of ethnology at the Brooklyn Museum in New York, visited the Pomo peoples living just north of Clear Lake. His goal was to collect materials that reflected the early life of these people, and with the help of two Pomo Indians, Penn and Susanna Graves, he amassed a collection of over 500 objects for his museum.

Among these things were several tule toys made by Susanna. She told Culin, "When the tule is ripe the women make them for their children. They call them di-gu-ba-hu." Diigubuhu *is an Eastern Pomo word for water bird or, more specifically, the American bittern.*

The bittern is a bird, a little larger than an egret, that lives in tule marshes and feeds on small fish. It's well camouflaged in brown and tan stripes and, when threatened, often sticks its head straight up in the air and either stands perfectly still or gently sways back and forth like the tules around it, making it very difficult for a predator to see.

The diigubuhu made by Susanna begins the same way we make our "dolls," but our "skirt" is actually a wrapped handle for the toy. A piece of tule is attached to the top of the figure, sticking strait up or slightly bent to one side. This creates a pear-shaped figure tapering up to the narrow neck and head of the bird in its defensive pose.

Pomo "Diigubuhu"
(American Bittern)

In 1952 Samuel A. Barrett published a book called Material Aspects Of Pomo Culture, *in which he printed pictures of several of these toys and listed three of them as "dolls woven of tule." The picture of this tule toy, with its misleading caption, evolved in people's minds to represent a human doll. When reproduced, the head of the bittern was ignored and the handle became the wrapping for the "doll's" waist. Then, because the resulting figure didn't look very much like a human, "arms" were added. Interpreters and teachers all over California, learning from each other, grabbed at this simple and unique Native American "doll" they could show children how to make.*

Well, native children did not make these toys, their mothers did. And the only people we know who made them were the Pomo north of Clear Lake. And it's not a doll representing a human form at all, but a representation of an American bittern in its hiding pose.

This is a common mistake that folks have been making for many years and it's taken on a life of its own, passing from one person to another throughout the state. But, as students and interpreters of Native cultures in California, we have an obligation to tell the truth, as best we understand it. Now we understand a little better, and it's hoped this truth will soon replace the misinformation about our "tule dolls."

For more about this, see an article by Beverly R. Ortiz entitled "Susanna Graves' Tule Bitterns" in News From Native California, *Volume 8 Number 1, Spring/Summer 1994.*

Closing

Processing acorns and working with tules can bring us a little closer to understanding the early Native Peoples of California and help us develop a deeper appreciation of the cultures that first developed these technologies. Their way of living was perfectly adapted to the world in which they found themselves and served them well for countless generations.

Their cultures still survive today in the proud descendants of these first Californians, who carry on these traditions, teaching their children, and us, the ways of their ancestors.

Santa Cruz
County
History Journal
Issue 5, 2002

Profile: Marie Wainscoat

Marie Wainscoat works on an abalone necklace, 2000.
Photo by Linda Yamane.

"Several years ago I had the pleasure of meeting a group of Butron descendants, who along with myself trace our Ohlone lineages back to the Carmel Mission and a village in Carmel Valley. It was so heartwarming to connect with all these people I'm related to. From there, I was able to begin filling in the missing links in my own genealogy. In addition to learning about my family, I began to learn the story of the Indian people, their absorption into mission life and their eventual cultural extinction. Now, I've become involved with a group of Ohlone people who are working to revive our cultural traditions through extensive cultural research. There's been an incredible revival of culture in the past several years, and I'm honored to now be a part of this community effort. I hope that this type of research will inspire both native and non-native people everywhere. My husband and I are independent filmmakers, and encourage everyone to document their history before it is lost. One thing I've learned in this process is if you don't make the effort now, it could be lost forever."

—Marie Wainscoat
(Rumsien Ohlone)

The Awáswas Language

by William Shipley

In pre-conquest times, there were eight languages spoken along the Central California coast, stretching from the Carquinez Strait in the north to the the Salinas Valley in the south. These languages were related to one another about as closely as, say Spanish and Italian, which indicates that they were descended from a single mother tongue spoken less than two thousand years ago. This language family, formerly called "Costanoan," is now known as Ohlonean.

One of these languages, Awáswas, was spoken more or less in what is now western Santa Cruz County, specifically along the coast from somewhere north of present-day Davenport to about the present area of Rio del Mar. The speakers, who probably numbered less than a thousand, lived in small village communities, often called "tribelets," for which a few names have survived: "Soquel," "Aptos" and "Zayante" are examples. The language itself has long been extinct.

Fortunately, three scholars came to the area at various times between 1878 and 1888, specifically to salvage what they could of the Awáswas language. Among them, they recorded just over seven hundred words including some words which undoubtedly represent slightly different dialects.

The most skillful and experienced of the three men was a Frenchman, Alphonse Pinart (1852 - 1911) who travelled widely over the world collecting language material from hundreds of little-known languages. His were the earliest recordings, made in just a couple of days. On August 23rd, 1878, at Mission Santa Cruz, he consulted a woman named Eulogia and on August 26th, in Aptos, a man named Rústico.

The second visitor was Jeremiah Curtin (1835 - 1906), a well-known figure in late nineteenth-century Amerindian studies, who collected extensive material on several Native American languages, partly in association with the Bureau of American Ethnology. His wordlist was obtained in Santa Cruz in November, 1884. The name of his Awáswas consultant is unknown.

H. W. Henshaw (1850 - 1930) was the last of the three. He worked with an unknown consultant from September 26th to 29th, 1888. It is possible that the Awáswas speaker from whom he obtained his wordlist was either Felipe Gonzales of Watsonville or Lorenzo of Santa Cruz. Both of these men spoke the language. Henshaw was not primarily an anthropologist. Most of his scholarly work was ornithological. At any rate, his ability to hear and record speech sounds was not as good as the other two investigators. Of the three, Pinart was clearly the most talented.

By comparing the recordings of the three different men and by checking the work of later, much more sophisticated scholars with related Ohlonean languages, notably Mutsun (spoken around San Juan Bautista) and Rumsen (spoken in the Carmel Valley), it has been possible for me to get very close to what the sounds of Awáswas were actually like. The wordlist which follows has been rewritten based on such an investigation.

Every written consonant and vowel is pronounced.
When consonants are doubled, both are pronounced,
as in Italian. The "x" is pronounced like "ch" in
German "Bach." The "ṭ" stands for a "t" sound made
with the tip of the tongue up in the roof of the
mouth. Stress is on the first syllable unless otherwise
marked.

The vowels are pronounced as follows:

"a" is like the "a" in "father."
"e" is like the "e" in "met."
"i" is like the "i" in "machine."
"o" is like the "o" in "note."
"u" is like the "oo" in "moon."

Awáswas Word List
Forms from Curtin are coded "C," from Henshaw, "H" and from Pinart, "P."

1. abalone, species of (P) *tuppenish*
2. abalone, red (a plural word) (P) *xasan*
3. abalone, another species of (plural) (P) *achkis*
4. abdomen (P) *huttu*
5. above (P) *rini*
6. acorn (P) *rappak*
7. Adam's apple (H) *tuhmur* (pronounce the 'h'); (P) *tukumur, tuxmur*
8. adobe (C) *alá*
9. afraid (P) *holmon, hoylmon*
10. afternoon (P) *wiyaks*
11. afterwards (P) *akkoy*
12. alder (P) *maara, mara*
13. angry (P) *hasseen, xassen*
14. ankle (P) *isment*
15. ankle (H) *hapán*
16. ant (C) *pashkaymin*
17. ants (P) *kasup*
18. antelope (C) *tiyuyen*
19. antlers (C) *chiri*
20. arm (H) *issu*, (P) *issu, isu*
21. armpit (P) *shomshom*, (H) *shumshum*
22. arrow (C) *tiyás*, (P) *tiyos*
23. arrow (P) *tyemmo*
24. arrow feathers (C) *sipós*
25. arrowhead (C) *tipe*
26. ashes (H) *yukí*, (P) *yukki, yuki*
27. ask (P) *chuuka*
28. atole (P) *atol*
29. aunt (P) *ansi*
30. baby (P) *allashu, alaso*
31. back (H) *kumes*
32. backbone (P) *rumuch, rumes*
33. bad (P) *hechtesh*
34. bad (P) *yuhán*
35. badger (P) *tayan*
36. bark of tree, outside (P), (C) *patá*

37. basket, kind of (P) *utis*
38. basket, kind of (P) *tipir*
39. basket, kind of little (P) *tipshin*
40. basket, little (P) *yasa*
41. basket, large burden (C) *chiwen*
42. bat [animal] (C) *wireknis*
43. battle (C) *hacchum*
44. beads (C) *maseh* (pronounce the 'h')
45. beak (C) *wakawepper*
46. beak (P) *weperx*
47. bear [animal. grizzly? brown?] (P) *oresh, ores*
48. beard (H) *heyis*, (P) *he eyes, eyes*
49. beard (C) *hayyek*
50. beat (P) *chimmi, chimmiw*
51. beaver (C) *hamíhl* (pronounce the 'h')
52. bed (H) *takó*
53. bedbug (C) *chaláw*
54. bee (C) *potukmin*
55. bee (P) *potxótmin*
56. bee [another species] (P) *o'opmin*
57. beetle (P) *humchushmin*
58. before (P) *wiakush*
59. begin (P) *huuyi*
60. belly (H) *hutu*
61. belly (P) *poshlok*
62. berry basket (C) *sawí*
63. bird (C) *púnis*
64. bird's eggs (P) *mochuen*
65. black (C) *multosmin, murtushmin* (questionable!)
66. black (P) *múrchun, murchu*
67. blackbird (P) *shukuri, sukxin*
68. blackbird, redwing (C) *shukrin*
69. black paint (H) *murtusamin ennér*
70. bladder (H) *ihí*
71. blind (P) *maahai, maxái*
71a. blind (H) *kulus*
72. blood (H) *payyán.*
73. blood (P) *payan*

74. blue (C) *héyu*
75. bluebird (P) *ashit, asit*
76. body (P) *hamma, huwara*
77. bone (H) *táyyi*
78. boots (C) *lahwén* (pronounce the 'h')
79. bow [of wood] (C) *liti*
80. bow (P) *liiti, liti*
81. bowstring (C) *ruk*
82. bowstring (P) *ruuk, rires*
83. boy (P) *chaarish, alaso*
83a. boy (H) *shinni*
   (the Monterey word is *'shin'*)
84. boy, little (H) *linmatsh*
85. brain (H) *halii*
86. branch [of tree] (P) *paklan*
87. bread [acorn?] (C) *sitnen, parémis*
88. break (P) *halle*
89. breast (P) *hettish, ettish* (probably 'chest')
90. breast, woman's (P) *mus*
91. breast, woman's (H) *mus*
92. bring forth (P) *hissuwin*
93. brother, elder (P) *taanan, taka*
   (nan = "my"?)
94. brother, my elder (C) *taknán*
95. brother, younger (C) *útek*
96. brother, younger (P) *uutek, tere*
97. brother-in-law (P) *ettenen, meres*
98. brush [on hillside] (C) *payáwa*
99. buckeye (C) *chayá*
100. buckskin (H) *hayyup*
101. bury (P) *yuri*
102. bush rat (C) *hinih*
   (pronounce the final 'h')
103. calf [of leg] (H) *sáyyan*
104. cane, wild (P) *ripan*
105. canoe (C) *wali*
106. cat [felis domesticus] (C) *penek* (! should
   be borrowed from Spanish or English)
107. chaparral (P) *huya*
108. chaparral cock [sp. grouse?] (H) *uyúy*
109. cheek (H) *utú*
110. cheek (C) *témash*
111. cheeks (P) *kachete, tsammush*
111a. chest [?] (P) (C) (H) *mini* (trans. 'heart'
   by all three sources, but see 'heart')
112. chin (H) *kihot*
113. chin (C) *hakúsh*
114. chin (P) *hakkus, chiktas*
115. cloud (C) *mótoshi*
116. cloud (H) *pishsha*

117. cloud (P) *pisha*
118. cold, a [sickness] (P) *tarshi*
   (from Span. *tosse*?)
119. cold, a [sickness] (H) *társin* (Span.?)
120. complete (P) *himmach*
121. cormorant (H) *saray*
122. corpse (P) *semmon chaaris*
123. corpse (H) *semon*
124. cottonwood (H) *popo*
125. cough (P) *toxoren*
126. cow (H) *pak* (fr. Spanish 'vaca')
127. coyote (H) *mayyán*
128. coyote (P) *wakshes, mayan*
129. crab (H) *tsuratumin*
130. crayfish (P) *karachmin*
131. crow [bird] (P) *shaaray, sharay*
132. crown of head (P) *charas*
133. cry out (P) *chirpi*
134. currant, red (P) *pachax*
135. cut (H) *warún*
136. cut (P) *waran*
137. cut wood (H) *tutski*
138. dance (P) *chittey, chitte*
139. daughter (P) *sinniw, kanaymi*
140. dawn (P) *awen, aruwa*
141. dawn (H) *áru*
142. day (H) *tuhis*
143. day (P) *tyunit, tuxis*
144. day after tomorrow (H) *awéntak*
145. day before yesterday (H) *uwikantis*
146. deaf (P) *tamhashmin, tamxán*
147. deep (P) *awno*
148. deer (H) *tote*
149. deer (P) *tooche*
150. diarrhea (H) *semoste*
151. diarrhea (P) *chukrin*
152. die (P) *semmon, semon*
153. dog (H) *chuku*
154. dog (P) *chuuku, chuku*
155. door (P) *hinnu, hayss*
156. doorway (H) *innu*
157. dove (H) *húnunu*
158. dove, ring (P) *ununi*
159. dream (P) *shuppen, shupen*
160. dress oneself (P) *richay*
161. drink (P) *weet*
162. dung (H) *irkó*
163. dust (C) *yuki*
164. dust (H) *hittin*
165. dust (P) *sheka*

166. eagle (P) *shiri*
167. eagle, golden (H) *soso*
168. eagle, bald (H) *siri*
169. ear (C) *túksus*
170. ear (H) *ótsho*
171. ears (P) *oocho, ocho*
172. ear, left (H) *awis otsho*
173. earth, ground (P) *pirren, pire*
174. earthquake (C) *yíne wérep*
175. earthquake (H) *imén*
176. east (H) *awetka*
177. eat (P) *hammay, amay*
178. eat supper (P) *hachsen*
179. eclipse of the moon (P) *kammun chaar*
180. eclipse of the sun (H) *uwikán*
181. eclipse of the sun (P) *kammun hismen*
182. egg (H) *oṭaw*
183. eggshell (H) *mote*
184. elbow (H) *kululis*
185. elbow (P) *kullulish*
186. elder [plant] (P) *chishsha, chisa*
187. elk (H) *siwu*
188. enemy [one of one's group] (H) *wayas*
189. enemy (P) *are, wayas*
190. enjoy (P) *heshkoon, heshkon*
191. eye (H) *hin*
191a. eye, left (H) *awis hin*
192. eye (C) *hin*
193. eye (P) *xiin*
194. eyebrow (H) *sunup*
195. eyebrows (P) *shunnux, shunup*
196. eyelash (H) *háyye*
197. eyelashes (P) *winas*
198. face (H) *hémet, hínep*
199. far (P) *waxi*
200. father, my (P) *apnan, kanapnan* (the *'kan'* means 'my')
201. father, my [child speaking] (P) *appa*
202. father, father's (H) *howó* (i.e., paternal grandfather)
203. father, husband's (H) *kan mákko ápnan*
204. feathers (P) (H) *sipos*
205. fever (H) *súisan*
206. fever (P) *chumrin, kayin* (Probably different kinds)
206a. few (H) *hemmet*
207. filbert (P) *shirak*
208. fingernail (H) *túl*
209. fingernail (P) *tuur*
210. fingers (H) *túyis*

211. fingers (C) *ishu etka*
212. fingers (P) *sarashin* (maybe all these are names of particular fingers?)
213. fire (C) *hiis*
214. fire (P) *shottow, sotow*
215. firedrill (H) *hílap*
216. firewood (H) *tápo*
217. firewood (P) *tappor, tapor*
218. finger, index (H) *púnluh* (pronounce the 'h')
219. fish (H) *wuyi*
220. fish (P) *wuy*
221. fish sp., large-headed (P) *mokoch*
222. fishhook (H) *wihí*
223. fishhook (P) *shawus, sawos*
224. fishline (H) *luk*
225. fish net (H) *shok*
226. flea (H) *por*
227. flies (P) *múmuru*
228. flint (P) *irek*
229. floor, ground (H) *ripun*
230. flour (probably acorn) (H) *muyyen*
231. flower (H) *tíwis*
232. fly (insect?) (H) *talku*
233. fly, to (H) *wínna*
234. foam (H) *kos*
235. fog (C) *sitis*
236. fog (H) *metsheknes*
237. food (H) *amá*
238. foot (H), (P) *kóro*
239. foot (P) *chipay*
240. forehead (H), (C), (P) *tíma*
241. forehead (P) *timma*
242. forget (P) *tonnen*
243. fox (H) *yuréh* (pronounce the 'h')
244. fox (P) *tupyun, apuk* (different species?)
245. friend (H) *tche*
246. frost (H), (P) *wákkan*
247. frost (P) *wakan*
248. fruit (H) *amsún*
249. full (P) *toolon* ('oo' is a long 'oh" sound)
250. get up (P) *hitmay*
251. girl (H) *atsháma*
252. girl (P) *achshiama, atsiama*
253. give (P) *haray*
254. go (P) *tuxay*
255. go out (P) *hiiyi, huyyuy*
256. good (P) *urse, orse*
257. gopher (H) *siwot*
258. granddaughter (P) *melen, appapich*

259. grandfather (P) *mele*
    (must be mother's father; see 'father's father.)
260. grandmother (P) *okko*
261. grandson (P) *appapich, meresh*
262. grass (H) *ʈarin*
263. grasshopper (H) *uruwa*
264. grasshopper (P) *uuruwa*
265. green (P) *chutku*
266. grizzly (bear) (H) *ores*
267. ground (C) *wúrep*
268. ground (H) *síka*
269. gull (H) *mawlóma*
270. gun (?!) (H) *taklep*
271. hail (H) *yópuk*
272. hail (P) *yuppak, charan*
273. hair (H) *ʈap*
274. hair (C), (P) *urí*
275. hand (H) *yawu* (fist? palm?)
276. hand (C) (P) (H) *isú*
277. hand (P) *issu*
278. hand, left (H) (P) *awísh*
279. hand, left (C) *étshum isú*
280. hand, left (P) *awishtat*
281. hand, right (P) *samma, sama*
282. haunches (P) *urek*
283. hawk, redtailed (H) *káknu*
284. head (C) *mótel*
285. head (P) *uri*
286. head (H) *ulí*
287. headache (H) *kayi uri*
288. headdress of feathers (H) *tiwi*
289. headman, village leader (P) *hushk, holom*
290. healthy, well (P) *hashsho, orsen*
291. hear (P) *ochok*
292. heart (P) *sire* (probably 'liver' as in other Ohlonean languages)
293. heart (P) (H) (C) *mini* (but see 111a.)
294. heel (H) *sayan*
295. here (H) *nomor*
296. hernia (P) *hookoy*
    (the 'oo' is pronounced long "oh")
297. high (P) *chiapash, chiaps*
298. hip (H) *chipay*
299. honey (H) *tumá*
300. honey (P) *chichi*
301. honeysuckle (P) *tuwiwan*
302. hoof (H) *kóro* (see 238.)
303. horn (H) *chiri*
304. hot (P) *tawa*

304. house (P) *ruwa*
305. house, my (H) *kan rúwa*
306. hummingbird (H) *humúnu*
307. hummingbird (P) *umuni*
308. husband, my (H) *polup*
309. husband (P) *mako*
310. husband, my (H) *kan makkó*
311. ice (H) *wákkan*
312. ill (P) *maalon, inxan*
313. infant (H) *aláshu*
314. intestines (H) *lituk*
315. intestines (P) *rishok*
316. intoxicated (P) *máchxen*
    (no alcohol before the Spanish came)
317. ivy, ground (P) *nisis*
318. jackrabbit (P) *cheyyesh*
319. jackrabbit (H) *cheyes*
320. jay, Steller's (H) *uyoy*
321. kill (P) *nemni, nimin*
322. knee (H) *tumish*
323. knee (P) *tummish, tumis*
324. knife (H) *sikke*
325. knife (P) *chippe*
326. knuckle (H) *yokán*
327. lake (P) *pawn*
    (like 'pound' without the 'd')
328. lame (P) *kooson*
329. lame (H) *alos*
330. lamprey (P) *uushu*
331. lamprey, brown sea (P) *wattuch*
332. large (P) *wétxesh*
333. laugh (P) *mayshi*
334. laurel (P) *shokkoche, shokochi*
335. leaf (H) *hapón*
336. leaf (P) *maruch*
337. leather (P) *wero* (from Spanish 'cuero')
338. left (H) *áwis*
339. leg (H) (P) *kóro*
    (see 'foot' and 'hoof.' This word probably meant everything from the knee down.)
340. leg (P) *chipay*
341. lightning (C) *wilka*
342. lightning (H) *willep*
343. lightning, flash of (P) *wilpen*
344. lip (H) *tánkar*
345. little (P) *kattit, kutush*
346. liver (P) (H) *sire*
347. lizard sp. (P) *weklap*
348. lizard (H) *haymin*
349. lizard (P) *mexeruwa*

350. look at (P) *hiriri, hiriiti*
351. louse (H) *kaháy*
352. low (P) *pachkil, numakis*
353. lung (H) *tawé*
354. lungs (P) *rummesh, minish* (but see 'chest')
355. madrone (P) *yukan*
356. magpie (H) *aré*
357. man (C) *táres, ṭales*
358. man (P) *chaarish, charish*
359. man, married (H) *háwsen*
360. mask (H) *tulúp*
361. mat (H) *tokó*
362. meadowlark (H) *tirichmin*
363. meal (of seed) (H) *muyén*
364. meat (H) *ris*
365. medicine (H) *unas*
366. medicine dance (H) *chaychi*
367. medicine man [shaman] (H) *soyés*
368. medicine song (H) *ason*
369. meteor (C) *lupkun ósi*
370. midnight (H) *halpiyen múrut*
371. milk [human] (H) (P) *mús*
372. milky way (P) *atsiam*
373. mist (P) *mechekenis, michken*
374. moccasins (H) *háta*
375. mole [animal] (P) *siwot*
376. moon (H) *hinépha*
    ('ph' as in English 'haphazard')
377. moon (C) *kurme*
378. moon (H) *ṭa*
379. moon (P) *chaar*
380. moon, eclipse of (P) *kammun chaar*
381. moon, full (H) *pumen ṭa*
382. moon, half (H) *álum*
383. moon, new (P) *ichaw chaar*
384. moon, three-quarter (P) *michiw chaar*
385. morning star (C) *atólo*
386. mortar (H) (P) *urwán*
387. mosquito (H) *hayyu*
388. mother (P) *aanan, anna, ana*
389. mother (H) *anán*
390. mountain lion (H) *mórus*
391. mountain lion (P) *tamal*
392. mountain range (P) *paranish*
393. mouse (P) *chooy, riina*
394. mounse (H) *rinya*
395. mouth (H) *wehéra*
396. mouth (C) *wiper*
397. mouth (P) *wepperx, weperx*
398. much (P) *irite*

399. mud (C) *shika*
400. mud (H) *lo*
401. mud (P) *hilok*
402. muscles (P) *chipay, chiipay*
403. mushroom (P) *potolmish*
404. muskrat (H) *ramés*
405. mussel (P) *sharo, saro*
406. naked (H) *riske*
407. navel (H) *lóho*
408. near (P) *hamatka, amatka*
409. neck (H) (C) *ranáy*
409a. neckace of shells (H) *maste*
410. necklace (P) *mas*
411. nephew (P) *sinsin, meres* (see 'niece')
412. nest (H) *hésin*
413. nest (P) *hesen*
414. net (P) *tekki*
415. nettle (P) *hapsun, táwhana*
416. new (P) *iichas*
417. niece (P) *meres* (see 'nephew')
418. night (H) *murrút*
419. night (C) *mur*
420. night (P) *murtey*
421. nipples (H) *mus* (see 'breast, woman's')
422. noon (H) *túhis*
423. noon [time to eat] (P) *yemak ammana, orpien tuxis*
424. north (H) *yákmuy*
425. north (P) *wakirx*
426. northwest (P) *wasar*
427. nose (H) (C) *hus*
428. nose (P) *huus, uus*
429. nostril (H) *púnṭuk*
430. now (H) *naha*
431. oak tree (P) *aruwe*
432. oak, black (H) *shatá*
433. oak tree, little (P) *sacha*
434. oak, live (H) *yúkis*
435. oak, live (P) *yukish, yukees*
    (pronounce 'ee' as in 'Beethoven')
436. oak, mountain (P) *rappak*
437. old; old woman (P) *mukiwkenish*
438. old man (H) *mitésmin*
439. old man (C) *huntátsh*
440. old man (P) *yexo* (from Spanish 'viejo')
441. old man (P) *inoknis*
442. old people (H) *uyakus ṭaris*
443. old woman (H) *shúlik*
444. old woman (C) *kétenetsh*
445. orphan (P) *leepe* (for 'ee' see 'oak, live')

446. orphan (P) *wikin*
447. owl, great horned (P) *umish*
448. owl, barn (P) *chaxi*
449. owl, screech (H) *tokóki*
450. pain (H) *kayis*
451. palm of hand (H) *númep*
452. palm of hand (C) *tarka*
453. pelican (P) *iyeiyen*
454. pelican, brown (H) *sawáya*
455. pepperwood (H) *sokotsh*
456. perforation in ear (H) *húlpu*
457. perspiration (P) *challa, challan*
458. pestle (H) *pakshan*
459. pestle (P) *paksan, pakshan*
460. pigeon, little [dove?] (P) *palatat*
461. pigeon, mountain (P) *xaran*
462. pine (P) *xiren*
463. pine, red (P) *xoop*
    (could this mean 'redwood'?)
464. piñon (P) *saak*
465. pipe, stone (P) (H) *torép*
466. pipe stem, of reed (H) *tshisá*
467. plain, flat place (P) *tyahatyak*
468. poplar (P) *porpoo*
469. pound, to (P) *huppay*
470. pulse (H) *nosó*
471. rabbit (P) *werwe*
472. rabbit, cottontail (H) *weren*
473. rabbitskin (H) *sillú*
474. raccoon (P) *sánxay, shashok*
475. rain, to (C) *aman*
476. rain (P) (H) *ámne*
477. rain (P) *amani*
478. rainbow (H) *sukúlay*
479. rainbow (P) *chikil*
480. rancheria, village (P) *ruwat* (see 'house')
481. rat (P) *hire*
482. rattle of snake (H) *hakan*
483. rattlesnake (H) *ipiwa*
484. rattlesnake (P) *hiippiwa, eppiwa*
485. raven (P) *kaakaru*
486. red (P) *patkat, patka*
487. remember (P) *hitmay*
488. return (P) *waate, ettuweni*
489. rib (H) *halém*
490. ribs (P) *tawe*
491. right arm (H) *sámma*
492. right arm above elbow (H) *issú*
493. right arm below elbow (H) *tawép*
494. right ear (H) *samma otsho*

495. right eye (H) *samma hin*
496. right hand (H) *samá*
497. ripe (H) *yiwun*
498. river (P) *rumme*
499. roast (P) *itkay*
500. rock (C) (H) *irék*
501. root and trunk of tree (P) *hiikoch, xikot*
502. rose [flower] (P) *ripin*
503. sage (P) *kashich*
504. sage, lime-leafed [chia] (P) *xélish, pati*
505. saliva (H) *ruswe*
506. salmon (H) *huraka*
507. salmon (P) *uraka, urak*
508. salt (C) *áwes*
509. salt (H) (P) *awés*
510. sand (C) *yukikutsuimi*
    (this is clearly something more complex)
511. sand (H) *wis*
512. sand (P) *wish*
513. Santa Cruz [this is some village name]
    (H) *amilinta*
514. scalp (H) *patá*
515. scar (H) *wasitsh*
515a. scar (P) *taharishmin*
516. sea (P) *kallen*
517. seagull (P) *mollom, mollomo*
518. seal (H) *súlan*
519. seal (P) *sullan, sulan*
520. seal, spotted (P) *awar*
521. seat (H) *ulís*
522. seaweed (P) *ayyi, rukchena*
523. seaweed [kelp] (P) *rukchena*
524. see (P) *hamne*
525. shark (H) *chuuch*
526. shivers, hot-and-cold (P) *tarshin*
527. shoes (P) *warach* (from Spanish 'huarache')
528. shoulder (H) (P) *olót*
529. shoulder (P) *olloch*
530. sick person (H) *semho*
531. sickness (H) *inhán*
532. silent person (H) *totósti*
532a. sinew (H) *hurek*
533. sinew [on back of bow] (H) *pechén*
534. sing (P) *shaawe, sawe*
535. sister, older (P) *taa*
536. sister, younger (H) *útek*
537. sister, younger (P) *uutek, tere*
538. sister, father's older (H) *ansí*
539. sister-in-law (P) *meres, ettenen*
540. skin (H) *patá*

541. skin (P) *pattax*
542. skunk (H) *yawi*
543. sky (C) *tarátak*
544. sky (P) *chara*
545. sky (P) *rini* (means 'above')
546. sleep (P) *echnen, hechen*
547. sling (H) *tawíp*
548. small (P) *numakshin, kutsiush*
549. smoke, to (H) *shukmuy*
550. smoke, to (P) *sukumuy*
551. smoke (P) *kar, kaar*
552. smokehole [of house] (H) *iyikas*
553. snails, small sea (P) *howesh, oos*
554. snake (H) *hintchiwa*
555. snake (P) *hinchiruwa*
556. snake, garter (H) *rayismin*
557. sneeze (P) *hashshinu, hashnu*
558. snow (H) *lo*
559. snow (P) *yuppak, charan, lixan*
560. sole of foot (H) *hátash*
561. son [man speaking] (P) *innis*
562. son [woman speaking] (P) *surkuw*
563. son [father speaking] (P) *tare*
564. son [mother speaking] (P) *tawre*
565. son, my (H) *kan innis*
566. son's son, my (H) *kan meres*
567. sore, a (H) *kayi*
568. south (H) *okes*
569. south (P) *watis*
570. sparrowhawk (H) *ilílu*
571. speak (P) *nonwe, nonwey*
572. spear (P) *hippur*
573. spine (H) *rumés*
574. spit (P) *russuy, rusuy*
575. spring [of water] (H) *konót*
576. squirrel (P) *ee*
577. squirrel, flying (P) *inni*
578. squirrel, ground (H) *e*
579. squirrel, grey (H) *hiré*
580. stab (P) *rippan, ripan*
581. star (P) *ushi*
582. star (C) *usí*
582a. star (H) *ussi*
584. star, morning [Venus?] (C) *atólo*
584a. star, morning (P) *awe*
585. starfish (P) *yaran*
586. stockings [?] (H) *ittú*
587. stomach (H) *píti*
588. stone (P) *irek*
589. storm (H) *yasi amni*

590. storm (P) *amne tarshi*
591. stream (P) *ittew*
592. street [?] (H) *yawun*
593. suckerfish (H) *chinwi*
594. sun (H) (P) (C) *hísmen*
595. sun, eclipse of (P) *kannun hismen*
596. sun, eclipse of (H) *uwikán*
597. sunrise (H) *ámel*
598. sunset (H) *ákun*
599. sweat (H) *talan*
600. sweathouse (H) *túpen*
601. swim (H) *yuha*
602. swordfish (P) *ukkush*
603. tail (H) *tupuy*
604. tail of bird (P) *tuupuy, tupuy*
605. take (P) *huweti*
606. there (P) *nuhu*
607. thief (H) *apsarasmin*
608. think (P) *hintas meshaxe*
609. throat (H) *hókos*
610. throat (P) *horkos*
611. thumb (H) *púnluh* (pronounce the 'h')
612. thunder (C) *túra*
613. thunder (H) *tula*
614. thunder (P) *chura, tura*
615. tide (H) *kaw*
616. tide, high (H) *hoppen*
617. tide, high (P) *mallen*
618. tide, low (H) *kawwen*
619. tide, low (P) *kawen*
620. toad (H) *kares*
621. toad (P) *wakachmin*
622. tobacco (H) *matér*
623. tobacco, native (P) *macher*
624. today (P) *naaha*
625. toe (H) *túyis*
626. toalache (Datura, Jimson Weed) (P) *monoy*
627. tomorrow (H) *múnsa*
627a. tomorrow (P) *munsha*
628. tongue (H) (P) *lasse, lase*
629. tooth (H) (C) *sit*
630. tooth (P) *siit*
631. toothache (H) *murus*
632. tortoise (P) *awnishmen*
633. tree (H) *huyya*
634. tree (P) *shipnan*
635. trees (P) *huya*
636. trout (P) *uuy, tammaria*
637. trout (H) *tamáya*
638. tule (P) *rookosh, haale*

639. twins (H) *palíchimin*
640. uncle [probably mother's brother]
      (P) *attenen*
641. uncle [father's elder brother] (H) *ét*
642. uncle (P) *ete*
643. under (P) *miw muy*
644. unripe (H) *asro*
645. urine (H) *ihi*
646. village (H) *usé*
647. vomit (H) *hachi*
648. wait (P) *suuti, elleypana*
649. walk (P) *chawe, chawey*
650. wall (H) *palér* (from Span. 'pared')
651. warrior (P) *súxxente*
      (prob. from Span. 'sergente')
652. water (H) (C) (P) *si, sii*
653. wave [of water] (H) *rúne*
654. weep (P) *warkay, warka*
655. west (H) *anós*
656. whale (H) *sikkil*
657. whale (P) *chimme*
658. whiskey (H) *kahas*
659. white (P) *loshko, losko*
660. widow (C) *huyyu*
661. widower (C) *lawen*
662. wife (P) *awnan*
663. wife, my son's [female speaking] (H) *pudi*
664. wildcat (H) *toróma*
665. wildcat (P) *xubish, torom*
666. willow (P) *ewi*
667. wind (C) *túye*
668. wind (H) *tárish*
669. wind (P) *tarshi*
670. wings (P) (H) *wima*
671. winnowing basket (H) *warsún*
672. wizard [probably 'shaman'] (P) *amtis*
673. wolf (P) *humniw, humu, heni*
674. wolf, gray (H) *umu*
675. wolf, large spotted (P) *humu*
676. woman (P) *kechkeyma, surkima*
677. woman (C) *aytaks*
678. wrist (H) *anpáyi*
679. year (H) *etéyaw*
680. yesterday (H) (P) *wikán*
681. young man (H) *koṯók*
682. young man (C) *kochó*
683. young woman (H) *acháma*

Numbers

one (P)	*immehen*
two (P)	*utchin*
three (P)	*kapxan*
four (P)	*katxowash*
five (P)	*missurx*
six (P)	*shaken*
seven (P)	*tupuytak*
eight (P)	*usha'atish*
nine (P)	*nukkun*
ten (P)	*iwesh*
eleven (H)	*imhen iyis*
twelve (H)	*utchin iyis*
thirteen (H)	*kappan iyis*
fourteen (H)	*katawash iyis*
fifteen (H)	*misul iyis*
sixteen (H)	*shakken iyis*
seventeen (H)	*tupuytak iyis*
eighteen (H)	*usatis iyis*
nineteen (H)	*nukku iyis*
twenty (H)	*utin iwes*

The Names of Santa Cruz: Santa Cruz Mission Baptismal Records for 18 Awáswas Villages

Introduction

As Native Americans were baptized at Santa Cruz Mission, each convert's name was entered into the book of baptisms. Along with the person's name were recorded his or her village and the names of both parents for a child convert. These names provide information concerning tribal distributions, the chronology of conversion for villages, and ethnic affiliation of villages. Analysis shows that speakers of two Costanoan languages (Awáswas and Mutsun) were among the earliest converts (1791-1810) and that later converts were Northern Valley Yokuts. Comparison of the names of parents with those of baptized adults suggests that on average less than 20% of the parents were ever baptized. This suggests extremely rapid population decline among the unconverted. The final dates of Awáswas baptisms suggest that the entire population ceased to exist outside the mission ten years after its establishment.

Population and Parents' Names

The 18 villages studied for this paper produced a combined total of 765 converts who were baptized at Mission Santa Cruz. The years of the baptisms, number of baptisms and the Awáswas and Spanish names of the 18 villages are listed below:

Awáswas Name	Spanish Name	Years	Baptisms
Achistaca	San Dionysio	1791-1795	75
Alistaca		1795-1800	2
Aptos	San Lucas	1791-1797	90
Chaloctaca	Jesus	1792-1796	34
Cajasta	San Antonio	1795-1802	5
Chitaca	San Juan	1795-1802	217
Cotoni	Santiago	1792-1800	80
Cupacta	Sta. Agueda	1795	1
Mitene	San Rafael	1793-1794	12
Partacsi	San Bernardo	1795	29
Ritocsi	San Jose	1793-1801	13
	San Gregorio	1791	2
Sayant	S. Juan Capistrano	1791-1795	54
Socon	La Candelaria	1795-1797	4
Somontac	Santa Clara	1793-1801	12
Suchesen	Del Corpus	1792	2
Tasun		1794	2
Uypi	San Daniel	1791-1795	83

These represent all 18 villages at which conversions began in the years 1791 through 1795. These probably were those settlements located closest to the mission. The villages of Aptos and Sayant were probably located on the land grants of the same name at Aptos and Felton respectively. Chitaca and San Gregorio may have been located on the coast in southern San Mateo County. The remaining villages cannot be located until some early Spanish map is discovered which shows the locations of various settlements.

In 1802 conversions from a new set of villages "en el parage de San Francisco Xavier" began. While these new converts were definitely Costanoan, it is not clear whether or not they are Awáswas. I suspect that they came from the area of Watsonville or San Juan Bautista but cannot be certain of this.

The last names of converts from the original 18 villages were recorded in 1802. It can be assumed that few if any survivors remained in the villages at this point in time. Because of the rapidity with which the native populations disappeared, it has usually been assumed by anthropologists that nearly all of the population was baptized and absorbed into the mission system and that the number of baptisms is a fair estimate of the original population. An examination of the Santa Cruz mission records suggests that this assumption is incorrect. The presence of parents' names allows us to check the baptism records to determine how many of the parents were baptized.

In the baptism records of Santa Cruz for the 18 Awáswas villages are listed 223 records which represent 223 child baptisms. In this number are 174 records which contain the names of both parents and 49 which contain the names of single parents. Baptisms began on October 9, 1791. By the end of that year 77 persons had been baptized. Children made up 75% of this group. Children accounted for more than a third of the baptisms in four of the next five years. In the first six years 200 children were brought to the mission from the 18 villages. In the next six years only 23.

Comparison of names of parents with the names of adults baptized reveals that most parents were never baptized. A total of 339 different individuals are mentioned as parents. An exhaustive study of the baptism records for each village reveals that only 72 (21.2%) of these individuals were ever baptized. The breakdown by village is as follows:

Village	Parents Baptized	Parents Mentioned	Percentage
Achistaca	6	36	16.7%
Aptos	10	48	20.8%
Cajasta	4	21	19.0%
Chitaca	20	81	25.0%
Cotoni	8	38	21.1%
Mitene	0	7	0.0%
Partacsi	4	6	66.7%
Ritocsi	0	2	0.0%
San Gregorio	0	1	0.0%
Sayant	6	40	15.0%
Somontac	0	2	0.0%
Uypi	9	40	22.5%

Many of these adults must have died after their children were baptized but before they themselves were baptized. It is also noticeable that many adults are listed who are not mentioned as parents (428 individuals). While some of these were old people without young children and others may have been young adults, it seems unbelievable that 428 of the 500 adults baptized had no children. My feeling is that there was a tremendous population decline of unbaptized individuals with more than 70% of the adults and perhaps a higher percentage of the children dying before being baptized.

We can only speculate as to the causes of this rapid decline in population. The nearly total disruption of the native economy which resulted from removal of many people to the missions must have played a role. I also suspect that epidemic diseases may have had an even larger role. Cook has discussed the role of measles in extremely high death rates (up to 30% in one year) at some missions.[2]

The data also seem to indicate a pattern whereby children were taken to the missions and probably immediately baptized. They were joined later by their surviving parents. In only 9 cases was a parent baptized before a child. In 77 others the child was baptized before the parent. The mission records seem to confirm the assertions of some authors that the principal means of recruitment to the missions was the stealing of children with the subsequent "conversion" of their parents.

Photograph of a page from the Santa Cruz Mission Baptismal Records, volume 1, 1791-1857. This first volume is bound in soft brown calfskin with a cord loop closure. The page shown here contains baptismal records 732 through 737 from the end of 1796 and the beginning of 1797. Photo courtesy of the Diocese of Monterey Archives.

Notes:

[1] This article is extracted from a paper of the same name presented by Richard Levy at the 5th annual California Indian Conference at Humboldt State University, October 12-15, 1989.

[2] Cook, Sherburne F., *The Conflict Between the California Indians and White Civilization I: The Indian Versus the Spanish Mission*; Ibero-Americana 21; Berkeley, California; 1943.

Santa Cruz Mission Baptismal Records for 18 Awáswas Villages
(Pinart Transcript)

Village	Year	Type*	#	Name	Sex	Parent or Spouse 2	and	Parent 2
Achistaca	1791	A	001	Moslon	(M) hija de	Y-noc	y	Trocsen
Uypi	1791	A	002	Suquest				
Uypi	1791	A	003	Yrien Russuen	(M)			
Sayant	1791	A	004	Salis	hijo de	Lachigui	y	Misip
Achistaca	1791	A	005	Zalan	hijo de	Chaiaire	y	Pinguini
Achistaca	1791	A	006	Zamisigua	hijo de	Guarop	y	Napen
Achistaca	1791	A	007	Chocon	hijo de	Pasicor	y	Octio
Sayant	1791	A	008	Caillec	hijo de	Nuiles	y	Omocol
Sayant	1791	A	009	Guisen	hija de	Zucumen	y	Salen
Sayant	1791	A	010	Chiquin	hija de	Zucumen	y	Salen
Sayant	1791	A	011	Sennasta	hija de	Mutaca	y	Guapet
Sayant	1791	A	012	Aycon	hija de	Chiquil	y	Zesen
Sayant	1791	A	013	Zeluem	hija de	Roresic	y	Titemis
Sayant	1791	A	014	Sorem	hija de	Ajaje	y	Nayem
Achistaca	1791	A	015	Guisant	hijo de	Gilus	y	Simos
Sayant	1791	A	016	Zaujem	hija de	Ysim	y	Cusemes
Sayant	1791	A	017	Chiquinan	hija de	Paquin	y	Guasapam
Achistaca	1791	A	018	Zuqulen	hija de	Talocasi	y	Uansin
Sayant	1791	A	019	Chiser	hijo de	Zamijin	y	Zocasen
Sayant	1791	A	020	Eles	hijo de	Mocole		
Uypi	1791	A	021	Puisas	hija de	Conejo	y	Oufate
Uypi	1791	A	022	Sipas	hijo de	Conejo	y	Oufate
Uypi	1791	A	023	Mistrec	hijo de	Conejo	y	Oufate
Uypi	1791	A	024	Masues	hijo de	Uvoques	y	Yeguen
Uypi	1791	A	025	Caussot	hijo de	Yscon	y	Sipan
Uypi	1791	A	026	Asuc	hija de	Curin	y	Cuquemis
Uypi	1791	A	027	Homombris	hija de	Curin	y	Cuquemis
Uypi	1791	A	028	Cu-nes	hija de	Zucumen	y	Caupan
Uypi	1791	A	029	Losinemen	hija de	Conejo	y	Ouratte
Aptos	1791	A	030	Zorone	hijo de	Molenis		
Uypi	1791	A	031	Suguit	hija de	Conejo	y	Laium
Uypi	1791	A	032	Panijen	hija de	Zumegst	y	Sajarete
Uypi	1791	A	033	Chusen	hijo de	Zumegst	y	Sajarote
Aptos	1791	A	034	Molegnis				
Uypi	1791	A	035	Uiaguis				
Uypi	1791	A	036	Ynaquin				
San Gregorio	1791	A	037	Archenis				
Aptos	1791	A	038	Solue	(M)			
Uypi	1791	A	039	Yegues	(M)			

Village	Year	Type*	#	Name	Sex	Parent or Spouse 2	and	Parent 2
Uypi	1791	A	040	Sallum	(M)			
Uypi	1791	A	041	Zalluc	hija de	Asois	y	Yminis
Uypi	1791	A	042	Guegues	hija de	Chusis		
Uypi	1791	A	043	Negpus	hijo de	Chusis		
Uypi	1791	A	044	Mutac	hijo de	Llames		
Uypi	1791	A	045	Chaguens	hija de	Licui	y	Alche
Sayant	1791	A	046	Zories	hijo de	Zocun	y	Salen
Sayant	1791	A	047	Sachat	hijo de	Paquin	y	Guasapat
Achistaca	1791	A	048	Charium	hija de	Ypejen		
Achistaca	1791	A	049	Suyul	hijo de	Pasicor	y	Rusuan
Achistaca	1791	A	050	Susnet	hija de	Chamagsi	y	Hujun
Achistaca	1791	A	051	Uprai	hija de	Pisa	y	Chitemis
Achistaca	1791	A	052	Sambray	hija de	Pisa	y	Chitemis
Sayant	1791	A	053	Zaujen	hija de	Guaris	y	Aui=ns
Uypi	1791	A	054	Chalognis	hijo de	Licui	y	Tasin
Uypi	1791	A	055	Ouguen	hijo de	Ayquiaso	y	Luiam
Uypi	1791	A	056	Ochos	hijo de	Sulan		
Aptos	1791	A	057	Atuquen				
Aptos	1791	A	058	Chagelis	hijo de	Puisat	y	Ysuent
Uypi	1791	A	059	Guaian				
Uypi	1791	A	060	Suguit				
Uypi	1791	A	061	Sausin				
Uypi	1791	A	062	Sllunem	hija de	Atess	y	Cuchipan
Uypi	1791	A	063	Ugchilli	hija de	Sachi	y	Pasur
Uypi	1791	A	064	Us	hija de	Aguis	y	Chuna
Uypi	1791	A	065	Llaquel	(M)			
Aptos	1791	A	066	Sasuen	hija de	Lasac	y	Rien
Uypi	1791	A	067	Chaitin	hija de	Maguen	y	Viles
Uypi	1791	A	068	Apis	(M) su madre			Ompuisp
Uypi	1791	A	069	Olchin	(M)			
Uypi	1791	A	070	En-nen	(M) su madre			Caujan
Uypi	1791	A	071	Guitas				
Uypi	1791	A	072	Usu	(M)			
Aptos	1791	A	073	Auem				
Aptos	1791	A	074	Chinntus	hija de	Paguechuqu		
Uypi	1791	A	075	Guesant	hija de	Lulles		
Uypi	1791	A	076	Ouiquinu				
San Gregorio	1791	A	077	Llagen	hija de	Chip		
Aptos	1792	A	078	Llolloc				
Uypi	1792	A	079	Ansate				
Achistaca	1792	A	080	Upejen	(M)			
Uypi	1792	A	081	Otuete	hijo de	Guites		
Sayant	1792	A	082	Guines	hija de	Mutac	y	Tauitin
Aptos	1792	A	083	Choget	hija de	Zenem		su madre
Sayant	1792	A	084	Nutem	hija de	Mutac	y	Tauitin
Aptos	1792	A	085	Zumumc				
Chaloctaca	1792	A	086	Ules				
Aptos	1792	A	087	Cuicheus				
Uypi	1792	A	088	Otiguen				
Chaloctaca	1792	A	089	Lluillin	hija de	Autraca	y	Gausemis
Uypi	1792	A	090	Misapat	(M)			

Village	Year	Type*	#	Name	Sex	Parent or Spouse 2	and	Parent 2
Chaloctaca	1792	A	091	Sirinte	hijo de	Gelelis	y	Ypasin
Chaloctaca	1792	A	092	Caturun	hija de	Gelelis	y	Ypasin
Uypi	1792	A	093	Chuculec	hija de	Lulcoxi	y	Sarot
Chaloctaca	1792	A	094	Zimorou				
Chaloctaca	1792	A	095	Zejos	hijo de	Cholmen	y	Nisipen
Uypi	1792	A	096	Zalelis				
Cotosi	1792	A	097	Tisic	hijo de	Echic	y	Ruris
Sayant	1792	A	098	Uehuc				
Achistaca	1792	A	099	Rishuc	(M)			
Achistaca	1792	A	100	Taeec				
Achistaca	1792	A	101	Sagiti				
Sayant	1792	A	102	Atest				
Cotosi	1792	A	103	Chanu	hija de	Guasquel	y	Echiem
Achistaca	1792	A	104	Oluem	(M)			
Achistaca	1792	A	105	Sauxcut	(M)			
Chaloctaca	1792	A	106	Guinuiti				
Cotosi	1792	A	107	Sasues	(M)			
Uypi	1792	A	108	Zunjen	(M)			
Uypi	1792	A	109	Yron	(M)			
Uypi	1792	A	110	Yellenti	hija de	Zurguin	(M)	
Achistaca	1792	A	111	Zuicam	(M)			
Achistaca	1792	A	112	Roiesic				
Aptos	1792	A	113	Yellaua				
Uypi	1792	A	114	Sipur	(M)			
Uypi	1792	A	115	Osoc=cihit	(M)			
Suchesen	1801	A	116	Laclah				
Uypi	1792	A	117	Chocsen	hija de	Axoc	y	Sichon
Sayant	1792	A	118	Cateran	hija de	Atxexi	y	Chiamis
Chaloctaca	1792	A	119	Uypoc	hijo de	Sujulin	y	Zemisan
Chaloctaca	1792	A	120	Chichical				
Chaloctaca	1792	A	121	Samit	hija de	Saumin	y	Ujate
Chaloctaca	1792	A	122	Zipan				
Chaloctaca	1792	A	123	Zunegecsi				
Chaloctaca	1792	A	124	Rauquin	(M)			
Chaloctaca	1792	A	125	Lassac				
Chaloctaca	1792	A	126	A-none				
Chaloctaca	1792	A	127	Ypasin	(M)			
Chaloctaca	1792	A	128	Nisipen	(M)			
Uypi	1792	A	129	Saroc	(M)			
Uypi	1792	A	130	Aspen	hija de	Lullas		
Cotosi	1792	A	131	Amorhol	hijo de	Guinitu		
Cotosi	1792	A	132	Uquem	hija de	Zugilua	y	Auslon
Cotosi	1792	B	133	Guisguilpu	y	Chiem		
Cotosi	1792	A	134	Cholgati	hija de	Callonimi	y	Quiquem
Aptos	1793	B	135	Zupas	y	Yutem		
Uypi	1793	A	136	Sincan	(M)			
Chaloctaca	1793	A	137	Saistenc				
Aptos	1793	A	138	Sitcome	hijo de	Gueltutu		
Aptos	1793	A	139	Cunete	hija de	Getruro	y	Antice
Uypi	1793	B	140	Guihiquis	y	Carseue		
Aptos	1793	A	141	Puisat				

Village	Year	Type*	#	Name	Sex	Parent or Spouse 2	and	Parent 2
Aptos	1793	A	142	Masies	hijo de	Chucoas	y	Chancoc
Aptos	1793	A	143	Sicualis				
Aptos	1793	A	144	Osilloc				
Aptos	1793	A	145	Sucut	hija de	Llucumut	y	Ymuta
Uypi	1793	A	146	Secut	(M)			
Sayant	1793	A	147	Paquin				
Cotosi	1793	A	148	Sapiquilo	hijo de	Zujilo		
Chaloctaca	1793	A	149	Usate	(M)			
Uypi	1793	A	150	Casseuc	(M)			
Sayant	1793	A	151	Chugiut				
Uypi	1793	A	152	Sumoxt				
Mitene	1793	A	153	Uctex				
Mitene	1793	A	154	Uayas	hijo de	Gurumis		
Uypi	1793	A	155	Simmimis				
Mitene	1793	A	156	Zuiguimemis	(M)			
Mitene	1793	A	157	Miscamis	su madre	Atssxan		
Aptos	1793	A	158	Puisat	(M)			
Achistaca	1793	A	159	Rechentis	hijo de	Llaguexi	y	Zimmicai
Cotosi	1793	A	160	Parses				
Sayant	1793	A	161	Suian	su madre	Zugullin		
Sayant	1793	A	162	Chelcon	hija de	Guarapat	(M)	
Ritocsi	1793	A	163	Questen	hija de	Josaie	y	Guascan
Cotosi	1793	A	164	Ymisun	(M)			
Uypi	1793	A	165	Lulluis				
Aptos	1793	A	166	Zan-nen	(M)			
Aptos	1793	A	167	Cactramis	(M)			
Sayant	1793	A	168	Socal				
Mitene	1793	A	169	Sumuras	hija de	Tajuile	(M)	
Mitene	1793	A	170	Japaxi	hijo de	Gueches		
Achistaca	1793	A	171	Cauchamis	(M)			
Cotosi	1793	B	172	Suipan	y	A-nanti		
Achistaca	1793	A	173	Yoson	(M)			
Cotosi	1793	A	174	Llenco	hijo de	Chas	y	Morchon
Cotosi	1793	A	175	Zuxila				
Cotosi	1793	A	176	Masilon	(M)			
Aptos	1793	A	177	Saquexi	hija de	Chilientu		
Aptos	1793	A	178	Ulas	hija de	Uxcanti	(M)	
Aptos	1793	A	179	Ulgen	hija de	Suxi	y	Rusuan
Cotosi	1793	A	180	Myait	hija de	Guequel	y	Echien
Aptos	1793	B	181	Zayan	y	Uget		
Achistaca	1793	B	182	Asusotuex	y	Cholget Rusan		
Ritocsi	1793	B	183	Gusay	y	Somcon=guaican		
Achistaca	1793	B	184	Lluegis	y	Zuncan=jimilin		
Mitene	1793	A	185	Cuchigite	(M)			
Chaloctaca	1793	A	186	Saunin				
Somontac	1793	A	187	Euxexi	hijo de	Ypuis	y	Tausus
Cotosi	1793	A	188	Sumeexi	hijo de	Guacham	y	Llullem
Mitene	1793	A	189	Juam	hija de	Choles	y	Zaniete
Cotosi	1793	A	190	Zosos	hijo de	Misteca	y	Ocxio
Cotosi	1793	A	191	Elupun	hijo de	Sipi	y	Parit
Cotosi	1793	A	192	Licsen	hijo de	Sucul	y	Sapen

Village	Year	Type*	#	Name	Sex	Parent or Spouse 2	and	Parent 2
Sayant	1793	A	193	Susiur				
Cotosi	1793	A	194	Sumen	(M)			
Cotosi	1793	A	195	Nuten	hija de	Soquen	y	Chasas
Sayant	1794	A	196	Mutac	hijo de	Lachi	y	Seuxan
Sayant	1794	A	197	Sequer				
Sayant	1794	A	198	Siquil	hijo de	Omochol	y	Zuiea
Sayant	1794	A	199	Zolos	hijo de	Lachi	y	Seurous
Sayant	1794	A	200	Chapirin	(M)			
Sayant	1794	A	201	Zeram	hija de	Cameset	y	Zallem
Sayant	1794	A	202	Guapet				
Cotosi	1794	A	203	Mocsam	hija de	Sipit	y	Parit
Achistaca	1794	A	204	Llapa	hijo de	Callon	y	Llapug
Cotosi	1794	A	205	Soros	hijo de	Chaguejoc	y	Pagmit
Tasun	1801	A	206	Ocot	(M)			
Mitene	1794	A	207	Sanit	(M)			
Cotosi	1794	A	208	Sapegan	(M)			
Achistaca	1794	A	209	Tacast	hijo de	Coton	y	Milguet
Sayant	1794	A	210	Niconexi	hija de	Zelos	y	Chaquirin
Cotosi	1794	A	211	Chichin	hija de	Lachimaxi	y	Chursan
Achistaca	1794	A	212	Zupigu:in	hijo de	Jares	y	Ocoit
Achistaca	1794	A	213	Yachaxi	hijo de	Lleguexe	y	Tungai
Achistaca	1794	A	214	Yllugaia	hijo de	Chamaisi		
Cotosi	1794	A	215	Nispani	hija de	Jemet	y	Parit
Cotosi	1794	A	216	Ziquiam	hija de	Mistrecat	y	Ocsion
Sayant	1794	A	217	U~nec				
Cotosi	1794	A	218	Asosc	hija de	Xalsaxi	y	Jomojon
Cotosi	1794	A	219	Zuipuna	(M)			
Uypi	1794	A	220	Cunchut				
Uypi	1794	A	221	Lachimaxi	(M)			
Aptos	1794	A	222	Olche	hija de	Chuot	y	Ulla
Achistaca	1794	A	223	Lloquen	(M)			
Sayant	1794	A	224	Uysuipet	(M)			
Sayant	1794	A	225	Zaximat	(M)			
Aptos	1794	A	226	Chomeret	(M)			
Aptos	1794	A	227	Gamisati	hijo de	Chilintu	y	Rissen
Aptos	1794	B	228	Zaran	y	Cachua		
Aptos	1794	B	229	Licui	y	Solot		
Aptos	1794	A	230	Sauten	hija de	Zupag	y	Yuten
Aptos	1794	A	231	Sugugue	(M)			
Cotosi	1794	A	232	Ocsion	(M)			
Cotosi	1794	A	233	Parit	(M)			
Cotosi	1794	A	234	Galan	(M)			
Mitene	1794	A	235	Zapsit	hija de	Lissi		
Cotosi	1794	A	236	Yaquamsi	(M)			
Uypi	1794	A	237	Suculam				
Uypi	1794	A	238	Osiet	(M)			
Achistaca	1794	A	239	Chaguex	(M)			
Aptos	1794	A	240	Oregit	(M)			
Achistaca	1794	A	241	Tutexexi	hijo de	Caiton		
Cotosi	1794	A	242	Chachoix				
Cotosi	1794	A	243	Chimachi				

Village	Year	Type*	#	Name	Sex	Parent or Spouse 2	and	Parent 2
Sayant	1794	A	244	Chaque	hijo de	Puchur	y	Sichan
Cotosi	1794	A	245	Mosseic	(M)			
Cotosi	1794	A	246	Jaissut	hija de	Chajas		
Cotosi	1794	A	247	Guisclani	hijo de	Guiguil	y	Moctun
Cotosi	1794	A	248	Sucut				
Cotosi	1794	A	249	Yimat				
Cotosi	1794	A	250	Chagax				
Mitene	1794	A	251	Quisnam	(M)			
Mitene	1794	A	252	Manem	(M)			
Aptos	1794	A	253	Rusuan	(M)			
Achistaca	1794	A	254	Chilini	hijo de	Peye		
Achistaca	1794	A	255	Ynos				
Achistaca	1794	A	256	Samecxi				
Achistaca	1794	B	257	Zursuquin	y	Ecceiot		
Cotosi	1794	A	258	Uspanti	(M)			
Achistaca	1794	A	259	Chiguil	hijo de	Genex	y	Ypsan
Achistaca	1794	A	260	Cheiten	hijo de	Camagsenim	y	Zabllem
Achistaca	1794	A	261	Llumita				
Achistaca	1794	A	262	Luruchac	(M)			
Sayant	1794	A	263	Oxpiti	(M)			
Achistaca	1794	A	264	Ustui	(M)			
Somontac	1794	A	265	Zuquion	(M)			
Cotosi	1794	A	266	Pussacsi	hijo de	Piltanc	y	Rusuan
Sayant	1794	A	267	Uchiun				
Chaloctaca	1794	A	268	Gemillin	hija de	Palas		
Cotosi	1794	A	269	Surin				
Cotosi	1794	A	270	Zunocsi	(M)			
Cotosi	1794	A	271	Chomor				
Cotosi	1794	A	272	Syccan				
Achistaca	1794	A	273	Satan	hija de	Viturun		
Chaloctaca	1794	A	274	Sonchel				
Achistaca	1794	A	275	Simos	(M)			
Sayant	1794	A	276	Salem	(M)			
Cotosi	1794	A	277	Jaischas	hijo de	Unsut		
Cotosi	1794	A	278	Sulic	hijo de	Morichon	(M)	
Achistaca	1794	A	279	Samen	hijo de	Suyputo	y	Pabon
Achistaca	1794	A	280	Rejes				
Achistaca	1794	A	281	Autraca				
Cotosi	1794	A	282	Llellege				
Cotosi	1794	A	283	Tuisan				
Cotosi	1794	A	284	Piltac				
Uypi	1794	A	285	Omiuispe	(M)			
Uypi	1794	A	286	Zumuru	hijo de	Atexi		
Uypi	1794	A	287	Ychiqui				
Uypi	1794	A	288	Guasapat	(M)			
Uypi	1794	A	289	Zursan	(M)			
Sayant	1794	A	290	Zuamesi				
Uypi	1795	A	291	Ansate	(100 ans)			
Uypi	1795	A	292	Sachi	(M)			
Uypi	1795	A	293	Ategi				
Uypi	1795	A	294	Uche				

Village	Year	Type*	#	Name	Sex	Parent or Spouse 2	and	Parent 2
Uypi	1795	A	295	Pasur	(M)			
Uypi	1795	A	296	Cuchipam	(M)			
Socon	1795	A	297	Luchuche				
Cajasta	1795	A	298	Mosoromnio	hijo de	Guarcalis	y	Cuinescus
Cajasta	1795	A	299	Zupac	hijo de	Guiltut		
Cajasta	1795	A	300	Yu~nan	hijo de	Tacunte	y	Chuivaste
Cajasta	1795	A	301	Crisin	hija de	Zia	y	Mirite
Aptos	1795	A	302	Alloi	hijo de	Chuchigite	y	Chigiuan
Cupacta	1795	A	303	Guilnut				
Cajasta	1795	B	304	Atix	y	Quinis		
Uypi	1795	A	305	Aguis				
Uypi	1795	A	305	Peliaste				
Cotosi	1795	A	307	Gusquil				
Aptos	1795	A	308	Geturust				
Aptos	1795	A	309	Yssuen	(M)			
Aptos	1795	A	310	Sajarot	(M)			
Uypi	1795	A	311	Amuis o/ Chana	(M)			
Cotosi	1795	A	312	Echien	(M)			
Aptos	1795	A	313	Sontot	hijo de	Chupas	y	Ysaiste
Aptos	1795	A	314	Palac				
Aptos	1795	A	315	Jetuas				
Aptos	1795	A	316	Sujuit	hija de	Sicastes		
Aptos	1795	A	317	Jacoit	(M)			
Aptos	1795	A	318	Ychinin	(M)			
Cajasta	1795	A	319	Lipus				
Cajasta	1795	A	320	Guiltute				
Cajasta	1795	A	321	Guisuut				
Socon	1795	A	322	Cuchup				
Cajasta	1795	A	323	Sachate				
Socon	1795	A	324	Siquirin				
Partacsi	1795	A	325	Ullec	hijo de	Chimus	y	Siquirin
Partacsi	1795	A	326	Onirmot				
Partacsi	1795	A	327	Guallac				
Achistaca	1795	A	328	Yurpen				
Partacsi	1795	A	329	Gualmosi	hijo de	Camexi	y	Taitait
Partacsi	1795	A	330	Chipos				
Partacsi	1795	A	331	Guatocni				
Chaloctaca	1795	A	332	Roguesi	hijo de	Palac	y	Uscan
Chaloctaca	1795	A	333	Usilli				
Chaloctaca	1795	A	334	Tanca	hijo de	Cholmes	y	Ullege/n
Partacsi	1795	A	335	Sapan	(M)			
Sayant	1795	A	336	Tairin	(M)			
Sayant	1795	A	337	Cascoit	hija de	Etoc	y	Rachuan
Sayant	1795	A	338	Zurjan	(M)			
Sayant	1795	A	339	Ginnen	(M)			
Partacsi	1795	A	340	Lacsen	(M)			
Aptos	1795	A	341	Guisiont				
Aptos	1795	A	342	Zayan				
Aptos	1795	A	343	Licumus				
Aptos	1795	A	344	Chupan				
Aptos	1795	A	345	Tupac				

Village	Year	Type*	#	Name	Sex	Parent or Spouse 2	and	Parent 2
Sayant	1795	A	346	Surimi				
Cajasta	1795	A	347	Moitoit	hija de	Ronoc	y	Sumurin
Chaloctaca	1795	A	348	Cholmos				
Partacsi	1795	A	349	Chusac				
Partacsi	1795	A	350	Aytop				
Sayant	1795	A	351	Ullegen	hija de	Lachi	y	Soron
Sayant	1795	A	352	Gousap	(M)			
Chaloctaca	1795	A	353	Ciscan	(M)			
Achistaca	1795	A	354	Rusuan	(M)			
Partacsi	1795	A	355	Jamos				
Chaloctaca	1795	A	356	Zalehes				
Partacsi	1795	A	357	Camexi				
Sayant	1795	A	358	Sepi				
Chaloctaca	1795	A	359	Jaicha				
Chaloctaca	1795	A	360	Tosausi				
Chaloctaca	1795	A	361	Siguem	(M)			
Somontac	1795	A	362	Sunuze				
Somontac	1795	A	363	Sucul				
Achistaca	1795	A	364	Samal				
Achistaca	1795	A	365	Pellecs	hijo de	Atuys	y	Uscan
Achistaca	1795	A	366	Sapax				
Cotosi	1795	A	367	Sentescu				
Cotosi	1795	A	367	Casllec				
Achistaca	1795	A	368	Tocon				
Cotosi	1795	A	370	Posmon	(M)			
Achistaca	1795	A	371	Chuyun	(M)			
Cotosi	1795	A	372	Raguan	(M)			
Achistaca	1795	A	373	Jusate	(M)			
Ritocsi	1795	A	374	Sipe/n	(M)			
Achistaca	1795	A	375	Moco~non	(M)			
Cotosi	1795	A	376	Tuniaze	(M)			
Cotosi	1795	A	377	Chirmit	(M)			
Ritocsi	1795	A	378	Mouyen	(M)			
Cotosi	1795	A	379	Jonea	hijo de	Chuges		
Chaloctaca	1795	A	380	Jimius	hija de	Y~noc	y	Uytirun
Somontac	1795	A	381	Ycuis				
Achistaca	1795	A	382	Jalsaxi				
Achistaca	1795	A	383	Susjun				
Sayant	1795	A	384	Ysin				
Cotosi	1795	A	385	Atuis				
Achistaca	1795	A	386	Etues				
Cotosi	1795	A	387	Charoc				
Cotosi	1795	A	388	Gui~nic				
Somontac	1795	A	389	Saguem				
Achistaca	1795	A	390	Olico				
Achistaca	1795	A	391	Zursu/n				
Partacsi	1795	A	392	Tijiris				
Somontac	1795	A	393	Usen	(M)			
Achistaca	1795	A	394	Uansi	(M)			
Achistaca	1795	A	395	Pussin	(M)			
Sayant	1795	A	396	Eusemis	(M)			

Village	Year	Type*	#	Name	Sex	Parent or Spouse 2	and	Parent 2
Achistaca	1795	A	397	Guitirun	(M)			
Cotosi	1795	A	398	Uesan	(M)			
Achistaca	1795	A	399	Ocoit	(M)			
Cotosi	1795	A	400	Yunsute	(M)			
Cotosi	1795	A	401	Pision	(M)			
Somontac	1795	A	402	Ausen	(M)			
Achistaca	1795	A	403	Yentas	(M)			
Partacsi	1795	A	404	Japo/n	(M)			
Cotosi	1795	A	405	Yspante	(M)			
Cajasta	1795	A	406	A~nar	(M)			
Achistaca	1795	A	407	Rusan	(M)			
Sayant	1795	A	408	Soron	(M)			
Ritocsi	1795	A	409	Guascan	(M)			
Achistaca	1795	A	410	Tomojon	(M)			
Uypi	1795	A	411	Solot	(M)			
Uypi	1795	A	412	Tasuet	(M)			
Ritocsi	1795	A	413	Jechuas				
Achistaca	1795	A	414	Zupitechimi				
Cotosi	1795	A	415	Llutui	(M)			
Aptos	1795	A	416	Zapsite	(M)			
Ritocsi	1795	A	417	Eciot	(M)			
Ritocsi	1795	A	418	Oguen	(M)			
Alistaca	1795	A	419	Orpon	(M)			
Chitaca	1795	A	420	Chacha	hijo de	Suajanas	y	Masuen
Chitaca	1795	B	421	Suchac	y	Echicos		
Chitaca	1795	A	422	Guasir	hijo de	Tojos	y	Meseren
Chitaca	1795	B	423	Caguicas	y	Auxen		
Chitaca	1795	A	424	Saturo	hijo de	Samans	y	Guasac
Chitaca	1795	A	425	Gichinaguis	hijo de	Zatimure	y	Rusiquis
Chitaca	1795	A	426	Cotoes	hijo de	Mosacris	y	Sacirate
Chitaca	1795	A	427	Joli/oit	hijo de	Topoc	y	Chocton
Chitaca	1795	A	428	Pujcu	hijo de	Ustis	y	Pujen
Chitaca	1795	A	429	Sipon	hijo de	Juniapis	y	Sisiron
Chitaca	1795	A	430	Pallac	hijo de	Oiorbac	y	Chilchac
Chitaca	1795	A	431	Lacig	hija de	Luchuchu	y	Yomscu
Chitaca	1795	A	432	Chision	hija de	Jamur	y	Guatuc
Chitaca	1795	B	433	Coja	y	Chupulluc		
Chitaca	1795	A	434	Cogpen	hija de	Lanis	y	Asirato
Chitaca	1795	B	435	Tatemure	y	Ymasta		
Chitaca	1795	A	436	Puras	hija de	Sayne	y	Nauquin
Chitaca	1795	A	437	Chachac	hija de	Jonsat	y	Temor
Chitaca	1795	A	438	Upesen	(M) de	Mugir	y	Josuat
Chitaca	1795	A	439	Luchuchu				
Chitaca	1795	A	440	Pusat				
Chitaca	1795	A	441	Juaxan				
Chitaca	1795	A	442	Suchac				
Chitaca	1795	A	443	Auxa				
Chitaca	1795	A	444	Jamus				
Chitaca	1795	A	445	Lanis				
Chitaca	1795	A	446	Alite				
Chitaca	1795	A	447	Tatimur				

Village	Year	Type*	#	Name	Sex	Parent or Spouse 2	and	Parent 2
Chitaca	1795	A	448	Majacris				
Chitaca	1795	A	449	Topoc				
Chitaca	1795	A	450	Caguisat				
Chitaca	1795	A	451	Cutamale				
Chitaca	1795	A	452	Sayne				
Chitaca	1795	A	453	Achat				
Chitaca	1795	A	454	Ustisal				
Chitaca	1795	A	455	Jourat				
Chitaca	1795	A	456	Gelle				
Chitaca	1795	A	457	Lonsin	(M)			
Chitaca	1795	A	458	Yabonas	(M)			
Chitaca	1795	A	459	Masuem	(M)			
Chitaca	1795	A'	460	Echicos	(M)			
Chitaca	1795	A	461	Chupullu	(M)			
Chitaca	1795	A	462	Guasin	(M)			
Chitaca	1795	A	463	Asixeto	(M)			
Chitaca	1795	A	464	Rusiquisi	(M)			
Chitaca	1795	A	465	Sauna	(M)			
Chitaca	1795	A	466	Chogot	(M)			
Chitaca	1795	A	467	Auxem	(M)			
Chitaca	1795	A	468	Nauquin	(M)			
Chitaca	1795	A	469	Rastam	(M)			
Chitaca	1795	A	470	Pujem	(M)			
Chitaca	1795	A	471	Temus	(M)			
Chitaca	1795	A	472	Quispim	(M)			
Chaloctaca	1795	A	473	Lugxuxi				
Partacsi	1795	A	474	Chupis				
Partacsi	1795	A	475	Mujuillil				
Partacsi	1795	A	476	Jusquis	hijo de	Laboc	y	Yastil
Partacsi	1795	A	477	Joros				
Partacsi	1795	A	478	Chimus				
Partacsi	1795	A	479	Josaie				
Partacsi	1795	A	480	Jenep				
Ritocsi	1795	A	481	Tarum	(M)			
Ritocsi	1795	A	482	Ypsan	(M)			
Ritocsi	1795	A	483	Tuntun	(M)			
Partacsi	1795	A	484	Ustis				
Partacsi	1795	A	485	Laboc				
Partacsi	1795	A	486	Zonqueus				
Partacsi	1795	A	487	Zerquen	(M)			
Partacsi	1795	A	488	Yastil	(M)			
Partacsi	1795	A	489	Guasen	(M)			
Partacsi	1795	A	490	Morchon	(M)			
Sayant	1795	A	491	Chaguen	(M)			
Cotosi	1795	A	492	Chupen	(M)			
Achistaca	1795	A	493	Tagcin				
Partacsi	1795	A	494	Melssoguini	(M)			
Achistaca	1795	A	495	Najam	(M)			
Achistaca	1795	A	496	Tineya	(M)			
Achistaca	1795	A	497	Ussuype	(M)			
Chitaca	1796	A	498	Zucis	hijo de	Guasochi	y	Ymana

Village	Year	Type*	#	Name	Sex	Parent or Spouse 2	and	Parent 2
Chitaca	1796	A	499	Seyute	hijo de	Toyop	y	Morejare
Chitaca	1796	A	500	Tallap	hijo de	Zallup	y	Aschi
Chitaca	1796	A	501	Camasin	hijo de	Pasan	(M)	
Chitaca	1796	A	502	Yrachis	hijo de	Taiup	y	Murejate
Chitaca	1796	A	503	Omuca	hijo de	Yaugussi		
Chitaca	1796	A	504	Mallolle	hijo de	Jamesta	(M)	
Chitaca	1796	A	505	Sotoro	hijo de	Januas	(M)	
Chitaca	1796	A	506	Tamgis				
Chitaca	1796	A	507	Aspuch	hijo de	Collop	y	Comoguen
Chitaca	1796	A	508	Lipoc				
Chitaca	1796	A	509	Piuan				
Chitaca	1796	A	510	Cuiseta				
Chitaca	1796	A	511	Jo~nore				
Chitaca	1796	A	512	Palsu				
Chitaca	1796	A	513	Sichirimas	hijo de	Toyop	y	Murejate
Chitaca	1796	A	514	Jisca	hija de	Urchesa	y	Chagsete
Chitaca	1796	A	515	Megeroa	(M)			
Chitaca	1796	A	516	Satyro	(M)			
Chitaca	1796	A	517	Sojoron	hija de	Ja~na	y	Lojou
Chitaca	1796	A	518	Zape	hija de	Jiniotic	y	Sayen
Chitaca	1796	B	519	Ajorbac	y	Chilchae		
Chitaca	1796	A	520	Tapiyun	(M)			
Chitaca	1796	A	521	Saitante	(M)			
Chitaca	1796	A	522	Coucan	(M)			
Chitaca	1796	A	523	Gualluc	hija de	Chausagua	y	Tomenme
Chitaca	1796	A	524	Jopinem	(M)			
Chitaca	1796	A	525	Satguit	hija de	Collop	y	Corusuer
Chitaca	1796	A	526	Yacharaste	(M)			
Chitaca	1796	A	527	Ayuen	hija de	Zoyop	y	Yumarasti
Chitaca	1796	A	528	Chegenem	hija de	Popolaste	y	Socton
Chitaca	1796	A	529	Zelanio				
Chitaca	1796	A	530	Quituste				
Chitaca	1796	A	531	Tallupo				
Chitaca	1796	A	532	Zatimuro				
Chitaca	1796	A	533	Rimis				
Chitaca	1796	A	534	Chaguila				
Chitaca	1796	A	535	Guelcas				
Chitaca	1796	A	536	Meseren				
Chitaca	1796	A	537	Sajuero	(M)			
Chitaca	1796	A	538	Aschi	(M)			
Chitaca	1796	A	539	Soncate	(M)			
Chitaca	1796	A	540	Moconon	(M)			
Chitaca	1796	A	541	Soquen	(M)			
Chitaca	1796	A	542	Paysan	(M)			
Chitaca	1796	A	543	Jamay	(M)			
Aptos	1796	A	544	Haugit	hijo de	Zilluacsi	y	Ssiuot
Aptos	1796	A	545	Ssacal	hijo de	Litcoa	y	Sunurcsi
Aptos	1796	A	546	Chunet	hija de	Pog~noya	y	Llata
Aptos	1796	A	547	Chusnanit	hijo de	Jalchin	y	Pergete
Aptos	1796	A	548	Lluliecsi	hijo de	Talchin	y	Apinat
Aptos	1796	A	549	Cipiar	hijo de	Rugussa	y	Ogellem

Village	Year	Type*	#	Name	Sex	Parent or Spouse 2	and	Parent 2
Aptos	1796	A	550	Jacinte	hijo de	Rugussa	y	Mayoasta
Aptos	1796	A	551	Chamam				
Aptos	1796	A	552	Ssumure				
Aptos	1796	A	553	Mascam	hija de	Tiuca		
Aptos	1796	A	554	Zauasta	hija de	Notoor	y	Tomel
Aptos	1796	A	555	Ssacar	(M)			
Aptos	1796	A	556	Aliquiel	(M)			
Aptos	1796	A	557	Uyunte	hija de	Notoor	y	Matue
Aptos	1796	A	558	Osnoite	hija de	Jalchic	y	Ursite
Aptos	1796	A	559	Ssumam	hija de	Litcoa	y	Sumurin
Aptos	1796	A	560	Jinuanis				
Aptos	1796	A	561	Potsen				
Aptos	1796	A	562	Napen	(M)			
Aptos	1796	A	563	Sonon	(M)			
Aptos	1796	A	564	Mayuasta	(M)			
Aptos	1796	A	565	Apenat	(M)			
Aptos	1796	A	566	Justan	(M)			
Aptos	1796	A	567	Apsan	(M)			
Chitaca	1796	A	568	Tupac				
Chaloctaca	1796	A	569	Tayon	(M)			
Aptos	1796	A	570	Tiuca	(M)			
Chitaca	1796	A	571	Sipus	(M)			
Aptos	1796	A	572	Jomel	(M)			
Aptos	1796	A	573	Saunet	(M)			
Aptos	1796	A	574	Moguesocoa	(M)			
Aptos	1796	A	575	Temug				
Aptos	1796	A	576	Luxoa	hija de	Lipo	y	Chauite
Aptos	1796	A	577	Guallon				
Aptos	1797	A	578	Chacsed	(M)			
Cotosi	1797	A	579	Maltani	(M)			
Cotosi	1797	A	580	Sumasta	(M)			
Chitaca	1797	A	581	Santaroa				
Chitaca	1797	A	582	Pasquite				
Chitaca	1797	A	583	Ronchete	(M)			
Chitaca	1797	A	584	Moctem				
Chitaca	1797	B	585	Cunumaspo	y	Tison		
Chitaca	1797	A	586	Palluai				
Cajasta	1797	A	587	Etop				
Cajasta	1797	A	588	Loyolis				
Chitaca	1797	A	589	Emiem	(M)			
Chitaca	1797	A	590	Palloc				
Socon	1797	A	591	Muyam	(M)			
Aptos	1797	A	592	Chagsete	(M)			
Cajasta	1797	A	593	Ejois	hijo de	Racunte	y	Chasxa
Chitaca	1798	B	594	Racunte	y	Mirote		
Chitaca	1798	A	595	Jijamis				
Chitaca	1798	A	596	Licoalis				
Chitaca	1798	A	597	Guazon	(M)			
Chitaca	1798	A	598	Ma-nicun	(M)			
Chitaca	1798	A	599	Ouen	(M)			
Chitaca	1798	A	600	Mascan	(M)			

Village	Year	Type*	#	Name	Sex	Parent or Spouse 2	and	Parent 2
Chitaca	1798	A	601	Zaapa	(M)			
Chitaca	1798	A	602	Zimurara	(M)			
Chitaca	1798	A	603	Sanguite	(M)			
Chitaca	1798	A	604	Palas				
Chitaca	1798	A	605	Pachguite	(M)			
Chitaca	1798	A	606	Tuyquesta	(M)			
Chitaca	1798	A	607	Pagnute	hija de	Rugussa	y	Ogellem
Chitaca	1798	B	608	Urchesa	y	Chacsete		
Chitaca	1798	A	609	Sunene	hijo de	Ellimoneme	y	Soton
Chitaca	1798	A	610	Oyorba				
Chitaca	1798	A	611	Rachcana				
Chitaca	1798	A	612	Pustupuy				
Chitaca	1798	A	613	Samana				
Chitaca	1798	A	614	Causute				
Chitaca	1798	A	615	Yucu/cus				
Chitaca	1798	A	616	Moyo/s				
Chitaca	1798	A	617	Tassimate	(M)			
Chitaca	1798	A	618	Socton	(M)			
Chitaca	1798	A	619	Jortiem	(M)			
Chitaca	1798	A	620	Chacsete	(M)			
Chitaca	1798	A	621	Otimoyca	(M)			
Chitaca	1798	A	622	Rucusta	(M)			
Chitaca	1798	A	623	Talemis	(M)			
Chitaca	1798	A	624	Llapama	(M)			
Chitaca	1798	A	625	Najam	(M)			
Chitaca	1798	A	626	Semgeti	(M)			
Chitaca	1798	A	627	Yutuam	(M)			
Chitaca	1798	A	628	Cisquin	(M)			
Chitaca	1798	A	629	Cuntute	(M)			
Chitaca	1798	A	630	Zipiron	(M)			
Chitaca	1798	A	631	Zaycnane	(M)			
Chitaca	1798	A	632	Zajun	(M)			
Cotosi	1798	A	633	Ssacal	hijo de	Causest	y	Mastem
Cotosi	1798	A	634	Lacium	(M)			
Cajasta	1798	A	635	Palas				
Chitaca	1798	A	636	Tulian				
Chitaca	1798	A	637	Jo~nicon				
Chitaca	1798	A	638	Ssalute				
Chitaca	1798	A	639	Calcam				
Chitaca	1798	A	640	Teina				
Chitaca	1798	A	641	Guallu				
Cajasta	1798	A	642	Pachguite	(M)			
Chitaca	1798	A	643	Yajuem	(M)			
Chitaca	1798	A	644	Asereto	(M)			
Chitaca	1798	A	645	Magtosu	(M)			
Chitaca	1798	A	646	Monguis	(M)			
Chitaca	1798	A	647	Pinissam	(M)			
Chitaca	1798	A	648	Matgui	(M)			
Chitaca	1798	A	649	Chuasta	(M)			
Chitaca	1798	A	650	Zatur	(M)			
Chitaca	1798	A	651	Iriguesta	(M)			

Santa Cruz
County
History Journal
Issue 5, 2002

Village	Year	Type*	#	Name	Sex	Parent or Spouse 2	and	Parent 2
Chitaca	1798	A	652	Pastam	(M)			
Chitaca	1798	A	653	Yutuam	(M)			
Cotosi	1798	A	654	Gucecsi	hijo de	Causut	y	Mastem
Cotosi	1798	A	655	Pi-namin	(M)			
Chitaca	1798	A	656	Tumullu				
Chitaca	1798	A	657	Tonem				
Cajasta	1798	A	658	Chigtou	hijo de	Uchucu	y	Gultegem
Cajasta	1798	A	659	Chilate				
Chitaca	1798	A	660	Pispin	(M)			
Chitaca	1799	A	664	Saseran	(M)			
Cajasta	1799	A	666	Racunte				
Cajasta	1799	A	667	Zuntuc				
Cajasta	1799	A	668	Uchuchu				
Cajasta	1799	A	669	Ullis				
Cajasta	1799	A	670	Casasmin				
Cajasta	1799	A	671	Quiasi				
Cajasta	1799	A	672	Ucsal				
Cajasta	1799	A	673	Jachin				
Cajasta	1799	A	674	Mirete	(M)			
Cajasta	1799	A	675	Agelate	(M)			
Cajasta	1799	A	676	Chiquem	(M)			
Cajasta	1799	A	677	Assiquim	(M)			
Cajasta	1799	A	678	Churem	(M)			
Cajasta	1799	A	679	Pellon	(M)			
Cajasta	1799	A	680	Quetepui	(M)			
Cajasta	1799	A	681	Sumajate				
Cajasta	1799	A	682	Quisiguam				
Cajasta	1799	A	683	Ynollati	(M)			
Chitaca	1800	A	685	Gepeson	hija de	Soirostte	y	Seyem
Chitaca	1800	A	686	Momen	(M)			
Chitaca	1800	A	687	Esquem	hija de	Aquins	y	Jamijin
Chitaca	1800	A	688	Lasin	hija de	Sipsip	y	Ochomosin
Chitaca	1800	A	689	Olola	hijo de	Guelloni	y	Llilon
Chitaca	1800	A	690	Tocote	hijo de	Santarua		
Chitaca	1800	A	691	Ca-nui	hijo de	Tecoyos	y	Simem
Chitaca	1800	A	692	Tapsiti	hija de	Jallon	y	Zalleguem
Chitaca	1800	A	693	Pertem	hija de	Jaruia	y	Conuem
Chitaca	1800	A	694	Yomuseti	hija de	Tancoi	(M)	
Chitaca	1800	A	695	Pullui				
Chitaca	1800	A	696	Chisem	hija de	Tancoi	(M)	
Alistaca	1800	A	705	Usture				
Cajasta	1800	A	706	Jatuas				
Cajasta	1800	A	707	Josoime	hijo de	Rojuisi	y	Ojollem
Cajasta	1800	A	708	Cholomos				
Cajasta	1800	A	709	Chilai	hijo de	Huichini	y	Chursan
Cajasta	1800	A	710	Chaulajate	hija de	Chiguil	y	Quimate
Cotosi	1800	A	711	Orusute				
Cajasta	1800	A	712	Touilme				
Cajasta	1800	A	713	Guimete				
Cotosi	1800	A	714	Causute	(M)			
Somontac	1801	A	716	Molloc				

Village	Year	Type*	#	Name	Sex	Parent or Spouse 2	and	Parent 2
Somontac	1801	A	717	Sosorona				
Somontac	1801	A	718	Untucula				
Somontac	1801	A	719	Morchon	(M)			
Ritocsi	1801	A	720	Milpan	(M)			
Chitaca	1801	A	721	Cunijoanco	(M)			
Chitaca	1801	A	722	Pichinchigui				
Chitaca	1801	A	723	A~nuis	(M)			
Chitaca	1801	A	724	Socoisiat	(M)			
Chitaca	1801	A	725	Pascom	(M)			
Chitaca	1801	A	726	Zaquis				
Cajasta	1801	A	727	Morem				
Chitaca	1802	A	728	Sesute	hijo de	Lelis		
Chitaca	1802	A	729	Sagian				
Chitaca	1802	A	730	Majas	hijo de	Tujal	y	Turpan
Chitaca	1802	A	731	Lucatuas				
Cajasta	1802	A	732	Aimiguiat	(M)			
Cajasta	1802	A	733	Asiati	hija de	Elilis	y	Sinam
Chitaca	1802	A	734	Cholposta	hija de	Rurecxi	y	Cosorom
Chitaca	1802	B	735	Rurecxi	y	Cullnun		
Cajasta	1802	A	736	Rujus				
Chitaca	1802	A	737	Jenes				
Chitaca	1802	A	738	Maxjas				
Chitaca	1802	A	739	Tupal				
Chitaca	1802	A	740	Yaum				
Cajasta	1802	A	741	Cuiset	(M)			
Chitaca	1802	A	742	Sumtum	(M)			
Chitaca	1802	A	743	Einasta	(M)			
Chitaca	1802	A	744	Culluem	(M)			
Chitaca	1802	A	745	Turpan	(M)			
Chitaca	1802	A	746	Jepi~nem	(M)			
Chitaca	1802	A	747	Yanuta	(M)			
Chitaca	1802	A	748	Usipu	(M)			
Chitaca	1802	A	749	Casorom	(M)			
Chitaca	1802	A	750	Sunuati	(M)			
Chitaca	1802	A	751	Simom	(M)			
Chitaca	1802	A	752	Upanix	(M)			
Cajasta	1802	A	754	Yamamti				
Cajasta	1802	A	758	Puchete				
Cajasta	1802	A	760	Jalsute	(M)			
Cajasta	1802	A	761	Lasium	(M)			
Cajasta	1802	A	763	Ojesi	(M)			

Santa Cruz
County
History Journal
Issue 5, 2002

200

Profile: Victor Mondragon

Victor Mondragon, 1928-1999. Courtesy of Charlie Higuera.

Recently a dear Amah, Victor Mondragon, left this world. Victor was born in 1928, a grandson of Ascencion Solorsano de Cervantes. Victor was the tribe's unofficial genealogist and, many of us felt, the heart of the Amah. His passing is mourned. Joe Mondragon, Victor's eldest brother, tells this story:

Shortly after Victor's death, Joe opened the front door of the family's home in Pacific Grove. There in the street in front of their house was a fox. It looked directly at the family as if it wished to talk to them. It stared for a moment and lingered on as loved-ones often do, not being able to express their feelings of love. Then, it gave one last glance and trotted off to the West.

Shortly thereafter, a hummingbird flew into the senior Mondragon's home. It flew quickly throughout the house as though it knew its way around. Then the bird circled each family member as though it was saying good bye and flew out the back door.

Finally, during the memorial gathering for Victor at Mission San Juan Bautista, as a Pomo medicine woman began a mourning prayer, overhead was heard a loud screech. After a pause, the Pomo medicine woman began her prayer again, only to be interrupted by another loud screech. This time, those in attendance looked up to see an eagle circling high overhead. The medicine woman was taken aback, as the eagle is a very powerful messenger. She waited as the eagle, circling again, screeched a third time before flying off.

Each of these animals, the number three, and the west direction are significant in Amah lore. We see the animals' signs as a fitting good-bye from Victor, a trusted friend to all he met and whose lives he touched.

—Edward Ketchum

Reburial Verses

by Linda Yamane

This is the day
    and here I am
    walking out to the mound
    past willows
    and grasses.
Toch, deer, has walked here too—
    I see tracks pointing the way.

The air is clean and a-buzz
    with sound of *mumure*, fly,
      and bee,
    both moving busily.
Butterflies on gentle breeze
      appear,
    then pass delicately.

So here I am
    and others, too, will come this day,
    each in his or her own way.
    Such different lives, different faces,
    from different directions, different places.
      Yes,
    more will come, but now it is a quiet time
      alone,
  to sit
    to watch
      to listen
        to feel the morning.

Ishmen, the sun, has warmed the earth.
    I touch it—this dirt so black and rich
    and full of tiny fluted oyster shells.
Did I say I was alone?
No, big black beetle marches here,
      resolute and intent.
Later I won't notice him,
    so busy will I be,
    but now I watch him carefully.

Hey, there's someone watching me
    with wary eye —cautiously
      moving closer, step by careful step,
      ready to flee
      should this giant, me,
        make a move.
But I sit still and watch
    this small sentry pause
      intermittently,
    doing push-ups, lizard-ly,
      and showing me
    the blue-ness people rarely see
      beneath his chin
    and on his belly.

Others now have come,
    and time for working has begun
      as we take you
        one-by-one
        out of boxes
    and lay you in the sun.

Soft depressions in the mound seem
    the perfect place to lay you down
      on beds of sage,
      in rows and rows,
    following the contours of the ground.
Round heads, long bones,
      vertebrae, jaw bones—
    I look at you and say,
"This is what we'll look like some day."

Well, some say we should keep you,
    to learn from your bones.
Once I longed for that kind of knowledge,
    thinking I had little else to connect me
      with my past.
    There was so much I just had to know.

But I love you enough to let you go,
    to do what my heart tells me is right—
    to return you to the ground.

No longer are you boxed and bagged,
    no longer specimens tagged.
And if we don't know the details of
    your bodies and lives, we are still rich
    with the knowledge that you are
        our people,
    that you were here before us,
    living in your own way.
You have indeed, left a legacy—
    we are still your family.
And so we've come,
    bringing the bones of you,
        our ancestors,
            home.

I take a moment to
    survey the scene—
    you look so peaceful,
        serene, and
    redwing blackbird sings.
Then best of all
    ummun, hummingbird,
    makes a call,
    hovering over you.
An auspicious blessing, I'd say,
    for one who helped create the world
        to visit us this day.
He sees that all is right,
    then redirects his flight
        and is gone.

It's back to work and
Ishmen burns, testing our resolve.
    Muscles strain
        sweat flows
            mouths thirst
            hours go.
This is no small task.
But we're not here for fun—
    a sacred job
    must be done …

Bones of woman
    I lay you down
        with cooking stones
            you once stirred 'round
                and 'round
        inside your cooking baskets.
Food warmed, then bubbled, boiled—
    meal and water
    thickening,
    rich and satisfying,
    nourishing
    bodies of family and friends.
No longer have you bodies to tend
    since just these bones remain,
    but we hope your spirits
        have been pleased
        and that this act
            has eased
            a bit of the pain.

Illustration by Linda Yamane

Big strong man-bones
        in my hands—
    femurs, humeri,
        pelvic fans.
I lay them down
        carefully
    recreating
        as best I can
    proper anatomy
        and symmetry.
What is this?
        A jaw of deer.
And look,
        a piece of antler here.
Perhaps this antler was a tool
        for flaking bits of stone,
        achieving proper sharpness and shape
        with skill and strength—
            and these bones.
Now these bones lie still,
        but once with weapons
        and hunter's skill
        brought venison home.

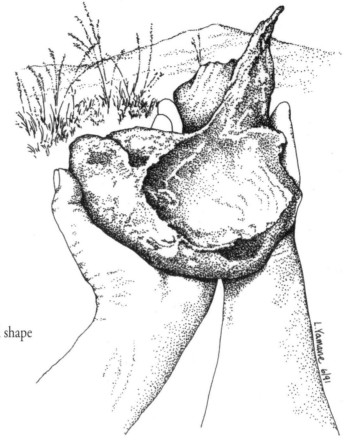

Illustration by Linda Yamane

Oh, this has to be
        the most difficult for me—
            to hold within my hands
                the bones of babies
                and older children—
                    treasured sons and daughters.
See, I'm a parent,
            too,
        and can feel how
        hard it must have been
            to lose you.
How those hearts must have ached
        at your early passing.

Now all I can do
        is return to you
        these tiniest of
            tiny
        olivella beads
        which your loved ones gave you—
            hundreds of
            perfectly rounded
            and perforated
            tokens of devotion.

Well, time has passed
        and now it is late in the day.
            Here you all lay
                nestled together,
            bones against bones
            in three depressions
            in the mound.

Santa Cruz
County
History Journal
Issue 5, 2002

Time to bring warm dirt around,
and so we lift it from the ground
and bring this blanket —brown—
to cover you.
This will be a big job, too,
but human brigade can see it through
with boxes and barrows
and fortitude.
Feet now tread carefully
back and forth,
aware of your fragility.

I stop to rest,
look down
and gasp.
I see a face
with mouth agape
and horror written there.
Yes, this mass grave also speaks
of travesty
upon a people—
not allowed to rest in peace
with dignity in
their final sleep.
And, oh, a skull
sliced by science
to peer within the very bone.
I can see the sadness here.
Yet there is also much to rejoice—
a healing,
a coming home.
I just can't let you leave that way.
And so I find myself
climbing
down
and changing that face,
putting peace in horror's place.

The time has come to say "Good-bye"
to those we love
but never knew
in life.

You're gone from view
but I doubt that few
here today
will ever forget you.
You've touched our lives
deeply,
and I felt here
only kindness and caring—
people sharing
in the fulfillment
of a common vision.
In the end we stand
waiting to be cleansed
before we leave this day.
We pray
for you
and ourselves.
And when I look to where I know you are
resting
I catch my breath,
for there I see
one final blessing
displayed
as Swallowtail
flutters deftly over all three depressions—
then circles back
and passes gently over our heads.

Now we go,
but we'll be returning,
bringing more
of our
ancestors home.

Statements by Local Indigenous Groups and Individuals

Editors' Note:

"We are still here" is a refrain heard from many California Indians including the indigenous peoples of the Monterey Bay region.

Over the years, however, we have heard that there is but one remaining person in a particular tribe or that there are only two speakers left of a particular Indian language. With stories like these it is easy to think that California Indians no longer exist. This is not true, as many of the articles in this journal show. The following articles are written by or about some of the local indigenous groups and individuals here in the Monterey Bay area today.

We invited all the known active groups of local indigenous peoples to say something about who they are and what they are doing currently. We hope that any group not included here will understand that it was not our intention to overlook them. These groups are a reflection of the diversity and richness of our area. In reading these articles one finds an underlying theme of honor and respect for the ways of their ancestors and of perseverance in the face of difficulty. They continue to research into their past to find ways to live as indigenous people in our modern world.

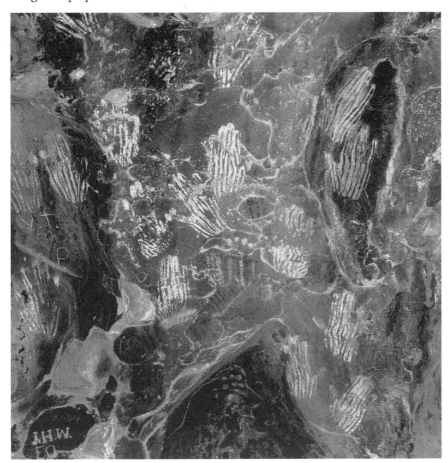

Handprints executed in white paint from the Cave of the Hands, Monterey County. Photo by Trudy Haversat & Gary Breschini.

Santa Cruz
County
History Journal
Issue 5, 2002

Amah/Mutsun Band of Ohlone Costanoan Indians

by Edward Ketchum

"Ekwe neppe human makke mehe, anyis trarah, numan trawra Hoole."
"It is not this one that we see, it is another heaven, where God lives."

We the Amah/Mutsun Band of Ohlone/ Costanoan Indians are happy to present to you this short message. The word "Amah" means "people" in the language of our forebears. We have been called Mutsun because one of the first villages encountered by the Spanish in our language area was named Mutsun. But we believe it appropriate to call ourselves Amah. The Amah are those who trace their lineage to the villages of Mutsun, Uñijaima, Xisca, Orestac, Ochentac, Pagsin, Teboatac, Ausaima, Tiuvta, Chitactac, and Tamarox.

The Amah were primarily indigenous to the Pajaro River drainage basin. The Amah called this land "Popeloutchom." This land known as Popeloutchom is special. The blood, sweat, and ashes of our forebears are part of the land. Neither we, nor Popeloutchom can be separated. This is a land of uncommon beauty and of great natural resources: salt for curing and shells to make money beads at the Western sea; asphalt and eternal water in the central region; flint for arrow points, mercury, soap, and clay in the North and South; stone for mortars and pestles to the East. It is a land of fertile soil and varying but mostly mild climate. Once it was home to great herds of elk and antelope, to streams filled with fish and valleys filled with plentiful plant foods.

We have been quiet in the past as the land was not overly developed and the most sacred lands were not in danger. However, recently there has been a great deal of change. We are concerned that if we do not act now, it will be too late. We wish to protect the Pajaro River and our most sacred places, which are still relatively unspoiled.

The hills to the West and North of San Juan Bautista are where the rocks, "Old One-Leg's Tunnel," and the Laayani are located, and where are found the medicine tree, the asphalt volcano, the spring of eternal water, and the "sacred hill of the Kuksui." Without protection these sacred places will not remain undamaged.

We believe we will be limited in our ability to protect this valuable heritage unless we are a federally recognized tribe. Once our anonymity served to protect us, now it is an impediment to our federal recognition. We now must expose ourselves so we may once again be the legitimate stewards of Popeloutchom. Obtaining federal recognition is very difficult, however, we have three very strong aids, and possibly a fourth.

First: In 1929 John Peabody Harrington, an ethnologist from the Bureau of American Ethnology of the Smithsonian Institution, visited our "grandmother," Ascencion Solorsano de Cervantes. Harrington described her as "a woman with all her five senses." Indeed, in her last years, she possessed an incredible memory and knowl- edge of the language, customs, and life both before and after Spanish contact. During most of Ascencion's life, she was a "doctora," healing all that she could from her little homes in Gilroy and San Juan Bautista. She is still a healer, as her memory serves to heal our community.

Second: We have the mission records. When fully interpreted and utilized, they will tell much of our history and genealogy. We have begun the process, but there are literally thousands of records still to be analyzed.

Third: We have the Amah people. We are small in number, but have a great desire to again be a recognized tribe. In 1998 we met at Mission San Juan Bautista to celebrate the life of Ascencion. A large group joined to dedicate a plaque in her memory. She was the last Indian buried at Mission San Juan Bautista. Joe Mondragon gave a short dedicatory speech in her memory. Then Mission priest, Father Ed Fitzhenry, told the following story:

A few days earlier, he was walking through the mission gardens on a beautiful day when he saw the mission's cat with a hummingbird in its mouth. The father thought that surely the hummingbird was dead as the cat pawed and threw its small frail captive in the air. However, when the cat put the hummingbird down, as cats do when they are playing with their prey, Father Fitzhenry rushed over and picked up the wounded bird in a napkin. Carefully he cleaned and examined it. He could find no physical harm. He gently raised the hummingbird aloft on the napkin. To his amazement the bird lifted its small head, raised its weakened body, fluttered its wings, and flew off as though nothing had happened. The hummingbird is Amah's symbol and the Father thought this was perhaps a metaphor for the Amah as we too are rising from our figurative captivity. He wished us God's blessings and then proceeded to bless Ascencion's plaque.

Surely this is a sign. Just as the cat held the small, weakened hummingbird in its mouth, ready to kill it, we have been in the mouth of a much stronger foreigner. Perhaps like the Father, you will be our fourth aid.

To learn more about the Amah or to aid us in this important work to protect Popeloutchom, please call or email:

Charlie Higuera, tribal council chairperson
(831) 375-5045
email: aerieways@aol.com

May the wild geese again rest in Soap Lake.

May we hear the elk trumpet in the highlands.

May the eagle and condor again fly overhead.

May the women make baskets.

May the Amah long-distance running game be played once again.

May the earth never stop quaking.

The eldest Amah, Aemitium (Carrie) Higuera, recently celebrated her 100th birthday on August the 8th, 2000. May Hoole's spirit be with you always, Carrie, and with your loving family. Photo taken August 8, 1990; courtesy of Charlie Higuera

Santa Cruz
County
History Journal
Issue 5, 2002

Costanoan-Ohlone
Indian Canyon Resource

by Russell Imrie for Anne Marie Sayers

Children run everywhere playing in the dusk, kicking up the earth in puffs. Young and old, friends mingle, telling stories and sharing news. Laughing women work around a table peeling apples. Stew simmers in a huge pot. We are all ready for a feast this evening. Natives from all over North America are gathered for a ceremony indigenous to these canyons and valleys. As has happened for thousands of years, the keeper of the Canyon is welcoming the community to share the Canyon as if it were their own land. Ann Marie Sayers, the present keeper of the Canyon, carries on the traditions of her mother, Elena Sayers, a full blood Mutsun woman, who told Ann Marie that as long as the songs are sung and the ceremonies continued, the earth would go on.

Anne Marie Sayers greeting visitors to Indian Canyon.
Photo by Russell Imrie.

In the heart of Costanoan territory, on the eastern flank of the Gavilan range in the San Francisco Bay area, the Canyon is the only truly Native land shared by all of us who have lost or left our own Native homes. The Canyon has been home to Native Californians for thousands of years as shown by oral tradition, by artifacts such as mortars and small lithic tools, and, most recently, by the human remains of a 12-year-old boy found there. The Canyon was first noted in Spanish records as an area of Agujes, for the springs that filled the marshy swamp or Cienega and is named Indian Gulch on old maps from the 1800s and marked as an "Indian Settlement."

As the mission system was imposed on the local people in the 18th and 19th centuries, many fled to the hills. Hidden behind swamps and inaccessible except for treacherous trails, the Canyon was a haven to these refugees. The area was labeled "steep and useless" in a 19th century map and so settlers did not take the land for ranches and farms. When California was absorbed into the Union (1850), most California Natives became homeless, uncounted, voiceless. With no human or legal rights, they were assimilated or went underground, ignored and marginalized. For better or worse, the Canyon was left to these Natives well into the 20th century. In 1914 a young man from Hollister, Howard Harris, visited the Canyon with his aunt to hire Indian labor. There they met a very old man who said "everyone is up at the falls." Harris tells of walking up the small creek, passing dwellings along the path, and then coming upon people gathered around the waterfall singing in their language.

How this magnificent canyon came to be Indian Country is a colorful story. It started in 1904 when 150 acres spanning the mouth of the canyon were allotted to Ann Marie's great grandfather Sebastian Garcia by the federal government. Ann Marie's mother, Elena, lived on this land until she passed in 1974. At that time, Ann Marie, her brother, Chris, and a small group of friends and family began an 8-year effort to claim the adjoining piece of land that included the waterfalls at the head of the Canyon. In 1988, she succeeded in gaining an allotment of 123 acres of trust land immediately below the falls where she now lives with her family. Thus, there are now two distinct parcels both of which are Indian Country: one the trust land allotted to Ann Marie, the other private land in control of an Indian person and within the traditional homeland of an indigenous population.

Ann Marie makes this property available for Natives from all over who want to celebrate or assemble on indigenous soil. The Canyon includes an ethno-botanical display of Costanoan culture and crafts. Traditional structures are scattered along the creek, including a large arbor, an underground sweat lodge, tule houses, and sweat houses. One of the larger activities is the annual Indian Canyon California Indian Storytelling Festival. Usually held the first Sunday of April, this one-day event brings together storytellers from all over the state in a small intimate setting. A unique opportunity to enjoy and sense the enveloping nature of Native stories, participants always remark on the setting and on the warmth they feel.

Ann Marie is involved in many activities that promote and educate about local indigenous people. Costanoan descendants connect to the community and their heritage through Ann Marie. Schoolchildren schedule trips to the Canyon. Visitors come from all over the world, including Europe, the Americas and around the Pacific. In 1999, Australian Aborigine artists whose work was exhibited at the Legion of Honor in San Francisco

asked that Natives from this land meet and welcome them. Ann Marie took part in this traditional welcome and then, before they left for home, welcomed them to the Canyon where they shared community values and enjoyed visiting Native land. Thus, the goal of acknowledging tribal status gains strength from the unique land-based perspective of Indian Canyon.

For further information, please contact:

Ann Marie Sayers and Costanoan Indian Research
PO Box 28
Hollister, CA 95024-0028
email: (c/o Russell Imrie) 1prieta@garlic.com
website: http://www.indiancanyon.org

Events:

Indian Canyon California Indian Storytelling Festival in May. Other events (some public, some private) take place throughout the year. Student field trips are always welcome and can be combined with a stop at Mission San Juan Bautista. For details visit the website listed above. Email contacts are forwarded to Ann Marie.

Tule House, Indian Canyon.
Photo by Russell Imrie.

Santa Cruz
County
History Journal
Issue 5, 2002

The Costanoan-Rumsen Carmel Tribe

by Tony Cerda

Documentary sources have clearly and consistently identified a community of Rumsen Indians living in the vicinity of the Carmel River in the Monterey Bay area. Through the documentation of Carmel mission priests, the Costanoan Rumsen Carmel Tribe can trace its lineage back to Mission San Carlos in the Carmel Valley. The original site of the village of Echilat, where our ancestors lived when they came to the mission San Carlos in 1775, is now known as Rancho San Carlos in Carmel Valley.

Recently, the tribe has begun research on the tribe's ancestry dating back to 1715 with Simon Francisco "Chanjay," progenitor of the present day Costanoan-Rumsen Carmel tribe. There are fifteen hundred direct descendants of Chanjay among the tribe's members. Other lineages include, but are not limited to, the descendants of Margarita, wife of Manuel Butron and Maria Espinoza.

Eighteen treaties between local California Indians and the United States Government were negotiated in 1851-1852. California congressmen rigorously opposed these treaties. The congressmen claimed that the treaties would be a "hardship" for whites who would be forced to move outside the reservations. Because of the opposition of California's Congressman, Congress refused to ratify the treaties and the Rumsen Band, as one of the parties, was thus denied Federal Recognition and reservation land.

Without federal status and under constant pressure from the influx of non-Indians, the Rumsen tribe moved southward: a migration that eventually led to settlement in the San Gabriel Valley of Southern California where most Costanoan Rumsen tribal members live today.

Membership in the tribe is based on lineage to the Costanoan-Rumsen tribe before 1850. The decision making structure is the tribal council of the Costanoan Rumsen Carmel Tribe, a governing body, elected by the general membership every two years. The elected tribal council is accountable to the membership through annual meetings, newsletters published quarterly, and one-on-one meetings if any member needs further clarification of the council's decisions. Members actively

Dancing on the grass at the Monterey Presidio, February 9, 2001.
Photo courtesy of Tony Cerda.

participate in determining priorities, decisions and strategies at tribal council meetings held monthly and at general membership meetings held annually. Special meetings are called for specific purposes that arise, from time to time, outside the regularly scheduled meetings.

At this time, the focus of our group is on community development, research, history, genealogy and documentation for status clarification. We provide the general public with information about the contributions of our tribe and other California tribes to California history. We celebrate Costanoan culture by demonstrating tribal dance and by sharing California native life with local elementary and secondary schools and with the general public. We assist Native Americans to identify their Indian cultural heritage through research in genealogy and history of the tribe.

We have had a number of significant accomplishments to date that include the following: We leased land in Webb Canyon, Claremont, California, for a ten year period with an option on an additional ten years to be used for ceremonial purposes and for presentations of the tribe's culture and history to the general public. We participated in stopping a major billion dollar development at Rancho San Carlos on land that was the original site of the village of Echilat; and we stopped a project at Los Padres Dam on the Carmel River that would have disturbed the tribe's ancestors burial ground. We have advanced cultural awareness at many sites in Northern and Southern California including the restoration of Crissy field at the Presidio of San Francisco.

Our measurable goal within the next three years is to continue the research on our genealogy and history necessary for federal recognition Our ultimate goal is to achieve federal recognition. Becoming a sovereign nation through federal recognition will change the economic strength and political power of the tribe. It will enable the tribe to control its own destiny within the tribal structure and to accomplish institutional changes that will provide better education and health care for all members and economic development that will lead to self-sufficiency for the tribe.

The history of the Costanoan-Rumsen Carmel tribe reflects a strong desire to maintain their culture regardless of many obstacles. This persistence in maintaining the culture of the tribe is evidenced by a continuing focus on the old ways (language, dancing, sweat lodges, and crafts). This is a major factor in the tribe's survival as a distinct community in today's modern society.

At one time, before the removal from the village of Echilat, the Costanoan-Rumsen people were self-sufficient. Families banded together for economic purposes as well as production. Becoming a federal tribe will once again empower all members of the tribe and future generations.

For more information, please contact :

Costanoan-Rumsen Carmel Tribe
3929 Riverside Drive
Chino, CA 91710

Tribal Office: (909) 591-3117

211

Tony Cerda.
Photo courtesy of Trudy Haversat and Gary S. Breschini.

Santa Cruz
County
History Journal
Issue 5, 2002

The Esselen Tribe
of Monterey County

by Tom Little Bear Nason and hummux

The Esselen made their home deep in the mountains of Big Sur. This was known as the center of the western world, a holy and sacred place of the tribe, where the Medicine People lived in a high mountain valley paradise filled with caves and surrounded by huge stone monoliths with faces of humans and animals. The Esselen had a vitally important job in the function of the Native world, for they were the keeper of the Western Gate, known as the "Window To The West." This window was known and honored for thousands of years as the site of exit from this world into the spirit world.

At the time the Carmel Mission was built, there were about 1000 Esselen people living at the Western Gate. They were forcibly removed to Carmel mission, as well as to Soledad and San Antonio, and soon began to die. They were the first tribe in California to be declared extinct. As they perished, the Window To The West ceased to function.

In the beginning of the 1960s, the Esselen people began to awaken. Tom Little Bear Nason, a seventh generation Esselen Indian was born at the entrance to the western gate. As he started to have visions at the age of eight, his life began to unfold. Over the years more and more was revealed about what would become the resurrection of the Esselen Tribe and the reopening of the Western Gate. At critical times in his life, elders and Medicine Teachers appeared, usually from one of the Hokan tribes, to guide and shape his life and work as the spiritual leader of the Esselen Tribe.

Little Bear has gathered around him a dedicated band of hard working students, teachers, and professionals of all races to assist in the resurrection of the Esselen Tribe. In 1989, Window To The West, Inc. was formed as a not-for-profit educational public benefit corporation dedicated to the study, preservation and teaching of California Indian culture and environmental perspective. With the blessing and assistance of his father, Grandfather Fred Nason, the oldest living tribal member, and his mother, Grandmother Anne Nason, a descendant of the Lambert family, Little Bear has transformed a portion of their ranch into Pachepus Ceremonial Grounds, located in a large fern-filled meadow at the elevation of 3200 feet, deep in the Santa Lucia Mountains in the back country of Big Sur.

The center piece of Pachepus is the Roundhouse, a subterranean 40 foot diameter ceremonial dance house made in the old way; that is, a prayer was said with every shovel full of earth and as each

Roundhouse in the Snow.
Photo courtesy of Trudy Haversat and Gary S.
Breschini.

lodge pole was put in place. At Pachepus are also a screened-in dining lodge, sweatlodge, kitchen, bathroom and shower. The ceremonial grounds are used by many tribes for events in a natural and sacred setting.

Research in a variety of fields continues. A rich collection of archaeological sites exist in Monterey County. Many of these sites are in Esselen territory. Cave pictographs provide a particularly rich cultural legacy from the past. Artifacts from the Isabella Meadows cave have been located and examined. Audio recording of Costanoan/Esselen songs, sung by Viviana Soto and collected by Alfred Kroeber in 1902, are available at the Phoebe A. Hearst Museum of Anthropology, University of California, Berkeley. The originals were recorded on Edison wax cylinders and have subsequently been transferred to tape. The Esselen Deer Dancing Song has been transcribed by Kumal and sung in ceremony. Some of the best specimens of artifacts from the early days in California exist in Russian museums and catalogs of these materials have been located.

Recent work by Randy Milliken and others using computer database analysis of the Mission records has given a fresh perspective to boundaries of the tribal territories. The lineage of the modern Esselen is being traced from the Mission records. All known published sources of recorded Esselen language have been collected, along with several unpublished sources. These range from the word lists of Kroeber through the more recent semantic work of Beeler and David Shaul and a dictionary and language lessons have been developed by hummux. The field notes of Harrington are being sifted for details. Much of this research has been prompted by the effort for federal recognition.

For further information contact:

Tom Little Bear Nason
38655 Tassajara Road,
Carmel Valley CA 93924
or visit our website at www.esselen.com

This is the Esselen Prayer:

Ike, nish I'apa	Aho, my Grandmother
Ike, nish Metxi	Aho, my Grandfather
Kwelmaxa, iniki asatsano	Thank you for this day,
lakai nish mepxeleno.	and for my life.
Lechs amisaxno alpa,	We pray for the deer,
lakai chapisino alpa,	and we pray for the birds,
lakai kalulno alpa,	and we pray for the fish,
lakai memneno alpa,	and we pray for the lizards,
lakai ami'chanaxno alpa.	and we pray for the plants.
Ikship Yakiskik,	Great Spirit,
lex mepxele namoeske,	purify our body,
lakai lex masianax.	and our soul.
Ike!	Aho!

Santa Cruz
County
History Journal
Issue 5, 2002

Ohlone/Costanoan
Esselen Nation Today

Excerpted from the O.C.E.N. Brochure

Vast and beautiful, Central and Northern Monterey County encompasses the ancestral homeland of the past and present day lineages of the Ohlone/Costanoan Esselen Nation. Our ancestors came from at least nine major Rancherias in the Monterey Bay Region.

In December 1602, Sebastian Viscaino sailed into what is now Monterey Bay for repairs and supplies during his long voyage to the mysterious reaches of California. Various tribal members from our coastal Rancherias met Viscaino's ship and provided well-needed food for Viscaino and his crew.

"The land is well populated with Indians without number, many of whom came on different occasions to our camp. They seem to be gentle and peaceful people; they say with signs that there are many villages inland. The sustenance which these Indians eat most of daily, besides fish and shellfish, is acorns and another fruit larger than a chestnut, this is what we could understand of them."
—Sebastian Viscaino

"The port is all surrounded with Rancherias of affable Indians, good natives and well disposed, who like to give what they have, here they brought us skins of bears and lions and deer. They use the bow and arrow and have their form of government. They were very pleased that we should have settled in their country."
— Fray Antonia de la Ascencion

For many years after Viscaino's voyage, trade ships heading east from the Philippines or coming north and south to and from the Vancouver region anchored in the Monterey Bay, and interacted with our ancestors.

In 1770, the Spanish made the decision to build a mission in Monterey, and they called it Mission San Carlos de Borromeo. This colonization effort by the Spanish changed our people's culture, language, government and lives forever. Once brought to a mission and baptized, our ancestors learned a new religion and a new language, were dressed in different clothes, and were not allowed to practice their centuries-old traditions. By December of 1770, the first baptism took place. It was of a young boy, five years old, from Achasta, one of our ancestral Rancherias.

The name "Esselen," the historical self-identification for some of our Rancherias, derives from *Ex'seien*, which means "The Rock." It specifically comes from the declaration: "*Xue elo xonia euene*" (I come from the rock). Contemporary tribal members, while no longer speaking the traditional languages, still use linguistic terms of Esselen origin. Many members refer to the mountainous interior of Carmel Valley, an area of profound spiritual and historical significance, as Cachagua, a name derived from the Esselen word *Xasiuan*.

Today, as a tribe representing this vast region, we have chosen a legal name that reflects the diversity in identification through the times. We are Ohlone/Costanoan Esselen Nation.

Esselen Nation currently consists of approximately 500 enrolled members, with many applications pending. Approximately 60% of our members reside in Monterey and San Benito Counties. We have a Tribal Council representing each of the nine original Rancherias within our territory.

The Ohlone/Costanoan Esselen Nation is currently in the process of reaffirmation with the Bureau of Indian Affairs (BIA). We submitted our tribal narrative to the Branch of Acknowledgement and Research (BAR) on January 25, 1995, during a White House meeting. The completed petition, which meets all recognition standards was hand delivered to BAR in August 1995. At present we continue to work towards the goal of reaffirmation as a federally recognized tribe with the the United States Government. Although unofficially terminated, the families of Ohlone/Costanoan Esselen Nation (historically recognized as the "Monterey Band") continue to thrive by revitalizing tribal government, community and heritage. We are only here because of those that came before us, and we will continue to fight for the rights that our ancestors were denied.

For ten thousand years, the Esselen, Rumsen, Achastian, and Guatcharrone Indians, among others, lived in the Monterey Bay Area without interruption. Despite missionization, government changes, broken treaties, devastation to their culture, and losing their land, their descendants survived. We are Ohlone/Costanoan Esselen Nation.

For additional information, please contact:
Ohlone/Costanoan Esselen Nation
P.O.Box 1301, Monterey, CA 93942
(831) 659-5831
Email: Acominos@aol.com

Web page address: www.talamasca.org/esselen

OCEN Tribal Council: Rudy Rosales, Richard Cominos, Jr., Rich Cominos, Gloria Ritter, Cheryl Urquidez, Marlene Baker, and Duane Thielman
OCEN Tribal Genealogist: Lorraine Escobar, CAILS
OCEN Tribal Administrator: Ann Cominos

215

"xue elo xonia eune"
"We come from the rock"
—Nesia Teyoc
as told to linguist Alphonse Pinart, 1878

Santa Cruz
County
History Journal
Issue 5, 2002

The Pajaro Valley Ohlone
Indian Council

by Lois Robin with Patrick Orozco

Grandmother told us many stories as we were growing up, and one of them was about the rancho San Andreas which was located on Trabing Road off Buena Vista. She spoke out that that was where she and all her brothers and sisters were born. Her story goes on to say that when her father, Francisco Rios, came to town on errands or business, he would hitch up the buckboard that was pulled by his horse, Babe. Grandma says,"he sat us down in the wagon and started down the old dusty road around five miles. Down the road he would always stop at a certain location, get off the wagon and tell us to wait. We could hear him singing chants and raising his arms and then he came back, looked at us and said, "Your people are buried there. Always respect them and protect them." She also told us that when she was about eight years of age, she was present at the burial of one of our relatives at this place.

It was in 1975 one late afternoon when I was near this same area. At this time I felt very strange knowing that I was not far from the Indian grave site that Grandmother told us about. There was some kind of whisper more like moaning or a cry. It was two weeks later that I saw an article that said an Indian burial site was discovered. We now have a deed to that sacred land, the land that holds the resting places of our ancestors. It was this event that opened up our eyes. We saw that we had a need to research our way of life and to learn what was left in regard to our songs and dances and traditional way of life. Grandmother told us what was left with her, but there was more to learn. Now here in 2000, we have regained many of our songs and dances and traditional practices, and the young ones are learning what was almost lost. Now we can say "yes," we are still here, the descendants of a people who walked these lands for 10,000 years.

—*Patrick Yana-Hea Orozco*

Above is a core story of the Indian culture that still exists in Watsonville. The group in Watsonville consists of about 100 persons, but about 350 affiliated members live elsewhere around the state. Ancestors of the present group came together in Watsonville in 1838. Grandma Rios' ancestry can be traced to a village located south of San Jose. These people were Ritoxci Ohlone. Her ancestors were taken into the Santa Clara Mission. Other significant family members are from the Carmel area. Although mission life was hard on the Indian people taken there, and most of them did not survive, ancestors of the present group did marry, found ways to leave the missions, had children and survived.

Ohlone people living in the Pajaro region at an earlier time built tule houses and lived close to the marshes, finding rich plant and animal resources there. Pajaro derives its name from the expedition of the Spanish explorer Portola. He described a visit to an Indian village on the Pajaro River. The Indian people may have been wary of the Spanish for when the explorers returned there, they found the village burned with only a large dead bird on a pole to mark the spot. The Spanish named the river Pajaro or "bird."

In 1996 the present group filed for federal recognition. The process of achieving recognition is lengthy because California Indian tribal groups do not readily fit into the federal standards, which were based on the nature of Eastern tribes. Without recognition, the group is precluded from many federal benefits, such as health, educational scholarship, and access to ritual materials.

The present day people find ways to acknowledge their culture and support each other. Native traditions honor births, deaths and marriages. With Patrick Orozco's leadership members of the group have learned songs and dances and are teaching them to the young. They create dance regalia and native musical instruments. They share their dances with the public, presenting at schools, parks, and community events.

Knowledge of plant material used for building, food, and medicine has been passed along to the present descendants. They know the uses of many native plants as well as plants brought here by the Spaniards and Americans. The Pajaro area is still rich in these natural resources. Members of the group conduct plant walks and seminars.

Patrick Orozco's Coyote song goes like this:

Sala Luni Sala Luni
Sala Luni Sala Luni
hea hea hea

Public Activities:
Ohlone Life in the Pajaro Valley: A Natural History Perspective
University of California at Santa Cruz Extension class, taught periodically by Patrick Orozco
Ohlone Day: Dance performance yearly, in late September, at Henry Cowell Redwood State Park in Felton, California
Ama-ka-Tura Dance Group available for performances
Plant Walks available on request

For further information, please contact:
Patrick Orozco
644 Pear Tree Drive, Watsonville, Ca 95076
Phone number and fax: (831) 728-8471

Ama-ka-Tura Dancers at the Carmel River. Photo by Lois Robin.

Santa Cruz
County
History Journal
Issue 5, 2002

T'epot'aha'l—the Salinan Nation: Always, Now, Forever

by Gregg Castro

Mother Earth is resilient as it yields to the forces of nature. Its soil will ooze and flow in the face of water; its mountains tremble to the shudder in the world's bones; it succumbs to the soft caress of the fog flowing in across its green brows from the great ocean. Yet it always remains, like adamant—strong, beautiful and true since the beginning of time.

Her children, T'epot'aha'l, the People of the Oaks, are of the same substance: strong as they yield to the forces of time and "civilization." They have flowed in the face of hatred and greed and withstood the harsh tremors of genocide and bigotry. They have endured the loss of their homes, their land and even their lives. Yet they also remain strong and true with a beauty born of the sorrow the People have endured with so much dignity. And also like Mother Earth, they have again blossomed in the warmth of the morning in the springtime of a new age. T'epot'aha'l—the People of Xolom —the Salinan Nation: always, now and forever.

The history of our people is long, honorable, and replete with stories of courage, love, integrity and, most importantly, perseverance. The deeds of our ancestors and even of our living Elders gives us the pride and strength to see our way through the odds against us. What has never been lost to us is our tie to the land which gave us birth and sustains us. It is a spiritual and emotional nourishment that impels us to preserve and perpetuate the ancient mysteries and learnings our ancestors sacrificed so much to sustain.

What sustains us is our faith and belief that this is but a moment, albeit an important moment, in time for our people. We believe we have always

been here, we are here now as an integral part of the community, and we will still be here when all that we see now is but a distant memory for our children's children and their descendants. Although we honor and respect the past and the teachings of the past, we do not live in the past. We are very much a people of now. What we do today, in this moment, is what we believe is most important— the past is a blocked path that we can learn from but not live in. The future is an unknown, but determined by what we do in the present.

It is good to have come to these days in the life of the Salinan Nation when many in the community have embraced our ideas and goals and some have helped to see them into reality. The public within our homeland, stretching from Monterey County to San Luis Obispo County, has supported our presence as we have educated them to our past. It has become a renaissance for our People as we have opened the doors to a gathering place, new projects and a new hope for our future.

Our tribal office, the Adobe Cultural Center, is the hub of the Salinan Nation's activities today. Within the center is a small display—a temporary museum of artifacts of the long history of the Salinan People in central coastal California. The center is a source of pride for our people in that we once again have a visible presence in our homeland—a place to call home.

But the center is only the beginning of yet greater dreams. We recently concluded an agreement between the Salinan Nation, the Monterey County Parks and Recreation and the Army Reserve at Fort Hunter Liggett to establish a Salinan Museum where our People's story can be shared and where the public can be educated about California indigenous people in general and our Jolon Indian story in particular. The museum will be in the Tidball Store Historical site in Jolon, CA.—a town whose name reflects an old Salinan word, "xolom". The old store building, to which some of our elders and ancestors have historical ties, will be restored. This will allow a larger portion of our artifacts and cultural collection to be properly archived and displayed for the community's enrichment. Along with the building itself is a nearby acre for such possibilities as a village replica, a "round house" and an indigenous plant garden.

We have other dreams. We dream of the growth of our annual tribal gathering, open to the public, so we can come together to share our heritage with each other and with the new communities now in our homeland. We dream of the continued protection of our ancestors' legacy through monitoring and consulting with private, business, and government agencies. And, our greatest dream: federal acknowledgement, so the United States will recognize their obligation and debt to our ancestors and our people for what has been taken from us. This is our most complex and burdensome work, yet we pray it will yield the greatest

harvest within the next few years. It will lend credence to our efforts to preserve our ancient heritage for all time.

We can certainly do no less than what Katol Kensha:nel, the Creator, called on our honored ancestors to do: Have respect for life, love the land and each other, have courage and strength to maintain the essential ingredients of our People that will renew and fortify our continuation as a unique and precious family on the land we have been gifted with.

If you are interested in more information or wish to help us achieve our goals, you can reach us as follows:

Gregg Castro
Salinan Nation Tribal Council Chair
email: glcastro@pacbell.net

Salinan Nation Adobe Cultural Center
10 Jolon Rd. King City, CA. 93930
Phone: (831) 385-1538   Fax: (831) 385-3436

219

Resources

If you want to read more about the Native Peoples of California and the Monterey Bay area, the following selected bibliographies provide a brief list of general-interest books on the subject and a separate list of books for children, which adults might also enjoy. (Books of specific interest are included in the bibliographies of many articles in this Journal.) In addition, a few web sites of interest are included here, as well as a list of places around the San Francisco and Monterey Bay areas that you can visit for further enrichment in Ohlone culture.

Books of General Interest

Tribes of California, Stephen Powers, University of California Press, Berkeley, CA, 1976
> A classic of American Indian ethnography, originally published in 1877. Stephen Powers visited the northern two-thirds of California in the summers of 1871 and 1872 and faithfully recorded what he saw and heard.

Handbook of the Indians of California, A. L. Kroeber, Dover Publications, New York, NY, 1976
> A monumental work based on more than 15 years of exhaustive research by A. L. Kroeber. It is a survey of each tribal group in California covering their social structures, folkways, religion, material culture, and much more.

Handbook of North American Indians; Vol. 8; California, Smithsonian, Washington, D.C., 1978
> One of a 20-volume series intended as an encyclopedic summary of what is known about the aboriginal peoples of North America. This volume contains chapters on each of the tribal groups found in California at the time of European contact.

The Indians of California, Time-Life Books, 1994
> An easy-to-read survey of the many different native cultures of California. It deals with the impact of the Missions and later gold miners on these cultures and how the People are surviving today. This book is illustrated with hundreds of photographs.

The Ohlone Way, Malcolm Margolin, Heyday Books, Berkeley, CA, 1978
> An easy-to-read, illustrated book that recreates the early life and landscape of the Ohlone People.

The Ohlone; Past and Present, Lowell John Bean, ed., Ballena Press, Menlo Park, CA, 1994
> A collection of papers by fourteen scholars from a conference on the Ohlone People that covers a wide range of topics from archeological research on bedrock mortars to what is happening to the Ohlone People living today.

A Time of Little Choice—The Disintegration of Tribal Culture in the San Francisco Bay Area 1769-1810, Randall Milliken, Ballena Press, Menlo Park, CA, 1995
> An engaging and easy-to-read ethnohistory that explores the effect of Mission life on the Ohlone, Miwok, Patwin and Yokuts tribal groups.

The Natural World of the California Indians, Robert F. Heizer, University of California Press, Berkeley, CA, 1980

A study of California's many different habitats and how the various Native Peoples adapted to these habitats, creating the great diversity of cultures found in the state.

It Will Live Forever, Beverly R. Ortiz, Heyday Books, Berkeley, CA, 1991

A practical manual on how to process acorns into a nutritious food. Julia Parker, a Miwok woman, shares the magic and lore of this ancient tradition.

The Fine Art of California Indian Basketry, Brian Bibby, Crocker Art Museum (Sacramento) in association with Heyday Books, Heyday Books, Berkeley, CA, 1996

Originally published as a catalog for a museum exhibition, this beautiful full-color book features over sixty examples of California Indian basketry.

The Costanoan/Ohlone Indians of the San Francisco & Monterey Bay Area—A Research Guide, Lauren S. Teixeira, Ballena Press, Menlo Park, CA, 1997

A bibliography and list of library sources for further research on Ohlone Indian culture.

Books for Children (and Adults)

When the World Ended, Linda Yamane, Oyate, Berkeley, CA, 1995

A translation of three Rumsien Ohlone stories of the in the 1920s by Smithsonian ethnographer, J. P. Harrington, who worked with some of the last native speakers of the Ohlone languages.

The Snake That Lived in the Santa Cruz Mountains, Linda Yamane, Oyate, Berkeley, CA, 1998

More Ohlone stories, told and illustrated by Linda Yamane.

Tjatjakiy-matchan (Coyote), Alex O. Ramirez, Oyate, Berkeley, CA, 1995

Another authentic Ohlone story recorded by Alex Ramirez, an Ohlone descendant who spent much of his childhood living in Carmel Valley, California. He was told this story as a child.

Indian Summer, Thomas Jefferson Mayfield, Heyday Books, Berkeley, CA, 1993

In 1850, six-year-old Thomas Jefferson Mayfield was adopted by the Choinumne Yokuts of the San Joaquin Valley and lived with these people for 12 years; he recounts his experiences in this book.

People At The Edge of The World, Betty Morrow, B. Morrow, Berkeley, CA, 1991

A book for young people about how the Ohlone lived in the old days and what happened to them after the "strangers" came.

The Way We Lived, Malcolm Margolin, ed., Heyday Books, Berkeley, CA, 1993

A collection of Californian Indian stories, songs, and reminiscences.

Native Ways, Malcolm Margolin & Yolanda Montijo, eds., Heyday Books, Berkeley, CA, 1995

This lively book, geared for younger readers, is full of humor and facts and gives readers of all ages a glimpse into how Indian people lived in the "old days" and how they are living today.

California Indians & the Gold Rush, Clifford E. Trafzer, Sierra Oaks Publishing Co., Newcastle, CA, 1989

An account of the little-known role that California Indian people played in the early stages of California's mining frontier.

Grass Games and Moon Races, Jeannine Gendar, Heyday Books, Berkeley, CA, 1995
> An illustrated collection of games and toys used by the Native Peoples of California with directions and anecdotes.

Weaving a California Tradition, Linda Yamane, Lerner Publications, Minneapolis, MN, 1997
> This book follows 11-year-old Carly Tex (Western Mono) through the process of gathering basketry materials with her family, making a basket, and showing it at the California Indian Basketweavers Gathering.

Web Sites

California Historical Society
> http://www.calhist.org/
> The California Hisorical Society's web site has links to Native American history and information.

California Indian Basketweavers Association (CIBA)
> http://www.ciba.org/
> CIBA preserves, promotes, and perpetuates California Indian basketweaving traditions; the website provides information on ongoing programs and activities.

News From Native California
> http://www.heydaybooks.com/news/
> A quarterly magazine devoted entirely to California's Native people that is written and produced by California Indians and those close to the Indian community.

Oyate
> http://www.oyate.org/
> A Native organization whose work includes evaluating texts, resource materials and fiction by and about Native peoples.

Parks & Museums

Chitactac Adams Heritage County Park
> South Santa Clara County on Watsonville Road between Morgan Hill & Gilroy; 408/842-2341.
> Visitor center: interpretive trail; bedrock mortars; rock art; educational programming by reservation 408/323-0107.

Coyote Hills Regional Park
> 8000 Patterson Ranch Road, Fremont, CA; 510/795-9285.
> Visitor center; mural; "shellmound" site with reconstructed traditional structures; educational programming; annual public event, "A Gathering of Ohlone Peoples," in the fall.

Henry Cowell State Park
> 525 N. Big Trees Park Road, Felton, CA; 831/335-3174.
> Annual public event, "Ohlone Day," in the fall.

Pacific Grove Museum of Natural History
> 165 Forest Avenue, Pacific Grove, CA; 831/648-3116.
> Two Ohlone baskets on display.

San Jose Historical Museum
    1650 Senter Road, San Jose, CA; 408/918-1047.
    Ohlone exhibit; educational programming; Ohlone basket.

Santa Cruz Museum of Natural History
    1305 East Cliff Drive, Santa Cruz, CA; 831/420-6115
    Ohlone exhibit, including mural; educational programming.

Santa Cruz Mission State Historic Park
    144 School Street, Santa Cruz, Ca; 831/425-5849
    Mission period exhibit.

Youth Science Institute Alum Rock Nature Center
    16260 Alum Rock Avenue, San Jose, CA; 408/258-4322
    Educational programming.

Youth Science Institute Sanborn Nature Center
    16055 Sanborn Road, Saratoga, CA; 408/867-6940
    Educational programming.

Youth Science Institute Vasona Nature Center
    296 Garden Hill Drive, Los Gatos, CA; 408/356-4945
    Educational programming.

Contributors

Linda Agren is Assistant Curator of Anthropology, Santa Barbara Museum of Natural History. She first became interested in John P. Harrington when she inventoried the collection of his fieldnotes, correspondence and photographs the museum had received from his daughter, Awona. Instead of simply filing the correspondence away in a folder, she read it all. In this way she came to know Harrington, his friends and family well. She was able to identify people in unlabeled photos, having looked at the other 1500 photos in the SBMNH collection and at the 10 microfilm reels of Harrington photos the Smithsonian recently published. She confesses, "I became a Harrington groupie."

Victoria Bobo worked with Dr. Robert R. Cartier for four years as the executive administrator of Archaeological Resource Management. She is currently working as a cultural resource specialist for an environmental firm, Geo InSight International, Inc. She received her BA in archaeological studies from Boston University and her MA in anthropology from the University of Wisconsin-Madison.

Lydia Bojorquez is an Ohlone Indian. She lives in Woodland, California where she enjoys life and sharing stories of her experiences with family and friends. Recently, she decided to write of her feelings and tell her stories. "Life is like a book and each day is an added chapter."

Gary Breschini, PhD, is certified by the Register of Professional Archaeologists (RPA) as a professional archaeologist and physical anthropologist. He has spent 30 years studying the prehistory of the Central California coast.

Robert R. Cartier, PhD, served as Principal Investigator for the excavations, research, and report writing carried out for the Scotts Valley Site. He completed his undergraduate work in anthropology at San Jose State University and earned his MA and PhD in anthropology from Rice University in 1975. From 1975, he has taught courses in archaeology and anthropology at De Anza College as well as other colleges and universities in the Monterey and San Jose regions. He is RPA certified in the categories of teaching, field work, and cultural resource management. Cartier organized the firm of Archaeological Resource Management in 1977. Since that time he has been directing archaeological and historical investigations in the central California area.

Edward D. Castillo is a Cahuilla and Luiseno Indian from Southern California. His academic training and graduate degrees are in United States Frontier History and American Anthropology. He was a founding member of the Native American Studies Department at both UCLA and UC Berkeley. He has taught Native American history and ethnography for over 30 years and is currently Professor and Chairman of Sonoma State University's Native American Studies Department. He has written five books, including *Native American Perspectives on the Hispanic Colonization of Alta California*, Garland Press, 1992 and has published many articles and chapters in professional journals and books, including the chapter "Native Response to the Colonization of Alta California" in the award-winning *Columbian Consequences, Archaeological and Historical Perspectives on the Spanish Borderlands West*, Smithsonian Press, 1989.

Gregg Castro is Chair of the Tribal Council of the Salinan Nation, an indigenous community of the central coast of California. Mr. Castro has been a council member since 1993 when the modern day council was established in its current form. Since 1995, Mr. Castro has worked with the Native American Programs Committee of the Society for California Archaeology, the state organization of cultural management professionals. The NAPC is involved in assisting Native American communities in California in the protection of their culture.

Tony Cerda is an elder of The Ohlone Bear Clan. He was elected Chairman of the Costanoan-Rumsen Carmel Tribe in July of 1994. He has been a Commissioner of the City of Pomona from July of 1996 to the present; he serves on the Historic Preservation Commission.

Geoffrey Dunn is a fourth generation Santa Cruzan who was raised in the watersheds of the San Lorenzo River and Soquel Creek. He is an award-winning filmmaker, journalist, historian and lecturer. He is the author of *Santa Cruz Is In the Heart*, currently in its fourth edition. His films include *Miss...or Myth?*, *Dollar a Day, Ten Cents a Dance*, and *Chinese Gold*. He also wrote the original screenplay for *Maddalena Z*. A lecturer in Community Studies at UCSC, he also serves as Executive Director of Community Television of Santa Cruz County.

Eduardo José (Joe) Freeman is a member of the Salinan Tribe. He currently serves on the Tribal Council and is coordinating the Tribe's efforts to obtain federal recognition. His main work is assisting to revitalize traditional Salinan culture and language.

Donna Gillette has an MA in Anthropology/Archaeology from CSU, Hayward and completed classes toward a Certificate in Archaeology from UCLA extension. She is on the Board of Directors of the American Rock Art Research Association and is a contributing member of the Society for California Archaeology, the Society for American Archaeology, the Santa Clara Archaeology Association, and the Santa Cruz Archaeology Association. After an avocational interest for many years in the pre-history of California and the Southwest, she returned to school to pursue an advanced degree in Anthropology/Archaeology. Her study area is the rock art of California, but she has traveled worldwide to view sites and attend international rock art meetings.

Trudy Haversat, MA, is an RPA certified professional archaeologist and physical anthropologist who has spent 25 years researching the archaeology and prehistory of the Central California coast.

David W. Heron is University Librarian Emeritus, University of California at Santa Cruz. His historical works include *Forever Facing South—The Story of the S.S. Palo Alto, "The Old Cement Ship" of Seacliff Beach* (Otter B. Books, 1991) and *Night Landing, A Short History of West Coast Smuggling*. (Hellgate Press, 1998). He is a volunteer at the Museum of Art & History Archives. He lives in Aptos with his wife, Winnie.

hummux has worked closely with Tom Little Bear Nason to help with the prophecy and life history of the Esselen people. During the past decade he has conducted extensive research in a wide variety of fields.

Russell Imrie is a Kahnawake Mohawk Indian living in Santa Cruz. He works with Indian Canyon and manages the Costanoan-Ohlone Indian Canyon Resource through his web site.

Jacquelin Jensen Kehl is a Mutsun Ohlone who has been active in the repatriation and preservation of Ohlone burials and cultural sites. She is a Most Likely Descendant registered with the State of California Native American Heritage Commission and also monitors and participates in archaeological projects in Ohlone territory.

Edward Ketchum, born in Marysville in 1949, often visited his extended family in the southern Santa Clara Valley where he heard his grandmother speak of her grandmother, Doña Ascención Solórsano de Cervantes, and of life in the past. He heard of the time when the ethnologist John Peabody Harrington came to her house. He listened as his father talked of the old recordings of Mutsun songs. These experiences enticed him to visit the Smithsonian Institute where he examined some of the Harrington collection and handled some of the Costanoan artifacts held there. He graduated from the University of California at Davis and has worked as a civil engineer throughout the west since 1972. His concern for the land and its people led him to participate in the Amah/Mutsun Band of Ohlone Costanoan Indian's tribal government.

Richard Levy is an anthropologist and linguist who works at Cal Trans as a district archaeologist. He received his Bachelors degree from the University of California at Santa Cruz in 1969 and his PhD from the University of British Columbia in 1973. Dr. Levy wrote the chapters on the Costanoans and the Coast Miwok in *The Handbook of North American Indians,* Volume 8 (California).

Sandy Lydon is Historian Emeritus at Cabrillo College where he taught local and regional history for over thirty years. An award-winning author and lecturer, he has focused most of his research and writing on the region's ethnic history. His most recent publication (as co-author) is *Coast Redwood: A Natural and Cultural History*, Cachuma Press, August 2001. His next publication (co-authored with Kurt Loesch) will be *Voices From the Edge of the World: Reclaiming the Human History of Point Lobos*, Capitola Book Company, 2002.

Stephen Meadows is a Californian of Ohlone and pioneer descent. He has degrees from UC Santa Cruz and San Francisco State University and he has long been active in public radio, where he hosts a political folk show called Meadow's Road on KZSC, 88.1 FM in Santa Cruz. More of his poems can be found in the anthology *The Sound of Rattles and Clappers,* edited by Greg Sarris (University of Arizona Press) as well as other anthologies and publications nationwide.

Randall Milliken is an ethnohistorian and research archaeologist currently working with Far Western Anthropological Research Group, Inc. in Davis, California. He specializes in the prehistory and contact-period history of California. He has a Masters Degree in Cultural Resource Management from Sonoma State University (1983) and a PhD in Anthropology from the University of California at Berkeley (1991).

Tom Little Bear Nason is a seventh-generation spiritual leader of the Esselen Tribe of Big Sur and a wilderness guide who is dedicated to helping others to mend the sacred hoop of life.

Patrick Orozco is a descendant who has always known he is Indian but twenty years ago knew little of his particular background or culture. Through these years he has recovered pieces of his identity and still continues his search. Patrick has been culturally active in the Santa Cruz, San Benito and Monterey County areas. He brings an Indian voice into the broader arena, testifying at civic meetings, monitoring with archaeologists and speaking for the needs and dreams of his neighbors and community.

Beverly R. Ortiz is an ethnographic consultant and contributing editor for *News from Native California*, for whom she has written a column about Skills and Technology since 1988. As a naturalist with the East Bay Regional Park District at Coyote Hills Regional Park in Fremont, she coordinates a series of public programs with Ohlone descendants, as well as an annual Gathering of Ohlone Peoples. She has written one book, several book chapters and entries, and more than 100 articles about California Indian lifeways and cultures. She is currently working on a PhD in Socio-cultural Anthropology from the University of California at Berkeley.

Douglas J. Petersen is an anthropologist who has studied and worked with the material culture of Native California for over twenty-five years. For many years he was the docent program coordinator for the Santa Cruz City Museum of Natural History. He currently lectures and teaches classes at schools, colleges, museums and state and county parks throughout the Monterey Bay area. He is also a storyteller and makes selected artifact reproductions for schools, museums and private collectors.

Santa Cruz
County
History Journal
Issue 5, 2002

Alex O. Ramirez has strong ties to his Rumsien Ohlone heritage, which he traces through both his maternal and paternal grandparents. As a youth, Alex lived first in Carmel and then in the Carmel Valley, each house a relatively short distance from Echilat, his family's ancestral village in the Carmel Valley. While growing up, Alex's parents and grandparents exposed him to the cultural traditions upon which he would draw throughout his life. He has served as cultural consultant to writers, anthropologists, and historians, has been a board member of several American Indian organizations, and has shared his cultural knowledge as guest speaker at schools, parks, and special events. He wrote and illustrated *Tjatjakiy-matchan (Coyote): A Legend from the Carmel Valley* in 1991, and translated Chocheño narratives which were published in 1994's *The Ohlone Past and Present*.

Lois Robin is a photographer and writer who ten years ago produced a photo story, *Indian Ghosts at California Missions*, depicting the presence of the Indian spirit within the California Missions. At that time she did not know any contemporary California Indian descendants, but by the time the exhibit finished traveling throughout California, she was acquainted with many. She has been photographing and writing about them ever since. Working closely with the Pajaro Valley Ohlone Indians and with support from the Santa Cruz Archaeological Society, she developed an interactive CD Rom, *First People of the Pajaro*, that tells the history of the local Ohlone people. She has produced several videos about local Ohlone life, including *Song for the River*. In 1997 she curated *The California Sesquicentennial: an Indian Perspective* for the Pajaro Valley Art Gallery.

William Shipley, Emeritus Professor of Linguistics, University of California at Santa Cruz, received his BA with a major in Anthropology from the University of California at Berkeley in 1948 and his PhD in Linguistics, also from Berkeley, in 1959. His dissertation was a grammar of Maidu, a native language of California, spoken in pre-conquest times at the northern end of the Sierra Nevada. In 1965, he joined the faculty of the new experimental campus, UC Santa Cruz, where he established a department of Linguistics. He remained at Santa Cruz for the rest of his active academic career. He retired in 1991, receiving at that time the University Award for Distinguished Teaching. His academic research focused on the Native Languages of California, particularly Maidu and, to a lesser extent, its two close relatives: Konkow to the west and Nisenan to the south. Since his retirement, he has worked with young Maidu, Konkow, and Nisenan people, helping them learn about their ancestral languages and how to write them.

Charles R. Smith is an amalgam that defies easy placement with roots spreading in many directions: part Danish Jew, part west country Irish, and part California Indian from the Choinimni people who occupy the lower and middle reaches of the Kings River in the foothills of the south-central Sierra Nevada mountains. He has a Master's Degree in Anthropology from the University of Arizona and combines a great deal of teaching experience with ethnographic and archaeological research in various parts of the world. He has published articles that deal with the Native Peoples of California, most notably in the Smithsonian's *Handbook of North American Indians, Volume 8,* (California). He is currently an instructor in anthropology at both Cabrillo and Hartnell colleges.

Ann Elizabeth Thiermann is a classically trained fine artist with a BA in Art from UCSC, three years of figurative and landscape study at the Art League of NYC, and an MFA from CSU, Long Beach. She has designed and executed over 55 murals in California. Her local public murals include a mural in Pearl Alley at Walnut Street in Santa Cruz, at the Waddell Creek Nature Center, and at the Santa Cruz Museum of Natural History, a detail of which appears as the cover of this Journal. Her Monterey Bay murals frequently utilize "field notes" from her "plein air" pastel paintings. She has taught at the college level since 1990 and currently offers a variety of painting and drawing courses through UCSC Extension and Monterey Peninsula College.

Linda Yamane is an independent scholar who traces her ancestry to the Rumsien Ohlone, the native people of the Monterey area. She has been active in researching and reviving Rumsien language, song, folklore, basketry and dance—traditions that were once thought lost. Linda is the newsletter editor for the California Indian Basketweavers Association (CIBA) and was a member of its founding board of directors. She has compiled and illustrated two books of Ohlone stories: *When the World Ended, How Hummingbird Got Fire & How People Were Made* and *The Snake That Lived in the Santa Cruz Mountains & Other Ohlone Stories*. She is the author of *Weaving a California Tradition*; co-author of *In Full View—Three Ways of Seeing California Plants*; and contributor to *The Sweet Breathing of Plants—Women Writing on the Green World*, edited by Linda Hogan and Brenda Peterson.

Index

Note: Page numbers of illustrations are in bold. "15n. 20" means page 15, note number 20.

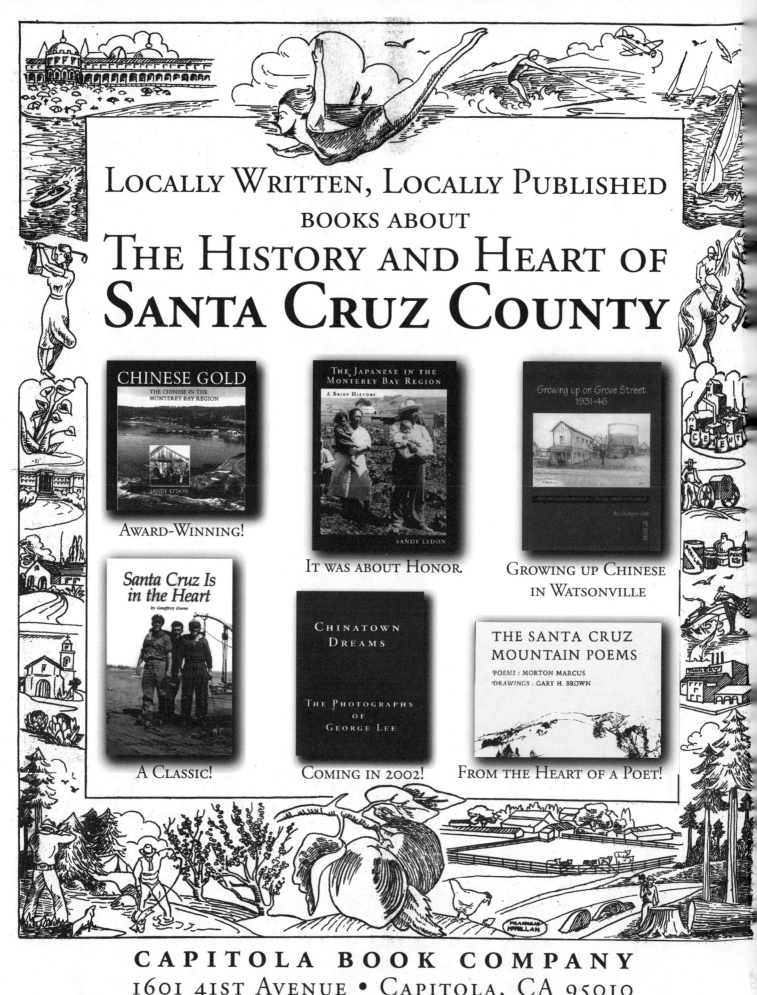